Interpretation of the Halstead-Reitan Neuropsychological Test Battery

A Casebook Approach

Interpretation of the Halstead-Reitan Neuropsychological Test Battery

A Casebook Approach

Charles J. Golden, Ph.D.
Associate Professor of Medical Psychology
University of Nebraska Medical Center
Omaha, Nebraska

David C. Osmon, Ph.D.
Assistant Professor of Psychology
University of Wisconsin
Milwaukee, Wisconsin

James A. Moses, Jr., Ph.D.
Staff Psychologist
Veterans Administration Medical Center
Palo Alto, California
and Assistant Clinical Professor of Psychiatry
Stanford Medical School
Palo Alto, California

Richard A. Berg, Ph.D.
Research Associate
St. Jude Children's Research Hospital
Memphis, Tennessee

 GRUNE & STRATTON
A Subsidiary of Harcourt Brace Jovanovich, Publishers
New York   London   Toronto   Sydney   San Francisco

Grune & Stratton, Inc.
111 Fifth Avenue
New York, New York 10003

Distributed in the United Kingdom by
Academic Press Inc. (London) Ltd.
24/28 Oval Road, London NW 1

Library of Congress Catalog Number 80-84839
International Standard Book Number 0-8089-1298-4

Printed in the United States of America

Contents

Preface

In recent years there have been extensive changes in the teaching of psychodiagnostics in clinical psychology and related professions. One of the major changes in this area has been the increasing interest in the field of clinical neuropsychology, the study of the relationship between the brain and behavior. This has been accompanied by increasing interest in and teaching of the Halstead-Reitan Neuropsychological Test Battery in over half of the clinical psychology training programs today.* In addition, the tests are extensively used in teaching by clinical internships as well as in a number of school psychology and other related programs.

Several major factors, however, have acted to restrict the scope of this training. The major problem has been the lack of case material: few programs or internships have the necessary amount of clinical material representing various forms of brain damage to present a fully comprehensive training program. In the same way, private practitioners and other clinicians wishing to use the test battery have found their training limited by the lack of adequate case material.

This volume is presented in answer to the problem. The text includes cases representing both left and right hemisphere injuries divided into specific localized disorders, as well as cases representing diffuse, psychiatric, and normal performance. Each case is presented so that the reader may diagnose the case blindly and then turn to the analysis provided by the authors. In addition, separate chapters present the basic empirical and theoretical results expected from injuries in different areas of the brain. The book also examines the complex question of differentiating psychiatric from brain injured patients.

*Golden, C.J., & Kuperman, S. Graduate training in clinical neuropsychology. *Professional Psychology*, 1980, *11*, 55–63.

Overall, the book includes 80 cases, each of which is presented in its entirety with all Halstead-Reitan scores reported. Used in conjunction with more theoretical books on neuropsychological diagnosis and the practical experience that can be offered in most settings, the book should give the interested reader a strong grounding in the clincial skills necessary for practice with the Halstead-Reitan.

The introductory four chapters of the book are written with the assumption that the reader is not highly versed in clincial neuropsychology or the Halstead-Reitan. However, we do not try to reproduce basic material in such areas as psychophysiology, neuroanatomy, neurological disease, and other related areas which have been covered comprehensively in other texts and in graduate school training courses. Our emphasis in these chapters is on the ways in which these basic conditions affect scores on the Halstead-Reitan Neuropsychological Battery. The reader wishing to become an expert in such interpretation, however, must also acquire the large body of knowledge referred to above, as well as gain practical experience under a competent neuropsychological supervisor. For this novice, this book is intended as a supplement to other work rather than an end in itself. For the reader with no background in clinical neuropsychology, reading Golden (1978)* is strongly recommended as minimal preparation for the current texts.

For the experienced neuropsychologist, most of the material in the first four chapters will be basic. However, even the expert should find challenging the wide range of cases available for interpretation. Cases have been chosen with a primary focus in each area of the neocortex as well as cases representing all the major neurological processes and the many complicating conditions that make neuropsychological diagnosis and assessment a major challenge. Mastery of these cases will lead to significant increase in skills for most psychologists using the Halstead-Reitan today.

Before turning to the text, a wide variety of acknowledgements are in order. Clearly, this book could not exist without the pioneering work of Ward Halstead, Ralph Reitan, and their students and colleagues for the past 35 years. It goes without saying that nearly every idea regarding the test battery first originated in these individuals, either in formal writing or more frequently in workshops, oral communications, teachings passed on to others, and in many other informal ways. As a result we have not, in general, attempted to thoroughly reference every idea to its original source (if that could even be determined), but rather have chosen to list the major work of this area in the Bibliography. Reading of all the material referenced in the Bibliography is highly recommended for the novice without background in this area. It is from these references as a whole that the ideas, rules, observations, and conclu-

*Golden, C. J. Diagnosis and rehabilitation in clinical neuropsychology. Springfield, Ill.: Charles C. Thomas, 1978

sions about the Halstead-Reitan have been integrated, along with the more oral traditional passed to the authors by their supervisors, colleagues, and students.

It is our hope that this casebook will aid in improving the interpretations of the Halstead-Reitan by both the novice and the experienced neuropsychologist. In this way we hope to both honor and extend the work of Halstead, Reitan, and others, and recognize the significance and importance of this work to modern clinical neuropsychology.

Charles J. Golden, Ph.D.

Interpretation of the Halstead-Reitan Neuropsychological Test Battery

A Casebook Approach

1
Administration

The Halstead-Reitan Neuropsychological Test Battery began with the work of Ward Halstead at the University of Chicago in 1935. Halstead carried out exhaustive studies of the behavior of brain-injured patients, developing and discarding hundreds of tests in the process. The results of his initial investigations were published in 1947 in *Brain and Intelligence: A Quantitative Study of the Frontal Lobes*. In that book Halstead introduced some of the tests that have become integral parts of the neuropsychological battery.

Subsequent to the publication of that book, one of Halstead's students, Dr. Ralph Reitan, established a neuropsychology laboratory at the Indiana University Medical Center. In 1951 Reitan established a test battery designed to measure a broad range of abilities. He included only tests believed to be valid indicators of brain dysfunction. The major goal with this test battery was to develop a variety of principles of inference that would permit diagnosis of individual subjects (Reitan, unpublished manuscript, undated).

Reitan began with Halstead's basic test battery and supplemented it with a number of additional tests to broaden the scope of the battery. Over the past 25 years Reitan has published a number of important studies that have validated and/or modified the battery. This initial work of Halstead and Reitan has led to the adoption of the test battery throughout the United States and around the world. Its acceptance is illustrated by the numerous studies that have appeared in major psychological and medical journals on the validity of the battery, as well as by the popularity of workshops on the use of the Halstead-Reitan test battery that have been presented by Reitan and others.

APPARATUS, ADMINISTRATION, AND SCORING

The Halstead-Reitan Neuropsychological Test Battery consists of a number of independent tests. In contrast to the situation with other tests mentioned in this volume, the exact procedures that make up the Halstead-Reitan test battery differ somewhat among neuropsychological laboratories. However, most users of the battery include the following tests: (1) Wechsler Adult Intelligence Scale (or its earlier form, the Wechsler-Bellevue); (2) Halstead Category Test; (3) Speech-Sounds Perception Test; (4) Seashore Rhythm Test; (5) Tactual Performance Test; (6) Trail-making Test; (7) Reitan-Klove Sensory-Perceptual Examination; (8) Reitan-Indiana Aphasia Examination; (9) Lateral Dominance Examination; (10) Halstead Finger Tapping Test. The Wechsler Adult Intelligence Scale is discussed extensively elsewhere (Golden, 1979). The remaining tests will be individually reviewed here.

Halstead Category Test

The Halstead Category Test was designed to measure an individual's capacity to deduce general principles from experience with specific items. The test involves 208 slides, each of which suggests a number from 1 to 4. When shown a slide, the subject must decide what number the slide suggests by attempting to deduce the principle represented by the slide. For example, the first slide contains the Roman numeral I. Almost all subjects deduce that this slide suggests the number 1. After deciding on an answer, the subject presses one of four levers numbered 1 to 4. If the subject has guessed the correct number, the pressing of the correct lever causes a pleasant door chime to ring, reinforcing the subject's guess as to the underlying principle. If the subject's guess is incorrect, the pressing of the incorrect lever is followed by a loud disagreeable buzzer. This indicates that the subject must deduce a different underlying principle in order to get the correct answer.

The test consists of seven different subtests, each with its own underlying principle. The first set of items suggests the correct answer by presenting the Roman numerals I, II, III, and IV. In the second set the correct answer is determined by the number of items on the page.

For example, if two circles are shown, the correct answer will be 2. In the third set, four items are always presented, however, one of the items is unique in some manner. For example, three of the items may be squares and the other a circle. The correct answer for this set is the position of the unique item. Thus if the unique item is the third figure the correct response will be 3.

In the fourth set, figures are presented each with a piece missing in one of the four quadrants: upper left, upper right, lower right, or lower left. For the first six items the quadrants are numbered I, II, III, and IV, moving clockwise from the upper left quadrant. The correct answer is the number of the quadrant in which something is missing. After the sixth item the numbers are no longer presented, and the subject must remember the correct numbering of the quadrants.

In the fifth set the correct answer is the proportion of the figure that is made up of solid lines rather than dotted lines. If the figure is one-fourth solid, the correct answer is 1. If the figure is three-fourths solid, the correct answer is 3. In the sixth set the principle is the same as in the fifth set, but the subject is not told this. The final set has no one principle but is made up of items from the first six sets. The subject must remember which principle applied to that item and must answer correctly. This serves primarily as a test of memory function rather than analytic ability.

The items for the Halstead Category Test are presented on a small viewing screen contained in a projection box. Because this apparatus is somewhat clumsy different investigators have devised alternative ways of presenting the items. At present there is no evidence suggesting the superiority of one method over the others, although some appear to be more convenient.

At the beginning of the test administration the subject is told that items will be presented that suggest a number from 1 to 4. The subject is told that the bell indicates a correct choice, whereas the buzzer indicates an incorrect choice. Finally, the subject is told that there is one principle running through each subtest that the subject must deduce.

At the beginning of each subtest the subject is again told that there is a principle that the subject must deduce, which may be the same as or different than the principles underlying the other subtests. Before the last subtest the subject is told that the answer to the item is the same answer as when the subject previously saw the slide.

The most serious problem in administering the Halstead Category Test is the time involved in carrying out the procedure. Whereas a normal subject may finish the test within an hour, a brain-injured patient may take 2 hours or more. Despite the value of the Halstead Category Test in the making of diagnostic decisions, the excessive time involved in conducting the test makes many clinicians reluctant to use it. Its length may also cause fatigue in a patient; answers may become random, or a patient may be unwilling or unable to finish.

Fatigue during the test may be lessened by giving the subject rest periods between subtests, although this may adversely affect performance on subtest 7 because the subject must remember the items for a longer period of time. This technique may also increase the length of the testing session. A second method to prevent fatigue is to use a short form of the test that involves fewer items. At present, however, there is no short form of the test that has been shown to be equivalent to the longer form for interpretation purposes.

A third alternative is to limit the duration of testing to a set time period. We have found that the prorated score after 1 hour of testing correlates highly ($r = 0.85, p < 0.001, df = 60$) with the overall score achieved by the subject. This procedure has the effect of eliminating the more difficult later items for those subjects who are unable to do them at better than a chance level, and serves as well as the longer test in discriminating among brain-injured, schizophrenic, and normal patients, although it does tend to underestimate the number of errors that will be made by patients with severe brain injuries.

It is useful in some cases to employ a "testing-the-limits" procedure. Here the subject who is unable to do the test initially has the items repeated, along with hints and suggestions that may lead the subject to the correct principle. Such a procedure sometimes illuminates the qualitative problems the patient may have.

The score for the Halstead Category Test is the number of items missed. If all items are not completed, the total score is prorated by the following formula:

$$\frac{\text{number of errors}}{\text{number of items attempted}} \times 208$$

Speech-Sounds Perception Test

The Speech-Sounds Perception Test, one of Halstead's original examinations, consists of six sets of 10 items each. For each item the subject hears a nonsense word (e.g., FEEP) that must be matched with one of four written alternatives (e.g., TEEP, FEEP, FEEK, TEEK). All nonsense words are formed by addition of a consonant before and after the vowels EE. Thus the discrimination made is between different consonant sounds.

The test administrator explains that the subject will hear nonsense words, each of which must be matched against its written equivalent. Three sample items are presented on the tape that correspond to the first three items of the first set. If the subject successfully matches the sample items, the test is then given by playing the tape. If the subject fails to understand the instructions, they are repeated. After the test items have begun the examiner has no role, since all items are presented by the tape. The test is begun at the first item of the first set.

Although the test presents no administrative problems, it does present some interpretive problems. If the subject's reading level is below that for the fourth grade, it is not possible to determine whether errors are due to deficits in speech perception or deficits in reading or spelling ability. Matthews (1974) suggested that the Boston Aphasia Examination, which does not require reading skills, would be a more effective test with a reading-impaired population.

The score for the Speech-Sounds Perception Test is the number of errors made among the 60 items. Inspection of the items missed is sometimes useful as an aid in determining specific speech sounds that cause the patient the most difficulty.

Seashore Rhythm Test

The Seashore Rhythm Test was taken by Halstead from the Seashore Battery of Musical Abilities. The test involves 30 items, each of which consists of a pair of rhythmic patterns presented by tape. The subject must indicate whether the two patterns in each item are the same or different. This is accomplished by having the subject place an S or a D in the appropriate space on the answer sheet.

The test administrator explains that the subject will hear two rhythmic patterns, one after the other. The subject is told that it is necessary to decide if the patterns are the same or different. Following this, the sample items are presented. After the samples are presented the subject is told to write S or D as appropriate. The examiner also writes S (= same) and D (= different) on the answer sheet to avoid misunderstandings. If the subject understands the directions, the tape is started and the 30 items are presented.

Once the test has begun, it should not be stopped even if the subject becomes confused because of the speed at which the items are presented. This procedure makes the test a more sensitive indicator of brain damage, but it also interferes with interpretation because a poor performance may result from inability to pay attention and work at a normal speed rather than from inability to remember and match rhythmic patterns. If this appears to be the case, it is often informative to repeat the items slowly (by stopping the tape recorder). This procedure allows a more detailed analysis of the results. The score for the test is the number of items missed during normal administration.

Tactual Performance Test

The Tactual Performance Test is a modification by Halstead of a standard Goddard-Sequin formboard. The formboard is a board with 10 removable cutouts, each cutout being a different geometric shape. In the standard formboard task the subject attempts to place each geometric shape into the position from which it came. In this modification the formboard is placed on a base that holds it at a 45° angle to the horizontal. In addition, the subject is required to do the test blindfolded. Consequently, many of the skills demanded by the Tactual Performance Test are quite different from those required by the standard visual formboard test.

Because no visual skills are to be used in this test it is imperative that the subject never be allowed to see the board or the geometric shapes. The subject must be fully blindfolded before any test apparatus is presented. It is extremely important to ensure that the subject is not able to see in any direction.

After the subject is blindfolded the board and geometric blocks are placed directly before the subject. The examiner then tells the subject the task that is to be done and has the subject feel the outline of the board. Then the subject is allowed to begin the test. Three trials are run: dominant hand only, nondominant hand only, and both hands together. Throughout the test the examiner keeps the shapes directly before the subject.

A number of problems may arise in the course of the three trials. First, the subject may attempt to use both hands during the single-hand trials. If this occurs, the subject immediately should be stopped from using the extra hand. In some cases this may require that the examiner hold the uninvolved hand in the patient's lap.

A second problem can arise if the subject wanders from the board to the base supporting the board or the table. If this occurs, the subject should be told and should be reoriented. Similarly, the subject may be on the board but may be ignoring a whole section, such as the upper third. In this situation the subject should be told to feel the whole board so that this error will be corrected.

There may also be problems with geometric blocks already placed. The most common problem occurs when the subject accidentally knocks out a block that has already been correctly placed. In this situation the examiner should replace the block for the subject and tell the subject that this is being done. A rarer problem may occur if the subject forces a block into the wrong hole. This is difficult to do, but it is not impossible if the subject persists. In this situation the examiner should have the subject feel both the block and the space, explaining that they are not of the same pattern. However, the examiner is not to explain in what manner they differ.

Problems may also arise with subjects who are afraid of being blindfolded. This is more common in settings where psychiatric conditions as well as organic conditions are seen. This problem may be handled by shortening the time period for each trial (see below) and allowing the subject to remove the blindfold between trials. When this is done, the examiner must ensure that the subject does not see the board or blocks. For some subjects even these measures may be ineffective, and it may be impossible to test such subjects blindfolded. Such subjects can be tested without being blindfolded, although interpretation of results in such a situation is greatly altered.

Similar kinds of problems can arise with the patient who cannot work for long periods of time or the patient who gets dizzy after being blindfolded for several minutes. In each case the examiner may make an adaptation by shortening the length of each trial or by providing "time-out" periods. If such rest periods are included within a trial, it is necessary to note this on the report and take it into consideration during interpretation.

If a subject is completely unable to use one hand, all three trials should be carried out using only the good hand. As might be expected, this procedure also considerably affects the interpretation of results.

The final problem is the length of each trial. As can be seen from the preceding considerations, there are specific problems that limit the time during which a subject can be tested. In addition to those considerations, there is the problem of subjects who, if allowed, would take 30 minutes or more on each trial. This is an inordinate amount of time to spend on a single trial within a test battery. Reitan (unpublished manuscript, undated) suggested that 15 minutes is a reasonable time in most cases, although in cases where the subject fatigues easily or becomes frustrated he suggested a time limit of 10 minutes. Russell, Neuringer, and Goldstein (1970) suggested a general time limit of 10 minutes for each trial.

We have found that use of the 10-minute time limit yields as much information as the 15-minute limit, as well as saving a significant amount of testing time. For subjects who are unable to work 10 minutes, we attempt to get at least a 5-minute sample; however, the shorter the time period, the less reliable the results produced.

After the three trials have been completed, the blocks and board are put away, and the subject's blindfold is removed. The subject is then given a clean sheet of paper and instructed to draw an outline of the board and then to draw each of the geometric shapes at its proper location on the board. Then the examiner should examine the drawing. If any of the shapes are not clear, or if the subject is unable to draw, the subject can indicate by verbal description and by pointing what the geometric shape is and where it goes. There is no penalty for poor drawing if the subject can indicate the correct shape and position by these alternative means.

Several scores are generated by the Tactual Performance Test. First, there are the three time scores, one for each trial. These are added to yield a total time score. Two additional scores are derived from the drawings after the test: one for Memory (a point being given for each shape correctly remembered) and one for Location (a point for each correct shape placed in its correct position).

Trail-making Test

The Trail-making Test consists of two parts: A and B. Each part involves 25 circles distributed randomly on a piece of white paper 8½ by 11 inches. In part A there is a number (from 1 to 25) written inside each circle. In part B there is either a number (from 1 to 13) or a letter (from A to L) written inside each circle.

Before beginning part A, the subject is shown a sample page that has seven circles on it, numbered 1 through 7. The subject is given a pencil and is told to connect the circles, progressing from circle 1 to circle 2 to circle 3 and continuing until the end is reached. The subject is also told to work as quickly as possible. If the sample is completed correctly, the subject is then given the test page to be completed.

If the subject fails to complete the sample correctly, errors must be explained. For example: "You did not complete the circles in order. You are to go from 1 to 2 to 3 rather than from 1 to 2 to 4." If the subject cannot complete the sample even after explanation, the examiner should guide the subject through the correct sequence; then the subject should again be allowed to try alone. This process can be repeated until the subject successfully completes the sample or until it becomes clear that the subject is unable to complete the test.

When the actual test for part A begins, the instructions are repeated, followed by the command to begin. The subject is watched closely by the examiner. Any time a mistake is made, the error is immediately pointed out to the subject, who is then allowed to continue from the point where the error was made. For example, the examiner might say, "You skipped a number," or, "You failed to draw your line all the way to the last circle." The test is completed when the subject correctly reaches the last circle. The score for the test is the number of seconds that elapse between the time of the command to begin and the time that the subject correctly reaches the last circle.

After part A is completed, the subject is given the sample from part B. The subject is told to connect the circles by going from 1 to A to 2 to B, doing first a number, then a letter, then a number again. The subject is then allowed to do the sample. If it is correctly performed, the examiner then presents the test page. If an error is made in the sample, the examiner follows the same procedure described for part A.

Except for the change in basic tasks, part B of the test is conducted exactly as part A. Scoring is the same for both parts. In some cases the examiner will find that the subject is unable to complete a section of the test (usually part B). In this situation the subject can be stopped after 300 seconds.

Reitan-Klove Sensory–Perceptual Examination

The Reitan-Klove Sensory–Perceptual Examination involves a number of separate procedures designed to measure sensory functions. The first test is for tactile imperception. The subject's hands are placed palms down on a table, and the subject's eyes are kept closed. The examiner touches the right and left hands using a random sequence. The subject must report which hand is touched. During these trials the examiner must determine the pressure required to produce a consistent and accurate response from the subject.

The method of reporting may be changed if the subject cannot say the words "right" and "left" reliably. For example, the subject could raise the hand that was touched or could point to the words

"right" and "left" after opening the eyes. The method of reporting is
not important as long as only tactile input is used by the subject.

Some subjects are unable to keep their eyes closed, especially
those with right-hemisphere injuries (Fisher, 1956). These subjects
may be blindfolded, or their hands may be hidden from view behind
a curtain or through a board. Again, the method is not important as
long as the subject is denied visual feedback.

After these initial procedures the subject is touched on the left
hand alone, right hand alone, or both hands simultaneously in a
random order. Each type of touch should be repeated four times. The
purpose of this procedure is to determine if the subject can correctly
report the touching of both hands simultaneously. Failure to do so is
indicative of *suppression*. Suppressions are rare but are of important
diagnostic value. However, if the apparent suppression is in reality
due to the subject's failure to sense a touch on one hand because of
inadequate pressure, the interpretation of the suppression will change
considerably. Thus it is important to continue to use the proper amount
of pressure determined in the initial phase of the examination.

Additional suppressions can be determined for the right-hand–left-
face combination and the left-hand–right-face combination. This is
done by applying the procedures described for the right and left hands.

A similar procedure may be used with auditory stimuli. The
subject's eyes are kept closed, and the examiner stands behind the
subject. The examiner tells the subject that a noise will be made in the
right ear (touching it) or the left ear (touching it). The subject must
report in which ear the noise is made. The examiner makes the noise
by rubbing two fingers together. The examiner determines the necessary level of loudness and then alternates the four left, right, and
simultaneous trials as was done for the tactile stimuli.

In order for the examiner to determine suppressions for visual
stimuli, the subject must fixate on the examiner's nose. If the subject
cannot do so consistently, items can be presented in the subsequent
trials only when the subject is fixating, and this must be determined
on a trial-by-trial basis by the examiner.

The visual trials are conducted by having the examiner sit 3 feet
in front of the sitting subject. The examiner's hands are extended, and
the examiner tells the subject that it will be necessary to identify
whether the hand on the patient's right or the hand on the patient's
left is moved. Then the sequences used for the tactile and auditory
procedures are employed. The procedures are administered three
times (examiner's hands above eye level, examiner's hands at eye
level, examiner's hands below eye level).

In some cases patients will have deficits in peripheral vision. In such situations the distance between the examiner's hands must be reduced so that the subject will be able to report stimuli on both sides accurately. Some subjects may have complete loss in one visual field (homonymous hemianopia), which will make it impossible to test for suppressions, or there may be partial loss in the upper or lower visual field on one side (upper or lower quadrantanopia). In cases of partial loss, either above or below eye level, trials must be omitted, depending on the locus of the loss.

In all testing for suppressions, irrespective of the modality, the subject is never told that there may be bilateral stimulation, although most subjects soon realize this. In some cases suppressions may appear to occur because the subject is not paying attention or because the subject gets confused. In such cases it is useful to conduct the trials for that procedure again to ensure reliability of results (Goldstein, 1974). For all suppression procedures, scores are the numbers of suppressions separately recorded for left and right. If more than four trials are given, this is indicated.

After completing the suppression procedure, the examiner begins the finger agnosia procedure. This tests the ability of the subject to identify which finger is touched by the examiner. In this test the subject's eyes are closed (or the subject's hands may be concealed in some other manner). The fingers of the subject's hands (first right, then left) are then touched four times each in random order. The subject reports by identifying the finger touched (e.g., thumb, forefinger, middle finger) or by use of a number assigned to each finger (1 through 5). The system of naming or numbering the fingers must be determined before the procedure begins, and it should be the method the subject prefers. If the subject cannot use verbal responses, response may be made by raising the appropriate finger or touching it with the other hand. The score for each hand is the number of errors among 20 trials (five fingers tested four times).

The next procedure is fingertip number writing. The examiner writes numbers (3, 4, 5, or 6) on the subject's hands that the subject must identify. The examiner begins the procedure by writing the numbers 3, 4, 5, and 6 on the subject's palm and identifying each number. If the subject wishes, the examiner can modify the manner in which the numbers are written. Then the subject's eyes are closed (other procedures previously discussed may be used for limiting visual information), and the examiner writes numbers on each finger of the right hand, proceeding from the thumb to the little finger. This is repeated four times. The number to be written at each trial is given on the scoring form. The procedure is then repeated for the left hand. The score for each hand is the number of errors among 20 trials.

In the coin-recognition procedure the examiner places a penny, a nickel, and a dime into the subject's right hand and then the left hand. The subject must identify each coin by touch alone and is not allowed to rub it on other objects or do anything except feel the coin. If the subject is able to identify coins in one hand alone, the examiner next places coins in both hands simultaneously, two pennies, two nickels, or two dimes. The subject is not told that the coins are the same. The score is the number of errors made for each hand.

The Tactile Form Recognition Test uses four shapes cut out of plastic: square, triangle, circle, and cross. These shapes are available for placing in the subject's hand, and they are also mounted at the top of a board with a hole in it. The subject alternately places the right and left hands through the hole, at which point the examiner places a plastic shape in the subject's hand, which is hidden from view. The subject feels the shape and points with the free hand to the same shape mounted on the board. Beginning with the right hand through the board, all four shapes are placed in the subject's hand, one at a time. The order of presentation of the shapes is given on the scoring form. The procedure is then repeated with the left hand, the right hand again, and the left hand again. Two kinds of scores are determined: the number of errors for each hand and the time measure. The time measure for each item is calculated as elapsed time from the time of placement of the shape in the palm of the subject's hand to the time of the subject's answer. These times are summed to get a total for each hand.

Reitan-Indiana Aphasia Examination

The Reitan-Indiana Aphasia Examination involves a survey of the major forms of aphasia. A booklet of items containing pictures and words to be recognized or read is necessary to administer the test. The test requires the subject to (1) name objects, (2) spell words, (3) draw shapes, including a Greek cross, (4) read letters and numbers, (5) read words, (6) read sentences, (7) write words, (8) pronounce words, (9) write sentences, (10) explain concepts, (11) do arithmetic, on paper as well as mentally, (12) discriminate body parts, and (13) tell right from left. Items must be presented exactly as described in the manual; any deviation from the correct answer is counted as an error. Two systems of scoring exist. In the first, the score is the number of items in which there is an error. The second is a weighted scoring system: more points are scored for items that are considered more significant. The weights for all items are presented in the book by Russell et al. (1970).

Lateral Dominance Examination

The Lateral Dominance Examination involves a set of procedures by which one attempts to establish the hand, eye, and foot dominance of the subject and the relative functioning of the right and left hands. The first items on the test determine the subject's ability to follow the instructions for the test. The subject is asked to do such things as, "Show me your right hand." The next section attempts to determine the subject's hand dominance. The subject is asked to demonstrate how to do seven things, such as throw a ball. The examiner makes note of the hand the subject uses. The subject is asked to write his or her name, the examiner noting the hand used and the time it takes. The subject is then asked to write the name using the other hand. The time to do this is recorded.

The subject is then asked to show how one would look through a toy telescope or shoot a toy rifle. The examiner notes the eye used in the first item and the shoulder used in the second. The subject is then asked to show how one would step on a bug and how one would kick a football. The examiner notes the leg used.

The next procedure is the Miles ABC Test of Ocular Dominance. The subject must look through V-shaped scopes at various times. Unknown to the subject, only one eye at a time can be used to look through the scope. The stimulus items are held directly below the eyes of the examiner. The subject looks through the scope, and the examiner determines the eye used. Ten trials are given. The scores are the number of trials in which the right eye is used and the number of trials in which the left eye is used.

The final procedure is grip strength, requiring a dynamometer, preferably one that can be adjusted to the size of the patient's hands. The subject takes the dynamometer in one hand. The hand is extended downward, and the subject is instructed to squeeze as hard as possible. Two trials are given for each hand. If the two trials differ by more than 5 kg (11pounds), additional trials are conducted until two trials produce results within 5 kg of one another. These two trials do not have to be consecutive. The final score for each hand is the average of the two trials selected.

Halstead Finger-tapping Test

The Halstead Finger-tapping Test uses a counter with an arm that is mounted on a flat board. The arm can be pressed down by the subject's index finger; it then returns to its original position. The subject is told to place one whole hand on the board, with the index finger on the arm of the counter. The examiner instructs the subject to tap the key down, allow it to return, and then tap it down again as quickly as possible. The proper method is demonstrated by the examiner.

The subject is then given five 10-second trials with each hand, starting with the preferred hand. The subject is given a rest after the third trial. Additional rest periods may be included if the subject appears fatigued.

To be acceptable, the scores for the two hands must be within five taps of one another. If this is not the case, additional trials are conducted until five trials produce results within five taps of one another. This is usually achieved within fewer than eight trials. The final scores are the averages of the five trials selected for each hand.

One major problem in this test is the tendency of some subjects to use the hand or arm in tapping instead of just the index finger. In this situation the subject should be made aware of this failure to follow instructions, and the trial should begin over again. In those few cases in which the subject is unable to tap with the index finger while keeping the hand and arm immobilized, the examiner must attempt to get as close an approximation as possible. Because these subjects generally do quite badly even with the nonstandardized administration this usually does not affect the interpretation of results significantly.

Cutoff Points

The most basic manner of looking at the components of the Halstead-Reitan test battery is to determine if a score falls in the "normal" range or the "impaired" range. This represents level-of-performance analysis, as Reitan has discussed it, and this is necessary in first examining the battery's scores. It should be noted that the cutoff points listed here (the score at which a performance becomes abnormal) are useful but not absolute (see Table 2-1, p. 23). For example, one might be highly suspicious of a normal but borderline score in speech perception for a subject with a Ph.D. degree but not at all bothered by such a score for a subject with a sixth-grade education. Keeping such factors in mind, the cutoff points and the normal and abnormal ranges provide excellent means by which one can compare scores to one another and compare subjects to one another.

2
Interpretation of Single Tests

The components of the Halstead-Reitan test battery attempt to measure different aspects of neuropsychological function. Thus each test can be thought of as representing different major skills. By examining scores on the different tests one is able to infer the presence of brain damage as well as the probable location, and, in some cases, the cause; however, it is important to recognize that no single test is a pure measure of any simple neuropsychological skill. All tests require the presence of at least several skills, with some skill requirements more prominent than others. Deficits in any of the skills can lead to deficiencies in performance. Thus it is important to be aware of the full range of abilities involved in the performance of a given test and to understand these factors thoroughly before attempting more complex analysis of the data. This chapter will deal with the interpretation of performance on each of the tests within the battery.

HALSTEAD CATEGORY TEST

The Halstead Category Test measures the subject's ability to form hypotheses and to validate them by experience. The test also relies heavily on the ability to form a general hypothesis from specific examples and to change the hypothesis when subsequent results are not in accord with the hypothesis. The test may also be affected by an individual's problem-solving skills (intellectual potential) and the individual's frustration-tolerance level.

Other abilities that the test items tap include visuospatial skills, attention, concentration, memory, and simple counting skills. Differential performance on the subtests may reveal some specific deficits in the subject's skill. For example, the fifth and sixth subtests have the heaviest emphasis on complex visuospatial skills.

This test is highly complex; very few subjects (normals included) attain fewer than 20 errors. There is a significant correlation between age and score on the Halstead Category Test (Vega & Parsons, 1967). The Halstead Category Test has been found to be up to 90 percent effective overall in distinguishing between brain-damaged subjects and normal nonpsychiatric subjects (Wheeler, Burke, & Reitan, 1963), possibly in part because of the effects of IQ on a subject's performance (Logue & Allen, 1971). Because the test relies on a wide variety of neuropsychological skills mediated by both the right and left hemispheres, it is sensitive to brain damage of all types. Consequently, it is best used as an overall indicator of pathological conditions.

The test may also be useful in left and bilateral prefrontal disorders (Halstead, 1947). The conceptual nature of the test and the requirement for good organizational and purposive behavior make the Halstead Category Test sensitive to localized prefrontal disorders (Luria, 1966). The existence of deficits on the Halstead Category Test, along with poor performance on most other parts of the battery, however, usually argue for involvement of other areas of the brain independent of the question of prefrontal involvement.

Qualitatively, this test is ideal for examining the subject's conceptual ability and problem-solving capacity. "Testing the limits" by providing hints and guiding the subject to the correct answer may yield information about the patient's strategy and thinking process.

SEASHORE RHYTHM TEST

Several basic abilities are important in the Seashore Rhythm Test. First, the subject must be capable of sustained attention. The test moves along quickly, with only slight pauses between items. No signal is given to indicate a new item. Second, the test requires good rhythmic skills. Rhythm relationships between tones must be clearly discerned. Finally, immediate auditory memory is also necessary to match the two rhythmic patterns in each item.

Deficits on the Seashore Rhythm Test have typically been associated with the right temporal lobe (Reitan, unpublished manuscript). Left-hemisphere injuries, however, are also associated with rhythm deficits (Osmon, Sweet, & Golden, 1978). Poor performance in either may be due to attentional problems or to rhythmic problems. Comparisons between the Seashore Rhythm Test and the Speech-Sounds Perception Test are often useful in determining the laterality of brain damage.

Because the rhythm test is highly dependent on the ability to generate sustained concentration it is quite effective (82 percent) in identifying brain-damaged subjects in general (Wheeler et al., 1963); however, Golden (1977) noted that an overall hit rate of only 70 percent was obtained when an acute psychiatric control group was used.

SPEECH-SOUNDS PERCEPTION TEST

The ability to discriminate phonemes and to match them to their written language symbols are the two most important skills on this test. The original test contains 60 items, and thus it is a rather boring task for many subjects. Our laboratory has found it useful, in regard to both efficiency and the subject's energy, to administer only the first half of the test. Golden and Anderson (1977) found no significant loss of accuracy in this practice.

It has been found that poor performance on this test generally indicates left-temporal-lobe dysfunction (Golden, 1978). Golden stated that mild deficits are reflected only by problems in distinguishing similar phonemes, whereas severe injuries more generally disrupt phonemic discrimination. Luria (1966) theorized that the secondary temporal areas of both hemispheres can decode speech and that the left (dominant) hemisphere is more specialized for this task. For example, Osmon and Golden (1978) reported poor performance on this test to be associated with dysfunctions of the right temporal lobe as well as the left. Apparently, poor performance can be associated with either temporal lobe, albeit more strongly with injuries to the left hemisphere. Golden (1977) found that 86 percent of left-hemisphere-damaged patients and 61 percent of right-hemisphere-damaged patients showed deficits in the Speech-Sounds Perception Test; however, very poor performance (more than 20 errors) is almost always associated with a left-hemisphere injury. Comparing performance on this test with performance on the Seashore Rhythm Test can be useful in distinguishing between right and left-hemisphere injuries.

HALSTEAD FINGER-TAPPING TEST

The Halstead Finger-tapping Test represents a measure of fine motor control. The test requires kinesthetic ability, motor speed, and visual–motor coordination to a mild degree. Inattention and inability to carry out instructions can also disrupt performance on this test.

Relative deficits for either hand reflect injury to the contralateral hemisphere, however bilateral deficits can indicate injury to the left (dominant) hemisphere because of its control of overall coordination. Deficits on the Finger-tapping Test may reflect injury to the motor strip area; however, disruption of sensory feedback because of parietal lobe dysfunction can result in decreased performance as well (Golden, 1978). Peripheral injuries to the hand or arm and subcortical disruption resulting in tremor or damage to the motor or sensory tracts can also be responsible for low scores on this test.

Both level-of-performance deficits and relative differences between the performances of the two hands can be indications of brain damage. Wheeler et al. (1963) found 79 percent hit rates in brain-damaged populations using the level-of-performance measurement alone. Control groups also show impairment with level-of-performance measurement about half of the time. Therefore a strongly lateralized deficit is more likely to be indicative of brain injury, since it rarely occurs in normal non-brain-damaged populations that are free of peripheral difficulties.

When comparing tbe left and right hands, one should generally expect that the dominant (usually right) hand will perform about 10 percent better than the nondominant hand. In cases in which the dominant hand performs only as well as the nondominant hand or less effectively than the nondominant hand, one should suspect a deficit in the dominant hand. In cases in which the dominant hand outperforms the nondominant hand by 15–20 percent or more, one should suspect impairment of the nondominant hand.

TACTUAL PERFORMANCE TEST

The Tactual Performance Test (TPT) is quite sensitive to brain damage in general because of the number of skills necessary to execute the test. Because the subject must complete the test blindfolded successful performance depends heavily on kinesthetic/proprioceptive skills (feedback from the joints and muscles) as well as spatial abilities. To achieve an adequate time score, the subject must use spatial and tactual skills to identify the shapes and their positions on the board and must also use purposive and organizational abilities to execute the task. Because subjects are not forewarned that they will later be required to draw the board from memory some measure of incidental spatial learning is obtained through the Memory and Location procedures (Golden, 1978).

Generally, the performance with either hand is assumed to reflect the status of the contralateral hemisphere. A decrease in the time score of one-third from the time required for completion by the dominant hand is usually to be expected on the second trial (using the nondominant hand) as a result of learning. A similar decrease is to be expected between the second and third trials. If the score for the nondominant hand is more than 40 percent better than the score for the dominant hand, a dominant-hemisphere lesion is likely; if the score for the nondominant hand is less than 25 percent better than the score for the dominant hand, a lesion of the nondominant hemisphere is likely.

The TPT may reflect dysfunction along anterior–posterior lines as well. If the tactile and/or spatial aspects of the test are responsible for poor performance, the damage is likely to be in the posterior aspect of the brain. Conversely, if poor performance is due to inadequate control and execution of behavior or a poor problem-solving strategy, then an anterior focus of injury is more likely. Indications of the location of damage can be obtained through qualitative analysis of TPT performance and by comparing the TPT with the Finger-tapping Test; TPT may reflect posterior while tapping suggests anterior lesions. Prefrontal lesions also cause low scores on the TPT, usually in the absence of basic sensory–perceptual deficits, thus allowing their identification by comparison of the TPT with the Sensory–Perceptual Examination. Care must be taken with both of these comparisons, because motor deficits will affect the TPT because of the loss of motor control, and prefrontal lesions may produce sensory deficits, although usually of a complex nature (e.g., fingertip number writing errors).

The TPT also appears to be useful in diagnosing psychiatric performance on the battery. Golden (1978) reported 70 percent effectiveness in differentiating brain-damaged subjects and acute schizophrenic subjects using the TPT. The memory score appears to be especially useful in this discrimination, yielding an 80 percent hit rate.

TRAIL-MAKING TEST

The Trail-making Test, part A, is a general measure of visuospatial scanning ability and motor and sequencing skills. The subject must also be able to count to 25 and keep track of the place of each number in the sequence. This part, like part B, requires the subject to draw connecting lines between circles. Thus it requires that the patient's dominant hand be used. Although the test was not normed this way, it may be administered by having the subject point or draw the lines with the nondominant hand. Care should be exercised in interpreting a test given this way.

In addition to the skills required for part A, some different abilities are necessary for part B. Alternating between numbers and letters requires more language skills of the subject. Ability to switch flexibly between the two different sets (a set of numbers and a set of letters) is also required.

The two parts are generally used in conjunction to help determine the laterality of brain injury (Reitan & Tarshes, 1959). Part A is generally considered more a measure of right-hemisphere integrity (i.e., visual scanning, spatial skills), whereas part B is more indicative of left-hemisphere intactness (i.e., language symbol manipulation and direction of behavior according to a complex plan). Therefore when one part indicates impairment relative to the other part, a lateralized injury may be present. Reitan (1958) also reported that part B was a sensitive indicator of brain damage in general. He found the test 81 percent effective in diagnosing brain-damaged subjects. The test is also sensitive to age and IQ, especially part B (Golden, 1977; Reitan, 1955a).

The Trail-making Test may be used to discriminate brain-injured subjects and psychiatric subjects at approximately 70 percent effectiveness (Golden, 1978; Goldstein & Neuringer, 1966). Qualitatively, the psychiatric subjects are likely to show bizarre performance signs (Goldstein & Neuringer, 1966). In populations where motivation and cooperation exist, the Trail-making Test may be used to make highly accurate discriminations among psychiatric subjects and brain-injured subjects.

In comparing the two parts of the Trail-making test, several rules of thumb may be used. First, if the score on one part is in the brain-damaged range (see Table 2-1) and the other is normal, the part whose score is in the brain-damaged range is considered to indicate greater impairment. Part A is considered to indicate greater impairment if the score on part B is less than twice the score on part A. Part B indicates

Table 2-1
Normal and Abnormal
Ranges for Halstead-Reitan Test Battery

Test	Normal Range	Abnormal Range
Halstead Category Test	0–50	51–208
Speech-Sounds Perception Test	0–7	8–60
Seashore Rhythm Test	0–5	6–30
Tactual Performance Test		
Total time	0–15.6	15.7–30+
Location	5–10	0–4
Memory	6–10	0–5
Right hand (time/block)	0–.82	.83+
Left hand (time/block)	0–.45	.46+
Both hands (time/block)	0–.27	.28+
Trail-making Test (A)	0–39	40+
Trail-making Test (B)	0–91	92+
Finger-tapping Test (dominant)*	50+	0–49
Finger-tapping Test (nondominant)*	46+	0–45
Impairment Index	0–0.4	0.5–1.0

Norms were adapted from Reitan (1959c), Halstead (1947), and Russell, Neuringer, and Goldstein (1970).

*Female norms are about 10 percent less.

greater impairment if its score is more than three times the score on part A. Tests in which the part B score lies between two times and three times the part A score suggest that performances on the two parts are essentially equal.

REITAN-KLOVE SENSORY–PERCEPTUAL EXAMINATION

The Reitan-Klove Sensory–Perceptual Examination measures both basic (suppressions and finger agnosia) and more complex (astereognosis and fingertip number-writing) sensory and perceptual processes. Besides these abilities, the subject's attention, cooperation, and peripheral injuries heavily influence the results obtained with this test; however, the presence of lateralized deficits is a highly reliable indicator of brain dysfunction in the absence of peripheral disorders. Sensory deficits may also indicate subcortical central nervous system damage, especially when they occur in the absence of other cognitive deficits.

Valid suppressions are rare, but when they are present they almost always indicate tissue damage in the contralateral hemisphere. To detect valid suppressions it is imperative to enlist the subject's undivided attention and cooperation. Tactile, visual, and auditory suppressions are indicative of damage to the primary projection areas in the parietal, occipital, and temporal lobes, respectively.

Lateralized deficits indicated by the remaining tests (Finger Agnosia, Fingertip Number-writing, Coin Recognition, and Tactile Form Recognition) are generally localized to the secondary and tertiary areas of the contralateral parietal lobe (Golden, 1978). Severe finger agnosia is typically seen in the presence of left parietal injuries, with bilateral deficits common; however, right parietal injuries do not usually result in bilateral deficits. Lateralized injury is usually not indicated unless there is a difference of three or more errors between the scores for the two body sides.

The Fingertip Number-writing Test is similar to the Finger Agnosia test, but it is much more sensitive. Thus injuries not actually in the parietal lobes can result in poor scores on this test without concomitant poor scores on the Finger Agnosia test. This test may also indicate anterior frontal injuries. Deficits on the TPT, with only Fingertip Number-writing problems or no sensory problems, are therefore likely to indicate prefrontal involvement. Lateralized deficits are indicated by a difference of three or more errors between the scores for the two hands.

The final two tests (Coin Recognition and Tactile Form Recognition), as measures of astereognosis, test the subject's ability to recognize objects by touch alone. Both tests are associated with parietal lobe functions; however, the Tactile Form Test is much more reliable. The Coin Recognition Test is poorly performed by many normal subjects. It is therefore difficult to interpret and should never be considered in isolation from the other sensory measures. Any errors on the Tactile Form Test are significant, and lateralized parietal injury is indicated when the performance with one hand is worse than that with the other. Many users of the battery no longer use the Coin Recognition Test because of its inherent problems.

WECHSLER ADULT INTELLIGENCE SCALE

The Wechsler Adult Intelligence Scale (WAIS) has been used as a neuropsychological device ever since Wechsler (1944, 1958) developed the "hold" and "don't hold" tests. Since that time, various indices using the Wechsler subtests have been developed to detect brain damage; for a review, see the work of Golden (1978). Because of the varied natures of deficits resulting from various types of brain damage no single index has been found that works in all populations.

In general, a pattern analysis of the WAIS subtests is more productive. The various deficits indicated on the WAIS are analyzed in comparison with each other to determine the basic problem underlying the profile. The WAIS deficits are also compared with the overall neuropsychological profile. This method is more in keeping with the rationale of using a comprehensive test battery than is interpretation of specific scores in isolation from other tests.

Information

As a measure of the subject's long-term general knowledge, the The Arithmetic Test can be suggestive of either right- or left-Zimmerman, & Rogal, 1971). The test is sensitive to the subject's educational level, and it may serve as a measure of the ability to acquire information. Scores are usually affected only by severe general deterioration, such as that seen in advanced organic brain syndrome or some other severe degenerative disorder. Thus the Information score is often considered to indicate the premorbid level of functioning against which deterioration indicated by other scores is measured. One major exception to this is the adult who has sustained serious injury early in life. Such individuals are unable to learn and will do poorly on many of the WAIS tests that are considered insensitive to adult injury.

Comprehension

Like the Information Test, the Comprehension (C) Test is quite stable (Russell, 1972), including scores on the understanding of everyday situations. This score can be used as a measure of premorbid functioning when scores on tests sensitive to brain damage are down and the comprehension score is not. The test, however, is affected by such things as the subject's social skills and breadth of experience. For this reason interpretation of this test as a measure of premorbid functioning should be made with caution if deficits in these areas are probable.

Arithmetic

The Arithmetic (A) Test is sensitive to a number of deficits. Besides requiring arithmetic skill, the test is sensitive to inability to translate a story problem into an arithmetic operation, inability to ember the story problem, difficulty in working a problem "in the ....d," spatial categorization, and anxiety. The anxiety of doing arithmetic often causes normal subjects to perform quite poorly.

The Arithmetic Test can be suggestive of either right- or left-hemisphere dysfunction. McFie (1969, 1975) noted the sensitivity of this test to left-parietal damage, presumably because of the association of numeric categorical ability with this area of the brain (Luria, 1966). Luria (1966) noted that the parietal area was involved in understanding the categorical structure of numerical positions. He also postulated a major role for the parietal area in comprehending mathematical operation signs.

Left-parietal verbal functions are also significant in the performance of the Arithmetic Test. In fact, any injuries affecting verbal skills may cause poor performance on this subtest. In addition, the attention and concentration needed to complete the test successfully make it fairly sensitive to brain damage in general. Finally, since spatial skills are important for many arithmetic processes, right-hemisphere injuries may also affect Arithmetic scores.

Similarities

The ability to identify abstract commonalities between two objects or ideas is required by the Similarities (S) Test. Poor scores on this subtest are highly related to dysphasia and are often seen in the presence of left-temporal and posterior parietal injuries (McFie, 1975). Occasionally, scores on this test will be low in left-prefrontal injuries because of the abstract categorical nature of the task. By and large, however, the test is highly associated with verbal ability, and as such it may be a good indicator of preinjury level of functioning when it is the highest verbal score.

Digit Span

The Digit Span (DS) test examines the subject's capacity for immediate auditory memory recall. Attention and anxiety also seem to be influential in the performance of this task. The task is quite sensitive to brain dysfunction in general (Woo-Sam, 1971). The digits-forward part of the test seems to be more indicative of left-hemisphere damage. However, the more sequential/spatial aspect of the digits-backward part seems to make it more strongly associated with right-hemisphere injury. If the digits-forward part is at least three digits longer than the digits-backward part, a right-hemisphere disorder is strongly indicated (Klove, 1959; Rudel & Denckla, 1974).

The basic sequential and auditory memory nature of the task makes the test especially sensitive to left-temporal-lobe involvement. The necessity for sustained attention and concentration makes the test sensitive to brain damage in general; however, for this same reason the test is sensitive to psychiatric disorders, especially where anxiety interferes with performance.

Vocabulary

Vocabulary (V) is a basic measure of verbal skills that are relatively insensitive to brain damage. Thus the Vocabulary subtest often serves as a measure of premorbid status; however, deficits will be detected in severe aphasics and in the presence of advanced degenerative disorders. A high correlation (about 0.8) is seen between this test and overall IQ. Therefore when large differences appear between scores on this and other tests, brain damage is likely (except in cases where cultural language deficits may be involved).

The test requires the subject to define each word orally, and it is therefore an expressive measure as well as a receptive measure. Oftentimes it is useful to compare this test with a purer measure of receptive abilities in subjects with expressive speech problems.

Digit Symbol

The Digit Symbol (DSy) test requires motor speed, visual–motor coordination, and the ability to associate numbers with nonverbal symbols. The test is generally sensitive to brain dysfunction and is considered the most sensitive indicator of brain damage on the WAIS. It is also sensitive to anxiety and psychiatric conditions (Rapaport, Gill, & Schafer, 1968). Because of the varied abilities important in this task, performance can be down in the presence of any type of injury, and it has little localizing value; however, it is often used to corroborate motor deficits.

Picture Completion

The ability to analyze complex visual configurations and determine missing parts is required in this test (PC). Woo-Sam (1971) has reported this test to be rather insensitive to brain damage; however, it has been noted that complex visual analysis of unfamiliar patterns is related to right-temporal-lobe function (Kimura, 1963). As a result, severe injuries to the right temporal area may cause occasional poor scores on this test.

Picture Arrangement

The Picture Arrangement (PA) measure examines the subject's ability to recognize a theme unifying several pictures and then the ability to sequence the pictures in the correct order to depict the theme in a logically developed fashion. Thus sequencing, visual analysis, and conceptual construction are tested.

The verbal and conceptual nature of the test gives it sensitivity to left-hemisphere dysfunction. The spatial sequencing and analysis of unfamiliar visual material gives it sensitivity to right-hemisphere damage. When the score on this test is poor relative to scores on the other performance tests in the absence of verbal deficits, an anterior right-hemisphere lesion is likely (McFie, 1975). When its score is poor along with those on a number of other tests, Picture Arrangement is of little localizing value.

Block Design

The obvious spatial nature of this test makes it most sensitive to right-hemisphere and diffuse brain damage (McFie, 1975). Spatial deficits resulting from left-parietal-lobe dysfunction can also produce poor scores on this test (McFie, 1960).

The Block Design (BD) Test seems most closely related to posterior right-hemisphere dysfunction. When accompanied by construction dyspraxia and left-body sensory signs, poor scores on this test usually indicate right-parietal damage. Deficits can also be produced by anterior lesions and are usually indicated when basic sensory signs, such as finger dysgnosia, are absent. Qualitatively, right-parietal dysfunction can be diagnosed when there are basic spatial deficits, such as those involving rotations or transformations. Anterior lesions are more strongly indicated when the subject lacks an overall strategy and when problem-solving skills are deficient; however, tactile, motor, and kinesthetic dysfunctions often complicate the picture, making qualitative analysis difficult if not impossible. Poor scores on the Block Design subtest may indicate left-parietal injuries as well, although right-parietal injuries generally cause more severe deficits. In evaluating Block Design performance, one must remember that errors caused by rotating the design have frequently been found to be associated with brain damage.

Object Assembly

Like the Block Design Test, the Object Assembly (OA) Test is basically spatial in nature; however, it is not as sensitive as the Block Design Test. The test involves jigsaw puzzles of common objects.

Thus it can be encoded verbally and can tap previously learned patterns. It is not as pure a measure of abstract spatial skills as is Block Design.

Poor scores can occur because of left-hemisphere injuries resulting in right-hand motor impairment and as a result of verbal and spatial deficits associated with left-parietal-lobe damage; however, the test is primarily sensitive to right-hemisphere disorders. Right-parietal dysfunction as well as temporal- and frontal-lobe dysfunction can result in poor performance on this test. The test usually has little localizing value.

REITAN-INDIANA APHASIA EXAMINATION

The Reitan-Indiana Aphasia Examination is designed to detect the numerous signs of language disorders. The test is quite sensitive to brain damage, with reports of 86 percent accuracy when two or more signs are present (Reitan, unpublished manuscript); however, there are brain-damaged subjects who show no dysphasia signs.

The Aphasia Examination is perhaps the most reliable indicator of left-hemisphere dysfunction. Wheeler and Reitan (1962) have classified each item on the test according to the strength of its lateralizing value. The strongest indicators of left-hemisphere involvement include inability to name objects (dysnomia), inability to read (dyslexia), inability to write (dysgraphia), and inability to recognize numbers and letters (visual letter and number dysgnosia). Other signs that may suggest left-hemisphere damage but that may also occur in the presence of right-hemisphere dysfunction include inability to calculate (dyscalculia), inability to spell (spelling dyspraxia), and inability to discriminate right and left without confusion (right–left disorientation).

Very poor performance is generally indicative of either left-temporal/parietal injury or generalized diffuse damage. Deficits may also occur as a result of left-frontal disruption. These problems are usually confined to expressive speech and writing, central dysarthria, and dysgraphia (Golden, 1978; Schiller, 1947). Right-hemisphere signs include construction dyspraxia (Wheeler, 1963) and left–right disorientation. For example, the drawings may be spatially distorted and the key may be reversed and/or asymmetrical, whereas in the drawings of left-hemisphere-damaged subjects the key may lack detail, with the spatial aspects preserved. These deficits, as well as the unilateral spatial neglect that often appears as inattention to the left side of the page or drawing, are typically indicative of right-parietal damage, but they may be associated with injuries anywhere in the right hemisphere

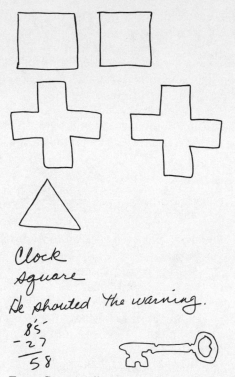

Fig. 2-1.   From Case 1 (all case numbers refer to Chapter
5). Performance of normal individual on Aphasia Test.

(Golden, 1978). Figures 2-1 through 2-14 illustrate various degrees of
construction dyspraxia. They were chosen from the cases presented
in Chapter 5.

IMPAIRMENT INDEX

The Impairment Index is a summary score representing performance on the tests in the battery most sensitive to brain dysfunction in
general. Anywhere from 7 to 12 tests are included on different versions
of the index. For the purposes of this book, the index is composed of
the following: the Category Test, the Total Time, Memory, and
Location scores on the TPT, the worst-hand score on the Finger-
tapping Test, the Speech-Sounds Perception Test, and the Rhythm
Test. The index was designed to provide an indication of the overall
level of functioning attained across the entire battery.

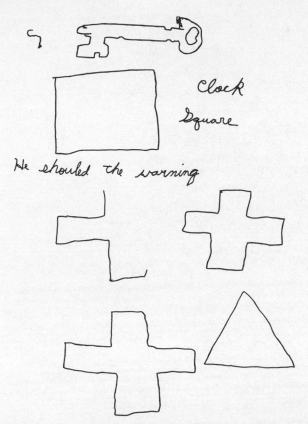

Fig. 2-2.   From Case 6. This subject shows mildly impaired
drawing, but within normal limits. There is more significant
impairment in the writing sample ("shouted," "warning").

The score on the index is calculated as the ratio of the number of
tests in the index that are in the brain-damaged range (Table 2-1) to
the total number of tests making up the index. For example, if four
tests are performed at or worse than the cutoff separating brain-
damaged performance and normal performance, then the ratio will be
4 divided by 7, or 0.57. An index score greater than 0.4 is generally
indicative of brain damage, although there are exceptions to this rule
that are discussed in the appropriate chapters of this book.

Because of the different effects that various types and severities
of lesions produce in the Impairment Index, statements about the
causes of brain damage are also possible. Type, severity, and chronicity of an injury are often reflected in the score on the Impairment
Index. For example, tumors cause various Impairment Index values,

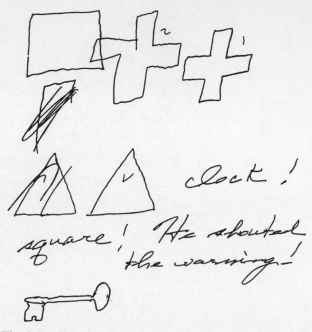

Fig. 2-3. From Case 9. This patient shows mild construction dyspraxia. Note overlapping of figures as well as
overdrawing on cross no. 2. The patient is somewhat aware
of his problems, as evidenced by the crossed out triangles.
Note the simplicity of the key as well.

depending on their locations and types (Golden, 1978). Fast-growing
destructive tumors cause the greatest neuropsychological disruption
and therefore the highest scores on the Impairment Index (usually at
least 0.9). Slow-growing nondestructive tumors cause less severe
impairment, earning Impairment Index scores in the range of 0.4 to
0.8.

The location of a lesion plays an important role in the score on
the index. For example, a destructive fast-growing tumor located in
the right prefrontal lobe may not affect the Speech-Sounds Perception
Test and the Category Test. Therefore an index value less than 1.0
would be earned, which is uncharacteristic of this type of lesion.

The chronicity of a lesion also affects the score on the index. In
general, the Impairment Index score is lower in older lesions. This
decrement in the index usually occurs as a result of spontaneous
recovery of function following an acute injury. In an acute injury

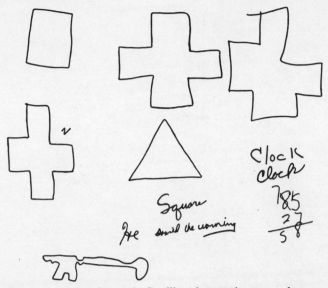

Fig. 2-4. From Case 12. Spelling dyspraxia, some dysgraphia, and construction dyspraxia can be seen in this example, although the construction dyspraxia is intermittent and is not obvious on all figures.

therefore the index score will be high initially and will decrease with time; however, in degenerative disorders the index score will increase with time.

COMPARISONS AMONG TESTS

The interpretation of any given test may vary from subject to subject because of the multiple abilities that may affect any single measure. As a result, comparison of test scores becomes an important method for identifying the underlying cause responsible for a given score or for determining its significance in terms of neuropsychological diagnosis. For example, poor performance on the TPT may be due to motor dysfunction; however, if a measure of motor performance (e.g., Finger-tapping Test) is normal, we are able to discard this hypothesis. As the reader might infer, these comparisons form a major part of the process of diagnosis.

Three types of comparisons have been found to be useful in neuropsychological work: first, comparisons among the various motor

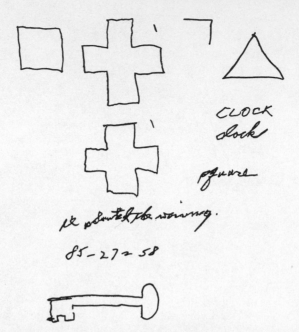

Fig. 2-5. From Case 15. There is borderline drawing impairment, but it is still within normal limits. Note the simplicity of the key, although it is correctly organized spatially.

and sensory measures on the battery; second, comparisons between the verbal and performance IQs on the WAIS; third, comparisons between tests representing either (theoretically) right- and left-hemisphere performances or posterior and anterior performances within a hemisphere.

Motor and Sensory Comparisons

Important comparisons can be made between the performances of the left and right hands on the Finger-tapping Test, the TPT, and the Finger Agnosia, Fingertip Number-writing, Grip Strength, and Tactile Form Recognition Tests. In general, deficits of the left hand suggest impairment to the right hemisphere, whereas deficits of the right hand suggest impairment to the left hemisphere. In each of these comparisons the actual level of performance is ignored; only the relationship between the two sides of the body is considered. This has the advantage of controlling for the subject's basic motor speed as

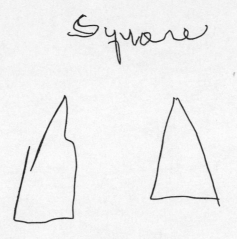

Fig. 2-6.   From Case 19. This output took two pages (see
Fig. 2-7) because of the size of the figures. In this first page,
construction dyspraxia is extremely evident, while
"Square" is copied legibly.

well as the attentional processes that may interfere with motor and
sensory processes.

The level of performance does play an important role, however,
in determining the likelihood of diffuse injuries. Subjects with diffuse
injuries will often show deficits on one side greater than those on the
other, as is true for many lateralized injuries, but they will also show
generalized decreases in the levels of both measures. Such a pattern
may also be seen in serious and widespread injuries to the dominant
(usually left) hemisphere because of the role of the dominant hemisphere in coordinating bilateral motor skills. As we shall see, these
conditions can be distinguished on the basis of what cognitive deficits
are also present and the degree of impairment.

Important comparisons can also be made between motor and
sensory tests. The most basic comparison can be made between the

Fig. 2-7.   From Case 19 (second part of Fig. 2-6). This page illustrates construction dyspraxia.

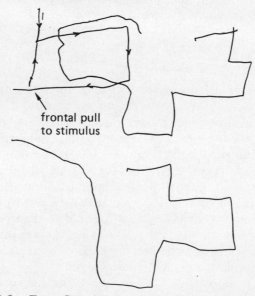

frontal pull
to stimulus

Fig. 2-8.   From Case 21. Severe construction dyspraxia.

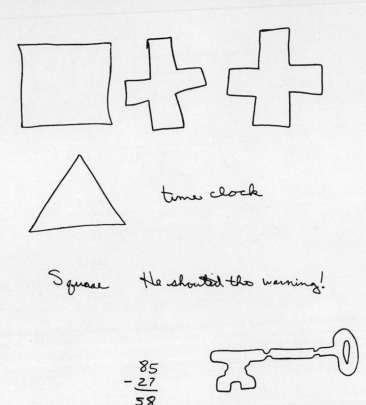

time clock

Square   He shouted the warning!

$$\begin{array}{r} 85 \\ -\ 27 \\ \hline 58 \end{array}$$

Fig. 2-9. From Case 23. Essentially normal performance, except for slight dyssymmetry of the cross. Excellent key.

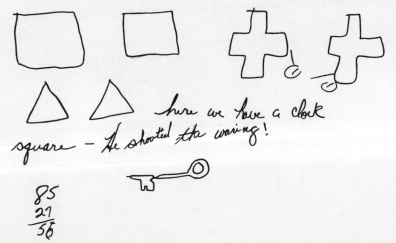

here we have a clock

square — He shouted the waring!

$$\begin{array}{r} 85 \\ 27 \\ \hline 56 \end{array}$$

Fig. 2-10. From Case 24. Mildly impaired drawings along with spelling dyspraxia ("waring") and dyscalculia.

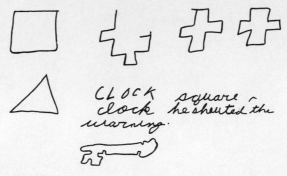

Fig. 2-11. From Case 26. Construction dyspraxia and dysgraphia.

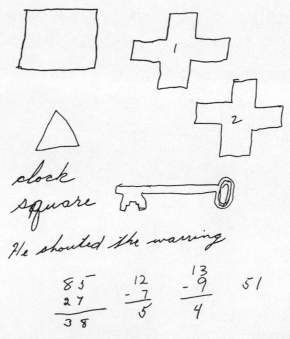

Fig. 2-12. From Case 29. Dyscalculia (85 − 27). Note tendency to confuse "r" and "n" in warning and problem with the "q" in "square."

Fig. 2-13.   From Case 31. Construction dyspraxia.

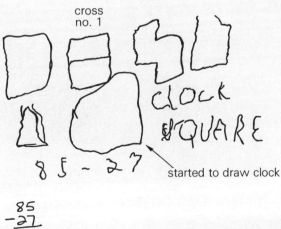

cross
no. 1

CLOCK

SQUARE

8 5 - 2 7   started to draw clock

Fig. 2-14.   From Case 34. Construction dyspraxia, dysgraphia, and dyscalculia in severe form. The patient was unable to write in script and could barely print. Note widespread tremor and the total loss of spatial configuration on the cross.

Finger-tapping Test and the TPT. For example, if the right hand performs normally on the Finger-tapping but not on the Tactual Performance Test, then we can say that there is worse performance on the TPT. This suggests an impairment away from the central motor–sensory strip of the brain, whether in the parietal, temporal, or prefrontal area of the brain. We can further localize such a disorder by looking at the Finger Agnosia score; if a deficit is indicated, then the injury is probably in the temporal–parietal area, but if no deficit is indicated, a temporal–prefrontal lesion is more likely.

On the other hand, if Finger-tapping performance is poorer, the lesion is likely to involve the sensory–motor area or adjacent areas in the temporal or frontal lobe. In general, the greater the deficit on the Finger-tapping score, the nearer the lesion is to the precentral gyrus. If both Finger-tapping and Tactual Performance scores are poor and there are deficits of Finger Agnosia as well, the lesion probably involves at least a good part of the parietal–frontal areas.

Verbal—Performance IQs

The difference between verbal IQ and performance IQ (VIQ–PIQ difference) has long been held to be a measure of lateralized cerebral dysfunction (Balthazar & Morrison, 1961; Goldstein & Shelley, 1973; Russell, 1972); however, there has been considerable controversy as to its effectiveness.

Two major factors have been identified that limit the usefulness of this comparison (Golden, 1978). First, as has been repeatedly stated, no measure is purely related to either hemisphere. The verbal subtests of Arithmetic and Digit Span are often influenced by right-hemisphere injuries. Conversely, the performance subtests rely heavily on motor coordination and the dominant hand, which is controlled by the left hemisphere in most cases. The Picture Arrangement subtest has a large verbal component that can be affected by left-hemisphere damage. Thus the VIQ–PIQ difference can be misleading; in fact, it can even suggest the wrong hemisphere.

Second, several process variables (such as recovery of function, severity and type of onset of the disease) affect the expression of WAIS IQs. Spontaneous recovery following acute injuries tends to obscure large initial differences between VIQ and PIQ. Thus chronic or older injuries may show little or no difference, depending on the amount of recovery that has taken place. Also, the more severe disorders and sudden-onset disorders tend to cause more pronounced deficits than slowly developing and less damaging insults. For example, a slowly developing hematoma or a low-grade tumor does not cause the strong PIQ–VIQ difference that is seen with a more quickly developing disease. Presumably, this is because the brain has more time to accommodate and reorganize the disrupted functions.

Given these influencing factors, the WAIS IQ comparison can provide some help in determining the laterality of brain damage. The VIQ–PIQ difference must be considered in light of the rest of the profile, however, before a diagnosis is made. Also, the reason for the IQ drop in each case must be closely examined before conclusions are drawn.

An alternative method of comparing groups of tests on the WAIS, given the limitations of the PIQ–VIQ comparison, is to concentrate on factors that have been reported in various factor analyses of the WAIS. Three factors are of particular interest to neuropsychological interpretation.

The first factor is a verbal comprehension factor. This factor is best represented by the Vocabulary, Information, Comprehension, and Similarities subtests. The score on the factor is determined by adding up the scale scores on these subtests and dividing by 4. As the reader has probably already seen, these four scales are generally the "hold" tests of the WAIS. Their average is often an excellent estimation of the subject's premorbid level of functioning. When poor performance is seen on this factor relative to the remaining factors, dysfunction of the left (dominant) hemisphere is almost always indicated, either as a lateralized deficit or in the context of a diffuse disorder.

The second factor is best represented by the Arithmetic and Digit Span subtests. This has generally been regarded as an attention/concentration factor, although it is clearly a numerical facility factor as well. This factor can be affected by injuries in either hemisphere because of disruption of concentration and attentional factors (common in disorders involving subcortical or frontal areas of the brain) or because of disruption of numerical skills (common in disorders of either parietal lobe). This factor is also more sensitive than the other factors to disruption by high levels of anxiety. Consequently, poor performance on this factor alone may simply reflect a psychiatric disorder.

The third factor is best represented by Block Design, Object Assembly, Picture Arrangement, and Picture Completion subtests. This can best be viewed as a spatial/perceptual factor. Like Block Design alone, this factor is most sensitive to parietal disorders, with poorer performance being seen in the presence of right-parietal dysfunction.

In general, differences of 3 or more scaled points among these factors are suggestive of relative dysfunction; however, caution must be exercised in older individuals, in whom such deficits are common on the Spatial factor. In these cases it is often best to use age-corrected scale scores.

Cognitive Test Comparisons

There are numerous cognitive test comparisons possible, given all the tests in the battery. Only a few of the more profitable ones will be examined here. Two types of comparisons are of benefit in attempting to pinpoint a focal lesion: (1) comparisons that help determine the laterality of the damage, and (2) comparisons that differentiate lateralized lesions along an anterior–posterior line. Again, it must be emphasized that any one of these comparisons in isolation is not strong enough to provide an accurate diagnosis. The profile must be interpreted as a whole.

Differential performance on the Rhythm Test and Speech-Sounds Perception Test is suggestive of lateralized injury. In conjunction with other signs, such as dysphasia, poor performance on the Speech-Sounds Perception Test relative to the Rhythm Test is fairly strongly indicative of left-hemisphere damage. In many cases, deficits will be found on both the Speech-Sounds Test and Rhythm Test. In these situations it is necessary to compare the levels of performance. This is best approximated by doubling the number of errors on the Rhythm Test and comparing that score to the number of Speech errors, a process that gives somewhat more weight to the speech-sounds measure, since it is, in general, a more reliable test. If rhythm errors (doubled) exceeds Speech errors and if Speech errors are fewer than 15, a right-hemisphere lesion is likely. If Speech errors exceed 20 or are greater than the doubled Rhythm errors, a left-hemisphere lesion is likely. In each case, however, the examiner must be alert for the possibility of a diffuse disorder when both Speech-Sounds scores and Rhythm scores are in the brain-damaged range.

A number of additional comparisons may be made between the WAIS subtests, a process that is aided by their common scoring system. In the presence of left-hemisphere injuries, poor performances are likely to occur on Digit Span (usually both backward and forward), Arithmetic, and Similarities, poor performance in the latter being almost always associated with left-hemisphere or diffuse injuries. In addition, performance in Picture Arrangement and Block Design may be down as well, in comparison with the other performance tests. Poor performance will also be seen in Digit Symbol; however, this is common in many kinds of brain injury. In general, a test score should be about 3 points below the general level for such tests as Vocabulary and Comprehension (among the verbal tests) or Picture Completion (among the performance tests) before a deficit is suggested.

In right-hemisphere disorders, the poorest scores are likely to be in Block Design, Picture Arrangement, Object Assembly, and Digit Symbol. Poor scores may also be seen on Arithmetic and Digit Span (Digits Backward when compared with Digits Forward, as discussed earlier), but the levels for these latter tests are seldom reduced as severely as the levels for the performance tests.

On a qualitative level, it is quite useful to determine the causes of the deficits indicated on the performance tests. If a significant motor impairment in the dominant hand is suggested by the subject's performance, an injury of the dominant (left) hemisphere or a diffuse injury is nearly always implied. Similarly, poor performance in Block Design, along with strong verbal deficits, suggests left-parietal involvement, whereas poor performance in Picture Arrangement alone, with verbal deficits, implies a left-hemisphere focus. Poor performance in Picture Arrangement and Digit Symbol, without any other deficits, suggests an anterior right-hemisphere focus.

Anterior–Posterior

Once the laterality of a lesion has been determined, there are several comparisons that help distinguish anterior and posterior lesions. In the left hemisphere, three basic comparisons are used. First, when dysphasia is present, the deficits may be largely either receptive or expressive in nature. Receptive dysphasia is caused by posterior lesions, and it involves difficulty in phonemic hearing discrimination as well as alienation of word meaning (Luria, 1973). Poor performance on the Speech-Sounds Perception Test is common, as are mild deficiencies indicated by the Aphasia Test.

Expressive language disorders are associated with anterior brain damage (the motor and premotor areas in particular). These disorders are manifested mainly as speech dysfluencies in which pronunciation is difficult or impossible. There is an inability to sequence speech sounds into words, phrases, and sentences. Perseveration and problems in writing (sequencing letters into words and words into phrases and sentences) are also often present.

Second, in the presence of left-hemisphere injuries, comparison of the Rhythm Test and the Aphasia Test can reveal an anterior or posterior focus (Osmon et al., 1978). It has been found that as the

Rhythm Test results become more impaired and the Aphasia Test results less impaired, lesions tend to be located more anteriorly. The third comparison involves the relationships between the TPT and the Finger-tapping Test discussed earlier.

There are, again, three fundamental comparisons of importance in localizing the focus of brain damage within the right hemisphere. Again, the Tapping–TPT comparison applies, just as in the case of the left hemisphere. The second comparison involves the relationship between poor performances in Block Design and Picture Arrangement. In mild to moderate right-hemisphere injuries, poor performance in Picture Arrangement in the absence of Block Design problems indicates an anterior locus. Likewise, poor performance in Block Design relative to Picture Arrangement suggests a posterior lesion. Caution is especially important in this case because of the number of influencing factors, such as severity and chronicity.

Finally, poor performance on the Rhythm Test has localizing value within the right hemisphere. Reitan (unpublished manuscript, undated) has noted a strong relationship between the right temporal lobe and the Rhythm Test. More posterior lesions generally do not cause rhythm deficits; however, frontal lesions sometimes do produce deficits. Overall, the Rhythm Test generally argues for an anterior location in mild to moderate cases.

CONCLUSIONS

In this chapter we have outlined the basic interpretations of the tests contained in the Halstead-Reitan Neuropsychological Test Battery. We have also examined the basic comparisons between tests that are used to determine lateralization and localization of brain dysfunction. These basic interpretations and comparisons must be regarded cautiously by the reader, and although each has some validity, all are influenced by numerous factors, the most important of which is the exact location of a lesion within a hemisphere. Consequently, the neuropsychologist must be alert not only to the interpretation of individual test scores and simple comparisons but also to the patterns of test results seen in specifically localized lesions in each hemisphere. The patterns to be expected in each specific location are discussed in the next three chapters.

3

Effects of Localized and Diffuse Brain Lesions

In order to understand the interpretation of the Halstead-Reitan Test Battery, one should begin with an understanding of how the major types of conditions affect the results of the tests. It is not within the scope of this book to provide a full description of brain function; see the work of Golden (1978) for an introduction to this topic or the work of Luria (1973) for a more detailed discussion. However, the basic effects of the various brain lesions will be discussed in the following sections. Our major emphasis is on the specific results yielded by the Halstead-Reitan Test Battery.

FRONTAL LOBES

The primary projection area of the frontal lobes is the motor strip. This area in the left hemisphere receives and transmits impulses predominantly from the contralateral body side. As the dominant side of the brain, the left hemisphere also controls the left side of the body to a moderate degree in the interest of overall coordination. Somatotopic organization affords each area of the body cortical representation in proportion to the fineness of control necessary in that body part. For example, the fingers require relatively large areas of the motor strip in accordance with the fine motor manipulation performed.

The premotor areas of the frontal lobes are directly anterior to the motor strip and are the secondary integrative areas for motoric behavior. That is, the individual motor impulses are sequenced into complex motor chains or "kinetic melodies," as Luria (1966) called them. For example, reaching for a cup of coffee, as a complex motoric behavior, requires the integration of numerous motor impulses into one smooth behavior. The premotor area enables this concatenation of motoric impulses to be executed smoothly and in the correct order.

The left-hemisphere premotor areas control the right side of the body as well as the expressive aspects of language. Broca's area is located low on the lateral surface of the premotor area and controls the sequential aspects of speaking. Whereas a lesion in the primary area disrupts control of the vocal mechanism, a lesion in the secondary area disrupts the flow of speech. If the lesion is severe enough, a person will be unable to say two sounds in a row. The subject perseverates on the first sound and is unable to switch the movements of the vocal apparatus to pronounce the second sound. The same inertia occurs in movements of the right-body limbs and the right eye with lesions located elsewhere in the premotor areas. The right premotor area controls the left-body side in the same manner, although it is not specialized in the expressive aspects of speech as is the left premotor area.

The tertiary areas are located in the most anterior part of the lateral aspects of the frontal lobes and are called the prefrontal areas. Originally these areas were believed to be "silent," but they have since come to be recognized as the most important part of the brain for controlling voluntary behavior. Luria (1966) recognized three broad functions of voluntary behavior these areas control: planning, structuring, and evaluating behavior. In other words, the prefrontal areas formulate a complex behavioral plan (planning). The necessary components of the behavior are then coordinated by the prefrontal area, and the behavior is executed (structuring). During execution, the prefrontal areas monitor the process to evaluate for necessary modifications in the behavioral act to adjust for ever-changing environmental conditions (evaluating).

Lesions in the tertiary area can disrupt voluntary behavior. Left-hemisphere dysfunction can result in loss of voluntary speech. The subject may be unable to plan or to generate a spontaneous verbal discussion. Likewise, spontaneous behavior may be greatly diminished because of inability to regulate behavior according to verbal instructions from oneself or from others (Luria, 1966). As a result of the lack of regulation of behavior the subject is likely to be distractable and unable to change flexibly between activities and thoughts (Luria, 1966; Milner, 1963). Right-frontal-lobe dysfunction is less well understood, although the right frontal lobe appears to direct behavior in similar but nonverbal ways. Difficulties with spatial problem-solving tasks appear to be the major deficits associated with dysfunction in this area of the brain.

Finally, the medial and basal portions of the frontal lobes are associated with emotional behavior. These areas are closely linked with the limbic and reticular activating systems, and lesions in this area have been associated with changes in cortical tone and emotional reaction (Luria, 1966; Sanides, 1964). No conclusive studies have been done to establish a personality reaction typical of damage to these areas. Several characteristics have been associated with severe lesions, both left and bilateral, however; for a review of this topic, see the work of Golden (1978). Generally, it appears that such persons show childlike immaturity and lack of concern for external conditions.

Left-Frontal-Lobe Halstead-Reitan Signs

Lesions in the primary area of the left frontal lobe affect right-hand performance on all motor tasks. The Finger Oscillation Test is the predominant motor measure, and a relative difference between scores for the two hands indicates dysfunction in the low-lateral surface of the motor strip. Differing levels of performance are obtained depending on the exact location, type, and extent of the lesion. Motor speed performance is sensitive to a wide variety of brain lesions; for example, a small decrement in performance can accompany a distant space-occupying lesion in which pressure effects are operative. The level of performance can also be useful in cases in which no relative difference between scores for the two hands is apparent. That is, bilateral deficits can occur with left-hemisphere injuries, and although the right hand is generally more severely impaired, this is not always the case. In cases in which performances with the two hands are approximately equal and are obviously impaired, a left-frontal lesion cannot be ruled out. These same considerations apply to the Grip Strength Test.

Motor deficits often show up on the Digit Symbol subtest as well. In fact, performance on the entire performance section of the WAIS (except for Picture Completion) can be lowered as a result of deficient dominant-hand motor speed. Therefore motor deficits should always be considered when evaluating tasks (such as the WAIS performance subtests) that require manipulatory skills.

Performance on the Tactual Performance Test (TPT) may also be affected by primary-area lesions in the left frontal lobe; however, more gross motor and sensory skills are important for this test. Because of these different requirements performance on the TPT is generally less impaired than that on the Finger Oscillation Test in the presence of these types of lesions. Reitan (1959d) suggested that poor performance on the TPT relative to the Finger Oscillation Test is indicative of posterior lesions, whereas the converse indicates anterior lesions; however, there is one important exception to this rule that will be explained later in this section.

Motor dysphasia as indicated by the Aphasia Test is the predominant symptom associated with lesions in the secondary frontal areas. Problems of sequencing phonemes into syllables and syllables into words indicate central dysarthria. Such persons are unable to pronounce the word "Massachusetts," for example; they lack the ability to control the speech apparatus in a manner that would permit individual sounds to be smoothly linked into a coherent vocalization. Premotor lesions, however, do not necessarily preclude the ability to enunciate individual sounds; in fact, less severe lesions may only cause these persons to slow their speech to concentrate more on making the transition between sounds and syllables. With more severe lesions, perseveration is common; such persons are unable to switch flexibly from sound to sound.

Dysgraphia, or difficulty in writing, may also occur in the presence of left-premotor lesions. Here, again, the deficit causes the problem of sequencing motor impulses into a "kinetic melody." The deficit is more likely to be manifested when writing from spontaneous generation than when writing from dictation or copying, in which the visual and auditory channels act as regulators of behavior. Again, perseveration is common. The subject may begin by writing the first letter and continue writing this letter, being unable to switch to the next letter in the sequence.

Lesions limited to the left frontal region show a typical deficit pattern involving the planning and structuring of behavior. Complex tasks in which an overall strategy must be used to regulate the execution of the test are typically poorly performed. The Category Test, the Trail-making Test (part B), and the third page of the Stroop Test all require constant conceptual regulation of behavior. They require both abstraction skills and cognitive flexibility for successful completion, and they are therefore poorly performed by subjects with left-prefrontal lesions.

Other deficits may occur in the presence of left-prefrontal lesions. Occasionally, poor performance is seen on the TPT because the subject is unable to develop an efficient strategy for executing the test.

In this case the comparison between TPT and Finger Oscillation Test does not indicate a posterior lesion. Also, the Digit Span Test may be poorly performed, but the overall IQ is relatively unaffected by these lesions. Although no sensory abilities are associated with frontal lobes, sometimes poor performance may occur on complex sensory tasks. The Fingertip Number-writing Test occasionally indicates deficits on the right hand or bilaterally in the presence of left-frontal lesions (Golden, 1978).

Lesions limited strictly to the orbital and medial areas of the frontal lobe do not produce typical neuropsychological deficits; however, patients with these lesions may, as a result of cortical tone disruption, show poor test performances because of lack of motivation. There are emotional characteristics that have been associated with damage in this region, but no typical Minnesota Multiphasic Personality Inventory (MMPI) profile has been identified. Frontal-limbic disruption seems to be associated much more with problems of motivation and arousal, whereas temporal-limbic damage correlates with more traditional psychopathological symptoms.

Right-Frontal-Lobe Halstead-Reitan Signs

As in the left hemisphere, lesions to the primary area of the right frontal lobe result in motor speed and strength deficits. These deficits are found almost exclusively on the left-body side, since the right hemisphere has very little ipsilateral (same body side) representation of motor functions. Absolute and relative dysfunctions are seen on the Finger-tapping Test and the Grip Strength Test. Motor dysfunction of the left hand may also be responsible for poor performance on those tasks that require coordinated effort of both hands. The TPT both-hands trial and the WAIS performance section (excepting the Picture Completion subtest) are examples. Similarly, in subjects where the left hand is dominant, all tests that are poorly performed and that require motoric execution must be evaluated in light of the motor problems. For example, in a subject with a poor score on the finger tapping test, poor performance on the Block Design test may reflect motor problems rather than a spatial dysfunction.

The TPT–Finger-tapping Test comparison is sometimes useful in establishing the presence of right-frontal-lobe dysfunction. The Finger-tapping test assesses function of the motor strip, whereas the TPT is more indicative of posterior right-hemisphere function; however, this comparison is less useful in the right hemisphere, since spatial skills constitute a large part of the TPT task. The TPT is often poorly performed by subjects with right-prefrontal disorders, where spatial integrative deficits occur, therefore obviating the comparison.

The Trail-making Test (part A) is often poorly performed by subjects with right-frontal disorders. The task requires purposeful visual scanning as well as basic spatial skills. A dysfunction in the right frontal lobe may result in a higher-order deficit in visual analysis ability that can affect the execution of the task; however, more posterior lesions that disrupt basic spatial skills can also result in poor performance on Part A of the Trail-making Test. Poor performance on this test is not necessarily indicative of a right-frontal disorder; however, poor performance often accompanies such a disorder.

The WAIS often reveals deficits that are associated with right-frontal-lobe dysfunction. The Picture Arrangement subtest is a complex visual problem-solving task that might be expected to indicate frontal disorders. Similarly, the Picture Completion subtest requires purposeful visual scanning such as that required by part A of the Trail-making Test, and it may also indicate right-frontal-lobe dysfunction. Finally, the Block Design and the Object Assembly subtests require basic spatial skills and the ability to evaluate a problem situation and generate a plan of solution. Poor performance on these two subtests may indicate right-frontal disorders in which problem-solving ability is impaired.

Poor scores on the Aphasia Examination may also occur in the presence of right-frontal dysfunction. Most often, drawing ability is affected, as the regulation of behavior by the right frontal lobe fails in spatial tasks. Whereas the perception of directionality and slope is controlled in the posterior right hemisphere, the ability to use these skills is dependent on the right frontal lobe. Therefore poor scores in drawing in the presence of right-frontal disorders reflect lack of spatial regulation of behavior rather than spatial perception problems. Likewise, motor responses to spatial items on the test (such as those required on items 28, 31, and 32) may also be deficient.

General tests may also be poorly performed by subjects with right-frontal dysfunction, although less dysfunction is generally seen with lesions in this area than anywhere else in the brain. The Category Test, because of its complexity and the wide range of skills necessary to execute the task, may indicate dysfunction caused by right frontal lesions. Likewise, scores on the Digit Span and Digit Symbol subtests may be affected by these lesions. Often times, mild to moderate deficits indicated by the Rhythm Test are seen in these disorders; they appear to result from either poor attention or sequencing deficits.

TEMPORAL LOBES

The basic sensory input to the temporal-lobe primary areas is auditory information. The primary area is located at the superior border in the posterior aspect of the temporal lobe. It is adjacent to the sensory–motor strip, positioned directly below and somewhat posterior to it. Input to the left lobe comes predominantly from the right ear, whereas input to the right lobe comes mainly from the left ear; however, auditory information from both ears reaches each temporal lobe. The elementary auditory signals are integrated in the secondary areas that surround the projection regions. Through both the left and right temporal lobes course parts of the optic-tract radiations on their way to the occipital lobe. Those parts of the radiations that represent the contralateral half of the upper visual field run deep in the posterior parts of the temporal lobes. Thus lesions in the left temporal lobe may result in upper-visual-field loss to the right side of the visual field. Conversely, upper-left-visual-field losses may be associated with right-temporal-lobe lesions. Specialized abilities accrue from different functions of the left and right lobes, and each will be discussed separately.

Simple and complex verbal functions typically are associated with the left temporal lobe. Simple phonemic discrimination is controlled by the secondary areas. The association with the parietal and occipital lobes makes clear the basis of more complex verbal functions. The tactile–kinesthetic functions of the parietal lobe contribute to verbal analysis and synthesis in terms of providing information about the vocal apparatus positions used in sounding out phonemes. Luria (1973) theorized that spelling is closely related to parietal-lobe function, inasmuch as tactile–kinesthetic information concerning the vocal apparatus contributes to the phonemic analysis of words. Likewise, the spatial function of the parietal lobe contributes to verbal processes that imply relations and spatial relationships.

The temporal–occipital connections are responsible for verbal processes that arise from auditory–visual integration. Reading requires the association of visual symbols (letters) with letter sounds and then letters into words. Verbal memory also seems to be related to the temporal–occipital and temporal–parietal–occipital regions.

The medial portions of the left temporal lobe are associated with the limbic system. As a result, this area is closely related to the acquisition of new long-term memories and to emotional behavior. Unilateral damage may result in psychiatric disorders, but it usually does not cause discernible disturbances in the acquisition of new long-term memories.

Primary and secondary right-temporal-lobe functions are responsible for the perception of nonverbal pitch and rhythm patterns (Luria, 1973). The more integrative areas of the right temporal lobe are more predisposed toward visuospatial analysis (Hebb, 1945; Luria, 1973). Kimura (1963) theorized that the secondary areas are more responsible for visual analysis of complex and unfamiliar stimuli. It appears that in the right hemisphere, temporal-lobe function is more closely integrated with occipital-lobe and parietal-lobe functions in the interest of nonverbal spatial abilities.

Although this brain area is predominantly geared toward nonverbal functions, Golden (1978) suggested that the right temporal lobe also appears to be involved in basic receptive verbal abilities. Clinical experience has shown that right-temporal-lobe injury often results in deficits involving typical receptive speech tasks. This fact is consistent with Luria's theory (1966) that both temporal lobes receive all types of auditory input and play roles in both verbal and nonverbal abilities.

Left-Temporal-Lobe Halstead-Reitan Signs

Basic auditory perceptual deficits are common in subjects with left-temporal-lobe injuries, showing up as poor performance on the Speech-Sounds Perception Test and the Rhythm Test. Osmon et al. (1978) found that poor scores on the Rhythm Test were highly associated with anterior-temporal-lobe injuries but that they also occurred in conjunction with poor scores on the Aphasia Test, indicating posterior injury. Deficits indicated by the Speech-Sounds Perception Test are generally associated with secondary temporal areas, where phonemic discrimination occurs.

Poor scores on the Aphasia Test are highly associated with left-temporal-lobe dysfunction. Reitan (1959d) reported 38, 86, 87, and 100 percent probabilities of brain damage associated with 1, 2, 3, and 4 errors on the Aphasia Examination. All manner of dysphasia symptoms are associated with left-temporal-lobe injuries, again depending on the severity and exact location of the damage. Certain lesions in the anterior temporal lobe are possible in which very few deficits are seen.

On the WAIS, poor performance is most often seen on the Digit Span and Similarities subtests (McFie, 1969, 1975). Disruption of the integrative auditory areas in the left temporal lobe is apparently responsible to a certain degree for deficits involving both immediate auditory memory and verbal conceptual ability. Of course, severe injuries can affect any WAIS subtest that contains a significant verbal component (including Picture Arrangement and Picture Completion).

Certain basic sensory-perceptual deficits are seen in subjects with left-temporal-lobe injuries. With destruction of tissue in the primary auditory projection area, right-ear suppressions occur. Because not all auditory fibers go to the left hemisphere central deafness does not occur; however, decreased acuity in the right ear can be associated with damage to the primary area of the left temporal lobe.

Loss of the upper quadrant of the right visual field is also possible with certain types of lesions of the left temporal lobe. From the relay in the lower brain, the optical radiations divide, with half (upper right visual field) going through the deep portions of the posterior temporal lobe and half (lower right visual field) going through the parietal lobe. Thus lesions in the left temporal lobe that compress or penetrate the optic radiations cause upper-right-visual-field losses.

Because of nearness to the motor strip deficits indicated by the Finger Oscillation Test are found to accompany some left-temporal lesions. Generally, the more posterior the lesion in the temporal lobe, the less the deficit that is seen; however, with posterior lesions, deficits indicated by the TPT and the Fingertip Number-writing Test appear, reflecting the close association of the temporal and parietal lobes in controlling complex sensory abilities.

Most left-temporal-lobe injuries cause severe speech and language deficits and therefore are associated with poor performance on many of the tests that are generally sensitive to brain dysfunction. Poor performance is common on the Category Test and the Trail-making Test (part B). Also, the Stroop Test, especially the first page, often indicates severe impairment as a result of the verbal deficit. Finally, the achievement tests generally are affected when a significant verbal deficit occurs. On the Wide Range Achievement Test (WRAT), all subtests can be affected, but the spelling and reading sections are usually most severely affected. The PPVT, as a measure of receptive language ability, is most sensitive to left-temporal-lobe dysfunction.

The MMPI will often indicate severe psychopathology in subjects with lesions involving the left temporal lobe. Neuropsychological research is beginning to demonstrate that lesions involving the temporal-limbic connections in the inferior and medial portions of the temporal lobes play a large role in symptoms like those of schizophrenia. A review of this research indicates that lesions involving the cortical-limbic system are related to arousal and orienting deficits characteristic of schizophrenics. These results, combined with neuropsychological data indicating left-temporal-lobe deficits associated with severe psychopathology (Purisch, Golden, & Hammeke, 1978), suggest a need for personality evaluation in providing a complete psychodiagnostic picture of the patient with left-temporal-lobe injury.

Right-Temporal-Lobe Halstead-Reitan Signs

Basic sensory losses caused by damage to the primary and secondary areas of the right temporal lobe produce both auditory and visual deficits. Performance on the Rhythm Test is most often disrupted in the presence of these lesions because of the basic sensory loss and integrative deficits that result from damage to the primary projection or the secondary areas; however rhythm deficits may occur with other lesions. The test is sensitive to brain damage in general because it requires good concentration.

Poor performance on the Speech-Sounds Perception Test is also characteristic of subjects with right-temporal-lobe injuries. In fact, the complex of Rhythm and Speech Sounds deficits is common in both temporal lobes. Usually, if the Rhythm Test indicates more severe impairment, then a right-temporal-lobe injury is more likely. Sometimes, however, this comparison is useless; the attendant deficits must always be examined before a localization diagnosis is attempted.

The disruption of visual analysis skills that results from damage in the secondary areas causes certain deficits on the WAIS. Meier and French (1966) noted problems with Picture Arrangement and Object Assembly in patients with these lesions. This deficit profile is easily distinguished from more posterior lesions in which more pure spatial deficits occur. Lesions in the posterior parietal area, for example, result in construction dyspraxia, with poor performance on Block Design and perhaps Object Assembly; exclusively temporal lesions, however, produce deficits which require analysis and synthesis of complex visual stimuli, especially unfamiliar tasks such as are required in the Picture Arrangement Test.

As the lesion moves further toward the occipital and parietal areas, more spatial deficits occur (Golden, 1978). Here, construction dyspraxia and a poor Block Design score may be evident. Also, the Tactual Performance Test may be poorly performed, revealed especially by the Memory and Location scores. Complex sensory deficits such as revealed by the Fingertip Number-writing Test, may also be more prevalent.

A typical neuropsychological profile associated with right temporal lobe dysfunction will include auditory and visual deficits. The Rhythm Test and possibly the Speech Sounds Perception Test will be disrupted. Typically the Picture Arrangement and possibly the Object Assembly subtests will be poorly done in the absence of relative deficits on the Block Design subtest. The presence of these few deficits, in the absence of other signs, strongly indicates a right-temporal-lobe disorder. Depending upon severity, chronicity, and exact location of the disorder, however, several other deficits may occur, as described above, and deficits may appear also on the generally sensitive tests. For example, TPT Total Time, Category, Digit Symbol, and Digit Span Tests and even the Trail-making Test (parts A and B) can all be performed in the brain-damaged range. This occurrence usually indicates a relatively severe and sudden-onset type of injury, however. In general, exclusively right-temporal-lobe disorder testing will yield a small and specified deficit pattern.

PARIETAL–OCCIPITAL LOBES

The basic sensory input into the parietal and occipital lobes is tactile and visual information, respectively. In the parietal lobe, the primary sensory-projection area (or where the basic sensory information impinges upon the cortical layer), is located in the anterior portion of the lobe and is called the postcentral sensory strip (Chusid, 1970). Conversely, the projection area in the occipital lobe is located in Brodmann area 17 at the back and medial portion of the lobe. In these areas the basic, point-by-point senses of touch and vision occur. Very little integration, and therefore little complex function, occur in these areas.

Parts of the visual tracts course through the parietal lobe after the relay at the lateral geniculate nucleus. The fibers representing the lower half of the contralateral visual field run through the deep parietal lobe on the way back to the occipital projection area.

In the parietal and occipital tissue surrounding the sensory-projection areas (secondary area) there occurs integration of information within each modality (Luria, 1966). In the left parietal lobe basic touch, kinesthetic, and proprioceptive information is combined to allow tactile stimulus localization and recognition of body position on the right side of the body. Likewise, the right parietal lobe handles integration of tactual information from the left body side. Luria (1966) also postulated that the left parietal lobe is provided this information for the left body side as well in order to allow control of coordinated movements involving both body sides. In the occipital secondary area integration of point-by-point visual information provides for complex visual perception. In the left lobe this perception is more specialized, detecting verbal symbols such as letters and numbers. The right occipital lobe, conversely, is specialized to interpret complex spatial configurations.

At the border of the parietal and occipital lobes the integration of both modalities occurs (tertiary area). The integration of tactile/kinesthetic abilities and visual abilities gives rise to spatial skills in both hemispheres. Luria (1966) noted that visual and tactile information is integrated into definite groups by "simultaneous" processing, thereby generating spatial function. The body parts are recognized and are oriented visually, and directional sense is also allowed. This area also is closely connected with the temporal area and its auditory functions.

Integration of tactile/kinesthetic and visual information with the temporal lobe verbal functions in the left hemisphere gives rise to a number of complex verbal capacities. The combination of spatial capabilities with verbal ones gives rise to relational words such as "above," "among," and others which have a large spatial component. Also, arithmetic ability and grammatical relationships are associated with this area. Verbal–spatial aspects of the body are understood here as well. The ability to name objects is also associated with this area and appears related to the tactile/kinesthetic function of the vocal apparatus controlled by the parietal area (Luria, 1966).

The integration of parietal and occipital lobe functions in the right hemisphere gives rise largely to spatial and complex visual analysis abilities, especially recognition of unfamiliar configurations. The integration of tactual and visual perceptions in the right hemisphere seems specialized to the understanding of spatial relations. McFie and Zangwill (1960) noted a relationship between this area of the right hemisphere and awareness of the left side of the body and environment. Damage to this area gives rise to the pathognomic sign known as unilateral spatial neglect. A person may completely "disown" his or her left arm, or she or he may ignore the left side of a page and therefore not understand printed words (Luria, 1966). The right parietal–occipital tertiary areas have also been associated with classification of nonverbal material (Warrington & Taylor, 1973). The recognition of faces and the sense of familiarity of objects seem to be two aspects of this ability (Hecaen & Angelergues, 1962; Luria, 1973).

Simple and complex spatial abilities are generally associated with this area as well. Determination of the slope and directionality of lines as well as construction of complex geometric figures and drawings are related to tertiary parietal functioning. Other spatial abilities, such as aligning multicolumn arithmetic problems, doing arithmetic calculation "in the head," and incidental spatial learning, are also highly dependent upon tertiary parietal functioning. The deficits associated with these areas will be fully delineated in the subsequent sections.

Left-Parietal—Occipital Halstead-Reitan Signs

The predominant deficits seen in this area are right-body motor and sensory problems. Deficits on the Finger Oscillation Test are common owing to a disruption in the sensory feedback necessary for execution of motoric tasks. Also, the sheer proximity to the motor strip and the fact that 20 percent of the neurons in the sensory strip are not tactile but are actually motor neurons also accounts for the poor performance (Luria, 1966). Low scores on the Grip Strength Test are also common for the same reasons. Sensory deficits include right-body errors on the Finger Agnosia, Astereognosia, and Fingertip Number-writing tests of the Sensory—Perceptual Examination. Bilateral motor and sensory deficits are not uncommon in left parietal disorders, especially in injuries involving the posterior aspect of the parietal lobe (Golden, 1978).

Tactile and visual suppression also occur in tissue-destroying lesions involving the sensory-projection areas of the parietal and occipital lobes, respectively. Confusion of left and right directions may also be noted on the Sensory-Perceptual Examination as well as the Aphasia Test.

The Tactual Performance Test (TPT) is often poorly performed in left-parietal lesions, and performance usually, in comparison with the Finger Oscillation Test, looks more impaired. The impairment may be the result either of reduced motor control, as reflected in the Finger Oscillation Test, or of impaired kinesthetic and spatial capabilities when the more integrative areas of the parietal and occipital lobes are disrupted. Only the right-hand score and perhaps the Location and/or Memory score are generally impaired when damage is confined to the left parietal lobe. The both-hands trial may also show disruption as a result of impairment to the right hand and overall coordination problems. Also, in cases of severe and sudden onset of disease, such as a fast-growing tumor or a hemorrhage in this location, the TPT may be generally disrupted.

In lesions involving the tertiary areas, the Aphasia Test may show considerable deficit, depending upon the severity and exact location of the lesion. Deficits on the Aphasia Test typically stem from problems differentiating left from right, an inability to name common objects (dysnomia), reading and writing difficulties (dyslexia, dysgraphia), misspelling (spelling dyspraxia), misidentification of numbers and letters (visual letter and number dysgnosia), inability to demonstrate the use of objects (ideokinetic dyspraxia), improper arithmetic operations (dyscalculia), and inaccurate recognition of body parts (body dysgnosia). In severe cases global aphasia may occur. The most common problems occur on the speaking and writing items when the lesion involves the anterior parietal areas, where simple tactile functions are controlled. Damage in this area causes poor oral and hand control, which interferes predominantly with the motor-sensory dysphasia items (i.e., speaking and writing). Conversely, more posterior parietal damage interferes with integrative functions such as arithmetic, naming, reading, body positioning, and spatial skills.

Deficits on the WAIS are also common in left-parietal–occipital dysfunction. McFie (1969; 1975) has indicated that deficits on Digit Span, Arithmetic, and Block Design are common. In patients with severe dysphasia, however, all verbal tests, including Picture Completion and Picture Arrangement, can be disrupted. The Stroop Test, especially the first page, will also be low in subjects with significant verbal deficit. These lesions appear to disrupt overall intelligence, including reasoning and verbal abstraction skills as well as achievement skills as measured by the WRAT and the Peabody Individual Achievement Test (PIAT).

Studies of personality reactions to lesions limited to this area or deficit patterns associated with this area have been sparse; however, studies using the MMPI have shown that left-hemisphere injuries often are associated with severe emotional distress, including psychosis. This reaction is especially common when dysphasia is present. Owing to the varied personality structures and personality responses to stress there is no one personality profile typical of left-parietal damage. Psychopathology does seem to be more likely with more severe cognitive deficits.

Right-Parietal–Occipital Halstead-Reitan Signs

As in the left-parietal–occipital area, damage to the primary and secondary areas results in motor and sensory problems. The deficits are incurred almost exclusively with the left body side and involve sensory signs more than motor signs. Deficits occur on the Finger-tapping, Finger Agnosia, and Fingertip Number-writing tests. Also associated with damage to the primary areas are suppression deficits, representing tissue-destructive lesions in the sensory-projection areas. Left-body tactile suppressions occur from damage to the parietal projection area, while left field visual suppressions come from damage to the occipital projection area.

Damage to the more posterior (tertiary) areas leads to several Halstead-Reitan deficits which involve spatial abilities. The WAIS, TPT, Trail-making, and Aphasia tests make manifest these spatial problems (McFie, 1969; 1975). The Block Design subtest is the predominant deficit on the WAIS; however, dysfunction may also be revealed by the Object Assembly, Picture Arrangement, and Picture Completion subtests. Digit Symbol scores are also depressed, although the score represents general dysfunction rather than specific spatial deficits. Construction dyspraxia is perhaps the strongest sign of posterior right-hemisphere damage. This deficit is best represented on the Halstead-Reitan Battery by the drawing items on the Aphasia Test. The Greek cross item and the key item are the most indicative of spatial difficulties. Errors which involve the other drawings may be more indicative of severe problems.

Lateralized deficits on the TPT left-hand trial are generally expected in posterior right-hemisphere injuries; severe and generalized dysfunction on the TPT, however, is also indicative of posterior right-hemisphere injuries, since manual–spatial cognitive abilities may be impaired. This impairment manifests as a general disability on the TPT across all trials, including the TPT Location score and often the Memory score as well. In the case of generalized spatial dysfunction a deficit is often apparent on part A of the Trail-making test, the difficulty being visually evaluating the task and having to connect the numbered dots rapidly.

Other minor deficits may also be associated with damage to this area of the brain because of the spatial components of the task. For example, the Arithmetic subtest of the WAIS involves some spatial skills to the extent that mental calculation and carrying and borrowing arithmetic functions are required. Consequently, Arithmetic subtest deficits may be associated secondarily with right-parietal–occipital damage. Likewise, some of the Aphasia Test items, such as right–left orientation, calculation, reading, and body-positioning items (items 15, 16, 25, 26, 30, 31, and 32), have a spatial component and may therefore show deficit when there is damage to this area of the brain.

DIFFUSE INJURIES

A diffuse disorder is taken to mean any injury which is not circumscribed in nature. Therefore cases will be described which involve either the entire brain or multiple focal areas. Examples of the former include diffuse arteriosclerotic disease, hydrocephalus, infectious disorders, and Alzheimer's disease. Examples of the latter may include multiple sclerosis, incipient Pick's disease, multiple metastatic tumors, and trauma with coup and contrecoup effects.

Generalized Diffuse Disorders

Generalized diffuse disorders cause a global depression of neuropsychological performance. There may be mild to marked deterioration on almost all of the tests in the battery, depending upon the type and severity of the disease process. For example, in patients with Alzheimer's disease the advanced stages are marked by extremely low scores on all tests. The WAIS IQs are in the 60s and below, the impairment index is 1.0, and several of the longer and more difficult tests, such as the Category Test and TPT, are often discontinued owing to the patient's condition. Suppressions in all modalities are not uncommon; however, whether they are the result of actual tissue destruction or the low comprehension and concentration levels of the patient is unclear and often impossible to determine. Even tests usually quite insensitive to brain damage, such as Vocabulary and Information, are severly disrupted.

There are diffuse disorders such as generalized atrophy which may not show any neuropsychological deficit. Golden (1978) has suggested that if the atrophy occurs gradually the brain is able to adjust its functioning, thus avoiding deficits normally caused when more rapid onset of the disease process occurs. The same applies to the arteriosclerotic process—rapidity of onset is related proportionally to the amount of deficit.

These types of diffuse disorders, which cause a certain amount of generalized depression across the profile, may often be superimposed upon a more focal deficit. An example of this phenomenon is seen in the elderly patient who experiences an occlusion of the left middle cerebral artery. On testing, a neuropsychological profile typical of a recovering middle cerebral artery disease is found, except that the level of performance is somewhat lower than would be expected. That is, overall performance is not really consistent with results as would be expected given the subject's age and education or scores on insensitive tests (such as Vocabulary). This set of results would then be suggestive of a generalized diffuse arteriosclerosis. This postulate would fit nicely with the primary diagnosis, since occlusions are often secondary to plaque formations in the arteries (arteriosclerosis).

In attempts to differentiate types of generalized diffuse disorders a good medical history is often necessary. With hydrocephalus, age of onset is typically quite young, which is not likely with arteriosclerosis or Alzheimer's disease. Also, most forms of hydrocephalus typically become apparent much more quickly and more dramatically than generalized arteriosclerosis. Attendant symptoms and disease processes are often helpful in distinguishing the various disorders. Hydrocephalus is often subsequent to insults such as trauma and tumor or other space-occupying lesions which obstruct the cerebrospinal fluid system. On the other hand, secondary to arteriosclerosis there are often various vascular disorders such as occlusion and hemorrhage, which may alert one to the likelihood of generalized arteriosclerosis. Infectious disorders causing diffuse symptomatology may present only a bacterial or viral infection historically. Other degenerative diffuse diseases, such as Alzheimer's disease, may present no historical evidence because they are disorders in and of themselves secondary to no other processes and not responsible for any other diseases.

Nongeneralized Diffuse Disorders

Unlike generalized diffuse damage, these disorders do not affect the entire brain equally. Thus only deficits associated with the affected areas are present. All manners of deficits are possible, however, depending on the location of the lesion(s). Therefore a number of these types of diffuse disorders will be considered.

Multiple sclerosis. Initially, multiple sclerosis attacks subcortically, causing motor and sensory deficits. The disease apparently causes damage by disrupting the myelin cover of the neuronal axons. This damage is often manifested in widely varying areas, thus creating "spotty" deficits. Motor and sensory deficits do not, as a rule, occur in nicely consistent patterns. Generally, visual deficits are common and auditory deficits are rare. Cortical involvement often occurs in the disease process. Motor and sensory deficits are often inconsistent with the cognitive difficulties. Cortical deficits are rarely circumscribed, and mild cognitive deficits without an apparent localized pattern should alert the test interpreter to the likelihood of multiple sclerosis. Cognitive deficits usually include the brain-damage-sensitive tests: Category, Total Time, and Location scores on the TPT, Digit Span, and Digit Symbol. The PIQ is usually less than the VIQ on the WAIS, and a typical conversion "V" on the MMPI is common in these patients (Cleeland, Matthews, and Hopper, 1970; Golden, 1978; Matthews, Cleeland, and Hopper, 1970).

Multiple metastatic tumors. Multiple tumors in the brain are generally metastatic (originating from primary carcinoma elsewhere in the body). They are usually fast growing and therefore quite destructive. They may occur within brain tissue or outside of the tissue in the meninges (Golden, 1978). Neuropsychological results vary widely depending upon the location, size, and rapidity of onset of the lesions. Owing to the severity of metastatic lesions there are typically suppressions when the sensory projection areas are involved. As would be expected with multiple severe lesions, all tests generally sensitive to brain dysfunctions show deficits. As with most tumors, a focal area of deficit is generally present as well. In the case of multiple tumors, more than one focal area of deficit should be present. With multiple focal areas of deficit, the pattern may appear like that of generalized deterioration, and the two may be indistinguishable.

Head trauma. The effects of head trauma are quite varied in severity. Mild insults may produce no significantly poor performances on the battery, whereas more severe injuries may cause dramatic neuropsychological effects. The losses due to trauma also may be transitory or permanent. A significant blow to the head will cause a focus of injury at the point of impact (coup effect) as well as a focus opposite the point of impact in the other hemisphere (contrecoup effect). Depending upon the severity of the injury, the brain may be just swollen, or it may be bruised or lacerated. Transitory deficits clear once the swelling and edema disappear, while tearing and bruising cause damage to the brain tissue.

Neuropsychological deficits vary depending upon the severity and exact location of the injured area(s). Generally, a relatively focal area of deficit occurs on the injured side, with a more diffuse and stronger deficit, if contusion and laceration has occurred, on the contrecoup side. The level of performance—as a result of the deficit incurred—appears to depend upon the length of time the patient was unconscious (Klonoff & Paris, 1974). Once the swelling and traumatic shock effects of the injury have worn off and the patient is conscious, alert, and cooperative, an impairment index above 0.7 is uncommon except in very severe cases and open head injuries. Most of the generally sensitive tests may fall into the brain-damaged range, and relatively focal deficit patterns may be apparent and associated with the coup and contrecoup insult. The localized deficit areas are usually less circumscribed than those of space-occupying lesions.

Incipient Pick's disease. Like Alzheimer's disease, this is a progressive degenerative brain disorder causing generalized atrophy of the brain. In its incipient phases a bilateral frontotemporal focus of dysfunction is discernible (Constantindis, Richard, and Tissot, 1974); in the later stages, however, there is generalized deterioration of all neuropsychological skills, as in Alzheimer's disease, and the patient almost completely lacks cognitive behavior.

Initial results on the battery often reveal the frontotemporal focus. The Category Test reveals great deficits in abstract conceptual intelligence, with scores above 100 errors being commonplace. Poor performance on the Trail-making Test (part B) shows the lack of conceptual flexibility characteristic of bilateral prefrontal lesions. Poor overall performance on the TPT reflects the deficits in planning behavior and problem-solving strategy also typical of prefrontal disease. Expressive speech deficits on the Aphasia Test may also be present. Several deficits also point out the temporal-lobe dysfunction. Auditory perceptual difficulties often show up in the form of deficits on the Rhythm Test and sometimes the Speech-Sounds Perception Test. Auditory memory problems are also associated with the disease. These deficits show up on the Digit Span subtest of the WAIS. Sequencing skills associated with the temporal–frontal areas are also evident in incipient Pick's disease and show up as deficits on the Picture Arrangement subtest of the WAIS and the Trail-making Test (part A.)

Parkinson's disease. Parkinson's disease and its several variants—see Golden (1978) for review—can be considered a diffuse brain disorder which is generalized only in its most advanced stage. The disease is located basically in the basal nuclei; however, as the process continues cortical deterioration progresses.

Tremor and micrographia—very small drawing and writing—are prominent pathognomic signs. General motor and sensory impairment is present and shows up on the Finger Oscillation, Grip Strength, TPT, and Sensory–Perceptual tests. Oftentimes the impairment is lateralized to one or the other hemisphere initially, and antiparkinsonian drugs such as L-dopa may mask these impairments, especially in the early stages of the disorder. Cognitive deficits occur on all generally sensitive tests, such as the Category Test. The patient's IQ scores often are normal, especially when pure motor deficits are taken into account in scoring of the performance sections. Again, as the disease progresses, neuropsychological performance declines until generalized deterioration occurs. In the terminal stages all but the most insensitive tests, such as Vocabulary, Information, and Comprehension, will be down.

PSYCHIATRIC DISORDERS

Perhaps the most prevalent referral question of neurological and psychiatric sources is that of functional–organic differentiation. Difficult diagnostic problems—subjects manifesting psychiatric as well as neurologic signs—are typical. The ability of the battery to succeed in this capacity is a controversial area, and research has been sparse and not directly "on target" in many respects.

The chronicity of schizophrenia appears to be an important aspect relating to the battery's success in this discrimination. Acute schizophrenics who show little drug effect and who cooperate with the examiner seem to present no problem in discrimination from brain-impaired subjects (Golden, 1978). Chronic cases, however, have been more difficult to distinguish. A level-of-performance method of data analysis has been the only procedure employed, and, as Golden (1978) noted, pattern analysis should be of benefit in discriminating chronic schizophrenics from brain-damaged patients. More clinically relevant research is needed with use of difficult diagnostic cases and chronic psychiatric populations. Data analysis should also be more like clinical interpretation and should include pattern analysis and qualitative methods. With use of controls for drug effects, hospitalization, and motivation, the battery's ability in this task can be better evaluated.

Diagnostic Steps

Once the above-mentioned variables have been controlled, the functional–organic differentiation is much clearer. Before a psychiatric cause can be entertained, however, all neurological disorders must be ruled out. For example, any profile demonstrating a focal pattern of deficit is more likely to be due to some sort of a localized neurological disorder, such as a neoplasm or a cerebrovascular lesion.

Most psychiatric profiles show varied deficits, and all diffuse injuries must be carefully ruled out. Multiple sclerosis (MS) is easily differentiated because of its characteristic deficit pattern. The predominant symptoms in MS are the motor and sensory signs. These signs often are inconsistently lateralized. In MS relatively few cognitive deficits are found. They are most often present in complex tests which are sensitive to brain injury in general or which involve motor and sensory skills, such as the Category Test, the Trail-making Test, and the TPT. The cognitive deficits usually indicate no focal damage; however, they follow from the motor and sensory deficits, which is not always the case with psychiatric profiles.

Likewise, the degenerative disorders, such as Pick's and Alzheimer's diseases, must be ruled out before a psychiatric etiology can be postulated. These diffuse injuries are easily distinguished from psychiatric profiles by their severity of deficit. In incipient stages Pick's disease presents an anterior locus of dysfunction that is also readily distinguishable from the diffuse psychiatric profile.

Parkinson's disease is a diffuse disorder that must be ruled out in organic–functional differential diagnosis. Like MS, Parkinson's disease is largely a motor and sensory disorder. Severity of cognitive deficit relates to the course of the disease. In general, tests sensitive to brain dysfunction overall are disrupted. The more advanced the disease, the more extensive is the neuropsychological deficit. In the terminal stages all but the most insensitive tests will show deficits. This profile, along with the unmistakable tremor which occurs in Parkinson's disease distinguishes this deficit pattern from one related to psychiatric dysfunction.

The diffuse deficits seen in closed head trauma can be confused with psychiatric disorders especially when the left hemisphere is predominantly involved and when significant psychopathology as a result of the brain damage is present. Careful examination of the profile usually reveals a highly focal deficit complex in one hemisphere with a less circumscribed but still localized pattern in the other hemisphere. Also, the motor and sensory deficits are entirely consistent with the cognitive defects, which is not always the case in psychiatric profiles. For example, a trauma to the parietal area is accompanied by sensory problems. In a psychiatric patient sensory deficits may be present without TPT deficits, thereby indicating the functional nature of the sensory problems.

Thus by analyzing the overall pattern of deficits in addition to simply noting the level of performance the tester usually can make an organic/functional differentiation. The psychiatric profile is not characterized by focal neuropsychological deficit patterns and can therefore be differentiated from localized neurological lesions. The pattern of deficits is also not consistent within itself and does not present a profile representative of any of the diffuse disorders possible. Significant neuropsychological deficit secondary to psychiatric etiology usually results in spotty deficits in which skills basic to some manifest deficit often remain intact. Manifest deficits usually result from impairment in attention and concentration. For this reason complex higher cognitive skills which require efficient cognitive processes, such as those tested by the Category, TPT, and Trail-making tests, are often disrupted. Otherwise, a test pattern may reveal some good performances which would, with a brain injury, be expected to be disrupted given other deficits and the localization of damage they suggest.

Goldstein and Shelley (1973) suggest that qualitative analysis often reveals signs indicative of psychiatric disorder. Certain "pathognomic signs" may be present which suggest a psychiatric diagnosis. For example, unusual answers to some items may indicate bizarre mentation. Oftentimes it may be found that wrong answers are due to poor concentration and motivation or bizarre thought processes rather than simply to an inability to execute the item. Consequently, inconsistencies in performance between testing is associated with psychiatric deficits. If for any reason the diagnosis is unclear, retesting of the patient may be useful in the making of a differential diagnosis.

4
Process Interpretation

The interpretation of the process, or cause, of a given neurological disorder is based on the pattern of the test deficits and the seriousness (level) of the test deficits. For example, fast-growing tumors typically will produce more impaired results across the board than will more benign disorders like aneurysms. Head traumas are more likely to produce multiple foci of damage (usually with one focus being the worst), while a static tumor will produce a highly localized, single focus. Thus armed with both a knowledge of the test results and an extensive knowledge of the patterns of effects caused by specific neurological disorders one can make reasonable guesses as to the cause of some disorders, especially those that produce highly unique patterns of deficits. When this information is combined with historical data one can make excellent interpretations in the area of process.

In general, results of testing can fall into a limited number of patterns, each of which can vary in intensity from very mild to extremely impaired. The major patterns one should learn to recognize include the following:

1. Overall good performance with no significant deficits;
2. Good or normal performance in one hemisphere but impaired performance in the other;
3. Impaired performance in both hemispheres, usually with one hemisphere more severe than the other;
4. Equal, diffuse impairment of both hemispheres;

5. Scattered deficits in which both hemispheres have focal dysfunctions but in which other areas are normal;

6. Bilateral or unilateral motor impairment without cognitive dysfunction; and

7. Bilateral or unilateral cognitive impairment without motor or sensory involvement.

In each of these cases, if one decides that there are other than diffuse deficits within a hemisphere, an attempt should be made at localizing the deficits, as described in the last chapter.

Each type of process will produce patterns of results consistent with one or more of the groups described in the list above. Many processes will produce several patterns, depending on the exact nature of the deficit, how long it took to develop, how long it has been there, age of onset, severity, premorbid intelligence, and other similar factors. It is not possible for us to give a full description of the neurology of all the possible disorders in this book; however, what follows is a short description of the most salient dimensions for the more common disorders. The reader should remember that expertise in this area is highly dependent upon both experience and familiarity with neurological disorders and their course. In the case examples given in Chapter 5 we will try to make clear the reasoning from theory to inferences. See also Chapter 3.

Tumors. Tumors occur in a variety of forms, each of which varies in the manner that it affects neuropsychological test results; however, there are several common findings. All tumors create an area of focal deficit surrounded by an area of more diffuse and less severe deficit. The area of focal deficit varies greatly in severity; the effects may be extremely mild in some tumors, extremely severe in others. In the most severe tumors brain tissue is destroyed, and suppressions will be seen if the tumor is in a sensory-reception area of the cerebral hemispheres.

The surrounding deficits may similarly vary in severity. In some tumors they are nonexistent; in others the entire function of the brain may be disrupted. These secondary effects may be the result of increased pressure, edema (swelling of the brain), or disturbances in cerebral circulation.

Abscesses—pockets of pus in the brain, caused by infection—may result in similar symptoms, as may hematomas, pockets of blood within the brain, and aneurysms (ballooning of a section of an artery of the brain).

A special type of tumor—metastatic tumors—results from the spread of cancer from other parts of the body to the brain. It is identifiable because it is usually multiple, causing pockets of focal deficit throughout the brain.

Head trauma. Head traumas are often characterized by a focal deficit in one hemisphere and a somewhat more diffuse and less severe deficit (countrecoup) in the opposite hemisphere. The severity of these deficits may vary considerably. In cases in which there is unconsciousness the severity generally correlates with the length of time that it takes a person to awaken.

Head trauma may also lead to localized or more severe bleeding in the brain. In these injuries there are usually more severe and permanent deficits; if the bleeding is severe, this may extend the area of injury considerably. In some cases, hematomas (pockets of blood) may form, sometimes several months after an injury because of slow bleeding in an artery. See also the discussion in Chapter 3.

Cerebrovascular disorders. Disruptions of the cerebrovascular system are a major cause of brain injury. A common disorder is infarction of an artery, which results in a lack of oxygen in tissue served by the artery. A common site for infarction is the middle cerebral artery, which supplies the motor, temporal, and parietal areas of each hemisphere. The infarctions can result in partial or complete loss of motor and sensory function on one side of the body. If the left middle cerebral artery is involved, there will also be extensive verbal deficits. If the right middle cerebral artery is involved, there will be severe spatial deficits (e.g., Block Design Test, drawings) and losses on the Rhythm Test. Similar results, in more severe form, will be caused by hemorrhage (rupture) of these arteries. In this case there will also be clear suppressions.

Many cerebrovascular disorders occur after the onset of arteriosclerosis. Since arteriosclerosis causes diffuse brain impairment, patients with cerebrovascular disorders may present a picture of diffuse impairment throughout the brain accompanied by an area of severe focal deficit.

Aneurysms are the result of a ballooning of a part of an artery. Aneurysms will cause mild, focal deficits where they are located; however, their effects rarely extend beyond this unless they hemorrhage. Aneurysms typically have impairment indices of 0.4–0.6, while infarctions will have indices of 0.6–1.0, and hemorrhages will result in indices of 0.9–1.0.

In many cases cerebrovascular disorders and tumors will produce similar results. For example, a severe tumor near the middle cerebral artery may be difficult to distinguish from an infarction or hemorrhage.

Epilepsy. Epilepsy is generally a secondary result of another neuropathological condition, often caused by the irritation of the brain by a scar, tumor, or other space-occupying disorder. There are also a large class of epilepsies labeled idiopathic—that is, of unknown origin. A series of articles on epilepsy (Matthews & Klove, 1967; Klove and Matthews, 1966, 1969, 1974) found that those with epilepsy of known causes showed more severe impairment on the Halstead-Reitan Battery than those with epilepsy labeled idiopathic; at present, however, there is no way to identify the presence of epilepsy with the test battery. Epilepsy is always a possibility, especially in clients with focal lesions.

Alcoholism. Chronic alcoholics have significant deficits on the Halstead-Reitan Battery (Gudeman, Craine, Golden, and McLaughlin, 1977). These deficits include tests of frontal lobe activity (Category Test, Trail-making Test, part B), spatial skills (Tactual Performance Test, Rhythm Block Design, Picture Arrangement, Object Assembly), and left-sided motor skills (Finger-tapping Test). The severity of the deficits depends on the chronicity and severity of the alcoholism.

Presenile dementia. The presenile dementias (Alzheimer's and Pick's diseases are the major forms) result in generalized deterioration of brain function, including deficits on those tests thought to be resistant to brain damage (e.g., Vocabulary). The impairment index in these disorders is usually 1.0. See the discussion in Chapter 3.

Parkinson's disease. As noted in Chapter 3, these patients show significant impairment on tests of drawing (including tremor) and on the Category Test, although WAIS scores tend to be normal (Reitan & Boll, 1971). Measures of motor and tactile skills are down, including the Tactual Performance Test and the Finger-tapping Test. These deficits may be bilateral or unilateral. Patients will also manifest very small writing in their attempts to reduce or compensate for motor problems. In the latter stages of this disorder there may be generalized impairment across Halstead's basic tests.

Multiple sclerosis. Multiple sclerosis (MS) is a degenerative disease of the central nervous system. MS produces sensory and motor symptoms that are often inconsistent and that may show periods of exacerbation and remission. As noted in Chapter 3, there are distinct deficits in performance IQ and on Finger-tapping, Tactual Performance, and other sensory tests. There may be mild cognitive losses reflected as a borderline score on the Category Test. Auditory problems are rare, but visual deficits may be caused by involvement of the optic nerve (Goldstein & Shelley, 1974; Matthews et al., 1970; Reitan & Boll, 1971; Robbins, 1974). MS patients may also show peaks on the Hypochondriasis and Hysteria scales of the MMPI, a pattern characteristic of conversion hysteria (Cleeland et. al., 1970). Because of the MMPI profile and the inconsistent symptoms MS is sometimes mistaken for a psychological disorder.

COMPLICATING FACTORS

Although process and location determine much of the pattern in the neuropsychological profile, a number of important factors must be recognized that complicate simple interpretation in most cases. Again, the reader should note that the present volume, concentrating on the interpretation of the Halstead-Reitan Battery, is limited to introducing these factors and their general effects. It cannot be emphasized enough that a knowledge of both the medical neurology of these diseases and the behavioral neurology associated with the disease processes is indispensible if one wishes to make accurate interpretations at this level. Readers are referred to several excellent books in this area, including those by Chusid (1970) and the Mayo Clinic (1976) and *Brain's Clinical Neurology* (Bannister, 1973), as well as many standard textbooks used in medical school neurology courses.

Acute Versus Chronic Disorders

Probably the most important of these additional factors is the consideration of the acuteness or chronicity of a given disorder. Traditionally, these terms are interpreted by many as referring to the time since onset of a disorder. Thus a disorder that started 10 years ago would be labeled chronic, while one that started 1 week ago would be labeled acute. Although this usage makes a great deal of common sense, the use of the terms in only this way adds some confusion to the neuropsychological interpretation.

A better way to consider these factors when doing neuropsychological testing is to consider the acute-versus-chronic dimension as actually representing a compensated versus an uncompensated disorder. Acute disorders look so bad in neuropsychological testing because they are uncompensated—that is, the natural ability of the brain to minimize the effects of any brain injury on a behavioral level has not taken place. This can happen in a wide variety of ways. First, any sudden-onset disorder that injures the brain will have a period during which the disorder will look acute. Examples of this would be a head trauma or an occlusion of a major cerebral artery. Because of the speed at which these disorders begin and because of their initial overwhelming effects the brain is unable to compensate. The time for which this may exist varies considerably from one disorder to another; a head trauma may show acute effects for only hours or even minutes (such as the athelete who has his "bell rung" on the football field) or may show these for months (such as the individual in a prolonged coma). The length of time is influenced by the severity of the injury as well as the presence of secondary effects, commonly grouped under the phase "diaschisis" (Smith, 1975). Diaschisis refers to a wide variety of secondary effects that prolong the acute phase of a disorder or intensify the deficits during the acute phase; this can include such phenomena as raised intracranial pressure, changes in blood-flow patterns, edema, hydrocephalus, and other similar effects.

Other acute injuries are prolonged by the growth of the lesion with time. Tumors are the best example of this category. A fast-growing tumor will develop so quickly that the brain is unable to compensate. Such a disorder will continue to look acute until it is arrested or until it kills the individual in question. A slower growing tumor may not produce these effects, however; patients have been identified who have had brain tumors for years that because they are slow growing give the brain time to compensate, which eliminates or minimizes acute signs on neuropsychological and neurological testing.

The third type of injury that continues to look acute is one in which the damage is so severe that the brain is simply unable to compensate in any way. Sudden, complete bilateral destruction of the prefrontal lobes can lead to total disintegration of behavior that is not followed by recovery. One patient seen by one of us (C.J.G.) had had complete removal of the left temporal lobe down to the level of the internal capsule. The severity of the injury made recovery impossible, and the patients' profile continued to look acute even 3 years later.

On the Halstead-Reitan Battery acute injuries will generally show much more severe effects overall. The impairment index will be considerably higher than in a chronic version of the same injury. If the injury is lateralized, the lateralization will often be quite marked, with the area of focus showing extreme dysfunction. Severe aphasic symptoms are more likely with acute injuries, as are highly lateralized motor and sensory deficits. Acute injuries are much more likely to show the classical picture associated with an injury in any given part of the brain. Thus an injury to the dominant temporal lobe that is not accompanied by significant speech deficits is not likely to be acute.

Chronic injuries, on the other hand, are those most likely to be compensated. Compensation occurs either as a result of the brain's recovery from the injury or from reorganization of the functional structure of the brain. In the first case recovery assumes that the injured areas of the brain are not totally destroyed but rather are only impaired in function. This situation can result from cells functioning at a below-normal level, changes in metabolism, changes in neurotransmitter levels, and other physiological alterations that can improve with time. Improvement in chronic disorders can also be traced to a lessening of diaschisis that has served to make the acute situation look worse.

Improvement in brain operation cannot take place when cells have actually been destroyed, however. There is as yet no evidence that destroyed nerve cells of the brain can regenerate. In these cases the brain is forced to undergo a functional reorganization. In this process tasks are done in a different way (using intact skills), or alternate areas of the brain take over the function of the injured areas. Using these processes the brain seeks to minimize the importance of any deficits associated with the brain lesion. When the lesion is circumscribed, this procedure is likely to be more successful. In more generalized injuries there are fewer ways for the brain to successfully reorganize.

The most obvious disorders that fall into chronic category are old injuries which have remained static (unchanged) for a significant period of time. An old occlusion, old head trauma, old removed tumor, or similar condition falls into this frequently used subcategory. The only exceptions here are injuries of the kind that have caused such destruction that recovery is not possible, as described above.

The second category includes those disorders that are not absolutely static but that change very slowly over a long period of time. Because the rate of growth is slow the brain is able to develop maximal compensation for these deficits. Depending on their location, this can result in there being no identifiable deficits in the patient. These disorders are exemplified by slowly developing degenerative disorders, slow-growing tumors, and congenital malformations or aneurysms of the cerebrovascular system. In the last case, for example, it is possible for a chronic disorder to become acute through hemorrhage or slow bleeding. If there is bleeding one can get the picture of a chronic disorder with a small focal area of acute injury. In the case of more massive hemorrhages the entire picture will look acute rather than chronic.

In general, chronic disorders look less severe on neuropsychological testing than do acute disorders. In the case of localized lesions, laterality and location will not be as sharply defined owing to recovery of some functions. Thus large right–left discrepancies are less likely to occur, as are large verbal–performance discrepancies on the WAIS. Acute aphasic symptoms are rarer, and pure syndromes are unusual. Symptoms that one would expect to be present are often missing, and overall performance is much more likely to be borderline or, in many cases, within normal limits overall. It should be noted, however, that acute disorders are not always worse than chronic disorders. The chronic residual effect of a widespread injury can be massive, as can be the cumulative effects of a long-term degenerative disorder.

Age of Onset

Another important variable is the age of onset of a given condition. Of most concern here are disorders that have their onset in childhood. In these cases one sees the effects not only of destruction of some skill areas but also of prevention of the development of some skill areas that later are dependent developmentally on the lost skills. Just to add to the complexity of the problem, however, a poorer result is not always the case; in some problems an early injury will cause less damage because the brain is less committed and is able to switch tasks to another part of the brain. This is especially true in very early injuries (prior to age 2). As a result these two sets of injuries must be considered separately.

With injuries occurring before the age of 2 years several possible outcomes are present. In a diffuse injury the child is generally impaired and severely restricted in learning skills. These children are often labeled mentally retarded. In the case of localized injuries, however, the outcome can be somewhat better; if the injury is in the temporal–parietal area of the brain and of sufficient size, the brain will transfer functions of the injured areas to the opposite hemisphere. This is especially true of damage to the left-hemisphere language areas if the injury occurs before the child has developed speech since it is about this time that these areas are committed to specialized language or nonlanguage function. The same phenomenon does not occur with frontal injuries, which the brain appears to ignore. These injuries do not show up immediately, however, unless there is injury to the motor areas, with cerebral palsy resulting. When only the cognitive areas are involved the deficit may not be noticed until late childhood or early adolescence.

Small injuries anywhere in the brain do not appear to invoke the mechanism of switching to the other hemisphere, which is apparently dependent on both size and location of the lesion. Thus these injuries will continue to interfere with function and skill acquisition throughout life. It has been theorized (Golden, 1978) that such injuries may be responsible for many specific learning disabilities.

Thus only with certain injuries prior to age 2 years is the brain able to take advantage of the fact that it is not fully committed in a functional sense at this stage of life. With those injuries that do not trigger advantage of this switchover effect the prognosis is usually poorer than at any other age because of the interference with future development. In injuries occuring later in life (after age 2), the severity of the injury is reduced because of the larger number of skills already learned by the child. The larger this learning base and the more extensive the brain development at the time of injury, the less will be the effects of the injury (Boll, 1976). As the child approaches maturity the injury comes closer to resembling that of the adult (see, e.g., Reed & Reitan, 1965, in the bibliography).

Dominance

In general, this book has proceeded with the assumption that the left hemisphere is the dominant hemisphere in everyone. By dominance is meant that the left hemisphere is more responsible for verbal processes as well as more responsible for bilateral coordination and overall planning and control strategies for the organism. In general, this assumption is true for well over 90 percent of all right-handed people and about 70 percent on all left-handed individuals (Milner, 1974). Thus right-hemisphere dominance and mixed-hemisphere dominance are rare conditions, especially in adults with no history of childhood brain injury.

The effects of right-hemisphere dominance on neuropsychological testing are obvious: they are exactly the reverse of what one would expect after reading the previous chapters, except, of course, for motor and sensory skills. Mixed dominance is a much more confusing problem, since the relative degree of dominance can vary considerably from case to case, making localization of processes in such patients nearly impossible.

One predictable relationship has generally been found in left-handed individuals that is not present in right-handed individuals: motor and sensory control of writing in these individuals is almost invariably a function of the right rather than the left hemisphere.

Premorbid IQ

Another important factor is premorbid intelligence. In general it is easier for the highly intelligent person to adjust to brain damage by finding an alternate way to do a task because generally the more intelligent person has more resources at his or her control than does the less intelligent person. This situation is similar to the effects described in children. As a child grows older, he or she has more resources and shows less damage from most injuries. Similarly, as a person becomes more intelligent, he or she has more resources and is better able to adjust to most injuries.

Emotional Reactions

Emotional reactions do not affect neuropsychological skills, but they do affect neuropsychological testing. Acute patients are often anxious, scared, depressed, and confused. These factors can significantly interfere with a patient's ability to perform on neuropsychological tests. The patient may refuse tests, especially in areas where he or she expects to do badly. Patients may pretend not to hear instructions or to understand them when they involve difficult tasks for them, although they will comprehend similar instructions in more rewarding circumstances. It is the responsibility of the neuropsychological tester to evaluate this situation and assess its impact on test performance. For example, the unmotivated or depressed patient may not be able to maintain performance over longer tests such as Category Test, Tactual Performance Test, or Speech-Sounds Perception Test. In these cases one must evaluate the cause of the deficit so as not to make assumptions of cortical injuries where none exist.

5
Case Examples

The interpretation of a neuropsychological battery can be learned only in part through the mastery of such data as contained in this volume and in other books on related topics in psychiatry, neurology, and neuropsychology. The actual interpretation process involves the organization of much data and the integration of the data with the known facts about localization of brain processes, process effects, chronicity, dominance, age, premorbid IQ, patient motivation, and all the other factors that may influence a given testing situation. Such a process can be learned only "by doing" and by subsequently receiving feedback on one's errors, and then "doing the whole thing over again."

Consequently, the remainder of the book is devoted to the presentation of 80 cases with a wide variety of diagnoses, problems, and performance. These cases have been selected either because they illustrate a certain type of injury or process or because they illustrate some difficult point in interpretation. All of these cases have been selected from actual clinical files. Each case example begins with a historical introduction. The amount of information presented here is the same amount that was available to the neuropsychologist upon original referral of the case. In some cases a diagnosis is included, while in others there is little information. Cases that have been included show all possible localizations, the major processes, and a wide variety of differences in such functions as chronicity or premorbid intelligence.

Associated with each case is a summary of the performance of the individual on each test of the Halstead-Reitan Battery. All measures should be familiar to those who have had any experience with the Halstead-Reitan Battery. (Those who do not have such experience should get such actual experience before reading these cases; we assume close familiarity with the techniques used in the battery and the scoring of the battery.) Note that for the Tactual Performance Test scores are given first at the top of the forms for total time taken, while scores for the right, left, and both hands are given as time per block (fractions of a minute) rather than in terms of the total time for the entire board. This allows one to compare performances where all blocks were not completed with those where all blocks were finished. At the bottom of each form is a list of aphasic symptoms, including construction dyspraxia. Not all drawings and pictures have been included because of space limitations, but examples for each disorder are provided in the figures in Chapter 2 (Figs. 2-1 through 2-14), which are taken from specific cases in this chapter, as indicated. The impairment index calculation has been left to the reader, as it would be after a normal test administration.

The reader should note that the reports were written for a wide variety of questions. This changes the type of response that we attempted to match to the referral question.

A final word on use of these cases: If you have some Halstead-Reitan experience, we suggest that you first try the cases "blind", and then attempt a second analysis with a knowledge of the case background. Only then should the writeup itself be read. If you have no experience in Halstead-Reitan interpretation, it is best to first read through the entire section, without studying each case in detail, to get an idea of how one can approach the cases. You can follow this with blind interpretations of each case and then with interpretation using the background information before you look again at the writeup. It has been our experience that both the novice and the person with some experience can go through the case series several times and still gain some information of importance each time without memorizing what each case represents. Repetition of these techniques will enable one to get the most out of the cases in terms of improving one's diagnostic skills. Certainly, 80 cases will not make one an expert (this depends on the acquisition of more knowledge in the areas described earlier in this volume), but this work can serve to significantly increase one's neuropsychological interpretive sophistication and awareness of the many factors affecting neuropsychological interpretation.

In those cases where such information is useful, the case reports refer to certain qualitative aspects of performance that cannot be interpreted from the standard scores. In addition, information on the subject that was obtained later may also be included in these sections. The reader should note that the interpretations in each case are correct as far as the neurological examination of the patient allows such determination.

Case 1

Background data. The subject is a right-handed, 28-year-old, single white female doctoral candidate with normal mental and neurological status. She volunteered to take the Halstead-Reitan Battery as part of a research project.

Case Example __1__ Age __28__ Sex __F__ Education __12__ Handedness __R__

General Tests:

    Category (errors) __45__ Trail-making: Part A __25__ Part B __45__

    TPT: Total time __11.6__ Location __3__ Memory __8__

Motor and Sensory Tests:

Finger-tapping	R __42__ L __37__	Fingertip	
Finger agnosia	R __0__ L __0__	number-writing	R ____ L ____
Supressions:		Tactile form	
Visual	R __0__ L __0__	(time)	R ____ L ____
Tactile	R __0__ L __0__	(errors)	R ____ L ____
Auditory	R __0__ L __0__		

    TPT: Time/Block R __.5__ L __.33__ Both __.33__

Cognitive Tests:

    Speech-Sounds Perception

      (errors) __2__   Rhythm (errors) __4__

    WAIS: (scaled score)

Information	__16__	Picture completion	__11__
Comprehension	__17__	Picture arrangement	__12__
Vocabulary	__15__	Object assembly	__17__
Similarities	__14__	Block design	__15__
Arithmetic	__15__	Digit symbol	__15__
Digit span	__15__		

        VIQ __133__   PIQ __125__   FSIQ __131__

Aphasia: None

Test results. Examination of the WAIS scaled scores shows an exceptionally intelligent young woman, with verbal skills that consistently rank near or above the 98th percentile. There is little variation in subtest scores, and that which is seen is within the range of normal variation. Analysis of nonverbal skills shows significant scatter, even though her overall nonverbal intellectual skills rank at the 95th percentile. Note that Picture Completion (PC) and Picture Arrangement (PA) are 1 standard deviation or more below the patient's other nonverbal subtest scores. This suggests some inefficiency in attentional focusing (PC) and planning and sequencing (PA). The relatively lower score on PA was due to average speed in completing the more difficult items and a minor reversal of two picture elements on the last PA item. This suggests that right-hemispheric intellectual skills are less practiced and efficient than those of the left hemisphere. This is a common finding in persons of very superior intelligence and has no particular significance for the integrity of cerebral functioning.

On the Halstead-Reitan measures the impairment index is well within normal limits, and the general level of functioning across subtests is within normal limits. Our expectation of intact cerebral functioning is confirmed. Here, as on the WAIS, one notes a pattern of relative strength and normal performance variation among the various measures. There are no aphasic errors, and the subject makes only two errors on the Speech-Sounds Perception Test. Her performance on a nonverbal auditory-discrimination measure, the Seashore Rhythm Test, is just within normal limits, the score probably reflecting less practice effect than do the speech-related items. Sensory–perceptual functions are intact. The Aphasia Test is normal (Fig. 2-1). Performance on the Trail-making Test is superior, particularly part B, in which her ability to verbally mediate the task is at a premium in working through the alphanumeric sequence. Nonverbal reasoning on the Halstead Category Test approaches the cutoff for impaired performance (51 or more errors); 31 of her 45 errors occurred on subtest III, which emphasizes the left-to-right position of the correct figure in the array. She had difficulty when the cues were nonverbal and presented a set which was contrary to her expectation and experience. When she was able to verbally mediate the other subtests she learned quite efficiently.

Motor-tapping performance is a bit too slow for the norms for women reported by Russell et al. (1970). The degree of slowing is mild. More important than the mild-slowing performance level is the relative efficiency of the two hands on this task. Note that the nondominant left hand is approximately 10 percent slower than the dominant right hand, as is expected in normals. Results of this kind may be seen within the normal range of variation. Some inefficiency of this kind is the rule rather than the exception, even among superior-functioning-level adults. Complex motor functioning is well within normal limits overall. The subject completed the TPT in a normal time with each hand. The third trial is mildly slowed compared to the other two trials; this may represent a mild fatigue effect, since each hand was competent to complete the task independently, and there is no basis for inference of an interference effect. Recall for the task is excellent (eight blocks), but location of the blocks in space is marginally impaired (three blocks). This recall inefficiency is mild but measurable. It is notable that it occurs on a measure that is nonverbal and difficult to encode verbally. Shapes can be given names easily if the patient is verbally skilled—star, oval, circle, square, rectangle, and the like—but locations are much more difficult to encode, particularly when they must be placed in relation to each other on a board that is kept from view. The shapes were very likely encoded verbally as a means of recognition during the formboard-solution portion of the task. An individual with superior verbal intellectual skills usually approaches this sort of task in a well practiced and effective manner. The failure of efficient encoding of locations thus appears to have been a matter of not expecting to be asked for such information. It appears that verbal encoding occured incidentally in the usual process of task solution, which would have made efficient recall of the shapes an easy matter.

Case 2

Background data. The subject is a right-handed, 30-year-old, single white male psychology technician with an M.A. degree in physiological psychology. He has normal mental and neurological status. He volunteered to take the Halstead-Reitan Battery as part of a research project.

Case Example __2__ Age _30_ Sex _M_ Education _18_ Handedness _R_

General Tests:

    Category (errors) _15_ Trail-making: Part A _15_ Part B _30_

    TPT: Total time _8.7_ Location _4_ Memory _8_

Motor and Sensory Tests:

Finger-tapping	R _51_	L _47_	Fingertip	
Finger agnosia	R _0_	L _0_	number-writing	R _0_ L _0_
Supressions:			Tactile form	
Visual	R _0_	L _0_	(time)	R _12_ L _11_
Tactile	R _0_	L _0_	(errors)	R _0_ L _0_
Auditory	R _0_	L _0_		

    TPT: Time/Block R _.31_ L _.34_ Both _.22_

Cognitive Tests:

    Speech-Sounds Perception

      (errors) _1_ Rhythm (errors) _1_

    WAIS: (scaled score)

Information	_15_	Picture completion	_16_
Comprehension	_16_	Picture arrangement	_14_
Vocabulary	_15_	Object assembly	_13_
Similarities	_16_	Block design	_12_
Arithmetic	_13_	Digit symbol	_16_
Digit span	_16_		

        VIQ _130_ PIQ _128_ FSIQ _131_

Aphasia: None

Test results.   The subject's verbal intellectual skills rank at the 98th percentile for age, and his nonverbal intellectual skills rank at the 97th percentile overall. This is clearly a highly intelligent individual, but even at this intellectual level there is some intertest scatter that is notable. Old learning on the verbal-comprehension factor (Information [I], Comprehension [C], Similarities [S], Vocabulary [V]) shows no significant variation from the high mean level. The attentional factor (Arithmetic [A], Digit Span [D]) shows a difference of 1 standard deviation that suggests variability in the efficiency of attention and concentration skills. At this level there is a premium upon speed of response as well as accuracy, so that a more careful manner of approach can penalize the subject. The perceptual organization factor among the nonverbal-scale skills (PC, BD[Block Design], PA, OA[-Object Assembly] also shows significant variation. PC is 1 standard deviation higher than the mean of the other three scales that compose the factor. The deviant score here is PC rather than the other three scales. The attention to fine detail seen in PC most likely shows some practice effect. The background information shows that the subject has an advanced degree in physiological psychology, which requires attention to much material that is microscopic in detail. There is thus good reason to infer that this high score reflects the effects of his specialized training. There is often a 2-standard-deviation difference between verbal and nonverbal skills in highly educated, verbally oriented persons of superior ability who have entirely normal cerebral functioning. This difference between the two skill groupings reflects their superior verbal ability rather than any deficiency in nonverbal skills as long as the nonverbal mean does not fall below the average level. We should expect that this subject has normal cerebral functioning from these results.

Examination of the level of performance on the Halstead-Reitan Battery tests, particularly the impairment index, confirms the expectation that the subject has normal cerebral functioning. He makes only 15 errors on the Category Test, demonstrating flexibility and efficiency in problem solving. Similar flexibility and efficiency of visual search as was seen on the WAIS PC subtest is seen on the Trail-making Tests, which were done very quickly and errorlessly. This also reflects efficient memorization, motor output, and cognitive flexibility.

Motoric skills for simple manual dexterity on tapping are within normal limits for males with a dominant right hand. The expected 10 percent difference between the tapping speed of the dominant and nondominant hands is closely approximated by the current results. More complex motor performance on the Tactual Performance Test shows very rapid TPT solution, efficient even on the first trial. The actual performance on the second trial does not fit with a reduction in speed by one third, as is usually seen in average-performance-level subjects expected since this is the trial-and-error learning of the first trial is eliminated and the efficiency is maintained on the second trial with the nondominant hand. The use of both hands in unison on the final trial shows the expected improvement of one-third when an advantage is added through practice effect and when one hand is freed to search the board while the other can search for matching blocks. As expected from this performance, the Sensory–Perceptual Examination is errorless. One would have to have highly efficient sensory and motor functioning to produce such a performance. Verbal encoding of the shapes typically occurs spontaneously with verbally oriented, highly intelligent subjects such as this. Recall of the shapes is thus often a relatively straightforward matter, and the subject did recall 8 of the 10 shapes. He recalled the locations of only half as many blocks, however, when he was asked to draw the TPT board on the postperformance incidental-recall phase. It is much more difficult to recall items for which there is no easily codable format, and there would be no necessary or spontaneous reason for the subject to carefully encode the locations verbally without prior knowledge that he would be asked to recall them later. His single marginally impaired performance thus occurred on this unexpected task.

Speech skills are most important in a person with graduate educational level, such as this subject. Thus the subject shows errorless performance on the Aphasia Screening Test and on the Speech-Sounds Perception Test. He also shows excellent aural discrimination on the nonverbal discrimination measure, the Seashore Rhythm Test.

Case 3

Background data. The subject is a right-handed, 33-year-old, single white male psychiatric technician with 14 years of education. He has normal mental status, and his neurological examination, done on a research-study screening basis, is within normal limits. He volunteered for the Halstead-Reitan Battery as part of a research project as a control subject.

Case Example __3__ Age __33__ Sex __M__ Education __14__ Handedness __R__

General Tests:

Category (errors) __50__ Trail-making: Part A __26__ Part B __88__

TPT: Total time __12.8__ Location __5__ Memory __6__

Motor and Sensory Tests:

Finger-tapping R __48__ L __48__ Fingertip
Finger agnosia R __0__ L __0__   number-writing R __0__ L __0__

Supressions: Tactile form
Visual   R __0__ L __0__   (time)   R __14__ L __19__
Tactile   R __0__ L __0__   (errors)   R __0__ L __0__
Auditory R __0__ L __0__

TPT: Time/Block R __.51__ L __.38__ Both __.39__

Cognitive Tests:

Speech-Sounds Perception

(errors)   __16__   Rhythm (errors)   __12__

WAIS: (scaled score)

Information   __12__   Picture completion   __11__
Comprehension   __11__   Picture arrangement __12__
Vocabulary   __12__   Object assembly   __11__
Similarities   __11__   Block design   __13__
Arithmetic   __10__   Digit symbol   __13__
Digit span   __10__

VIQ __105__   PIQ __114__   FSIQ __109__

Aphasia: Spelling dysparaxia,. dysarthria, dyscalculia

Test results. The WAIS scores for this subject show uniform consistency in level of performance. Whereas many subjects with college-level training show a superiority of verbal over nonverbal intellectual skills, this man shows the reverse pattern. It is well to remember that VIQ–PIQ differences do not reach significance until there is a 15-point difference between them; thus variation of the kind seen here does not provide any cues to this man's cerebral functioning impairment.

Careful evaluation of the Halstead-Reitan scores leads to a different impression than might be obtained from a casual observation of the impairment index, which is within normal limits. A number of the test scores are barely within normal limits. When the scores are taken in total one notes that tests passed are often marginal passes for this individual, and his scores on the whole show borderline impairment of cerebral functioning for a man of average intelligence. This is true of the Category Test, TPT Memory, TPT Location, Finger-tapping–right hand, Trail-making–part B, and the Aphasia Screening Test. Slightly greater performance decrement on each of these subtests would raise the impairment index well into the brain-damaged range, with only TPT total time within normal limits. It is always necessary to carefully examine how the patient reached the overall impairment index score, since a measure that relies upon cutoff scores for classification may be insensitive to false positives and false negatives that fall in the borderline range, as with this case.

The Category Test error total was due primarily to difficulty with subtests III and IV, with excellent performance on the other subtests. This shows inefficient learning on tasks with a spatial component (left-to-right position for subtest III and quadrant position for subtest IV). Performance on the Trail-making Test–part A (Trails A) is within normal limits, but the Trails B score is barely within normal limits. The subject appears to be able to deal with the sequencing, visual-search, and motor-output tasks for Trails A. Transformation of the numerical sequence of Trails A into an alphanumeric progression on Trails B called for more flexibility in the integration of these skills that lowered his efficiency to a marginal level. These hypotheses require further evaluation in the light of the other test results to identify which skills are central to the patient's performance difficulty.

Simple manual motor speed and dexterity, as measured by the Finger-tapping Test, show equal performance with the two hands. The normal cutoff for this test with the dominant hand is 50 taps. The nondominant hand should be 10 percent less efficient than the dominant hand. One would infer that left-hand performance is consistent with normal performance, but right-hand performance is too slow. Given the left-hand performance of 48 taps as a standard for this patient, the right hand should be tapping 52–53 taps instead of 48. This is the first clue to some inefficiency of left-hemispheric functioning. One then would also want to compare the patient's performance efficiency on a more complex measure of motor function, the Tactual Performance Test. Note that the TPT total time is within normal limits and that the times for the dominant and nondominant hands are individually within normal limits. The expected transfer from the dominant to the nondominant hand trials is seen. The test of cooperation of the two hands on the third trial, however, reveals significant impairment, which suggests either difficulty with interhemispheric transfer or fatigue. Recall of the TPT task on the incidental memory measures (TPT Memory and Location) was barely within normal limits, as noted above.

Nonverbal aural discrimination on the Seashore Rhythm Test is moderately impaired. The subject also shows difficulty with verbal aural discrimination on the Speech-Sounds Perception Test. The Aphasia Screening Test shows multiple errors that should not have occurred in a man with 2 years of college if left-hemisphere functioning were intact. He spelled the word square as "skor," cross as "corss," and triangle as "trolangle." Pronunciation difficulty with a literal paraphasic error was seen when the phrase "Methodist Episcopal" was mispronounced as "Methodist Episcobal." On the written arithmetic problem $85 - 27 = ?$, the patient carried one digit from the tens column correctly but arrived at the answer 48 initially and then changed the answer to 47. Failure to complete the calculation despite preservation of the overall plan of attack on the problem suggests left-hemisphere dysfunction in a man of this education level. More important was perseveration of the foregoing response answer as the solution to the subsequent mental calculation $17 \times 3 = ?$.

This patient has boderline-to-mild left-hemisphere dysfunction. This was confirmed independently by other neuropsychological tests, but a discussion of those results is beyond the scope of this report. The etiology of the disorder has not been established.

Case 4

Background data. The patient is a right-handed, 54-year-old, divorced white male with an eighth-grade education. He has worked as a licensed practical nurse and bus driver. He underwent bilateral prefrontal lobotomy for treatment of chronic, intractable anxiety 21 years prior to the time of testing. He experienced some palliative relief of his symptomatology to the point that he was able to return to work after the operation. He completed the Halstead-Reitan Battery as part of a clinical neuropsychological evaluation.

Case Example __4__ Age __54__ Sex __M__ Education __8__ Handedness __R__

General Tests:

Category (errors) __109__ Trail-making: Part A __65__ Part B __182__

TPT: Total time __22.7__ Location __3__ Memory __6__

Motor and Sensory Tests:

Finger-tapping R __54__ L __45__   Fingertip

Finger agnosia R __0__ L __0__   number-writing R __7__ L __2__

Supressions: Tactile form

    Visual R __0__ L __0__   (time)   R __14__ L __14__

    Tactile R __0__ L __0__   (errors)   R __0__ L __0__

    Auditory R __0__ L __1__

TPT: Time/Block R __.95__ L __.69__ Both __.63__

Cognitive Tests:

Speech-Sounds Perception

(errors)   2   Rhythm (errors)   8

WAIS: (scaled score)

Information	13	Picture completion	13
Comprehension	9	Picture arrangement	9
Vocabulary	12	Object assembly	9
Similarities	11	Block design	7
Arithmetic	12	Digit symbol	5
Digit span	11		

VIQ 110   PIQ 103   FSIQ 107

Aphasia: Dysnomia

Test results.   This patient's intellectual skills are relatively well preserved. The verbal comprehension factor (I, C, S, V) on the WAIS, however, shows significant scatter and relative lack of sophistication in practical, insight-oriented, commonsense applications of knowledge (C) that he has learned formally (I, S, V). This is consistent with his history of labor for over two decades in fields that emphasize routine work and minimize novel, insightful, or creative applications of old knowledge. Given the history of prefrontal lobotomy, there is also a likelihood that this man has been unable to effectively formulate plans for task solution when faced with novel task demands. He thus functions best in a position that emphasizes routine activity and makes little demand upon him for innovation. There are sufficient items within the comprehension subtest to allow him to earn an average score on the basis of old learning and premorbid socialization. His attention and concentration skills, reflected in the attentional factor (A, D), are remarkable intact for a man with chronic anxiety. The perceptual-organization factor (PC, BD, PA, OA) is best evaluated from the age-corrected scaled scores for a patient of this age, since there is a significant underestimate of functioning level if the age-uncorrected scaled scores are used for this purpose. There is considerable intertest scatter even among the age-corrected scores. Note that the PC score, which is the least sensitive to organic deficit among the nonverbal subtests, is also the highest score by a margin of 1–2 standard deviations over the remainder of the subtests in the perceptual-organization factor. While the patient's functioning is adequate for everyday routine living, he appears to be adapting at a level which is well below his potential.

Examination of the overall pattern of the Halstead-Reitan Battery results reveals highly variable performance. The overall impairment index of 0.572 is relatively mild, but this patient is markedly impaired on skills which are particularly sensitive to the prefrontal cortical area's role of organizing complex behavioral programs for task solution. When this function is disturbed or eliminated through damage to the diffuse cortical projection system that originates in the prefrontal area, as with prefrontal lobotomy, there are generalized disruptive effects on behavior. One of the most important of these is a return to a more primitive, often trial-and-error sort of learning and problem solving. This haphazard approach is seen here across a variety of measures.

This patient learned very inefficiently on the Category Test. Complex sequential visual tracking on the Trail-making Test shows marked impairment. This is typical of frontally lesioned adults, since they are unable to form a stably organized plan of analysis for visual search of the stimulus field. When the sequential order of the task is made more complex from part A to part B of the test, frontally lesioned patients such as this man have increasingly greater difficulty with integration of the sequencing on part B; in particular this may be simplified from the alternating alphanumeric sequence (1–A–2–B–3–C . . .) to a stereotyped series of counting or alphabetical recitation. After a few items (usually those that are cued) the patient loses the task.

Simple motor behavior is adequate for speed and coordination bimanually, but the left hand is a bit too slow as compared with the superior performance of the right. This is a clue to right-hemisphere impairment that is greater than that of the left hemisphere in this modality. More complex motor behavior on the Tactual Performance Test shows mild slowing with the dominant right hand on the initial trial and a rather slow performance with the left hand as compared to the right on the second trial with the formboard. This is further evidence of right-hemisphere deficit. In this context of impaired frontal-lobe functioning it shows a continuation of the trial-and-error approach that occurs in the absence of an overall plan for solution of the problem. The performance on the final trial with both hands in unison is the poorest of the three trials and shows no practice effect or benefit from the use of the hands together. Marginally adequate recall on the TPT Memory score is attributable to "passive imprinting" of those shapes that the patient could easily encode verbally as he worked with them. His failure to achieve a passing score on the TPT location measure shows that he lacked an active strategy for encoding locations and that he was not able to mobilize this information spontaneously, since he could not form an intention or plan to do so systematically.

Sensory examination shows normal tactile and visual responding unilaterally and no suppression with double simultaneous tactile stimulation. Auditory stimulation revealed borderline impairment of the hearing with unilateral stimulation of the left ear. The patient was able to reliably report the stimuli that were presented unilaterally to each ear. Bilateral simultaneous stimulation, however, revealed consistent suppression of stimuli presented to the left ear only. This is another piece of evidence that the right cerebral hemisphere is functioning less well than the left. Inconsistent and scattered Fingertip Number-writing Test errors were made on the fingers of the right hand (seven errors), but these were more frequent than those for the left hand (two errors). Stereognosis was intact bilaterally for speed and accuracy on the Tactile Form Recognition Test.

Aphasia Screening Test errors were remarkable primarily for one instance of dysnomia, in which the patient called a triangle a rectangle. This was a form of perseveration with minor variation on the previous item, a square. He misread item 16, demonstrated slurring on the repetition of the word "Massachusetts," and misspelled "square." Discrimination of speech sounds was nearly errorless on the Speech-Sounds Perception Test, since the task was more structured and involved only multiple-choice recognition. The more rapid Seashore Rhythm Test was apparently a bit more stressful for the patient, since he made more errors and scored in the mildly impaired range.

Case 5

Background data. The patient is a 58-year-old, right-handed, single white male with a baccalaureate degree. He underwent bilateral prefrontal lobotomy for intractable schizophrenia 16 years prior to the present examination. He has been psychiatrically hospitalized most of his adult life, and he has been unable to adapt to or tolerate community life despite numerous attempts to provide him with a home outside of the hospital. There was little change in his mental status after the lobotomy. He completed the Halstead-Reitan Battery as part of a followup clinical neuropsychological evaluation to assess his functioning status.

Case Example _5__ Age _58_ Sex _M_ Education _14_ Handedness _R_

General Tests:

  Category (errors) _88_ Trail-making: Part A _35_ Part B _125_

  TPT: Total time _18.4_ Location _4_ Memory _6_

Motor and Sensory Tests:

  Finger-tapping   R _35_ L _35_   Fingertip

  Finger agnosia   R _0_ L _0_   number-writing R _2_ L _2_

  Supressions: Tactile form

    Visual   R _0_ L _0_   (time)   R _0_ L _0_

    Tactile   R _0_ L _0_   (errors)   R _0_ L _0_

    Auditory   R _0_ L _0_

  TPT: Time/Block R _.86_ L _.56_ Both _.42_

Cognitive Tests:

Speech-Sounds Perception

(errors)   3   Rhythm (errors)   5

WAIS: (scaled score)

Information	12	Picture completion	8
Comprehension	8	Picture arrangement	7
Vocabulary	14	Object assembly	9
Similarities	12	Block design	13
Arithmetic	9	Digit symbol	5
Digit span	10		

VIQ 109   PIQ 106   FSIQ 108

Aphasia: Dysarthria, dyscalculia

Test results. The extreme scatter that typifies his performance
has been reported repeatedly in the literature on schizophrenia. Not
only are schizophrenics highly diverse as a clinical group, they are
also individually quite uneven as a rule in cognitive-functioning skills.
The level of performance on the comprehension subtest, for example,
is six scaled score points or 2 standard deviations below the patient's
vocabulary scaled score. This discrepancy reflects deficient capacity
for insight in a man of his intellectual ability. This is not unexpected
in a man who has been chronically institutionalized as an adult and
who has undergone prefrontal lobotomy.

Deficient awareness of the wider range of alternatives in the
world outside of an institutional setting is to be expected with
ignorance of and lack of exposure to them. The surgical frontal lesions
also impair the patient's ability to control impulsive guessing at the
most obvious or idiosyncratically appealing alternatives without adequate ability to consider other choices which may be more relevant.
His ability to reason in terms of cause and effect and to anticipate the
likely consequences of his intended actions is thus rather weak on the
PA measure, but it is within the range of normal variation for age. The
norms become liberal in this area as the sixth decade is approached,
and this man had premorbidly higher functioning ability which apparently included good socialization. He came from a professional family
and functioned reasonably adequately as a child. His intelligence and

social-learning history help him to compensate for his organic deficit, but his PA performance is clearly deficient when compared to the standard of his BD performance by a margin of 2 standard deviations. The relative elevation of the Block Design score over the PC and PA scores by four or more scaled score points may indicate schizophrenia. Supposedly the schizophrenic subject does much more efficient work on an impersonal task without social cues (BD) than on those which have interpersonal connotations (PA, PC). Visual search on the PC subtest is deficient to a degree that is nearly equal to the deficit on PA. This, too, is expected with a bilateral frontal lesion, since the patient is unable to inhibit guessing at the first salient feature of the stimulus that catches his attention. He has difficulty with attentional focusing, since this requires the inhibition of extraneous details from attention and narrowing down to the most appropriate alternative, which may not be the most obvious one. Enough of the easier items are obvious to a man of potentially superior ability that he is able to earn an average-range score for age, but this is only a hint of what he could have done premorbidly.

The Category Test performance is well into the brain-damaged range. This result, in combination with poorer performance on Trails B than on Trails A and impairment of TPT performance in the absence of Sensory–Perceptual Test errors, is typical of patients with prefrontal lesions.

Simple motor speed on the Finger-tapping Test shows equal performance speed with both hands. The performance of the dominant right hand should be approximately 10 percent greater than that of the left hand. Failure to find the expected relationship shows somewhat less efficient left-hemisphere functioning, although the performance with either hand is by no means within the normal range. It is, however, a pattern of relative deficit. Comparison of simple motor functioning with complex motor skills on the Tactual Performance Test (TPT) shows mild slowing with each hand tested separately.

Performance on the Aphasia Screening Test was diagnostically noncontributory. The patient mispronounced "Massachusetts" and was unable to calculate 17×3 mentally. (He did the simpler calculation 6×8 correctly during a testing-the-limits procedure.) Aural discrimination of nonverbal speech sounds was within normal limits, with only three errors in 60 trials. The more rapidly presented Seashore Rhythm Test produced a borderline performance, since it calls for closer attention and more rapid response. It is faster and is not cued item by item as is the Speech-Sounds Perception Test, where the patient did well. His relative attentional difficulties have been noted above.

Case 6

Background data. The patient is a 56-year-old, single white male with a seventh-grade education who works as a janitor. He underwent bilateral prefrontal lobotomy for management of intractable schizophrenia 24 years prior to the time of the current examination. He completed the Halstead-Reitan Battery as part of a followup evaluation of his mental and neurological status.

Case Example __6__ Age __56__ Sex __M__ Education __7__ Handedness __R__ (n/a)

General Tests:

Category (errors) __125__ Trail-making: Part A __72__ Part B __308__

TPT: Total time __30__ Location __4__ Memory __5__

Motor and Sensory Tests: min.

Finger-tapping	R __42__	L __30__	Fingertip	
Finger agnosia	R __6__	L __6__	number-writing	R __5__ L __4__

Supressions:

Tactile form

Visual	R __2__	L __0__	(time)	R __20__ L __19__
Tactile	R __0__	L __0__	(errors)	R __1__ L __1__
Auditory	R __0__	L __4__		

TPT: Time/Block R __5.0__ L __5.0__ Both __5.0__

Cognitive Tests:

Speech-Sounds Perception

(errors) ____6____   Rhythm (errors) ____7____

WAIS: (scaled score)

Information	12	Picture completion	8
Comprehension	7	Picture arrangement	5
Vocabulary	14	Object assembly	7
Similarities	10	Block design	7
Arithmetic	7	Digit symbol	7
Digit span	6		

VIQ __100__   PIQ __96__   FSIQ __98__

Aphasia: Dyslexia, dyscalculia

Test results. This individual is functioning at an average level for age in the verbal and nonverbal domains currently, but there is evidence that he once was capable of more efficient functioning. His subtest scatter among the verbal-comprehension subtests (I, C, S, V) shows seriously impaired capacity for insight and social judgment (C) in a man who formerly had learned well in formal training and academic settings (I) as well as from general life experience (V). The good verbal skills seen in V suggest a relatively rich exposure to English and a sophisticated range of concepts and ideas. In this context the low score on C, over 2 standard deviations below that for V, suggests decline from a higher functioning level. Unevenness of performance level of this kind is not uncommon in chronic schizophrenics. Abstraction ability and concept-formation skills (S) appear to be reasonably adequate for current functioning level, but they are well below the patient's potential-ability ceiling. One would expect that this man formerly functioned more efficiently in this area as well, since intact ability to abstract and generalize would be necessary to obtain and store information as well as to learn to express oneself as effectively as was noted in his V performance. The insensitivity of V to organic impairment makes it a useful premorbid-functioning-level estimator for verbal skills in the absence of cultural disadvantage or the use of English as a second language. The results appear to be free of such bias in this case.

The attentional-factor subtests (A, D) show consistent lowering of concentration and attention span for a man of above-average ability. One would expect that he is distractable, and this is seen behaviorally. After correction for normal aging effects these scores remain near the lower limit of the average range. The perceptual-organization factor (PC, BD, PA, OA) should be evaluated only from the age-corrected scores in a man of this age, since these scores fluctuate greatly with age. They are all timed measures, and speed of motor output varies significantly with age. Examination of scatter for this factor shows a fairly even performance level that clusters near the mean, with the exception of PA, which is four scaled score points below the mean. The patient shows fairly good preservation of visuopractic and perceptual-organization skills (BD, OA), but he has difficulty with forsight and planning ability (PA). Such an individual would have difficulty anticipating the consequences of intended actions. He would function more efficiently in a position which was fairly routine, unstressful, and highly structured. His work as a janitor meets these needs.

From the Halstead-Reitan results one notes generalized impairment across almost all of the original Halstead indices, but there is variable performance. The poorest performances come on forebrain-function tasks, as one would expect from the history, but there is additional mild generalized brain dysfunction. This has been reported in long-term neuropathological followup of prefrontal lobotomy cases that came to autopsy 15, 20, or more years after the lobotomy was performed. As with the other two prefrontal lobotomy cases presented in this series (Cases 4 and 5), this man shows marked impairment of ability to abstract, generalize, and form concepts on the Category Test.

Simple motor speed on the Finger-tapping Test shows mild slowing with the dominant right hand and moderate slowing with the left hand. The difference in speed between the two hands is 29 percent and reflects a significant lateralized motor deficit. This implies dysfunction in the sensorimotor region of the right cerebral hemisphere. More complex motor functioning on the Tactual Performance Test shows inability to complete the task with either hand alone or with both hands in unison on successive trials. There is no improvement in performance level with practice. It is interesting to note that although this man never placed more than two blocks into their appropriate spaces on the board for any single trial, he was able to recall five of the shapes correctly. He located four of them correctly in space in relation to each other according to the formboard scheme. Also noteworthy is the fact that he placed only three of the blocks in their spaces on all of the trials combined; he correctly placed the circle and rectangle on the first trial and the circle and cross in their places on each of the subsequent two trials. Clearly he could not have mastered the information from feeling the blocks alone, since he recalled their relative positions on the board as well as their shapes. That information could have been obtained only from examination of the board itself. This implies that he has retained at least a modicum of sensory integration and haptic information-storage ability. It also calls for an explanation of the occurrence of the errors on the Sensory–Perceptual Examination.

Review of the Sensory–Perceptual Test findings shows intact response to unilateral tactile stimulation without suppression on double simultaneous stimulation. There was consistent confusion on the third and fourth fingers of both hands (12 errors), but this is not seen uncommonly in nonclinical populations, and confinement of errors to this manual area is diagnostically unremarkable. There were inconsistent scattered errors with indentification of numbers written on the fingertips of both hands (nine errors in all); no consistent pattern emerged here. One stereognostic recognition error was made with each hand on the Tactile Form Recognition Test. Auditory stimulation of the ears was intact with unilateral stimulation, but consistent suppression of the left ear occurred with double simultaneous stimulation; this reflects right-temporal dysfunction. Inconsistent suppression of the right inferior visual quadrant occurred with double simultaneous stimulation; this is associated with right-parietal dysfunction. The marginal performance on Fingertip Number-writing perception and stereognosis are also consistent with mild bilateral parietal dysfunction.

The Aphasia Screening Test results show some diagnostically remarkable errors. The patient read the item "7 SIX 2" as "seven ess-eye-ex two," and he calculated $85 - 27 = ?$ as 118 on paper. The simultaneous synthesis error of reading "SIX" as "S-I-X" suggests left-parietal dysfunction. This is supported by the finding that the patient approached the subtraction problem quite idiosyncratically. Adding the numbers produces 112, a result seen in some prefrontal-lobotomy patients who have intact calculation skills but who fail to make a preliminary investigation of the problem and impulsively guess at the solution. This man, in contrast, explained his reasoning as follows: "Take 15 away from 27 and add 85 to equal 100. I play cribbage." He could not explain how he reached his solution, 118. Inability to deal with arithmetic symbols when carrying (borrow 1 from the tens column and add to the ones column, so that 5 becomes 15) and reversal of the minuend and subtrahend (27 - 15) when it becomes clear that subtraction would yield a negative number (15 - 27) shows confusion of arithmetic processes and number structure. Note that the patient also had lost the idea of number placeholders, so that he tried to subtract 27 from 15 instead of 7 from 15, as would have been appropriate in the ones column. The confusion apparently progressed when he could not see how to proceed and added 15 to 85 to reach 100. By this time he had lost track of the problem entirely. He then went on an idiosyncratic association about his use of calculation in a favorite pastime ("I play cribbage"), as is not infrequently seen in frontally dysfunctional patients. The inferred calculational errors are typical of deficits seen in parietal acalculia, a dominant-left-hemisphere syndrome.

As expected with a frontally lesioned patient there is impairment on Trails A and B, more on the latter with its more complex alternating sequence in addition to the visual-tracking and motor-output requirements of the task. The slowed performance on the Digit Symbol (DS) test of the WAIS gave an initial cue that the performance on Trails would be slow and inefficient. As noted in the other prefrontal lobotomy cases discussed in this series, there is difficulty for these patients in visually tracking a series through an array with an efficient, goal-oriented strategy. As with their other problem-solving behavior, the absence of frontally mediated control leads to a disorganization and randomness of the visual-searching task and a return to trial-and-error attempts at information processing. This becomes accentuated when the task requires attention to alternating sequencing requirements. The numerical sequence of part A produced a moderately slowed performance, while the addition of letters to create an alphanumeric sequence (part B) led to severe impairment of performance speed. The patient easily lost the task and had to be reoriented to it by the examiner.

The Speech-Sounds Perception Test is barely within normal limits, and the Seashore Rhythm Test is barely over the cutoff level for brain dysfunction in this individual. This differential performance on the two tests is often seen in persons who respond well to a multiple-choice test which cues and helps to narrow the response choices. Task structure is thus increased, and level of performance usually improves as a result. The Seashore Rhythm Test is faster and is uncued, but it calls only for the subject to make the distinction of same or different between arrays of nonverbal sounds. The higher task structure with more alternatives seems to elicit better performance than the more rapid task with fewer alternatives for this individual.

Note also this patient's mildly impaired drawing (Fig. 2-2).

Case 7

Background data. The subject is a 28-year-old, single white male professional mathematician with normal mental and neurological status. He volunteered to complete the Halstead-Reitan Battery as part of a research project.

Case Example __7__ Age __28__ Sex __M__ Education __12__ Handedness __R__

General Tests:

Category (errors) __13__ Trail-making: Part A __23__ Part B __67__

TPT: Total time __12__ Location __8__ Memory __9__

Motor and Sensory Tests:

Finger-tapping R __53__ L __50__   Fingertip

Finger agnosia R __0__ L __0__   number-writing R __0__ L __0__

Supressions: Tactile form

Visual R __0__ L __0__   (time) R __18__ L __16__

Tactile R __0__ L __0__   (errors) R __0__ L __0__

Auditory R __0__ L __0__

TPT: Time/Block R __.63__ L __.40__ Both __.23__

Cognitive Tests:

Speech-Sounds Perception

(errors) __7__   Rhythm (errors) __1__

WAIS: (scaled score)

Information	17	Picture completion	16
Comprehension	16	Picture arrangement	16
Vocabulary	18	Object assembly	17
Similarities	16	Block design	16
Arithmetic	15	Digit symbol	14
Digit span	16		

VIQ __137__ PIQ __139__ FSIQ __140__

Aphasia: None

Test results.   This case is included in the clinical case review to
show an idealized level of performance. Note that the subject has no
deficiencies on any of the test measures and that his level of performance is consistently superior. There is very little scatter among the
WAIS subtests, almost all of which rank at the 98th or 99th percentile
level. Note that at this extremely high level of functioning efficient
learning occurs without the individual variations that can be seen in
the performances of persons of normal functioning level but lesser
ability. The progression across subtests of the Category Test is very
nearly errorless on any one subtest, and the subject is able to discard
unreinforced hypotheses quickly and readily. There is none of the
stimulus-bound reasoning that is so often seen in brain-dysfunctional
cases. Basic adaptive abilities are intact, and performance is nearly
errorless on brain-related measures. Note also that there is a reduction
in performance time by approximately one-third on each successive
trial of the Tactual Performance Test and that incidental recall of the
formboard is highly efficient on the Memory and Location indices.
Motor and sensory skills are intact. There are no aphasic errors. This
is the sort of performance that one would expect of a professional
who is functioning at a high level in his or her field, as is the case with
this person. Integrity of basic adaptive abilities, such as those that are
measured by the Halstead-Reitan Battery, are prerequisite to such an
achievement level.

Case 8

Background data. The subject is a 42-year-old, single white male with 14 years of education who works as a maintenance man. He volunteered to be a control subject in a research study with the Halstead-Reitan Battery. He was found to have normal mental and neurological status on clinical examination.

Case Example $\underline{8}$ Age $\underline{42}$ Sex $\underline{M}$ Education $\underline{14}$ Handedness $\underline{R}$

General Tests:

Category (errors) $\underline{15}$ Trail-making: Part A $\underline{13}$ Part B $\underline{31}$

TPT: Total time $\underline{8.5}$ Location $\underline{3}$ Memory $\underline{6}$

Motor and Sensory Tests:

Finger-tapping	R $\underline{53}$	L $\underline{46}$	Fingertip number-writing	R $\underline{0}$	L $\underline{0}$
Finger agnosia	R $\underline{0}$	L $\underline{0}$			

Supressions:

Tactile form

Visual	R $\underline{0}$	L $\underline{0}$	(time)	R $\underline{19}$	L $\underline{17}$
Tactile	R $\underline{0}$	L $\underline{0}$	(errors)	R $\underline{0}$	L $\underline{0}$
Auditory	R $\underline{0}$	L $\underline{0}$			

TPT: Time/Block R $\underline{.29}$ L $\underline{.43}$ Both $\underline{.13}$

Cognitive Tests:

Speech-Sounds Perception

(errors) $\underline{2}$ Rhythm (errors) $\underline{2}$

WAIS: (scaled score)

Information	$\underline{13}$	Picture completion	$\underline{14}$
Comprehension	$\underline{11}$	Picture arrangement	$\underline{12}$
Vocabulary	$\underline{13}$	Object assembly	$\underline{17}$
Similarities	$\underline{15}$	Block design	$\underline{15}$
Arithmetic	$\underline{9}$	Digit symbol	$\underline{15}$
Digit span	$\underline{10}$		

VIQ $\underline{111}$ PIQ $\underline{135}$ FSIQ $\underline{122}$

Aphasia: None

Test results.   The patient's WAIS IQ scores are unusual in that there is a 24-point difference between the verbal and performance IQ scores, with the higher score on the nonverbal component. This is a statistically significant difference. Intellectual functioning of the right cerebral hemisphere of this individual ranks at the 99th percentile for age, while the functioning of his left cerebral hemisphere ranks only at the 77th percentile. His choice of work as a maintenance man may be a function of relative lack of channels for expression of his superior right-hemispheric skills. With the barely-above-average left-hemisphere skills of this individual it would be difficult for him to succeed in advanced work as an engineer or architect, for example, but he might do well as a master mechanic or tradesperson.

His scores on the verbal comprehension factor (I, C, S, V) show significant scatter. He has learned efficiently for a man of his educational level, and he has a fairly diverse fund of background information, concepts, and ideas (I, V). His ability to do verbal-abstraction and concept-formation tasks (S) is his strongest ability among the verbal skills. In sum, these skills show excellent verbal-learning potential, but the verbal IQ score still ranks barely above the average range. Note that C is significantly below S—by four scaled score points—but that it falls below V by only two scaled score points. This pattern suggests that this man has the potential for more sophisticated and insightful practical social judgement (S − C differential) but that his capacity for commonsense reasoning and insight is adequate for one of his functioning level (V − C differential).

One would want to explore the possibility of situational anxiety in this man, since he shows suppression of both of the elements of the attentional factor (A, D) below the V score by 1 standard deviation or more. Other factors that lead to distractibility, such as lack of motivation, fatigue, or mild cerebral dysfunction, are contraindicated by the excellent performance level on the other WAIS and Halstead-Reitan Battery measures. A history of arithmetic or numerical problem-solving difficulty is a common feature in even intelligent subjects, and it may play an important role in setting up an avoidance reaction to any task that involves calculation.

The nonverbal subtests are generally elevated to a high performance level, with the exception of PA. This suggests specific difficulty relative to the overall performance level in foresight and planning ability. Note that such a level of performance might be quite adequate and efficient in a person with average right-hemispheric functioning, but it is not sophisticated and efficient enough for this man to actualize his potential adequately. As a result he is likely to experience difficulty when he tries to plan on a long-range basis that is consistent with his intellectual potential. When he finds that he has overlooked important facts and that he has difficulty keeping his mind on the task even though he can carry through the work, he is likely to become discouraged and to doubt his ability.

The Halstead-Reitan Battery results show an excellent overall level of performance, with efficient abstraction and learning on the Category Test, which provides the patient with an opportunity to make use of his excellent right-hemispheric skills in conjunction with verbal mediation. Unexpected findings occur on the motor measures; there is normal speed with both hands, but the left hand is a little too slow on tapping in comparison with the right. Also, there is a reversal of the normal practice effect on the first two trials of the Tactual Performance Test, with a significantly poorer performance of the nondominant left hand after a superior initial performance with the right hand. The TPT and Finger-tapping Test performances in the absence of sensory deficit with either hand suggest lateralized pre-motor inefficiency in the right hemisphere. The times are within normal limits in all of these instances, but the normal learning sequence does not appear, particularly with more complex motor behavior.

The relatively poor performance on the PA subtest of the WAIS also may be consistent with relatively static forebrain dysfunction, particularly in the right anterior temporal area, but there is no associated motor deficit of significance on tapping with the left hand, as would be expected if this were the case. The excellence of the remainder of the patient's functioning contraindicates significant brain dysfunction, and the developmental history is negative for trauma or disease. This is an example of a normal variant that may signal residual dysfunction in an otherwise high-functioning-level subject, particularly one who has suffered an old head injury which has healed well. Results must be considered in context and in the perspective of the history before diagnostic classification is accepted or rejected. If doubt exists about the results, the patient should be referred for a complete medical and neurological workup. These were negative in this individual before he was seen for neuropsychological evaluation.

Case 9

Background data. The patient is a 46-year-old, divorced white male who formerly worked as a shoe salesman and was unemployed at the time of testing. He has a baccalaureate degree. There is a history of implusive and intermittently explosive anger that dates to the onset of neurological symptoms. These behavioral anomalies are related to his brain lesions. The patient was in the Palo Alto VA Medical Center Neurosurgery Service for the third time in 6 years for a craniotomy procedure. Twice previously he had had large meningiomas surgically removed from the right frontal area of his brain. The first of these extrinsic tumors was removed 6 years previously and was the size of a grapefruit at operation. The second tumor was located in the same area and was surgically resected a year later. It had developed and attained the size of a navel orange in the interval between the first and second operations. The patient underwent a course of radiotherapy to the tumor bed and was free of recurrent tumor until just before the time of this neuropsychological examination, 5 years after removal of the second tumor. We were called to consult on the case for neuropsychological evaluation after the third craniotomy had been done for removal of a small meningioma from the left frontal area 2 weeks previously. At the time of testing the patient was ambulatory, well motivated, and cooperative with test procedure. He had tolerated the operative procedure well and had experienced no medical complications. Seizures were well controlled on dilantin. In the first two instances the development of the tumor had been insidiously slow until it had reached a large size and the patient became symptomatic.

Case Example 9   Age 46 Sex M   Education 16 Handedness R

General Tests:

    Category (errors) 95   Trail-making: Part A 59 Part B 98

    TPT: Total time 22.4 Location 5 Memory 8

Motor and Sensory Tests:

    Finger-tapping   R 55 L 45   Fingertip
    Finger agnosia   R 0   L 0   number-writing R 0   L 0
    Supressions: Tactile form
        Visual   R 0   L 0   (time)   R 21   L 19
        Tactile   R 0   L 0   (errors)   R 0   L 0
        Auditory   R 1   L 2
    TPT: Time/Block R 1.1 L .84 Both .40

Cognitive Tests:

    Speech-Sounds Perception

        (errors)   8   Rhythm (errors)   5

    WAIS: (scaled score)

        Information   13   Picture completion   11
        Comprehension   11   Picture arrangement   10
        Vocabulary   13   Object assembly   11
        Similarities   12   Block design   6
        Arithmetic   12   Digit symbol   9
        Digit span   11

                VIQ 114   PIQ 108   FSIQ 112

Aphasia: Construction dyspraxia (mild)

Test results.   Examination of the WAIS scores reveals an individual with remarkably good intellectual preservation after recovery from a very serious series of brain lesions. This is to be expected when lesion onset is slow and the patient is relatively young. Brain function often is sufficiently plastic that recovery can occur with relatively little residual deficit. There is also experimental evidence that the functions of the right cerebral hemisphere are more diffusely organized than are those of the left cerebral hemisphere. This allows other parts of a functional system to take over skills that have been impaired by extrinsic-tumor pressure effects, ischemia, edema, and other complications that are associated with large meningeal tumors such as those from which this man has suffered.

Note that the level of left-hemisphere-dependent intellectual skills is often quite even and shows no performance-level decrement. This is to be expected because the left prefrontal tumor was discovered early and was surgically removed before it could damage the perisylvian speech areas. The prefrontal locus of this tumor is also consistent with reports that such lesions are usually "silent" in their effects on cognitive functions.

Examination of right-hemisphere-dependent intellectual skills shows a level of performance comparable to that of the left hemisphere with one notable exception, the BD subtest. This is a very important clue to one of the patient's primary complaints, that of getting lost in a system of spatial coordinates. This is a frequent complaint of right-parietal patients. This patient had to wait until a parking lot was almost empty before he could find his car. He had to search on all four sides of a city block because he could not remember the side of the block on which he had parked his car if he had not written down the cross streets at the nearest corner when he left it. He spent several hours with assistance from garage staff looking for his car in a multilevel garage after he had become lost and confused. He often arrives late for appointments because he cannot remember how to find his way to the clinic or other appointment destinations. He has to spend a good deal of time searching for personal possessions such as keys, and he has to allow himself extra time to be sure that he can locate them in time to stay on schedule. If he leaves something in a new place, in short, it is as good as lost as far as this man is concerned. These disabling difficulties might be overlooked if one considered the Halstead-Reitan results alone. The patient complained, "People say that I'm fine because my speech is good, but I'm *not* fine!"

Note that the BD score is approximately 2 standard deviations below the mean of the patient's nonverbal subtests and his WAIS profile as a whole. This is attributable to mechanical-pressure effects of the massive tumors that recurrently grew in the right frontal area of his brain. The brain in the frontal area was able to adjust and to compress adjacent, more posterior structures until there was pressure of the right parietal area of the brain against a rigid closed space, the back of his skull. This is where the major and irreversible damage by the right prefrontal lesion occurred on intellectual functions. Such far posterior dysfunction is not associated with sensory loss, and the problem is easy to miss even with sophisticated neuropsychological evaluation if one is not aware of the mechanism by which it may occur.

Examination of the Halstead-Reitan Battery results shows a typical prefrontal pattern of results. There is impairment of abstraction and concept formation on the Category Test, which is most pronounced on tests with a spatial component. This is consistent with the parietal effect of the primary lesion. The patient showed a lack of cognitive flexibility, with the usual concrete reasoning that is typical of patients with static frontal lesions such as this. This does not impair old learning, attention, or concentration on the intelligence test, as had been noted for many years in the literature; however, there is a loss of the ability to form a general plan and to abstract and test general solution principles or strategies based on experience so that they can be applied and evaluated on a new series of examples.

There is a deficit on simple motor speed and manual dexterity that is lateralized to the right cerebral hemisphere on the Finger-tapping Test. Note that the patient has superior speed with the dominant right hand, but his performance deficit on tapping with the left hand is twice what it should be for a normal 10 percent differential performance between the dominant and nondominant hands. This is consistent with pressure effects of the recurrent large right frontal tumors, the first and largest of which extended from the frontal pole to the area just anterior to the sensorimotor region. If one were to examine the performance of the hands on the basis of level of performance alone, the deficit might be missed, since both scores are within normal limits. As Reitan has emphasized, it is necessary to compare the "functional efficiency of the two sides of the body" to demonstrate focal deficits relative to the individual's level of performance as well as relative to that of averaged data for normative groups.

More complex motor performance on the Tactual Performance Test shows an unexpected finding, with inability of this man to complete the task within the allotted 10-minute period with the dominant right hand. This was followed by a slow and labored performance on the next trial with the left hand that led to completion of the task. Note that there is less than the usual one-third reduction in time on the task over trials; this shows dysfunction of the prefrontal area when it occurs in the absence of tactile or visual imperception or suppression, as is the case here. There is also mild construction dyspraxia on attempts to copy an outline of a Greek cross (see Fig. 2-3); fingertip number writing, tactile finger identification, and stereognosis, however, are all errorless. The massiveness of the recurrent right frontal tumors appears to have had lateral as well as anterior–posterior damaging effects on the right side of the brain. The patient shows inconsistent binaural auditory suppression with double simultaneous stimulation, but there is no aural imperception with unilateral auditory stimulation. This indicates serious bilateral temporal-lobe dysfunction. The inference is supported by the finding of marginal performances on the Seashore Rhythm Test and the Speech-Sounds Perception Test, both of which rank at the cutoffs for brain dysfunction.

Case 10

Background data. The patient is a 26-year-old, white married female homemaker with a high school education. She has a psychiatric diagnosis of borderline personality. During the psychiatric admission on which this neuropsychological workup was completed, electroencephalographic (EEG) studies confirmed the presence of bilateral and independent temporal-lobe epilepsy. The inference of bitemporal dysfunction was made from the neuropsychological workup independent of and prior to the receipt of the EEG results. A computer tomographic (CT) brain scan was ordered on the basis of the combined medical and neuropsychological findings. Focal white-matter degeneration was demonstrated in the temporal lobes bilaterally.

Case Example __10__ Age _26_ Sex _F__ Education _12_ Handedness __R__

General Tests:

    Category (errors) _29_ Trail-making: Part A _29_ Part B _70_

    TPT: Total time _7.7_ Location _6__ Memory _9__

Motor and Sensory Tests:

Finger-tapping	R 42	L 40	Fingertip			
Finger agnosia	R 0	L 0	number-writing	R 0	L 0	
Supressions:			Tactile form			
Visual	R 0	L 0	(time)	R 0	L 0	
Tactile	R 0	L 0	(errors)	R 0	L 0	
Auditory	R 2	L 1				
TPT: Time/Block	R .30	L .26	Both .21			

Cognitive Tests:

  Speech-Sounds Perception

    (errors)   _2__   Rhythm (errors)   _0__

  WAIS: (scaled score)

Information	13	Picture completion	14
Comprehension	17	Picture arrangement	13
Vocabulary	12	Object assembly	13
Similarities	13	Block design	9
Arithmetic	10	Digit symbol	10
Digit span	14		

        VIQ _119_   PIQ _112_   FSIQ _117_

Aphasia: None

Test results. Examination of the WAIS results shows an intelligent individual with marked cognitive inconsistency in her intrafactorial subtest scatter. This is an important clue to diminished cognitive efficiency. Her overall ability level appears to be reasonably well estimated by her IQ summary scores, but she could be functioning cognitively much more efficiently, aside from her psychiatric disturbance. The verbal-comprehension factor (I, C, S, V) shows remarkable scatter with no frankly deficient performances; however, there is a spiked score on C that suggests unusual awareness of social norms, rules, expectations, and appropriate behavior in practical, common-sense-reasoning situations. There is abstract-level proverb interpretation and excellent intellectual capacity for insight. There appears to have been some special training or investment in learning such information as a means of living up to conventional standards or expectations, since the score on C is more than 1 standard deviation above the patient's relatively high verbal-scale mean. The remainder of the verbal-comprehension scores (I, S, V) cluster in the bright-normal range.

    The attentional factor (A,D) shows considerable variability of almost 2 standard deviations between the subtests, despite the fact that these subtests are factorially related and should therefore approximate each other in functioning level. The much higher D than A score shows intact attention span (D) in a person with concentration difficulty (A). Such an individual can attend but has difficulty keeping her mind on one thing at a time for an extended period.

Cognitive visuopractic skills subserved by the right cerebral hemisphere that are measured by the perceptual-organization factor (PC, BD, PA, OA) also show cognitive inefficiency. The patient has an even performance on all subtests of this factor with the exception of BD, which is 1–2 standard deviations below the subtest mean for this grouping. The examiner noted that the patient felt self-conscious about the time limit on the final items in the series, and the patient may have performed more poorly because of performance anxiety. Some situational factor such as this would have to be inferred in the absence of supportive evidence of right-parietal or visuospatial difficulty elsewhere in the test-battery findings. It is also of interest to note that the subject maintained the square outline configuration of the block designs but had difficulty with analysis and reproduction of internal details of the designs. This is typical of dysfunctional left- rather than right-hemispheric solution strategy.

With the Halstead-Reitan results one notes a rather good level of performance overall. This is the lowest level of inference, and it would be unwise to dismiss results such as these without a thorough review of performance to be sure that there are no deviant functions that might signal cortical dysfunction among the results. Frontal-lobe functioning as reflected by Category Test concept-formation skills is adequate. Normal TPT performance in the absence of tactile or visual sensory impairment shows normal learning and incidental recall on the Memory and Location phases of TPT administration. Progression over trials is satisfactory in this case. The Trail-making Tests are done quickly and accurately. There are no significant deficits on the Aphasia Screening, Seashore Rhythm, or Speech-Sounds Perception Tests.

The other tests, however, give clues to this woman's neuropsychological status. Note that tapping is suppressed bimanually below the level that is normal for women with the dominant hand (46 taps minimum) and that the level of performance with the nondominant left hand is at the lower limit of the normal range for women (40 taps) according to the norms of Russell et al. (1970). There is preliminary evidence of mild motor deficit with temporal lesions that is reported by Halstead. Note also that there is normative slowing of the right hand. The comparison of the two hands on tapping speed for this woman shows mild slowing of the right hand compared to the left. The difference in performance level between the two hands is 10 percent in favor of the dominant hand for the normal individual. The observed pattern suggests somewhat greater right- than left-temporal dysfunction, although by itself this evidence is relatively weak. Strong supportive evidence comes from the finding that the patient has inconsistent auditory suppressions in the presence of normal monaural hearing with unilateral stimulation. The suppressions occurred twice as often in the right ear as in the left. This is a very important clue to serious temporal-lobe dysfunction, since it implies structural-lesion changes bilaterally in the temporal lobes. Note that the consistency of suppression is greater in the right ear and that the tapping-speed deficit was somewhat greater in the right hand. This implies that the dysfunction, while subtle, is somewhat greater in the left than in the right temporal lobe.

Case 11

Background data. The patient is a 53-year-old, married right-handed, white male with a high-school education. He was employed as an animal technician at a research facility at the time of this evaluation. There had been a 33-year history of headache and a 31-year history of "blackouts" which were reinterpreted as memory lapses after careful history taking. Neurological evaluation revealed a psychophysiolgical basis for the headaches, but no interpretation was given by the neurologist for the "blackouts." The referring medical student suspected temporal-lobe seizures on the basis of the history and requested neuropsychological evaluation to help in the assessment of the patient's higher cortical functioning.

Case Example 11   Age 53   Sex M   Education 12   Handedness R

General Tests:

    Category (errors) 74   Trail-making: Part A 34   Part B 105

    TPT: Total time 9.5 Location 3   Memory 9

Motor and Sensory Tests:

Finger-tapping	R 50	L 45	Fingertip		
Finger agnosia	R 1	L 1	number-writing	R 0	L 0
Supressions:			Tactile form		
Visual	R 0	L 0	(time)	R 23	L 20
Tactile	R 0	L 0	(errors)	R 0	L 0
Auditory	R 0	L 0			

    TPT: Time/Block R .46 L .32 Both .17

Cognitive Tests:

  Speech-Sounds Perception

  (errors)   _3_   Rhythm (errors)   _8_

  WAIS: (scaled score)

    Information   _12_   Picture completion   _12_

    Comprehension   _10_   Picture arrangement   _9_

    Vocabulary   _13_   Object assembly   _10_

    Similarities   _12_   Block design   _13_

    Arithmetic   _17_   Digit symbol   _9_

    Digit span   _14_

        VIQ _120_   PIQ _116_   FSIQ _119_

Aphasia: Dysnomia (but corrected spontaneously)

Test results. The verbal and performance IQs for this patient show an intelligent individual with selective performance decrements that reveal mild cognitive inefficiency. Evaluation of the WAIS verbal-comprehension-factor subtests (I, C, S, V) with the age-corrected scores shows that all scores in this group cluster within 1 standard deviation of each other and show no decrement. The attentional factor (A, D), in contrast, shows a 1-standard-deviation difference between its elements, A and D. The patient seems to vary in attention-span length (A versus D), but he shows superior concentration ability (A). The perceptual-organization factor shows relatively greater performance on PC and BD than on PA and OA.

Consideration of the Halstead-Reitan Battery results shows a similar pattern of selective deficit. The patient made 74 errors in all on the Category Test, but 60 of these errors are confined to the third and fourth subtests, where he performed at random. He did poorly only on those subtests with a spatial component. Performance on Trails B was mildly impaired, but performance on Trails A was adequate. There was a mild temporal impairment on the Seashore Rhythm Test, where the patient's performance was marginal. Aphasia Screening Test findings are remarkable only for an instance of questionable dysnomia in which the patient identified an outline drawing of a Greek cross as an "insignia" and then changed his response to cross. Sensory examination is unremarkable. The results are consistent with a mild frontotemporal syndrome. There was no confirmation of the suspected temporal-lobe epilepsy after neurological examination of this individual.

Case 12

Background data. The patient is a right-handed, 19-year-old, single white male with 11 years of education. He had had a 2-year history of proven bilateral temporal-lobe epilepsy with violent outbursts, depression, and suicidal attempts at the time of testing. He was nonpsychotically depressed and nonsuicidal at the time of this neuropsychological evaluation. The workup was done as a clinical neuropsychological assessment of the patient's current functioning status.

Case Example __12__ Age __19__ Sex __M__ Education __11__ Handedness __R__

General Tests:

    Category (errors) __45__ Trail-making: Part A __16__ Part B __61__

    TPT: Total time __12__ Location __6__ Memory __7__

Motor and Sensory Tests:

Finger-tapping	R __49__	L __39__	Fingertip		
Finger agnosia	R __3__	L __2__	number-writing	R __0__	L __0__
Supressions:			Tactile form		
Visual	R __0__	L __0__	(time)	R __18__	L __16__
Tactile	R __0__	L __0__	(errors)	R __0__	L __0__
Auditory	R __0__	L __0__			

    TPT: Time/Block R __.68__ L __.28__ Both __.30__

Cognitive Tests:

  Speech-Sounds Perception

    (errors) __11__   Rhythm (errors) __9__

  WAIS: (scaled score)

Information	8	Picture completion	6
Comprehension	7	Picture arrangement	5
Vocabulary	8	Object assembly	7
Similarities	9	Block design	11
Arithmetic	10	Digit symbol	10
Digit span	7		

        VIQ __92__   PIQ __86__   FSIQ __89__

Aphasia: Spelling dyspraxia, dysnomia, dyslexia, construction dyspraxia

Test results.   This patient is functioning in the borderline to low-average intellectual range overall, and he appears to have functioned at this level for some time preceding the onset of his seizure disorder 2 years ago. The relatively low scores on WAIS I and V suggest a man who is experiencing relative difficulty with academic work and verbal expression generally. This is consistent with his failure to complete high school. His age at leaving school also is coincident with the onset of the seizure disorder. The verbal-comprehension factor (I, C, S, V) shows essentially no scatter and suggests relatively limited native endowment in the verbal realm. There is better concentration than attentional ability on the attentional factor (A, D), which suggests more ability to attend and learn than is being shown by current results. The perceptual-organization factor (PC, BD, PA, OA) shows marked elevation of BD over the remainder of the subtests that compose the factor. It has been noted by Reitan (unpublished manuscript) that BD greater than PA to a degree greater than 1 standard deviation in the presence of brain dysfunction suggests a more anterior lesion locus. Outstandingly poor scores on BD may be associated with right-parietal dysfunction. The very poor score on PA may be associated with right-anterior-temporal dysfunction in this case. This is consistent with the known temporal-lobe seizure disorder.

In addition, there is defective perceptual scanning (PC) and visual organization (OA) that suggests weakness of the patient's right-hemispheric cognitive functioning as a whole; however, one must interpret these results in the context of his depression, which was significant enough to require psychiatric hospitalization during the period when the testing was done. He was not motorically retarded on DS or Halstead-Reitan motor measures, which strongly emphasize motor-output speed, but his motivation can be presumed to have been relatively low throughout the test session. Perseverance in the face of problem-solving difficulty was doubtless reduced to some degree.

The Halstead-Reitan Battery results show subtle evidence of dysfunction without striking level of performance deficits overall. The Category Test score is borderline, which suggests difficulty with abstraction and conceptualization on an inductive-reasoning task. The pattern of performance, while somewhat inefficient, parallels the patient's inefficient low-average to borderline intellectual-ability level.

Important clues to left-frontotemporal dysfunction are seen in the mildly impaired score on the Speech-Sounds Perception Test and in numerous errors on the Aphasia Screening Test. The patient misspelled square as "sqeura," he misspelled cross as "croos," and he misspelled triangle as "tryuangle." He identified the Greek cross as a "series of squares." This shows an interesting perceptual fragmentation of the figure into squares, with the central portion of the cross and each of the four arms forming a series of five squares. This fragmentation process is typically seen with total left-hemisphere information processing of perceptual details when the right hemisphere is severely dysfunctional or is isolated surgically, as in a commissurotomy patient. The item "7 SIX 2" was misread as "2-6-2" and then spontaneously reread correctly. There was intermittent mild constructional dyspraxia in attempts to draw a Greek cross. See Figure 2-4.

Simple motor speed and coordination on the Finger-tapping Test show borderline-normal speed with the right hand but excessive slowing with the left hand. The difference in speed between the hands is approximately twice the normal 10 percent margin in favor of the dominant hand. This reflects right-hemisphere dysfunction. TPT performance with the dominant right hand is too slow by approximately a full minute in comparison with the performance with the left hand. The performance with both hands also shows a somewhat poorer performance than that with the left hand alone. It appears that the addition of the right hand to the performance of the left hand on the third TPT trial served more as a form of distraction than as an aid to task solution. This suggests mild left-hemispheric premotor-area dysfunction in the absence of tactile sensory deficit, as is seen here. Incidental recall of the TPT task is adequate on both the Memory and Location measures.

The mildly impaired score on the Seashore Rhythm Test can occur with dysfunction of either or both temporal lobes. There is independent evidence cited above that both temporal lobes are dysfunctional in this individual. The Sensory–Perceptual Examination is remarkable only for a very few errors on the identification of the fingers of the right and left hands. The overall patterning of test results is consistent with a bilateral mild frontotemporal syndrome.

Case 13

Background data. The patient is a left-handed, 29-year-old, single white male with 12 years of education. He had had a left-frontotemporal-lobe intrinsic brain tumor surgically removed 6 years prior to this neuropsychological examination. He complained of on-going left-frontotemperoral headache and word-finding difficulty. Since the surgical operation there had been aphasia, a right homonymous hemianopsia, psychomotor retardation, irritability, temper tantrums, and questionable temporal-lobe seizure disorder. The patient was evaluated on a clinical basis to provide information that would aid treatment staff to assess his readiness for vocational retraining versus outpatient speech therapy and brain-injury cognitive retraining.

Case Example 13 Age 29 Sex M   Education 12 Handedness L

General Tests:

Category (errors) 81   Trail-making: Part A 42   Part B 143

TPT: Total time 14.1 Location 2   Memory 5

Motor and Sensory Tests:

Finger-tapping   R 40 L 52   Fingertip
Finger agnosia   R 0   L 9   number-writing R 6   L 1

Supressions: Tactile form

Visual   R 0   L 0   (time)   R 10 L 10
Tactile   R 0   L 0   (errors)   R 0   L 0
Auditory R 1   L 0

TPT: Time/Block R .63 L .33 Both .45

Cognitive Tests:

Speech-Sounds Perception

(errors)   11   Rhythm (errors)   3

WAIS: (scaled score)

Information   5   Picture completion   7
Comprehension   7   Picture arrangement   9
Vocabulary   5   Object assembly   10
Similarities   10   Block design   12
Arithmetic   8   Digit symbol   5
Digit span   9

VIQ 83   PIQ 93   FSIQ 87

Aphasia: Dysnomia, spelling dyspraxia, dyslexia,
dysarthria, construction dyspraxia,
right homonymous hemianopsia.

123

Test results.   The generalized suppression of the patient's verbal skills reflects his aphasic disorder, which will be discussed in more detail when the Halstead-Reitan results are reviewed, below. The relative sparing of Similarities subtest items is usually the result of the patient's ability to provide overlearned answers to these questions. These items can be answered briefly enough that it is possible for a patient to earn a passing score despite obvious difficulty on the other verbal subtests. In the presence of a serious speech disorder such as this it is unclear what the patient's premorbid level of functioning might have been from verbal psychometric results alone. Judging from the BD score on the nonverbal portion of the WAIS and his completion of high school, it appears fair to infer that he probably had average native ability.

It is of interest that the patient's attention and concentration skills appear intact on the attentional factor (A, D). His low score on DS reflects the psychomotor retardation noted clinically. It is of interest that this is a lateralized motor deficit, as will be seen in the discussion of the Halstead-Reitan results that follow. Visuopractic skills are relatively intact, but they vary in performance level on the perceptual-organization factor (PC, BD, PA, OA). There is difficulty with attentional focusing (PC), stemming in part from slowness of response. Foresight and planning skills are remarkably intact on PA. The patient seems to have retained much of his ability to think in terms of cause and effect despite relative difficulty with verbal expression of the general principles on C that he knows intuitively and demonstrates on PA. Allowance for psychomotor retardation with the right hand and the asphasic speech deficit would place the right-hemispheric skills near the mean for age, whereas left-hemispheric verbal skills are more generally suppressed by the aphasic deficit.

Since the speech disorder will influence many of the other Halstead-Reitan results to a significant degree, it will be discussed first. The patient shows inconsistent dysnomia. Spelling was too difficult for the patient on most items. He replied with a forceful "No!" when asked to spell the words "cross" and "triangle." When he was asked to read "7 SIX 2" on a card, he at first read only "six" and then read the entire item. Repetition of more complex words ("Massachusetts," "Methodist Episcopal") led to paraphasic errors. There was agraphic writing with cursive script but not with printing. The patient performed simple written and mental calculations adequately. Aural discrimination of speech sounds on the Speech-Sounds Perception Test was mildly impaired.

The Sensory–Perceptual Examination is remarkable for a right homonymous hemianopsia and one auditory suppression of the right ear in the presence of intact monaural hearing. Fingertip number writing showed six errors on various fingers of the right hand but only one error on the fingers of the left hand. Stereognosis was intact bimanually. There was mild construction dyspraxia in drawing of an outline of a Greek cross. Tactile sensation was intact bimanually, and no suppression occurred on tactile testing with double simultaneous stimulation. Sensory findings are consistent with the left-hemispheric temporal-lobe component.

There is moderate impairment of abstraction and inductive-reasoning ability that is seen on the patient's Category Test performance. The patient's motor speed with the dominant left hand is within normal limits. Motor speed with the right hand shows mild slowing that is significantly greater than the normal 10 percent lower speed of the nondominant hand below the dominant hand. The difference in speed between the hands in this individual is approximately twice normal. A similiar reversal is seen for the more complex motor behavior on the TPT formboard task. Here the patient had an unusually efficient initial performance with the dominant left hand, which was followed by an almost doubled time on the subsequent trial with the right hand (an improvement of a one-third reduction of speed for each subsequent trial is the rule for a normal performance over trials on TPT). This patient shows a dramatic reversal of the expected pattern. This is a strong indicator of premotor area dysfunction in the left cerebral hemisphere when there is no associated tactile sensory deficit that accompanies the TPT motor deficit, as is the case here. Incidental recall of the task on the memory and location measures was impaired, which reflects that patient's inefficiency of approach to the task despite his ability to complete it on each trial. This is typical of the frontal component of the lesion, such that only those features which are passively recognized as familiar are recalled. Inability to effectively mediate the task solution verbally, as is often seen for nonaphasic subjects, also probably contributed to the difficulty with incidental recall.

Trails A performance is just above the brain-dysfunctional cutoff, whereas Trails B is well into the impaired range. This performance pattern of normal or near-normal performance on Trails A with clearly impaired performance on Trails B has been noted by Golden (1978) as indicative of left-hemispheric dysfunction. It is also typical of frontal-lobe dysfunction, since the more complex and difficult alphanumeric-alternation sequencing task presented by Trails B creates much more of a challenge to the frontally impaired patient (particularly the patient with a left-sided lesion) than does the simpler numerical sequence of Trails A. These expectations are borne out in the present case. Intensive speech and cognitive neuropsychological retraining were recommended for this patient.

Case 14

Background data. The patient is a 55-year-old, left-handed, married white male with a high-school education. He was working part time as a senior mechanical designer at the time of testing. The patient was alert, oriented, ambulatory, and free of obvious deficit on initial presentation. He was referred for followup evaluation of a severe closed head injury which had occurred 6 years previously.

Case Example 14   Age 55 Sex M   Education 12   Handedness L

General Tests:

    Category (errors) 104 Trail-making: Part A 55 Part B 91

    TPT: Total time 30 Location 1   Memory 8

Motor and Sensory Tests:

Finger-tapping	R 35	L 37	Fingertip
Finger agnosia	R 2	L 2	number-writing R 0 L 1
Supressions:			Tactile form
Visual	R 0	L 0	(time) R 10 L 10
Tactile	R 0	L 0	(errors) R 0 L 0
Auditory	R 0	L 0	

  TPT: Time/Block R 10 L 10 Both 10

Cognitive Tests:

  Speech-Sounds Perception

    (errors)   6   Rhythm (errors)   5

  WAIS: (scaled score)

Information	12	Picture completion	8
Comprehension	4	Picture arrangement	6
Vocabulary	9	Object assembly	9
Similarities	7	Block design	10
Arithmetic	12	Digit symbol	7
Digit span	11		

       VIQ 99   PIQ 104   FSIQ 101

Aphasia: None

Test results. This patient's average functioning level currently shows significant decline from his premorbid functioning level. Note that there is tremendous scatter among the subtests that compose the verbal-comprehension factor (I, C, S, V). This unevenness of functioning level, with an outstanding deficiency on C in particular, highlights the patient's cognitive inefficiency. Since he is not aphasic, one can use the I and V scaled scores as a rough estimate of his premorbid functioning level. Note that I is 1 standard deviation greater than V; this pattern is frequently seen in overachievers of average ability who work to gain specialized information that goes beyond their general level of knowledge and experience; the difference of five scaled score points between V and C and the low level of C, however, show very serious impairment of this patient's capacity for insight and practical social judgment that may be viewed by peers as a posttraumatic personality change. Only information which is old and formalized (I, V) seems to have remained fairly intact. It is unusual to find intact attention and concentration skills (A, D) in a patient with such striking deficits in most other cognitive areas. There apparently had been sufficient time for the patient to recover these skills between the time of the accident and this examination.

The perceptual-organization factor (PC, BD, PA, OA) also shows the pattern of marked cognitive inconsistency. The PC subtest is thought to be relatively insensitive to organic cerebral dysfunction and probably reflects the patient's average premorbid ability for age on this measure of attentional focusing. He still reasons well nonverbally and intuitively (BD), which probably makes it possible for him to carry out his work in conjunction with his retained old verbal-information store and his intact attentional skills. When he must show social judgment, however, serious difficulties arise. This is compounded by the social shortsightedness on PA, which reflects difficulty with planning and anticipation of the likely consequences of intended actions. Visual–motor speed (Digit Symbol [DS]), coordination (BD), and organization (OA) are all within normal limits for age. The relatively weak abstraction skills (S) will probably lead to some stereotyping of response strategy and reliance upon old learning to compensate for the felt efficiency loss.

As expected in a case of severe closed head injury, this man's neuropsychological test results reflect diffuse impairment of higher cortical functions. The patient has inconsistent problems.

Simple motor-output speed on the Finger-tapping Test shows moderate slowing bimanually, with approximately the expected 10 percent performance difference between the dominant and nondominant hands in favor of the former. More complex motor performance on the TPT formboard task shows identical performances with the right and left hands on successive trials and failure to complete the task on the final trial with both hands. The left-hand performance on TPT shows moderate impairment, but the right-hand and both-hands trials are severely dysfunctional. Memory for the shapes of the formboard was well within normal limits, but the more sensitive spatial-location measure was done very poorly. It is important to note that there is no significant sensory loss in this individual. The patient showed only minor finger agnosia, and he made one fingertip number-writing error. Stereognosis was intact. There were no suppressions or sensory-loss findings in visual, tactile, or auditory modalities. TPT performance decrement of this kind in the absence of sensory loss indicates premotor-area dysfunction of the hemisphere that is contra-lateral to the dysfunctional hand. In this case the impairment is bilateral.

Performance on the Trail-making Tests is impaired, more so on Trails A, which is moderately slowed, than on Trails B, which shows only borderline impairment. The Speech-Sounds Perception Test and the Seashore Rhythm Test also reflect the pattern of mild, residual impairment some years after the head injury. The overall results confirm the expectation of bilateral residual cerebral dysfunction that is consistent with the history of closed head injury.

Case 15

Background data. The patient is a 51-year-old, right-handed, divorced white male with 13 years of education. He works as an insurance salesman and real estate broker, but he was unemployed at the time of this examination. The referral was made by a psychiatrist who was treating this man for depression and anxiety reaction that had had a 30-year intractable history and that was resistant to medication with minor tranquilizers. The clinical diagnosis was characterological depression. Neuropsychological evaluation was requested to rule out a possible organic cerebral component to the syndrome, since the patient had been beaten by vandals during a robbery attempt 2 years previously. He suffered multiple closed head injuries as a result of that attack.

Case Example _15_ Age _51_ Sex _M_ Education _13_ Handedness _R_

General Tests:

Category (errors) _77_ Trail-making: Part A _46_ Part B _90_

TPT: Total time _22.3_ Location _4_ Memory _6_

Motor and Sensory Tests:

Finger-tapping R _26_ L _26_ Fingertip

Finger agnosia R _1_ L _1_ number-writing R _2_ L _2_

Supressions: Tactile form

Visual R _0_ L _0_ (time) R _18_ L _18_

Tactile R _1_ L _1_ (errors) R _0_ L _0_

Auditory R _0_ L _0_

TPT: Time/Block R _.73_ L _1.0_ Both _.50_

Cognitive Tests:

Speech-Sounds Perception

(errors) _6_ Rhythm (errors) _3_

WAIS: (scaled score)

Information	11	Picture completion	11
Comprehension	9	Picture arrangement	6
Vocabulary	12	Object assembly	9
Similarities	12	Block design	10
Arithmetic	13	Digit symbol	8
Digit span	10		

VIQ _109_ PIQ _104_ FSIQ _107_

Aphasia: None

Test results. The WAIS results show an individual with high-average intelligence and relative weaknesses in the social-judgment and insight (C) and the foresight and planning (PA) areas. Despite the generally high cognitive-functioning level, these scores show relative weakness. The PA score is particularly low, remaining so even after age correction. The difference between this score and the mean of the factorially related perceptual-organization subtests (PC, BD, PA, OA) is statistically significant. This may be an important clue to brain dysfunction in this case. The Category Test results show mild overall impairment.

The Aphasia Screening Test was performed errorlessly. There was mild intention tremor when the patient drew the plane geometric outline figures (Fig. 2-5), but there was no tremor at rest. The Sensory–Perceptual Test revealed one suppression of the left side of the face with double simultaneous stimulation of the right and left face with light touch. Auditory examination was within normal limits. Bitemporal visual-field narrowing was noted on visual-field confrontation testing. Referral to the Ophthalmology Service was recommended in order to rule out a lesion in the area of the optic chiasm which can cause bitemporal hemianopsia with narrowing of the visual fields to approximately the width of the shoulders when the optic chiasm is compressed medially. There was one tactile fingertip number-writing error noted with each hand.

Simple motor speed on the Finger-tapping Test showed marked bimanual slowing, more so with the dominant right hand than with the left hand. At this low motor-output level the difference between the motor speed of the hands becomes smaller on a percentage basis, but the relationship of superior performance for the dominant hand should be preserved. This is a relatively subtle clue to the left-hemispheric dysfunction in this case. On the more complex motor problem-solving Tactual Performance Test the initial trial with the dominant right hand is within normal limits and the task is completed. The subsequent trial with the left hand proceeds to the time limit, at which point only *half* of the blocks have been placed in their appropriate positions. In the absence of tactile sensory deficit this is a very strong indicator of right-premotor-area damage. A kick or fist blow to the right frontotemporal area of the head could account for the observed deficit pattern, and this is consistent with the history.

A variety of general functioning indicators rank at a marginal-impairment level, either just above or just below the cutoff for brain dysfunction. These are TPT Memory, TPT Location, Trails B, Seashore Rhythm, and Speech-Sounds Perception Tests. Generalized, relatively mild, residual dysfunction on such measures is consistent with serious closed head trauma several years after onset of injury, since the brain has had an opportunity to heal by this time from the concussive injury.

Case 16

Background data.   The patient is a 54-year-old, right-handed, married white male with an M.A. degree in speech pathology. He had been unable to work as a speech pathologist for the past 6 years, during which time he had shown progressive personality change, decreased memory, and presenile dementia. The computer tomographic scan that was completed just before this neuropsychological examination was done revealed frontal-lobe atrophy. The clinical diagnosis was Pick's disease.

Case Example 16 Age 54 Sex M Education 17 Handedness R

General Tests:

Category (errors) 119 Trail-making: Part A 30 Part B 67

TPT: Total time 32.0 Location 0 Memory 6

Motor and Sensory Tests:

Finger-tapping R 46 L 46 Fingertip

Finger agnosia R 0 L 0 number-writing R 3 L 1

Supressions: Tactile form

Visual R 0 L 0 (time) R 12 L 11

Tactile R 0 L 1 (errors) R 0 L 0

Auditory R 1 L 2

TPT: Time/Block R 12 L 10 Both 10

Cognitive Tests:

Speech-Sounds Perception

(errors) 8 Rhythm (errors) 2

WAIS: (scaled score)

Information	13	Picture completion	7
Comprehension	13	Picture arrangement	8
Vocabulary	15	Object assembly	9
Similarities	7	Block design	11
Arithmetic	12	Digit symbol	9
Digit span	12		

VIQ 114 PIQ 104 FSIQ 110

Aphasia: None

Test results.   The WAIS subtests show selective decline of intellectual skills with relatively better preservation of the patient's over-
practiced verbal skills. One would expect better functioning in the
verbal area as dementia proceeds in a man whose academic training
had been in speech pathology. Note, however, that the lowest verbal
score comes on S, and this score is significantly below the verbal
mean. Reitan (unpublished manuscript) has indicated that such results
often are seen with dysfunction of the left temporal lobe. One would
want to be attentive for other evidence of temporal-lobe dysfunction
in the Halsead-Reitan Battery as well, where it will be manifested on
several measures. There is relatively better preservation of the general
level of performance on the right-hemispheric nonverbal intellectual
skills. The mean performance level here is somewhat lower than that
on the left-hemisphere-dependent verbal-scale items, where the patient's native endowment and formal educational training contribute
to the higher functioning level.

There is a remarkably poor performance on S for a person of
even average ability, and it is extremely poor for an individual with
graduate-level professional education. Even in isolation this score
should raise the question of a dementive process to the mind of the
observant examiner. The preservation of old learning and the breadth
of premorbid intellectual mastery allows the patient to still maintain
fairly good scores on the WAIS. The need to abstract and apply novel
solution principles, however, highlights this man's concrete, stimulus-
bound thinking and his difficulty with shifting of cognitive set.

The Sensory–Perceptual Examination is remarkable for one
suppression of the left hand with double simultaneous tactile stimulation of the hands. There are also inconsistent aural suppressions
with double simultaneous auditory stimulation. These occurred twice
as frequently in the left ear as in the right ear. The visual fields were
full to confrontation testing, but no visual suppression was elicited
with double simultaneous stimulation. Intermittent errors of both
hands were noted on fingertip number-writing perception, with three
times as many errors for the right hand as the left. Tactile finger
identification and stereognosis were errorless. There were no aphasic
errors. The left tactile suppression and fingertip number-writing errors
indicate right-parietal dysfunction. The fingertip number-writing errors
with the right hand were too few and too inconsistent for one to infer
significant left-parietal dysfunction without supporting evidence.

Simple motor speed on tapping shows mild slowing with the right
hand and adequate performance with the left hand in comparison to
Reitan's norms. This is a clue to mild dysfunction in the left sensori-

motor region. Comparison of these findings with the more complex motor functions measured by the Tactual Performance Test shows much more pronounced deterioration of TPT performance. The TPT performance with the right hand is very much poorer than that with the left hand. This is expected because the premotor area is anterior to the sensorimotor area, and the dysfunction should increase as the frontal pole is approached in a man with a circumscribed frontal-lobe disease. The patient was unable to place any of the blocks in their places on the TPT formboard during the first 10 minutes of the initial trial with the right hand. The left-hand performance required the full 10 minute period and again the patient failed to complete the task, but he placed seven blocks correctly within the allotted time limit. The failure to complete the task on the third trial with both hands and production of a poorer performance on the third trial than on the second (left hand alone) again shows severe functioning impairment. There is probably interference of the right hand with performance of the left hand and/or a fatigue effect that accounts for the poor performance on the third trial. This pattern is expected with frontal-lobe damage, since the patient with such a lesion cannot form an active, integrated plan of attack on the problem and reverts instead to a random, trial-and-error approach. The excellent performances on the Trail-making Tests are thus unexpected and paradoxical.

The Speech-Sounds Perception Test shows mild impairment, with a score that ranks at the cutoff for brain dysfunction. This is consistent with other evidence (WAIS S subtest decrement, right-ear auditory suppressions) of left-temporal-lobe dysfunction. Performance on the Seashore Rhythm Test shows "a" remarkably good functioning level for a man with serious bitemporal-lobe dysfunction. The Seashore Rhythm Test is a nonlateralized aural discrimination measure. It is likely that the right temporal lobe is able to compensate for the poorer functioning of its left-hemisphere counterpart, so that the overall Seashore Rhythm Test score is within normal limits. The absence of acutely destructive damage to the temporal lobes is indicated by this performance and by the absence of aphasia.

Case 17

Background data. The patient is a 40-year-old, right-handed, divorced white male with 12 years of education. He is employed as a landscape designer. The history is remarkable for anoxic encephalopathy secondary to carbon monoxide poisoning and two subsequent automobile accidents. The patient suffered a head injury in one of these accidents. Neurological examination revealed short-term-memory loss, bilateral dysdiadochokinesis, dysgraphia, and mild dysnomia. Neuropsychological testing was done to evaluate this man's higher-cortical-functioning status as requested by the neurologist.

Case Example __17__ Age __40__ Sex __M__ Education __12__ Handedness __R__

General Tests:

Category (errors) __50__ Trail-making: Part A __33__ Part B __86__

TPT: Total time __21.5__ Location __0__ Memory __7__

Motor and Sensory Tests:

Finger-tapping R __45__ L __20__   Fingertip

Finger agnosia R __0__ L __0__   number-writing R __0__ L __0__

Supressions: Tactile form

     Visual R __0__ L __0__   (time) R __14__ L __12__

     Tactile R __0__ L __0__   (errors) R __0__ L __0__

     Auditory R __0__ L __0__

TPT: Time/Block R __7__ L __10__ Both __4.5__

Cognitive Tests:

Speech-Sounds Perception

(errors) __6__   Rhythm (errors) __9__

WAIS: (scaled score)

Information	12	Picture completion	14
Comprehension	10	Picture arrangement	10
Vocabulary	11	Object assembly	10
Similarities	13	Block design	10
Arithmetic	9	Digit symbol	7
Digit span	6		

VIQ __101__ PIQ __106__ FSIQ __103__

Aphasia: Dysgraphia, dyscalculia, dyslexia

Test results.   Other than the lowering and inconsistency of the attentional-factor subtests (A, D)—which reflects short attention span and concentration difficulty—and the slowed motor output on DS, the WAIS results are fairly noncontributory to the diagnostic evaluation of this individual. The remaining intellectual skills are well preserved, and the patient appears to have lost little of his cognitive-function ability on this measure. The relatively lower scores on BD, PA, and OA were due to lack of rapid solution, although the patient failed very few items on any of these subtests. His attentional difficulty and the slowed motor-output speed are consistent with this mild reduction of performance efficiency.

There is reduced problem-solving efficiency on a variety of Halstead-Reitan Battery measures on which the patient's performance approaches the dysfunctional range or is mildly impaired. These include the Category Test, Trails B, Speech-Sounds Perception Test, Seashore Rhythm Test, and Finger-tapping Test–dominant (right) hand. There is inefficiency of inductive reasoning ability (Category Test), visual tracking and sequencing (Trails B), aural discrimination (Speech-Sounds, Rhythm), and motor speed (Tapping) with the dominant hand to a lesser degree than with the nondominant hand.

The Aphasia Test finding are remarkable for dysgraphia, mild calculation difficulty, and a reading error. The dysgraphic errors are the most important of these errors—even the patient's signature, a motor stereotype, was illegible. He evidenced no dyslexic errors, which would be expected in an angular gyrus lesion of the dominant hemisphere. He did misread the item "7 SIX 2" initially, however, after which he reread the item correctly. The categorical structure of number and symbolic arithmetic operations that are dependent upon left-posterior-parietal functioning were intact. The patient made a carrying error on the 85 - 27 = ? problem and gave his answer as 48 instead of 58. These symptoms and the mild tapping-speed decrement with the right hand are all consistent with mild dysfunction in the left posterior frontal and adjacent temporal areas.

The Finger-tapping Test performance is mildly impaired with the right hand, but it is markedly impaired with the left hand. The performance of the left hand is 55 percent slower than that of the right hand. This is dramatic evidence of right-hemispheric sensorimotor-area dysfunction. It is supported by the TPT performance difference between the hands on subsequent trials. The right-hand initial performance is within normal limits, but the patient takes 43 percent more time to complete the task with the left hand. This result shows marked premotor dysfunction in the right cerebral hemisphere. The more severe right- than left-hemisphere dysfunction in this man is consistent with a coup and contrecoup injury mechanism. A blow to the anterior right side of the head and contrecoup injury to the left frontotemporal region is consistent with the neuropsychometric findings. The mild, generalized dysfunction is consistent with the history of carbon monoxide poisoning.

Case 18

Background data. The patient is a 56-year-old, right-handed, divorced white male with a baccalaureate degree and 1 year of graduate work. He works as a social security disability evaluator. The history is remarkable for chronic alcoholism, several episodes of delirium tremens, and chronic depression. The patient was admitted to the Psychiatry Service for treatment of alcohol-related symptomatology. Neurological examination revealed cerebellar ataxia. Cerebral atrophy secondary to chronic alcoholism was suspected. The patient had had episodes of amnesia and confusion prior to this admission. He could not remember any of three objects for 5 minutes, and he could not perform mental subtraction of serial sevens from 100. Luria (1973) has reported that the latter symptoms are typical of left-temporal-lobe dysfunction. One would thus want to be observant for evidence that would confirm or disconfirm that hypothesis from the present results.

Case Example 18 Age 56 Sex M Education 17 Handedness R

General Tests:

Category (errors) 55 Trail-making: Part A 35 Part B 73

TPT: Total time 14.5 Location 7 Memory 9

Motor and Sensory Tests:

Finger-tapping R 51 L 41 Fingertip

Finger agnosia R 0 L 0 number-writing R 0 L 0

Supressions: Tactile form

Visual R 0 L 0 (time) R 22 L 21

Tactile R 0 L 0 (errors) R 0 L 0

Auditory R 4 L 0

TPT: Time/Block R .57 L .66 Both .22

Cognitive Tests:

Speech-Sounds Perception

(errors) 5 Rhythm (errors) 2

WAIS: (scaled score)

Information	17	Picture completion	11
Comprehension	16	Picture arrangement	12
Vocabulary	15	Object assembly	9
Similarities	13	Block design	11
Arithmetic	15	Digit symbol	8
Digit span	12		

VIQ 132 PIQ 118 FSIQ 127

Aphasia: None

Test results.   Cursory examination of the IQ scores for the WAIS
and the impairment index might lead the novice examiner to conclude
that this man has no significant deficits; level of performance alone,
however, is only the starting point for a thorough examination of
testing findings. In a man who has had a very high level of functioning
premorbidly (IQ levels, WAIS subtests I and V), there is a very great
deal of information that has been stored in long-term memory which
is thus resistant to organic deterioration. Material which becomes
elementary and routine or automatized to such an individual may
resist decline even with onset of serious cerebral dysfunction, as in
this case. Patterns and relationships among the test scores must be
examined to determine if there is deviant performance on an intra-
individual basis.

This man shows significant losses and inconsistencies of performance, but these would be missed if he were to be compared to a group
of subjects with average intelligence such as Reitan's original reference
group. The impairment index becomes of relatively little use in the
absence of separate norms for superior-intelligence-level subjects,
since average performance in a premorbidly superior subject can
indicate considerable cognitive slippage and dementia. As noted, the
basic adaptive skills are very likely to be resistant to serious erosion
in such persons until they are very much more advanced in their
degenerative course than is the case when symptoms become evident
in the average individual.

The Category Test score of 55 errors shows mild impairment for
an average-intellectual-level control population. Only about 3 percent
of Reitan's original controls made as many as 55 errors. When one
compares this man's performance to that of the mean average control,
the result shows significant cerebral dysfunction. When one recalls
that this is a superior subject, there is no satisfactory explanation for
the result other than that of impaired cerebral functioning.

This man's excellent premorbid left-hemispheric skills were sufficient to compensate for his cognitive difficulties noted on tasks that
he must have found rather elementary. The Aphasia Screening Test,
Speech-Sounds Perception Test, and Seashore Rhythm Test results
therefore were diagnostically noncontributory. The relatively well
preserved scores on the Trail-making Tests suggests that the compensation of preserved right-hemispheric intellectual skills for sequencing
(PA) and visual-motor coordination (BD) were sufficient for the patient
to complete Trails A and B without difficulty. Sensory examination
was significant for auditory suppression of stimuli to the right ear,
which confirms our suspicion of left-temporal dysfunction.

There is also unexpected strong lateralization of motor deficit on simple and complex motor tasks. Note that the tapping speed with the dominant right hand is within normal limits, but the speed with the left hand is 19 percent slower than that with the right hand. On the Tactual Performance Test a similar pattern is seen. The initial trial on TPT with the right hand is within normal limits, but that with the left hand shows a practice effect reversal and moderately impaired performance. There is clear lateralized dysfunction on the sensorimotor and premotor frontal areas of the right cerebral hemisphere. The Category Test findings are consistent with the frontal aspect of the syndrome and the erosion of cognitive efficiency that has been likened to a premature aging effect of frontolimbic structures in chronic alcoholic patients. The short-term amnestic difficulty demonstrated clinically for this patient is consistent with the expected limbic component of the syndrome. The lateralized motor symptoms suggest a process other than ethanol abuse alone, possibly a head injury from a fall when the patient was drunk. This could not be definitively established from the history, but it has been seen to apply in other similar cases.

Case 19

Background data. The patient is a 49-year-old, right-handed, divorced white female with a baccalaureate degree in art. She has a history of chronic depression and chronic alcoholism and is at risk for Huntington's chorea. Involuntary facial grimacing had appeared by the time of testing, but the diagnosis had not been definitely established at the time of testing. Neuropsychological evaluation was requested to evaluate the degree and type of dementia that this patient exhibited. She had been hospitalized on a long-term inpatient chronic-care unit for several years at the time of this examination.

Case Example __19__ Age __49__ Sex __F__ Education __16__ Handedness __R__

General Tests:

Category (errors) __118__ Trail-making: Part A __195__ Part B __653__

TPT: Total time __33.7__ Location __1__ Memory __3__

Motor and Sensory Tests:

Finger-tapping	R __33__	L __23__	Fingertip		
Finger agnosia	R __8__	L __9__	number-writing	R __12__	L __13__
Supressions:			Tactile form		
Visual	R __2__	L __2__	(time)	R __23__	L __24__
Tactile	R __2__	L __2__	(errors)	R __3__	L __4__
Auditory	R __0__	L __2__			

TPT: Time/Block R __10.0__ L __10.0__ Both __2.0__

Cognitive Tests:

Speech-Sounds Perception

(errors) __12__   Rhythm (errors) __11__

WAIS: (scaled score)

Information	__9__	Picture completion	__7__
Comprehension	__6__	Picture arrangement	__4__
Vocabulary	__11__	Object assembly	__7__
Similarities	__9__	Block design	__4__
Arithmetic	__5__	Digit symbol	__4__
Digit span	__7__		

VIQ __89__   PIQ __80__   FSIQ __84__

Aphasia: Construction dyspraxia, spelling dyspraxia, confusion, dysarthia, R-L confusion, dyscalculia

147

Test results. The patient's WAIS performance shows dull-normal functioning with considerable cognitive erosion for a college graduate. One might infer that an art major would have at least average-level right-hemisphere skills; thus a decline of approximately 1.5–2 standard deviations may be expected to have occurred in these skills. This is a much greater decline than we would be able to attribute to chronic alcoholism alone. Even with 20 or more years of heavy drinking there is primarily a dulling of inductive-reasoning skills, particularly abstraction, but not a drastic erosion of adaptive abilities to this degree. The level of performance is consistent with additional dementia caused by degenerative brain disease.

The verbal comprehension factor (I, C, S, V) reveals at least a high-average level of premorbid ability (V). When there is atrophic cerebral disease (such as that which is suspected in this case) the rule of thumb that V does not decline with "organicity" must be set aside. The senile and presenile dementias, as well as Huntington's chorea, may cause long-term memory loss and confusion as the atrophic disease process progresses. Aphasia may also develop in such cases, and it certainly can destroy the patient's ability with verbal expression and thinking, which is based on "inner speech." If Wernicke's area is damaged, speech comprehension may also be affected adversely. This woman's ability to abstract should not be assumed to be intact based on the average score on S, since such a performance level may be due to overlearned associations to the first five responses, as is commonly seen in intelligent individuals such as this person. If dementia ensues thereafter, the patient may show preservation only of the overlearned material, as in this case with the I, S, and V subtests. Capacity for social judgment (C) is deficient even for the demonstrated level of V. Even more pronounced is the deficit on foresight and planning ability (PA). This woman thus should have great difficulty with making and executing appropriate plans and in implementing them independently. Her inability to function outside of a sheltered institutional setting for the past several years is consistent with her expected grave-disability status. Her attention span (D) is fairly well preserved for age, but her ability to concentrate (A) is seriously impaired. There is relatively better preservation of the patient's visual-search and attentional-focusing skills (PC) than of nonverbal skills that are dependent upon speed of motor output (DS, BD).

The Halstead-Reitan Battery results are so generally and severely impaired that there is little to offer in the way of pattern analysis for this case. The patient's performance on the Category Test was random throughout most of the test.

Motor examination shows gross deficits in visual tracking and sequencing when these skills must be employed on a speeded motor task, the Trail-making Test. Complex motor examination with the Tactual Performance Test led to essentially no progress with either hand by itself on successive trials. This woman also shows marked sensory disturbance. This implies parietal rather than prefrontal dysfunction as the basis of the TPT performance deficits. Simple manual motor speed and dexterity on the Finger-tapping Test shows moderate bimanual slowing that is more pronounced in the left hand than in the right hand.

The Aphasia Test results were remarkable for spelling difficulty, right–left confusion, dysarthria, and confusion on simple computational items that were to be done mentally or in written form. There was moderate constructional dyspraxia in attempts to copy a Greek cross (Figs. 2-6 and 2-7). The Sensory–Perceptual Examination was remarkable for inconsistent bilateral tactile suppression, inconsistent aural suppression of stimuli presented to the left ear, and inconsistent bilateral visual suppression in the superior visual quadrants. The bilateral visual and auditory suppressions are consistent with temporal-lobe damage. The tactile suppressions are consistent with TPT evidence of parietal-lobe damage. Further support for bilateral parietal-lobe damage is seen in bimanual dysstereognosis, agraphesthesia, and finger agnosia.

Results are consistent with severe, probably progressive degenerative brain disease that is much beyond what one could attribute to the alcoholic history. The results are consistent with moderately advanced dementia of the generalized kind seen in Huntington's chorea.

Case 20

Background data.   The patient is a 46-year-old, right-handed, married white male retired obstetrician gynecologist. He had shown depression and progressive dementia for approximately 1 year at the time of this evaluation. He was at risk for Huntington's chorea when the testing was done, since there was a proven family history of the disease. The diagnosis was later proved for this patient as well. There were no choreiform movements at the time of this examination. The neuropsychological evaluation was done as a clinical workup to examine the degree and extent of the cognitive impairment.

Case Example _20_ Age _46_ Sex _M_ Education _22_ Handedness _R_

General Tests:

Category (errors) _122_ Trail-making: Part A _63_ Part B _113_

TPT: Total time _27.7_ Location _3_ Memory _9_

Motor and Sensory Tests:

Finger-tapping R _57_ L _43_   Fingertip

Finger agnosia R _3_ L _3_   number-writing R _3_ L _3_

Supressions: Tactile form

Visual R _0_ L _0_   (time) R _14_ L _16_

Tactile R _0_ L _0_   (errors) R _0_ L _0_

Auditory R _0_ L _0_

TPT: Time/Block R _.64_ L _1.0_ Both _.78_

Cognitive Tests:

Speech-Sounds Perception

(errors) _3_   Rhythm (errors) _0_

WAIS: (scaled score)

Information	17	Picture completion	16
Comprehension	12	Picture arrangement	8
Vocabulary	13	Object assembly	10
Similarities	12	Block design	15
Arithmetic	9	Digit symbol	7
Digit span	10		

VIQ _115_   PIQ _118_   FSIQ _117_

Aphasia: None

Test results. The WAIS results confirm the presence of mild dementia in a man of formerly superior intellectual ability. His medical specialty requires surgical as well as medical skill; thus one would expect that he should have superior verbal and nonverbal intellectual skills to have succeeded at it. His premorbid expertise in his specialty was attested by his attainment of board certification. The verbal-comprehension factor (I, C, S, V) shows tremendous scatter that encompasses almost 2 standard deviations. Note that there is an indication of an extremely rich fund of background information, concepts, and ideas (I) that are not now expressed in a highly sophisticated way (V). Abstraction-ability and concept-formation skills (S) also seem mundane for a man of formerly very superior ability. There is significant decline of attention span and concentration ability (D, A), which now rank at the mean but formerly would have had to have been at or near the superior range if the patient were to have been able to function at an effective professional level, as he did. The perceptual-organization factor (PC, BD, PA, OA) shows even more cognitive inconsistency. The attentional-focusing measure (PC) remains very superior, and it is thought to be resistant to most effects of organic cerebral impairment. This result is consistent with the score on I and the history of high-level achievement. The visual–motor coordination and nonverbal-reasoning measure (BD) is also still in the superior range. Factorially related intellectual measures of foresight and planning ability (PA), as well as visual organization (OA), however, vary from the PC–BD level by 2 standard deviations or more, unequivocal evidence of intellectual decline.

The Halstead-Reitan Battery results show selective impairment overall, but the level of performance on some of the measures is markedly impaired. One would not necessarily want to conclude that all of the dysfunction is mild because the impairment index is relatively low. The Category Test performance, for example, is markedly impaired.

Simple motor speed on the Finger-tapping Test shows a lateralized motor deficit. Tapping speed with the dominant right hand is superior, but that with the left hand is mildly impaired. The difference in speed between the hands is of more importance in this case. The speed with the left hand is approximately 25 percent slower than that with the right hand. More complex motor behavior on the Tactual Performance Test shows a reversal of the normal learning sequence over trials. The first-trial performance with the dominant right hand is within normal limits, but on the second trial with the nondominant left hand the patient could complete only 40 percent of the task within the time limit allowed. There was also marked impairment on the final TPT trial when he was allowed to solve the task with both hands in unison.

There was no aphasia, and aural discrimination tasks (Rhythm and Speech-Sounds Perception tests) were performed well. The Sensory–Perceptual Examination showed no tactile or auditory sensory loss or suppression. There was a marginal hearing problem in the right ear with tinnitus, so that testing for aural suppression could not be done. There were mild and intermittent finger-identification errors with both hands. Mild bimanual dysgraphesthesia was also found, but stereognosis was intact. Several general cortical indicators show mild to moderate impairment. Consideration of the fact that this is a premorbidly superior-intellectual-level subject suggests at least moderat overall impairment. Overall the results are consistent with relative sparing of sensory functioning and primary dysfunction of the frontal lobes, right greater than left.

Case 21

Background data. The patient is a 60-year-old, right-handed, married white male who was retired from a career Army position with the rank of sergeant. He has 12 years of education. The history is remarkable for chronic alcoholism and a rapid course of dementia with disinhibited and socially vulgar behavior for the past 6 months. The neurologist who referred the patient for neuropsychological examination noted a "florid right-parietal syndrome and excessive anosagnosia" in addition to the other features listed. Computer-tomographic brain scanning with and without contrast medium showed moderate, diffuse cortical atrophy and "moderate symmetric dilation of all ventricular structures." The impression on the basis of the radiographic findings was moderate, diffuse cerebral atrophy. The clinical diagnosis made by the neurologist was Alzheimer's disease.

Case Example 21 Age 60 Sex M Education 12 Handedness R

General Tests:

Category (errors) 113 Trail-making: Part A 117 Part B 300 and

TPT: Total time 30. Location 0 Memory 3 stopped

Motor and Sensory Tests:

Finger-tapping R 34 L 14 Fingertip

Finger agnosia R ___ L ___ number-writing R ___ L ___

Supressions: Tactile form

Visual R ___ L ___ (time) R ___ L ___

Tactile R ___ L ___ (errors) R ___ L ___

Auditory R ___ L ___

TPT: Time/Block R 10.0 L * ___ Both * ___

Cognitive Tests:

Speech-Sounds Perception

(errors) 15 Rhythm (errors) 13

WAIS: (scaled score)

Information	8	Picture completion	2
Comprehension	11	Picture arrangement	6
Vocabulary	10	Object assembly	2
Similarities	6	Block design	2
Arithmetic	4	Digit symbol	0
Digit span	4		

VIQ 87 PIQ 67 FSIQ 77

Aphasia: Spelling dyspraxia, dysgraphia, dysarthria, dyscalculia, right-left confusion, construction dyspraxia

*-Discontinued

Test results.   Examination of the WAIS profile shows significant dementia with variable performance. The verbal-comprehension factor (I, C, S, V) shows significant scatter. The V and I scores appear to be consistent with the patient's educational and occupational attainment. The relatively good performance level on S after age correction masks consistent concrete conceptualization. There is remarkably good preservation of long-term memory for socially conventional principles (C), which shows that the patient once was capable of and aware of socially conventional behavior. Significant residual foresight and planning ability (PA) that might provide a basis for semi-independent functioning in the home setting now unfortunately are masked and negated by frontal-lobe disinhibition that consistently leads to socially inappropriate behavior. The attentional factor (A, D) shows consistently impaired attention and concentration skills of marked degree. Visuopractic skills show severe, generalized impairment (PC, BD, PA, OA), which is consistent with the proven diffuse degenerative brain disease.

The Halstead-Reitan results speak for themselves. The patient was not able to earn a single score in the non-brain-damaged range. There is variable performance on the Finger-tapping Test, with greater impairment of the right cerebral hemisphere than the left on this measure, but the patient's ability to express himself, to interpret his experience, to plan and execute goal-directed behavior, and to even care for his own basic needs are severely compromised. He is gravely disabled. A brief review of some of the more outstanding deficits he demonstrated is in order to show the nature of his information-processing difficulty.

His performance throughout most of the Category Test was random, and he never progressed beyond a 50 percent learning rate. He could not complete Trails A on the first attempt, but he was able to work through it very slowly after additional instruction. Trails B confused him, and he had to be stopped after numerous attempts to reexplain the task to him. He could make no progress on the Tactual Performance Test even though maximal time limits were allowed. There was no possibility of testing for sensory or perceptual disturbance, since he became confused with the concepts right and left, and he could not tell reliably when his hand or his face was being touched on the double simultaneous tactile-stimulation items. Stereognosis was grossly impaired bimanually, with impulsive guessing at the stimulus array that was provided for nonverbal response.

The Aphasia Screening Test showed some education-related deficits such as omission of the silent letter "e" at the end of the word "square." The cross was named as a "Red Cross," which is a concrete image–symbol association. Spelling of the words "cross" and "triangle" was adequate, but square was copied as "sguake" from the card presented. The patient could not write in script. He wrote the word clock as "clook," and he misread "7 SIX 2" as "2-6-2". "Massachusetts" was mispronounced as "massachususses," and "Episcopal" was misprounced as "episodal." There was consistent right–left confusion. The patient copied the problem $85 - 27 = ?$ from the card as $25 - 27 = ?$ at first, but he recopied the item correctly when the error was noted for him by the examiner. When he attempted to do the calculation he arrived at the solution 38 instead of the correct answer of 58. He explained that he had carried a one from the tens column to make the minuend in the ones column a 15. He then subtracted $15 - 7$ and reached 8. Then he lost the spatial configuration of the problem completely and subtracted the original numbers in the minuend from each other ($85: 8 - 5 = 3$). He juxtaposed these two numbers and confidently read his answer as 38. There was marked construvional apraxia in attempts to copy a Greek cross. When the patient focus passed into the left visual field, across the perceptual midline, his gestalt disintegrated on repeated attempts. He also overlapped his crosses and incorporated the elements of one cross into those of a second one. The concrete stimulus pull of the other line caught his attention, and he could not disengage himself from it perceptually to complete the task that he had begun. (See Fig. 2-8) Despite these gross errors, the patient showed glimmers of his former self, as when he was asked to explain the phrase, "He shouted the warning." The patient quickly replied, "That means there's a danger."

In a man with gross and disabling brain disease such as this it is well to seek out the threads of his remaining adaptive ability, however sparse they may be, since they may be sufficient to keep open a line of communication with him. Through this contact he can make his needs and fears known, and he can be helped to adjust to his declining ability with dignity. Major role structure with firm limits on social behavior and simple self-occupation in the garden were recommended for this man until the time came when he could no longer be cared for at home and institutionalization would become necessary. That time appeared to be approaching when this evaluation was completed.

Case 22

Background data. The patient is a 66-year-old, right-handed, married white male with a high-school education. He had worked as an automobile salesman and radio announcer, but he had been unemployed for some months prior to the present examination. He had been able to find only seasonal work selling betting forms at a horse-race track. The patient had noted personality change with irritability, ready onset of confusion and frustration with inability to do routine tasks, and inability to do any but the simplest forms of logical reasoning. He was interpersonally pleasant, agreeable, and cooperative with testing until he experienced difficulty early in the test series, at which point the hostile behavior was seen, but it was directed mostly at himself. After the testing he was as agreeable and polite as he could be given the situation, which he had found confusing and emotionally draining despite frequent rest breaks. He apologized for his social inappropriateness and was well aware of his cognitive deficits. A computer-tomographic brain scan without contrast medium was obtained a few weeks after the neuropsychological studies were completed. It showed "mild prominence to the Sylvian cisterns and the sulci over the convexities; ventricles are normal in size for age." The impression from the brain scan was mild cerebral atrophy. The clinical diagnosis was Alzheimer's disease.

Case Example _22_ Age _66_ Sex _M_ Education _12_ Handedness _R_

General Tests:

    Category (errors) _132_ Trail-making: Part A _126_ Part B _300_ and

    TPT: Total time _30_ Location _0_ Memory _3_ stopped

Motor and Sensory Tests:

    Finger-tapping   R _51_   L _41_   Fingertip

    Finger agnosia   R _5_   L _5_   number-writing   R _0_   L _0_

    Supressions: Tactile form

        Visual   R _0_   L _0_   (time)   R _11_   L _12_

        Tactile   R _0_   L _0_   (errors)   R _0_   L _0_

        Auditory   R _0_   L _0_

    TPT: Time/Block   R _1.7_ L _3.3_ Both _1.4_

Cognitive Tests:

    Speech-Sounds Perception

      (errors)   _3_   Rhythm (errors)   _11_

    WAIS: (scaled score)

Information	_8_	Picture completion	_8_
Comprehension	_8_	Picture arrangement	_2_
Vocabulary	_10_	Object assembly	_8_
Similarities	_9_	Block design	_3_
Arithmetic	_5_	Digit symbol	_0_
Digit span	_10_		

         VIQ _96_   PIQ _82_   FSIQ _90_

Aphasia: Dysnomia, right-left confusion, construction dyspraxia, dyscalculia (mild)

Test results. Examination of the age-corrected verbal-comprehension factor of the WAIS (I, C, S, V) shows a fairly even performance level which approximates the patient's estimated average premorbid functioning level. His concentration ability (A) is quite poor, but his attention span (D) is high-average for age. These two measures (A, D) comprise the attentional factor of the WAIS, and a discrepancy of this magnitude between them shows cognitive inefficiency. They should approximate each other in performance level, since they are factorially related. The third factor, perceptual organization (PC, BD, PA, OA), shows even greater scatter, which reaches the magnitude of 2 standard deviations. PC is relatively well preserved and is consistent with the estimated average premorbid functioning level. This is not uncommon in cases of dementia with variable performance. There is severe impairment of ability to think sequentially in terms of cause and effect (PA) and to solve problems inductively or nonverbally (BD). The very poor performance on PA with the relatively well preserved score on C presents the clinical picture of a man who has a fairly good grasp of general principles in formal terms but who is unable to put the information to practical use in constructive novel and practical problem solving. Such an individual may be said "to know better but not to do better." This is not a matter of poor motivation or contrariness but rather an inability to perform that may have an organic (right anterior temporal and/or right frontal) basis. Here there is relatively good preservation of old learning and difficulty with novel applications of it.

The patient shows pronounced and generalized impairment of adaptive abilities subserved by organic brain functions. The performances throughout the Category Test, for example, were at or very near a random-response level. Visual-tracking and sequencing tasks of Trails A and B confused the patient to such a degree that he could not attend to the task for long before he became disorganized and agitated over his inability to proceed. Another supporting finding for the inference of right-anterior-temporal dysfunction at the basis of some of the patient's sequencing and planning difficulties is the moderately impaired score on the Seashore Rhythm Test, a nonlateralized temporal-lobe indicator, in the presence of a normal performance on the Speech-Sounds Perception Test. The patient seems to have become lost with the Rhythm Test, which went too quickly for him and which was uncued. He did well on Speech-Sounds, apparently because it was much slower and was structured with a multiple-choice format that listed all possible answers for the item. Announcement of each item on Speech-Sounds before it was presented also helped him to attend to the task on each item.

Motor speed with the dominant right hand is remarkably intact, while the slowing with the left hand is approximately twice the normal differential. Performance level was halved instead of improved when he proceeded from the first TPT trial, with the right hand, to the second trial, with the left. The third trial, with both hands, approximated his performance on the first trial with the right hand alone. Recall for the block shapes and their locations was consistently poor. The Sensory–Perceptual Examination was remarkable for mild bimanual finger dysgnosia and dysgraphesthesia. Stereognosis was intact with both hands. There was no suppressions in any sensory modality, and there was no sensory loss.

The Aphasia Screening Test was remarkable for dysnomia, when the patient called a cross a square at first and then corrected himself spontaneously. He showed a literal paraphasia when he repeated "Episcopal" as "episcobal." He was able to do the calculations $87 - 58 = ?$ on paper and $17 \times 3 = ?$ mentally, but the first item required over 2 minutes of calculation time, and the second item required 90 seconds. There was consistent right–left confusion. Visual praxis was mildly impaired in attempts to draw a Greek cross, and the patient perseveratively drew two of each geometric figure presented when he was asked to copy each of them, one at a time, for a card.

There is generalized brain dysfunction in this individual that is consistent with the clinical diagnosis of Alzheimer's disease and the computer-tomographic brain-scan findings. Since there is no available therapy for this degenerative brain disease, it is best for the patient and his family to support his remaining cognitive strengths so that he can be kept active and alert as long as possible. His remaining long-term memory skills make him a reasonably good conversationalist in light social discourse, and he is personable. He dresses well and presents a good superficial appearance to the casual observer. He can manage a simple routine job, such as selling forms or programs from a stationary booth at sporting events. His age and physical condition are such that much walking is ill advised. He can still make change adequately, but this is slow and he might need some assistance in this regard. One might see him as an assistant or associate to another person who handled the monetary transactions. This was suggested to the family and the patient, who pursued the option. This man requires family support at home now, and he is fortunate to have it. While his medical prognosis is poor and while further cognitive deterioration is certain, his rate of dementia progression is fairly slow, and structural changes are not yet advanced. He may be able to live out his remaining years in fair personal satisfaction and simple productivity which keeps him active in a routine, low-stress, sheltered position. He will have a position of respect in his family and can serve the useful role of a grandparent with the aid of his wife.

Case 23

Background data. The patient is a 27-year-old, left-handed, single white male with 13 years of education who works as a production manager. He was undergoing biofeedback therapy for management of severe migraine headache in the right temporal region. The therapist was aware that this condition is sometimes associated with focal cerebral atrophy when it becomes severe, as it was in this case. Referral for neuropsychological evaluation was made to rule out focal brain dysfunction in the right temporal area.

Case Example _23_ Age _27_ Sex _M_ Education _13_ Handedness _L_

General Tests:

Category (errors) _48_ Trail-making: Part A _27_ Part B _67_

TPT: Total time _9_ Location _8_ Memory _9_

Motor and Sensory Tests:

Finger-tapping	R 48	L 46	Fingertip		
Finger agnosia	R 0	L 0	number-writing	R 2	L 1
Supressions:			Tactile form		
Visual	R 0	L 0	(time)	R 16	L 18
Tactile	R 0	L 0	(errors)	R 0	L 0
Auditory	R 0	L 0			

TPT: Time/Block R .45 L .26 Both .19

Cognitive Tests:

   Speech-Sounds Perception

      (errors)   _2_   Rhythm (errors)   _3_

   WAIS: (scaled score)

      Information   _13_   Picture completion   _12_

      Comprehension   _10_   Picture arrangement   _11_

      Vocabulary   _10_   Object assembly   _15_

      Similarities   _10_   Block design   _14_

      Arithmetic   _13_   Digit symbol   _11_

      Digit span   _15_

              VIQ _110_   PIQ _118_   FSIQ _114_

Aphasia: None

   Test results.   The WAIS results show a high level of performance
with some inconsistency in functioning level across subtest factor
groups that suggests cognitive inefficiency. The verbal comprehension
factor (I, C, S, V) shows I at 1 standard deviation higher than the
other three subtests in this group. This pattern is usually seen in an
overachieving individual of average ability who works to master
special knowledge (I) that is beyond his general level of ability and
knowledge gained from experience (V) as well as his typical level of
intellectual (S) or social (C) conceptualization. This may create significant tension due to self-imposed demands for high goal striving. The
attentional factor (A, D) shows that the patient is able to attend and
concentrate diligently. Such attention to task that far exceeds general
ability level helps to maintain this man's work-oriented style unabated.
The perceptual organization factor (PC, BD, PA, OA) shows significant scatter as well. Note that PA, a right-temporal indicator, is the
lowest of the four subtests composing the factor; it is 1 standard
deviation below BD and four scaled score points below OA. This
latter comparison is a statistically significant difference that suggests
specific mild right-temporal dysfunction. Reitan (unpublished manuscript) found that there is a marked decline of the PA score with an
acutely destructive lesion of the right anterior temporal area. With
less severe but significant impairment of this cortical region such as

this man displays, there may be only a deficit relative to the other factorially related scales.

The Halstead-Reitan Battery results are remarkable for three deficit performances in this individual. The first and most important is the appearance of a mild motor deficit with the dominant left hand. The nondominant right hand taps at a speed that is within normal limits; the left hand, however, shows a reversal of the usual dominant-hand superiority. With the right hand as a standard, the left hand should be tapping at approximately 53 taps to maintain the usual performance differential between the hands. This specific motor deficit is mild, but it may occur with focal right-temporal lesions. There is consistent empirical evidence from Halstead, Penfield, and others that the temporal region contains an accessory motor area and that disruption of anterior-temporal function disturbs fine motor speed and coordination to a mild degree such as that seen here.

The second remarkable performance is the score on the Category Test, which is barely within normal limits. The third deficit is mild slowness with the left hand on the first TPT trial as compared with the subsequent right-hand performance. There is a 42 percent improvement from the first to the second trial, whereas the level of difference should approximate 33 percent. This suggests a 9 percent performance decrement with the dominant left hand. Right premotor dysfunction is implied and is consistent with the sensorimotor inefficiency seen with left-hand tapping. Overall the results are consistent with right-hemispheric frontotemporal motor functioning that is marginally impaired. This may be associated with the migraine symptomatology. and it should improve if that syndrome can be alleviated by means of biofeedback treatment. See also Figure 2-9.

Case 24

Background data. The patient is a 36-year-old, right-handed, twice-divorced white male with 14 years of education. He works as a forklift operator. The history is quite complex, but relevant diagnoses are chronic paranoid schizophrenia, alcohol and heroin addiction, polydrug abuse, and left supraorbital skull fracture 13 months prior to this examination. One might expect a generally very suppressed performance level in such an individual. There is relatively good intellectual preservation in paranoid schizophrenia, however, and recovery is often good in young people after acute head injury. The case is presented to show the utility of neuropsychological assessment in the evaluation of strengths and deficits in a complex clinical case.

Case Example 24   Age 36   Sex M   Education 14   Handedness R

General Tests:

   Category (errors) 66   Trail-making: Part A 64   Part B 250

   TPT: Total time 30   Location 0   Memory 5

Motor and Sensory Tests:

   Finger-tapping   R 51   L 52   Fingertip

   Finger agnosia   R 8   L 14   number-writing   R 5   L 5

   Supressions: Tactile form

      Visual   R 0   L 0   (time)   R 18   L 21

      Tactile   R 0   L 0   (errors)   R 0   L 1

      Auditory   R 0   L 0

   TPT: Time/Block   R 5.0   L 10.0   Both 2.5

Cognitive Tests:

   Speech-Sounds Perception

      (errors)   20   Rhythm (errors)   4

   WAIS: (scaled score)

      Information   12   Picture completion   7

      Comprehension   10   Picture arrangement   6

      Vocabulary   12   Object assembly   6

      Similarities   13   Block design   7

      Arithmetic   9   Digit symbol   7

      Digit span   7

                  VIQ 103   PIQ 83   FSIQ 94

Aphasia: Dysarthria, spelling dyspraxia,
           dyscalculia, R-L confusion

Test results.   The difference between the verbal and performance IQ scores in this individual is statistically significant and shows less intellectual functioning of the right cerebral hemisphere on cognitive measures. One should be cautious not to jump to the conclusion that he may have a lateralized right-hemispheric brain lesion. All of the nonverbal subtests of the WAIS are timed, while only the arithmetic subtest of the verbal scale is timed. In a patient with multiple medical, toxic, and psychiatric problems such as this, there are likely to be situational as well as organic reasons for the decline in performance level.

Examination of the WAIS verbal-comprehension factor (I, C, S, V) shows mild cognitive inconsistency, with a 1-standard-deviation difference between the S and C subtests. None of the subtests in the factor deviate markedly from their mean, however, and the scatter is certainly well within expected limits for a schizophrenic individual. There is mild impairment of the attentional factor subtests (A, D) relative to the general ability level that is reflected in the V score. This is consistent with the situational distress that this man was experiencing at the time of testing. One would expect mild distractibility and concentration difficulty given these scores, and these were seen during the test administration. Energy level was also relatively low because of situational depression. These are important factors to keep in mind when the nonverbal subtests are evaluated.

For the perceptual-organization factor (PC, BD, PA, OA) one finds a generally suppressed level of performance. There is a slow rate of motor output (DS), and some fatigability is likely, with falling off of the scores as the final two subtests in the factor are reached. The patient declined to do the WAIS in two sessions and preferred to complete it at one sitting; thus this effect could not be circumvented. There are relatively weak performances on measures of attentional focusing (PC), visual–motor coordination (BD), and visual organization (OA). Demonstrated foresight and planning skills (PA) are limited, as is commonly found in chronically psychotic individuals. WAIS data in some provide a picture of a reasonably intelligent individual with weak attentional, organizational, planning, and integrative skills. The intellectually dulling effects of alcohol and drug abuse and the disorganizing elements of the thought-process disorder have probably contributed to the overall result. The patient might be expected to be somewhat haphazard in his approach to complex and challenging problem-solving tasks. Such hypotheses and inferences should be kept in mind as the Halstead-Reitan Battery results are considered.

Reitan and associates often refer to four tests from their battery as the most sensitive and clinically important for establishing the presence of brain damage. These are the Category Test, TPT Location component, Trails B, and the impairment index. This man scores in the brain-damaged range on all four of these indices.

On the Category Test, one notes that the level of impairment is relatively mild. Simple motor speed on the Finger-tapping Test is easy to dismiss as within normal limits with both hands for this man, but one must note that the dominant hand shows a slight inferiority in tapping speed when compared to the nondominant hand. Use of the left hand as a standard for comparison shows that the right hand should be tapping at approximately 56 taps instead of only 51 taps. This is of special clinical significance when one recalls that this man has had a left-frontal head injury. The left-hemispheric dysfunction in the sensorimotor area that is reflected by the reduced right-hand tapping speed is very likely a residual effect of the head injury. Note that it is a selective and lateralized deficit; the level of functioning on this ability is excellent overall.

Consideration of the Tactual Performance Test, a more complex motor task, shows grossly impaired performance. There is no denying that the performance is at a low level, but this is not necessarily related to organic deficit alone. Consistency must be demonstrated across results to point to a sensible clinical syndrome. Note that performance goes to the 10-minute time limit with only two blocks placed. On the subsequent trial the patient is unable to place any of the blocks in the allotted time, and his final-trial performance with both hands in unison is little better than the initial performance. Incidental learning occurred from feeling the blocks and the board, since the patient was able to recall the shapes of five blocks even though he never placed more than four of them in the board on any one trial.

Sensory examination reveals intact tactile sensation without suppression under double simultaneous stimulation. The other sensory modalities were also intact and free of suppression phenomena. There was dysgnosia of the second finger of the left hand and of the second and fifth fingers of the right hand. Mild dysgraphesthesia was found bimanually, and there was one stereognostic error with the left hand. The intact and relatively-high-level motor functioning of the hands on tapping and the mildness of the sensory imperception without suppression phenomena gives no support to a primary organic basis for the TPT deficit. Also, postulation of a premotor syndrome to account for the deficit does not agree with the lack of lateralized deficit as noted on the Finger-tapping Test or the mild frontal symptoms on the

Category Test. One is led to the conclusion that the TPT deficit probably has a functional basis and that the patient motivationally lagged when he found the task to be too difficult. The fatigue effect that is seen on the final two subtests of the WAIS also is consistent with the failure to place any of the blocks on the second trial of the TPT formboard task.

The Aphasia Screening Test is remarkable for paraphasia, as when the patient mispronounced "Massachusetts" as "massatussess" and when he repeated "Methodist Episcopal" as "methodiss episcobal." He wrote the dictated "shouted" as "shooted," and he made a calculation error on the subtraction of $85 - 27 = ?$ when he gave the answer as 56. The overall plan of execution that was dependent upon left-frontal functioning was intact, and the answer was not done impulsively. The categorical structure of number was intact and is dependent upon left-posterior-parietal mediation. He mentally calculated $17 \times 3 = 51$ accurately. There was mild right-left confusion, which is a left-hemisphere symptom. There was no significant constructional dyspraxia (Fig. 2-10). Supportive evidence for mild left perisylvian dysfunction is seen in the moderately impaired score on the Speech-Sounds Perception Test. The score on the Seashore Rhythm Test, in contrast, is marginally within normal limits and suggests mild difficulty with fine language-related aural discrimination as reflected in the Speech-Sounds performance.

The overall results in this case are suggestive of mild, generalized cerebral dysfunction with a superimposed lateralized left-frontotemporal component stemming from the history of left supraorbital skull fracture 13 months prior to the neuropsychological examination.

Case 25

Background data. The patient is a 34-year-old, right-handed, divorced white male with 18 years of education. He was working as a salesman at the time of this neuropsychological evaluation. The patient's history is remarkable for "dyslexia" and manic–depressive illness which is well controlled with lithium carbonate medication. The "dyslexic" syndrome was described by the referring psychologist as "difficulty matching numbers with items, trouble sequencing items, and backwards writing under fatigue or stress." The patient reported great difficulty with completion of the nonverbal WAIS items when he was tested 8 years previously. The "dyslexic" symptoms had been present since childhood and had not interferred with the patient's ability to achieve academically, but they had reappeared intermittently when he felt stressed. The possibility of anxiety-related symptomatology was entertained, but an MMPI administered to the patient was diagnostically noncontributory. The Halstead-Reitan Battery was part of a more extensive battery of tests that was administered in an attempt to elucidate the nature of this man's difficulty.

Case Example 25 Age 34 Sex M Education 18 Handedness R

General Tests:

Category (errors) 48 Trail-making: Part A 60 Part B 120

TPT: Total time 14.4 Location 2 Memory 8

Motor and Sensory Tests:

Finger-tapping R 49 L 42 Fingertip

Finger agnosia R 0 L 0 number-writing R 2 L 1

Supressions: Tactile form

Visual R 0 L 0 (time) R 0 L 0

Tactile R 0 L 0 (errors) R 0 L 0

Auditory R 0 L 0

TPT: Time/Block R .75 L .49 Both .20

Cognitive Tests:

Speech-Sounds Perception

(errors)   5   Rhythm (errors)   6

WAIS: (scaled score)

Information   15   Picture completion   9

Comprehension   18   Picture arrangement   9

Vocabulary   17   Object assembly   8

Similarities   12   Block design   8

Arithmetic   13   Digit symbol   8

Digit span   7

VIQ 121   PIQ 95   FSIQ 111

Aphasia: Dysarthria, spelling dyspraxia

Test results. There is a 26-point difference between the verbal and performance IQ scores for this patient, which is a statistically significant difference. The more significant scatter from the interpretive viewpoint, however, occurs from a review of the subtest scaled scores themselves, since they give insight into the patient's relative areas of cognitive strength and deficit. Inconsistent cognitive performance is immediately evident from examination of the verbal-comprehension factor (I, C, S, V), on which there is a range of 2 standard deviations. The patient has learned very efficiently from both formal training (I) and exposure to a rich and verbally oriented life experience (V). He has a diverse fund of background information, concepts, and ideas. He also has a good grasp of social conventionalities (C), and one would expect that he has high achievement motivation to have learned this efficiently and consistently. Variation among the very-high-ranging verbal subtests reflects primarily the patient's somewhat uneven mastery of esoteric information that is educationally mastered. This might be expected with his reading difficulty, which very well might make it difficult for him to learn with full efficiency on such difficult material. Of more importance is the inconsistent conceptualization difficulty on Similarities items that are within his ability level.

This man's attention and concentration skills are quite inconsistent on the attentional factor (A, D). Note that he also shows a 2-standard-deviation difference between these scores. Normally one would expect the reverse patterning, with better attention span (D) than concentration ability (A), and the scatter here is extreme. Clearly this man is functioning well below his intellectual potential. He has considerable difficulty keeping his mind focused on one thing at a time. His nonverbal intellectual skills cluster in the low-average range for age, which seems to be a bit too low for a person with his towering intellectual potential. It is likely that the attentional difficulty lowers the patient's ability to perform well under time pressure and that he falters as a result. He was noted to give up in response to frustration with an incomplete solution on some of the nonverbal subtest items. He expected to do poorly on them, recalling his performance of years before, when he had also encountered difficulty on these tasks.

Examination of the four key neuropsychological measures for the Halstead-Reitan Battery provides equivocal evidence of brain dysfunction. The impairment index and category Test are both on the boderline of brain-dysfunctional performance ranges, while Trails B and the TPT Location component are clearly into the brain-damaged range. The performance on the Category Test showed relative inefficiency.

The Aphasia Screening Test is remarkable for errors on only two items. The patient mispronounced "Methodist" as "methodiss," and he made an error in writing the word "square"—he wrote it as "sqwre" and then spontaneously corrected the item as soon as he saw his error.

The Sensory–Perceptual Examination is remarkable only for two fingertip number-writing errors on the thumb and index finger of the right hand and one such error on the little finger of the left hand. These results are within normal limits.

Motor performance on the Fingers-tapping Test shows slightly-below-average performance with the right hand and slightly excessive slowing with the left hand in comparison with the right hand. The difference is very small and probably is a normal variant. It is certainly not sufficient to make an inference of lateralized motor deficit. The TPT performance shows the normal speed of solution on the first trial with the dominant right hand and a reduction of solution time by approximately one-third on the second trial, as is reported by Reitan in normals. Note, however, that the time for the third trial is reduced by almost 60 percent over that of the second trial. The patient had learned the task after the first two trials. He benefitted greatly in solution efficiency when he had one hand free to search for blocks while the other hand searched the board for spaces or anchored an identified space while the appropriate block for it was sought with the free hand. Recall of the block shapes was quite efficient, but ability to localize them in space was not. The TPT Location score, a sensitive general-functioning-level indicator, was well into the brain-damaged range. The Trail-making Tests were done rather slowly and inefficiently.

The patient learned well as long as he was goal directed and particularly when he could verbalize a solution strategy. When he could not anticipate the task, however, his limited attentional skills made his ability to recall incidental information quite inefficient. This man may be considered to have borderline cerebral dysfunction, of the "minimal brain dysfunction" variety that has been associated with learning disability. There is no unequivocal evidence of structural brain damage in medical workups or in the psychometric results. Referral was made to an adult learning-disability center for further, in-depth evaluation of the patient's reading and perceptual difficulty, which could not be definitely corrborated as a brain-related deficit on this examination.

Case 26

Background data. The patient is a 51-year-old, right-handed, legally separated white male with an eighth-grade education. He works as a landscaper. The history is remarkable for excessive drinking, five myocardial infarctions, and an episode of cardiac arrest. There was evidence of gross neurological dysfunction on the mental-status examination, including long-term memory loss. Dementia was suspected clinically. There was moderate situational depression. Neuropsychological evaluation was requested to determine the degree and extent of dementia.

Case Example 26   Age 51   Sex M   Education 8   Handedness R

General Tests:

    Category (errors) 120   Trail-making: Part A 80   Part B 216

    TPT: Total time 25.9 Location 0   Memory 6

Motor and Sensory Tests:

Finger-tapping	R 15 L 15	Fingertip	
Finger agnosia	R 4 L 4	number-writing	R 4 L 3
Supressions:		Tactile form	
Visual	R 0 L 0	(time)	R 18 L 21
Tactile	R 2 L 10	(errors)	R 1 L 2
Auditory	R 1 L 4		

    TPT: Time/Block R 1.0 L 3.3 Both .53

Cognitive Tests:

  Speech-Sounds Perception

    (errors)   25   Rhythm (errors)   11

  WAIS: (scaled score)

    Information   8   Picture completion   4

    Comprehension   7   Picture arrangement   2

    Vocabulary   10   Object assembly   4

    Similarities   6   Block design   3

    Arithmetic   6   Digit symbol   4

    Digit span   7

            VIQ 86   PIQ 69   FSIQ 77

Aphasia: Spelling dyspraxia, dysnomia, dyscalculi
          R-L confusion

Test results.   Use of the WAIS V subtest as a rough indicator of
premorbid-intellectual-level estimation in this case appears to be the
most reliable option, even though there are some aphasic symptoms.
If one considers V to be a conservative estimate of this man's
premorbid ability level, then one might place his minimum premorbid
IQ at 100 for verbal and nonverbal skills. Use of that standard shows
decline of the verbal IQ by almost 1 standard deviation and decline on
the nonverbal IQ by twice that amount. This would imply a decline
from the 50th percentile in both cases to a functioning level at the
18th percentile for verbal skills and at the 2nd percentile for nonverbal
skills. These results provide evidence of gross dementia due to
generalized intellectual decline that has an organic basis, as is demonstrated by the Halstead-Reitan Battery results and the history.

The WAIS verbal-comprehension factor (I, C, S, V) shows generalized decline from the baseline-performance level shown by V. The
patient has limited ability to draw upon formal stored information (I),
but this store may not have been much greater premorbidly, considering his educational level. Note that capacity for insight and practical
social judgment (C) is relatively weak, as is his capacity for abstraction
(S). The patient would thus be expected to be aware of few options
and to be attempting to compensate for his intellectual losses on the
basis of a modicum of understanding gained from general personal

experience (V, C). Attentional skills and concentration ability, as reflected by the attentional factor (A, D), are consistently poor. This man has trouble attending to a task for long, and his mind wanders to whatever seems to catch his attention or interest at the moment. The perceptual-organization factor (PC, BD, PA, OA) is generally suppressed, and the rate of motor output is low (DS). Of particular interest in this factor is the very low score on PA, which shows essentially no mobilized capacity for foresight and planning. This man lacks an integrated plan for social action (low C) and the means for carrying out activities that he chooses or those that are arranged for him (low PA).

Examination of the Halstead-Reitan Battery scores shows a generally suppressed level of performance that is consistent with the WAIS results. The patient's performance on the Category Test was grossly impaired.

Simple manual motor speed on the Finger-tapping Test is markedly impaired bimanually. The relative slowing of the right hand compared to the left is of no clinical consequence at this level of performance, since the impairment is severe and bilateral. More complex motor behavior on the Tactual Performance Test shows remarkably greater impairment of the left hand than the right. There is negative transfer from the first trial with the dominant right hand to the second trial with the left hand. Performance with both hands on the final trial remains at the moderately-to-markedly-impaired level. The TPT findings, in conjunction with the Sensory–Perceptual Examination data, reflect bilateral parietal-lobe dysfunction, since there is evidence of structural brain damage from the suppression findings.

Tactile perception is intact, with unilateral tactile stimulation of the hands producing consistent suppression of the left hand. Similar simultaneous stimulation of the right hand and left face produces consistent suppression of the facial stimulus. Stimulation of the right side of the face and the left hand produces inconsistent suppressions of either hand or face on various trials, more often with suppression of the facial component. Suppressions rarely are seen without serious structural damage to the cortex, and their occurrence with frequency such as this is pathognomonic of such damage. There was consistent suppression of the left ear and one suppression of the right ear with double simultaneous auditory stimulation. Visual confrontation testing was intact, and no visual suppression occurred with testing in any portion of the visual field. Mild dysgnosia of each hand was noted. There was also very mild and inconsistent dysgraphesthesia and mild dysstereognosis.

The Aphasia Screening Test shows spelling and naming errors consistently (Fig. 2-11). The patient spelled the world "triangle" as "trieangele," which suggests some grasp of phonetic analysis if not spelling ability. He called a triangle a pyramid and a fork a spoon. He misread the arithmetic problem 85 − 27 as 85 × 27. He was also unable to calculate 17 × 3 mentally. There was a right–left confusion, as when the patient was asked to place his left hand to his right ear and he placed his right hand to his right ear. Aural discrimination on the Speech-Sounds Perception Test was moderately impaired. Performance on the Seashore Rhythm Test was no better with nonverbal aural stimuli.

This man shows generalized, disabling brain disease which spares almost none of his higher cortical functions. Referral for neurological examination was suggested to the referring psychiatrist. The patient appeared to be approaching the point at which he would require constantly supervised, sheltered, long-term care.

Case 27

Background data. The patient is a 27-year-old, right-handed, single white male with 6 years of college education but no degree. He has worked as an electronics-assembly-line employee and draftsman. The medical history is remarkable for a concussive head injury that the patient suffered 8 years prior to the present examination. At that time he was unconscious for 3 days and experienced a transient left hemiparesis with transient crossed aphasia. Residual symptoms at the time of the current neuropsychological examination involved incoordination of the left hemisoma and dysarthria. There was some paranoid gradiosity noted clinically, and diagnostic personality testing confirmed the presence of borderline personality disorder by DSM-III criteria. The workup was done as a baseline estimate of the patient's current neuropsychological cognitive-retraining needs.

Case Example __27__ Age __27__ Sex __M__ Education __18__ Handedness __R__

General Tests:

    Category (errors) __37__ Trail-making: Part A __57__ Part B __150__

    TPT: Total time __15.2__ Location __5__ Memory __9__

Motor and Sensory Tests:

Finger-tapping	R __38__	L __25__	Fingertip
Finger agnosia	R __0__	L __0__	number-writing R __0__ L __10__
Supressions:			Tactile form
Visual	R __0__	L __0__	(time) R __12__ L __14__
Tactile	R __0__	L __0__	(errors) R __0__ L __0__
Auditory	R __0__	L __0__	

  TPT: Time/Block R __.74__ L __.50__ Both __.28__

Cognitive Tests:

Speech-Sounds Perception

(errors) __4__   Rhythm (errors) __2__

WAIS: (scaled score)

Information	12	Picture completion	12
Comprehension	13	Picture arrangement	11
Vocabulary	11	Object assembly	13
Similarities	9	Block design	14
Arithmetic	9	Digit symbol	6
Digit span	11		

VIQ __104__   PIQ __108__   FSIQ __106__

Aphasia: Dysarthria, spelling dyspraxia.

Test results. There is remarkably little cognitive deficit for a man with so serious a history of head trauma. This is often the case at a long interval after head injury in a young person. There is some evidence of residual cognitive inefficiency that is seen in subtest scatter on the verbal-comprehension factor (I, C, S, V). This is relatively mild and is confined to the Similarities subtest, which is significantly lower than the other subtests that compose the factor. The rest of these skills have remained in the high-average range. The attentional factor (A, D) shows somewhat better attention span (D) than concentration ability (A), but both skills are adequate for the subject's intellectual-functioning level. The perceptual-organization factor (PC, BD, PA, OA) again shows the pattern of mild cognitive inconsistency, particularly with BD 1 standard deviation higher than PA. This pattern has been noted by Reitan (unpublished manuscript) as indicative of a more anterior than posterior dysfunction. The relatively small difference between these two scores here suggests mild right-anterior-temporal dysfunction. This is of particular interest because the S subtest score was also relatively low on the verbal-comprehension factor with S having been noted by Reitan (undated manuscript) to be related to the integrity of left-temporal functioning. These are relative deficits and they are both mild, but such subtle relationships take on greater significance long after head trauma when there has been good recovery of general functioning, as in this case.

Motor functioning on the Finger-tapping Test shows bimanual slowing, significantly more so with the left hand than with the right. This is consistent with the history of right-hemisphere injury and the inference of bitemporal dysfunction, since there is evidence of a supplementary motor area in the superior temporal lobe, as reported by Halstead (1947). Inferior sensori-motor-region or superior-temporal dysfunction could also account for the patient's residual dysarthria, since there is representation of the lingual and buccofacial portion of the Penfield homunculus in this area of the cortical map. The Aphasia Test results are contributors for verbal paraphasia (repetition of "shouted" as "felted"), dysarthria ("Methodist" repeated as "methodiss" and "Massachusetts" repeated as "Massachusutt"), and a spelling error ("square" copied as "sqare," self-corrected thereafter). Sensory-Perceptual findings were entirely unremarkable. The Category Test findings show a normal overall performance.

The results show, in sum, a residual bitemporal syndrome with greater involvement of the right temporal area than the left. The bilateral involvement is consistent with contrecoup injury mechanisms. The recovery from the brain injury has been excellent. Cognitive retraining was begun to alleviate the residual symptoms and is continuing. Psychiatric treatment will be begun when the patient's neuropsychological recovery is more advanced in an attempt to help him work out a more satisfactory adjustment.

Case 28

Background data. The patient is a 24-year-old, right-handed, single white male with 12 years of education. He formerly had worked as a clerk, but he was unemployed and drawing disability benefits for chronic paranoid schizophrenia at the time of this examination. The Halstead-Reitan Battery was administered as part of a general evaluation of the patient's mental status.

Case Example 28   Age 24   Sex M   Education 12   Handedness R

General Tests:

   Category (errors) 34   Trail-making: Part A 65 Part B 50

   TPT: Total time 14.1 Location 6 Memory 8

Motor and Sensory Tests:

   Finger-tapping   R 41   L 50   Fingertip
   Finger agnosia   R 0   L 0   number-writing   R 0   L 0

   Supressions: Tactile form

      Visual   R 0   L 0   (time)   R 20   L 21
                                       (errors)   R 0   L 0
      Tactile   R 0   L 0

      Auditory   R 0   L 0

   TPT: Time/Block   R .55 L .60 Both .26

Cognitive Tests:

   Speech-Sounds Perception

      (errors)   4   Rhythm (errors)   3

   WAIS: (scaled score)

      Information   14   Picture completion   8
      Comprehension   10   Picture arrangement   6
      Vocabulary   16   Object assembly   7
      Similarities   13   Block design   11
      Arithmetic   11   Digit symbol   6
      Digit span   11

               VIQ 114   PIQ 83   FSIQ 101

Aphasia: None

Test results. There is a 31-point difference between the verbal and performance IQ scores of this individual, which is a statistically significant difference. There is often a dramatic variability of cognitive-subtest performance in schizophrenic persons; thus one must be particularly careful about the inference of neuropsychological deficit from such findings alone. Note in this case that the patient is natively quite intelligent, but he is functioning below his intellectual potential. His chronic psychosis is certainly contributory to this overall result. The deviant score that produces the large discrepancy between the verbal and performance IQ scores is the lower performance IQ; the higher verbal IQ score is consistent with this man's verbal-ability level, while the performance IQ clearly underestimates it.

Consider the scatter among the verbal-comprehension-factor subtests (I, C, S, V) as an instance of cognitive inconsistency. Here there is a range of fully 2 standard deviations between V and C, a difference which shows deficient capacity for insight (C) in a man of this ability level (V). It is important to note that the patient does not lack the rudiments of common sense; rather, he is sufficiently pedestrian in his capacity for insight so that he does not use judgment that is commensurate with his ability level. He has a good fund of background information (I), concepts, and ideas (V) that is considerably greater than that found in the usual high-school graduate. Attentional-factor subtests (A, D) show no variation, but results are both relatively inefficient for a man of this ability level as well. The perceptual-organization factor (PC, BD, PA, OA) shows inattention to detail (PC), poor foresight and planning ability (PA), and weak visual organization (OA) in the context of good capacity for intuitive reasoning and visual–motor coordination (BD). The combination of C and PA with a large difference between them shows that this man does not exercise good judgment for his ability level. He does not even implement those options of which he is aware. His chronic psychotic status and frequent rehospitalization because of bizarre behavior and inability to provide for his basic needs for food, clothing, and shelter bespeak his difficulty in coping despite his potential intellectual superiority.

The Halstead-Reitan Battery shows very few results that deviate from normative expectations; however, there are three reversals of expected speed-of-performance tasks that point to subtle bilateral hemispheric dysfunction in this man. The first is the reverse practice effect on the first two trials on the Tactual Performance Test. The patient scored within normal limits on the first trial with the dominant right hand, but he took half a minute longer to do the same task on the next trial with the nondominant left hand. An improvement in time of one-third should have taken place if normal learning were occurring. In the absence of sensory loss, this reflects right-hemisphere premotor-area dysfunction. There is also a reversal of expected motor-output speed on parts A and B of the Trail-making Test. This man shows an above-average score on Trails B but a markedly slowed performance on Trails A. This pattern has been noted by Golden (1978) to be typical of patients with right-hemispheric dysfunction. There also is a reversal of the pattern of right-hemispheric dysfunction in the Finger-tapping Test results. The tapping speed with the dominant right hand is slower than that of the left hand by a factor of 18 percent. Left rather than right motor-strip dysfunction is indicated by this finding.

There is no history of head trauma for this individual, and thorough neurological examination was within normal limits. The deficits are fairly mild and may represent the residual of bifrontal chronic residual trauma. Birth trauma is one possibility, but there was no definitive medical diagnosis.

Case 29

Background data. The patient is a 55-year-old, right-handed, single white male with 12 years of education. He is self-employed as a house painter when he is able to work. There is a history of chronic undifferentiated schizophrenia, and the patient was significantly depressed at the time of this examination. Neuropsychological evaluation was requested on a clinical basis to rule out organic cerebral dysfunction.

Case Example _29_ Age _55_ Sex _M_ Education _12_ Handedness _R_

General Tests:

Category (errors) _107_ Trail-making: Part A _90_ Part B _270_

TPT: Total time _30_ Location _0_ Memory _5_

Motor and Sensory Tests:

Finger-tapping	R _42_ L _30_	Fingertip	
Finger agnosia	R _0_ L _0_	number-writing	R _0_ L _0_
Supressions:		Tactile form	
Visual	R _0_ L _0_	(time)	R _18_ L _20_
Tactile	R _0_ L _0_	(errors)	R _0_ L _0_
Auditory	R _0_ L _0_		

TPT: Time/Block R _1.7_ L _5.0_ Both _5.0_

Cognitive Tests:

Speech-Sounds Perception

(errors) _12_   Rhythm (errors) _6_

WAIS: (scaled score)

Information	_9_	Picture completion	_9_
Comprehension	_12_	Picture arrangement	_6_
Vocabulary	_9_	Object assembly	_8_
Similarities	_12_	Block design	_8_
Arithmetic	_6_	Digit symbol	_0_
Digit span	_9_		

VIQ _101_   PIQ _92_   FSIQ _97_

Aphasia: Dyslexia, dysarthria, dyscalculia (mild)

Test results. Examination of the WAIS subtest scatter suggests that the patient has probably always functioned in the average intellectual range. The verbal-comprehension factor (I, C, S, V) shows remarkably little scatter on age-corrected scores for a chronic schizophrenic. The range of concepts and ideas (V) and formal background information (I) is adequate for a high-school graduate. Capacity for insight and practical social judgment (C) is intact, and there is good abstraction ability (S). In sum, these skills suggest good ability to learn from experience. Attention span (D) is adequate for age, but there is mild concentration difficulty (A). This discrepancy on the attentional factor (A, D) shows mild cognitive inefficiency. The perceptual-organization factor (PC, BD, PA, OA) subtest scatter is also fairly consistent, with no significant cognitive impairment after correction is made for age.

The Halstead-Reitan Battery results for this individual show generalized chronic and static cerebral dysfunction. There is no lateralized sensory deficit. No frank aphasic symptoms are seen, but errors are made with pronunciation of more complex words and reading of more complicated sentence-length material (Fig. 2-12). For example, the patient read "famous" as "williams" in the sentence "He is a famous animal, a friendly winner of dog shows." He mispronounced "Massachusetts" as "massatusetts," and he mispronounced "Episcopal" as "epispopal." His handwriting was somewhat illegible on one word, and he made a calculation error that was not diagnostically remarkable.

Motor speed on the Finger-tapping Test is bimanually slowed, and the nondominant left-hand performance is excessively slowed in comparison with that of the right hand. The moderate slowing and failure to complete the TPT tasks on the first trial with the right hand were followed by a severely impaired performance with the left. No improvement was made on the final trial, when both hands were used in unison. Incidental recall for the TPT task on the Memory and Location components was in the brain-dysfunctional range. None of the neuropsychological measures administered to this man produced a performance within normal limits. There is generalized decline of organically based adaptive abilities. The patient required a sheltered board-and-care living situation when he returned to the community upon hospital discharge.

Case 30

Background data. The patient is a 38-year-old, right-handed, single white male nurse–anesthetist with 13 years of formal education and medical corpsman training in the armed services. The history is remarkable for head trauma suffered 4 years previously in a fall that caused a right-temporal contusion and a right-temporoparietooccipital depressed skull fracture. The lesion was treated by right-anterior-temporal lobectomy, and the skull defect was repaired by cranioplasty with replacement of the bone flap where possible. The patient suffered from posttraumatic psychomotor seizures, which were well controlled by medication. There was an additional psychiatric diagnosis of borderline personality disorder according to standardized DSM-III criteria.

Case Example __30__ Age __38__ Sex __M__ Education __13__ Handedness __R__

General Tests:

    Category (errors) __91__ Trail-making: Part A __30__ Part B __73__

    TPT: Total time __19·3__ Location __6__ Memory __8__

Motor and Sensory Tests:

Finger-tapping	R 51	L 41	Fingertip		
Finger agnosia	R 0	L 0	number-writing	R 0	L 0
Supressions:			Tactile form		
Visual	R 0	L 0	(time)	R 12	L 11
Tactile	R 0	L 0	(errors)	R 0	L 0
Auditory	R 0	L 0			

TPT: Time/Block R __·91__ L __·73__ Both __·29__

Cognitive Tests:

Speech-Sounds Perception

(errors)   9___   Rhythm (errors)   6___

WAIS: (scaled score)

Information	16	Picture completion	10
Comprehension	10	Picture arrangement	9
Vocabulary	13	Object assembly	10
Similarities	10	Block design	11
Arithmetic	8	Digit symbol	8
Digit span	10		

VIQ 107   PIQ 103   FSIQ 105

Aphasia: None

Test results. There is remarkably little deficit associated with the head injury in this man, but he was young at onset and he had excellent neurosurgical care immediately after the injury. Examination of the IQ scores shows average measured ability, which is consistent with the level of performance on most of the age-corrected scaled scores. A notable exception among the subtests of the verbal-comprehension factor (I, C, S, V) is the difference between the scores on I and V. The higher score on I in this pair points to a fund of formally acquired information that is greater than this man's general range of concepts and ideas based on experience. This is consistent wih his specialized medical corpsman training. The patient's capacities for abstraction (S) and practical judgment and insight (C) are barely adequate for general intelligence level (V). The attentional factor (A, D) shows rather short attention span (D) and significantly impaired concentration capacity (A) for his ability level. The perceptual-organization factor (PC, BD, PA, OA) shows a general clustering of scores about the mean of the patient's age group.

The Halstead-Reitan Battery results show mild residual impairment of the head injury and the right-temporal lobectomy. Note that as expected the tapping speed with the left hand is slightly slowed in comparison with that of the right hand, but the deficit seen here with the right-anterior lobectomy is much less than would be expected. It appears that the functional motor system of the right cerebral hemisphere has reorganized so that the sensorimotor area has taken over the supplementary motor function that is normally subserved by the resected right anterior temporal area. The PA score is the lowest of the subtests in the perceptual-organization factor, but its difference from the remainder of the subtests in that group is not significant. Speed of performance on a more complex motor problem-solving task, the Tactual Performance Test, reveals slowed performances with each hand individually, consistent with dysfunction in the adjacent premotor area. There is no aphasic disorder, but the patient shows borderline performance impairment on the Seashore Rhythm and Speech-Sounds Perception tests, both of which are sensitive temporal indicators. The Seashore Rhythm Test is a nonlateralized temporal-lobe-function indicator, whereas the Speech-Sounds Perception Test is sensitive to left-temporal functioning. These results are consistent with intellectual measures (low S, PA) that suggest mild, residual bilateral temporal-lobe dysfunction.

There is also a prefrontal component to the syndrome that is seen in the Category Test response pattern. The overall results are consistent with a mild right-temporofrontal syndrome with a trace of left-temporal dysfunction. The bilateral indications are attributable to the contrecoup mechanism which may be seen in severe head injuries such as the one that this man suffered.

Case 31

Background data.   The patient is a 32-year-old, ambidextrous, single white male with 12 years of education. He formerly worked as a bartender and as a taxicab driver. The history is remarkable for the nonpenetrating right-temporoparietal shrapnel wound received 9 years prior to this examination, chronic alcoholism, and paranoid schizophrenia by history that was completely in remission at the time of testing. Evaluation by a speech pathologist, whose consultation was sought for further evaluation after the neuropsychological evaluation was completed, confirmed the syndrome of dyslexia with dysgraphia. This is due to a lesion of the angular gyrus of the dominant hemisphere.

Case Example _31_ Age _32_ Sex _M_ Education _12_ Handedness _A_

General Tests:

Category (errors) _107_ Trail-making: Part A _60_ Part B _210_

TPT: Total time _17.2_ Location _4_ Memory _7_

Motor and Sensory Tests:

Finger-tapping R _50_ L _50_

Finger agnosia R _0_ L _0_

Fingertip number-writing R _3_ L _3_

Supressions:

Tactile form

Visual   R _0_ L _0_ (time) R _18_ L _20_

Tactile R _1_ L _2_ (errors) R _0_ L _0_

Auditory R _0_ L _0_

TPT: Time/Block R _.58_ L _.71_ Both _.43_

Cognitive Tests:

Speech-Sounds Perception

(errors) _35_   Rhythm (errors) _12_

WAIS: (scaled score)

Information	10	Picture completion	8
Comprehension	8	Picture arrangement	8
Vocabulary	9	Object assembly	8
Similarities	11	Block design	8
Arithmetic	8	Digit symbol	7
Digit span	6		

VIQ _91_   PIQ _86_   FSIQ _88_

Aphasia: Dyslexia, dysgraphia, R-L confusion, dyscalculia, construction dyspraxia

Test results. Examination of WAIS subtest scatter shows an individual of average native ability (I, S, V) who is functioning somewhat below his potential now. There is greater loss of right- than left-hemisphere-dependent congnitive skill, consistent with the history of lateralized head trauma. There is reason to suspect bilateral involvement in serious head trauma cases such as this one, but evaluation of dysfunction lateralization is made more difficult by this patient's ambidexterity. Laterality of cerebral function is usually less complete in persons with mixed dominance; thus one should consider the possibility of some bilateral contribution to intellectual and neuropsychological skills and deficits for this individual that are usually considered to be strongly lateralized in right-handed persons. Speech and related functions are among important elements in this category for this case.

· This patient shows adequate social judgment and insight capacity (C) for general ability level (I, V), but he has somewhat weak foresight and planning skills. An index of his concentration ability (A) ranks at the lower limit of the average range, and his attention span (D) is significantly impaired. Factorial analysis of the test results shows no significant cognitive inefficiency from a scatter analysis of the attentional (A, D), verbal-comprehension (I, C, S, V), or perceptual-organization (PC, BD, PA, OA) groupings. There is fairly consistent but generally suppressed level of functioning across cognitive skills.

The markedly impaired performance on the Category Test is due to random responding on subtests III and IV, which produced 67 of the 107 errors he made.

Simple manual motor speed with the dominant right hand is normatively average but not faster than the left-hand speed. Note that this relative motor deficit occurred on the opposite side of the head from the point of injury to the posterior right hemicranium. This suggests a contrecoup injury mechanism which should be evaluated in the light of the other findings. More complex motor problem solving on the Tactual Performance Test shows a normal initial performance with the dominant right hand and mild but significant slowing with the left hand on the subsequent trial. The third trial performance—in which both hands are used in unison—is moderately slowed. Since the task is completed on each trial and since there is no strong lateralization effect, these are again only relative performance deficits consistent with long-term residual effects of closed head trauma. The lack of normal transfer from the dominant to the nondominant hand is consistent with posterior right-hemispheric dysfunction due to the direct effect of the wound. The speed with the left hand on the TPT for the second trial is 18 percent faster than that on the initial trial with the right hand.

Confirmatory evidence for the inference of right-posterior dysfunction comes from the Sensory–Perceptual Examination. The patient shows intermittent suppression of tactile stimulation to the left side of the face with double simultaneous stimulation to the right hand and left face. There is intermittent suppression of the left hand when the procedure is reversed and the right face and left hand are touched in unison. These results indicate a right-parietal lesion with probable structural changes in the cortex. There is also one suppression of the *right* hand with the right hand–left face combination, which points to a probable structural lesion in the left-parietal area. This is a very important finding, since the results of the evaluation by the speech pathologist and the Halstead-Reitan Aphasia Screening Test show dyslexia with dysgraphic errors that are associated with a lesion of the *dominant* angular gyrus, in the left parietotemporal junction. This is the mirror-image position of the point at which this man was wounded. There was also a bilateral superior-visual-field defect that would be consistent with bilateral trauma to the temporal-lobe portion of the optic radiations. There was mild bimanual dysgraphesthesia, while tactile finger identification and sterognosis were within normal limits.

The Aphasia Screening Test revealed dysgraphia that was seen in fusion and omission of letters, even in his personal signature. Paragrammatism was seen in disturbance of syntax when the patient was reading. For example, the patient read the phrase "see the black dog" as "see the dog black." He misread "MGW" as "MW" and then corrected himself spontaneously. He misread "place left hand to right ear" as "please left hand go right ear." "Square" was misspelled "squar," but the omission of the final "e" on this word is commonly seen in persons with a history of school difficulty. Right–left confusion was seen in attempts to comply with the command to place his left hand to his right ear. He placed the right hand to the right ear, and then he placed the left hand to the left ear in an attempt to correct his error. Calculation errors to written problems involved minor mistakes in carrying from one number column to the other (For $85 - 27 = ?$ he answered 68 instead of 58). More complex mental calculations also showed initial errors (For $17 \times 3 = ?$ he answered "59, no, 51"). There was marked construction dyspraxia in attempts to draw a Greek cross (see Fig. 2-13), and the patient could not complete even the drawing of a developmentally simple figure such as a triangle without several attempts. The patient denied that such difficulty had been present before the head injury.

The Seashore Rhythm Test, a nonlateralized temporal-lobe indicator, shows moderate impairment. The Speech-Sounds Perception Test, in contrast, shows severe impairment of auditory verbal discrimination, consistent with the Aphasia Test results. The overall patterning of results is consistent with bilateral temporoparietal lesions, including those of the angular gyrus of the left hemisphere. While some of the speech findings are less confidently lateralized in a person with manual ambidexterity, the sensory and motor findings in this case are consistent with the history and a contrecoup mechanism of injury. This mechanism is fairly common in severe closed head injury such as this patient received, and the alert examiner will not fail to search for evidence of it among the results in such cases.

Case 32

Background data. The patient is a 52-year-old, right-handed, divorced white female with 15 years of education who works as a medical secretary. The history is remarkable for chronic and severe migraine headache, chronic alcoholism, sinistral deafness, and a burst aneurysm of the right posterior communicating artery which was surgically clipped. EEG findings revealed a pattern of right-hemispheric "multifocal epileptogenic activity and damage pattern . . . with damage evidence primarily posterior." A computer-tomographic (CT) brain scan revealed the surgical clip in the region of the lesion of the right posterior communicating artery. There was no midline shift or intracranial blood noted at the time of the CT scan, which was done shortly before the neuropsychological workup and the EEG study. At the time of the neuropsychological evaluation the patient still had a third-nerve palsy of the right eye, which was patched. The psychiatric diagnosis was depressive disorder, agitated. The patient was alert, very cooperative, and well motivated to perform to her capacity.

Case Example 32   Age 52   Sex F   Education 15   Handedness R

General Tests:

    Category (errors) 88   Trail-making: Part A 33   Part B 75

    TPT: Total time 14.4 Location 4   Memory 8

Motor and Sensory Tests:

Finger-tapping	R 41	L 39	Fingertip		
Finger agnosia	R 1	L 0	number-writing	R 0	L 10
Supressions:			Tactile form		
Visual	R 0	L 0	(time)	R 18	L 17
Tactile	R 0	L 0	(errors)	R 0	L 0
Auditory	R 0	L 0			
TPT: Time/Block	R .61	L .50	Both .33		

Cognitive Tests:

Speech-Sounds Perception

(errors)   5   Rhythm (errors)   1

WAIS: (scaled score)

Information   14   Picture completion   8

Comprehension   15   Picture arrangement   7

Vocabulary   17   Object assembly   11

Similarities   16   Block design   9

Arithmetic   13   Digit symbol   9

Digit span   14

VIQ   133   PIQ   109   FSIQ 124

Aphasia: (Patched right eye, left ear deafness)
        None

Test results. Examination of the IQ scores shows a highly intelligent woman who is well educated and highly verbal (VIQ, I, V). She has superior capacity for insight and practical social judgment (C). Her attention span is appropriately above average for a person of her ability level (A, D). Factorial groupings among the age-corrected verbal subtests show isolated scatter. Note that for the verbal-comprehension factor (I, C, S, V) there is a difference of four scaled score points between S and I, and I also lags behind V by 1 standard deviation of three scaled score points. The lower score on I is related to a relatively lower level of formal background knowledge that is educationally acquired. The level of performance remains very high even on I, but this woman's lack of the full college education and graduate training of which she was capable is reflected in the level of performance on I. In a very-high-level sense she is undereducated for a person of her ability level. Her higher ability level is seen in the scores that reflect general experiential background (V) and abstraction–conceptualization ability (S). Given her high conceptual-ability level, one would want to be particularly aware of any clues to impaired ability with concept formation or generalization from experience when the other test results are considered. Such skills may be presumed to have been intact premorbidly.

The perceptual-organization factor (PC, BD, PA, OA) does show significant intertest scatter, with OA four scaled score points above PA and three scaled score points above PC. This is a reasonable finding in the light of the arterial-lesion site, which is adjacent to the anterior medial temporal area. PA is sensitive to dysfunction of the right anterior temporal area, and its relatively low position compared to the other perceptual-organization-factor subtests is to be expected. If OA is taken as the most likely estimate of the patient's premorbid-functioning level, there would appear to be a generalized decline in right-hemispheric cognitive function of approximately 1 standard deviation. This is consistent with the EEG findings and the inference that this woman premorbidly functioned at a high level intellectual level with comparably high cognitive efficiency. The difference between her verbal and nonverbal IQ scores, now 24 points, was probably considerably less premorbidly, but this result by itself would not necessarily make one suspect right-hemispheric dysfunction. Results of this magnitude can be seen in verbal overachievers who have no cerebral-functioning impairment. In such cases the difference between verbal and nonverbal skill levels simply reflects the subject's verbal superiority as compared with an average level of nonverbal functioning. The findings must be interpreted in the light of the history to make the reason for the level-of-performance difference clear.

The patient's motor functioning on the Finger-tapping Test, a simple manual motor-speed measure, is in the mildly impaired range with the dominant right hand. This result suggests a very mild motor deficit of the sensorimotor region of the left hemisphere. More impressive is the patient's haptic-motor performance on the Tactual Performance Test. Here there is a normal performance with the dominant right hand on the first trial. This is followed by a reduction of performance speed on the next trial by a factor of only one-sixth; the time reduction should be twice that amount if there were normal learning. This reflects premotor dysfunction of the right cerebral hemisphere in the absence of tactile sensory impairment.

Performance on the Sensory–Perceptual Examination was seriously compromised by the patient's multiple sensory deficits. She has normal visual acuity in both eyes, but the right eye was patched during recovery from the third-nerve palsy. She was also neurally deaf in the left ear. It was therefore impossible to test for double simultaneous stimulation in these two modalities. Hearing and vision in the unaffected ear and eye were intact. Graphesthesia, tactile finger identification, and stereognosis were within normal limits.

The Category Test performance produced no random responding, but the patient performed poorly. Such results are typical of prefrontal dysfunction with its stimulus-bound "concrete" reasoning. This is to be expected in a person with a history of chronic alcoholism; there is a likelihood for such cognitive skills to decline with such a history.

In overview the four most sensitive measures of the Halstead-Reitan Battery show equivocal evidence of cerebral dysfunction in this woman. The Category Test and TPT Location component show poor incidental learning, but the score on Trails B is normal and the impairment index is only on the borderline of the brain-dysfunctional range. There is evidence of mild complex motor dysfunction of the right hemisphere and a trace of motor-speed loss in the left hemisphere. In a person with an intracerebral vascular lesion such as this it is perhaps not too surprising that there are equivocal findings found on tests that were designed primarily for functions of the cerebral hemispheres proper. The EEG findings were not associated with structural cerebral changes on the CT scan that was obtained at the time of neuropsychological evaluation. The Halstead-Reitan Battery nevertheless was sensitive to subtle hemispheric dysfunction, including the patient's alcohol-related cerebral deficits. This case was included to show some strengths and limitations of the technique in assessment of cerebral functioning integrity.

Case 33

Background data. The patient is a 30-year-old, right-handed, single white male college student with 15 years of completed education. His major field is English, and his minor area is speech. He was hospitalized for treatment of a delayed stress reaction that manifested in adjustment difficulties and "Vietnam flashbacks." Neuropsychological evaluation was requested by a counseling psychologist who found that the patient had scored lower than had been anticipated on a battery of vocational-aptitude tests.

Case Example _33_ Age _30_ Sex _M_ Education _15_ Handedness _R_

General Tests:

Category (errors) _28_ Trail-making: Part A _39_ Part B _92_

TPT: Total time _18.6_ Location _2_ Memory _4_

Motor and Sensory Tests:

Finger-tapping   R _60_   L _60_   Fingertip

Finger agnosia   R _0_   L _0_   number-writing R _0_ L _0_

Supressions: Tactile form

   Visual   R _0_   L _0_   (time)   R _0_ L _0_

   Tactile   R _0_   L _0_   (errors)   R _0_ L _0_

   Auditory   R _2_   L _0_

TPT: Time/Block R _1.0_ L _.38_ Both _.48_

Cognitive Tests:

Speech-Sounds Perception

(errors)   10   Rhythm (errors)   3

WAIS: (scaled score)

Information   10   Picture completion   12

Comprehension   12   Picture arrangement   8

Vocabulary   11   Object assembly   10

Similarities   10   Block design   7

Arithmetic   5   Digit symbol   9

Digit span   12

VIQ 99   PIQ 95   FSIQ 97

Aphasia: None

Test results.   The patient currently exhibits average intelligence, and he appears to have always functioned near this overall level. Examination of the subtest results shows good verbal-skill preservation with fairly even performance on the verbal-comprehension factor (I, C, S, V). All of the scores here are within 1 standard deviation of the mean for age and of each other. The attentional factor (A, D), however, shows considerable concentration difficulty (A) in a man with intact attention span (D). His distractibility may contribute to the lowered performance on the aptitude measures noted by the referring psychologist. There is also considerable inefficiency on the perceptual-organization factor (PC, BD, PA, OA). Here the highest score occurs on PC, which is expected because this is the least sensitive measure of cerebral dysfunction among the subtests of this group. There appears to have been a significant decline in right-hemisphere-dependent cognitive skills from a formerly high-average level. It is important to note that this patient is currently in the hospital with manifest symptomatology of anxiety and depression. He performs less well when the task requires rapid performance and serial reasoning, since his energy level is relatively low and his concentration ability is significantly impaired (A). One would want to be cautious with interpretation of the nonverbal WAIS items until the neuropsychological test results are considered.

The Halstead-Reitan Battery results show borderline overall cer-

ebral functioning with fairly specific dysfunction of the left frontotemporal area. Simple motor speed on tapping is superior bimanually. One
does not make the inference of impaired laterality of motor functioning
at this extremely high level of performance when there is not a
superior performance level of the dominant hand. This man simply
was very dextrous with both hands on this task. The performance
with the dominant right hand on the first trial of the Tactual Performance Test, in contrast, is mildly to moderately slowed, while that of
the left hand on the subsequent trial is within normal limits. There is
a worsening of performance level from the second trial to the third,
when the hands are used in unison. This suggests a disruptive effect
of the right hand on the performance of the left when they are used in
unison. Incidental recall for the task is deficient on the TPT Memory
and Location components. In the absence of tactile sensory impairment or suppression and with intact graphesthetic and stereognostic
function, the impaired TPT performance with the right hand shows
left-hemisphere premotor-area dysfunction. Marginal speed on the
Trails A and B visuopractic sequencing tasks is also consistent with
this inference.

The Sensory–Perceptual Examination findings are remarkable for
inconsistent auditory suppressions of the right ear with double simultaneous aural stimulation. Recognition of nonsensical speech sounds
on the Speech-Sounds Perception Test is mildly impaired, while
perception of nonverbal acoustic patterns is adequate. This also points
to a left-temporal component to the syndrome. The Aphasia Screening
Test findings are noncontributory. Findings are consistent with a left
frontotemporal syndrome with probable structural damage in the left
temporal lobe.

Case 34

Background data. The patient is a 31-year-old, right-handed, divorced unemployed white male. The patient is hospitalized for cognitive rehabilitation of his postencephalitic state. The workup was done as part of the baseline evaluation for the rehabilitation-program planning team.

Case Example __34__ Age __31__ Sex __M__ Education __12__ Handedness __R__

General Tests:

    Category (errors) __117__ Trail-making: Part A __80__ Part B __360__

    TPT: Total time __30__ Location __1__ Memory __2__

Motor and Sensory Tests:

Finger-tapping	R __24__ L __23__	Fingertip	
Finger agnosia	R __8__ L __12__	number-writing	R __9__ L __9__

Supressions:

Tactile form

			(time)	R __30__ L __34__
Visual	R __3__ L __0__			
Tactile	R __9__ L __5__	(errors)	R __2__ L __2__
Auditory	R __3__ L __0__		

    TPT: Time/Block R __10.__ L __10.__ Both __10.0__

Cognitive Tests:

Speech-Sounds Perception

    (errors) __18__   Rhythm (errors) __19__

WAIS: (scaled score)

Information	9	Picture completion	7
Comprehension	8	Picture arrangement	4
Vocabulary	8	Object assembly	3
Similarities	8	Block design	4
Arithmetic	3	Digit symbol	3
Digit span	2		

        VIQ 77   PIQ 63   FSIQ 69

Aphasia: Dysnomia, spelling dyspraxia, dyslexia, dysarthria, dycalculia

Test results.   The patient's verbal-scale score pattern shows a clear factorial separation in which there is good preservation of old learning on the verbal-comprehension-factor subtests (I, C, S, V) and severe impairment of both components of the attentional factor (A, D). This man appears to have functioned in the average/low-average range premorbidly; currently, however, there is gross inability to attend (D) and to concentrate (A). As expected there is relatively good preservation of PC among the nonverbal subtests and marked falling off of the other subtests that compose the perceptual-organization factor (BD, PA. OA). With a patient such as this who has suffered a severe, generalized brain dysfunction due to infectious disease, it is often helpful to give the nonverbal subtests of the WAIS on a timed and untimed basis to determine if there is residual ability which is being masked by the time limits on these measures. Note that the only timed test of the verbal scale (A) is also one of the poorest performances that this man produced. If this testing-the-limits procedures is used, the test must be scored in the usual way with credit allowance only for those items that are completed within the time limit. A separate, supplementary calculation of estimated IQ can be obtained from the tests given on an untimed basis, and the difference between these two measures can then be compared. A review of the scores that differ by 1 standard deviation or more provides a rough index of latent potential masked by the time factor. The poorer performance on the nonverbal subtests also probably reflects their novelty for this individual. He does relatively well on measures that are dependent upon old learning, but he has difficulty with items that require novel application of such information, particularly where speed of solution or motor output is a factor.

The Halstead-Reitan Battery results show generalized impairment, with none of the scores on the Battery within normal limits or even close to those levels. Note that there is a differential performance level between new learning with the Halstead-Reitan Battery tests and the old learning reflecied on the WAIS verbal-comprehension subtests, just as there was between these WAIS subtests and those of the WAIS perceptual-organization and attentional sub-test factor groupings. The decline in performance level on the Halstead-Reitan tests show this man's loss of ability to solve problems effectively, to apply old knowledge in innovative new ways, to remember and apply new information, and to understand and respond quickly to verbal commands. All of these "adaptive abilities," as Reitan has called them, have been markedly compromised in this patient. The generalized suppression of performance is consistent with our expectations in a case of infectious disease that diffusely infiltrates the brain.

The Aphasia Screening and Sensory–Perceptual tests require special discussion, since the errors that are made here provide insight into this man's difficulty beyond the level-of-performance measures that have been reviewed. The most consistent deficit among the aphasic errors this man makes is word-finding difficulty. Attempts to name a square on a visual confrontation task produced this response: "ta . . . too . . . sk . . . square." He called a cross a "cube something" at first, but he was able to give the correct name with much effort. He named a triangle correctly, but he named a fork as a "cross, thor, fork." Spelling was also affected, but there is retention of some phonetic analytic ability. Square was spelled correctly on the first attempt. Cross was misspelled as "crouse," and triangle was misspelled as "tralies." (See Fig. 2-14.) Reading at sentence level was partially preserved, mostly at the simpler level without dependent clauses. For example, the patient read "see the black dog" correctly. He misread the more difficult sentence, "He is a friendly animal, a famous winner of dog shows" as "he is a friendly animal in a famous dog show." The phrase "place left hand to right ear" was misread as "place the left hand in right ear." The patient had no difficulty carrying out the correction action in response to verbal command. When he was asked if he could perform the logical absurdity of placing his left hand on his left elbow, he first placed his left hand to his left shoulder. When he was asked to try the item again after repetition of it during a testing-the-limits period, he realized the absurdity. The patient could not write in cursive script, but he was able to print legibly. Pronunciation was remarkably good. He showed only slight slurring in repetition of "Methodist Episcopal," but he mispronounced Massachusetts as "mathachusetts."

He was confused by the problem $85 - 27 = ?$ at first, and he gave 11 as his answer. He asked, "You can't take 7 from 5, can you?" Then he recognized the number structure and the need to carry from the tens column: "Oh, if you borrow 1 from the 8 you could." This is an important clue to this man's hemispheric functioning, implying that there is at least a basis for the categorical structure of number and an ability to deal with symbolic arithmetic operations. This is unstable, however, since the patient added rather than multiplied on the dictated problem $17 \times 3 = ?$ answering 20 instead of 51. Such errors show that the patient has difficulty attending to task and that he may simplify tasks that he finds confusing. He seems to guess at simpler substituted tasks that he finds are still within his ability range. He gave the same answer again after the examiner repeated the question to be sure that the patient had understood it. The preservation of the rudiments of calculation implies that there is at least a modicum of left-posterior-parietal functioning that is intact, upon which retraining of such skills can proceed to build.

The Sensory–Perceptual Examination shows inconsistent suppression in tactile, auditory, and visual modalities. Double simultaneous tactile stimulation of the hands produced consistent suppression of the right hand only. Simultaneous tactile stimulation of the right face and the left hand produced twice as many suppressions of the right facial as the left manual stimulus. Reversal of the procedure, so that the right hand and left face were touched simultaneously, produced three times as many right-hand as left-face suppressions. Clearly there is much greater impairment of the right side of the body on tactile sensation under double simultaneous stimulation, but there are bilateral suppression errors with all combinations tested. This reflects bilateral parietal-lobe damage, which is much more pronounced in the left parietal area. Inconsistent suppressions of each ear were demonstrated with double simultaneous aural stimulation. Inconsistent suppressions of the left superior visual quadrant were also found with double simultaneous visual stimulation. The sinistral visual and aural suppressions reflect right-temporal-lobe damage, while the dextral aural suppressions reflect left-temporal-lobe damage. There were no associated deficits for sensory testing of tactile, visual, or auditory functions that were done with unilateral stimuli. Bimanual agraphesthesia was demonstrated for the identification of numbers that were written on the fingertips, but the patient was able to recognize numbers that were written on the palms of the hands. There was also bimanual dysstereognosis and finger dysgnosis, which was greater for the left hand than the right hand.

Case 35

Background data. The patient is a 49-year-old, right-handed, married white male mechanical-engineering technician. He suffered a severe right-hemispheric cerebrovascular accident a month previously that left him with a left homonymous hemianopsia, left hemiparesis, and dressing apraxia. The patient was alert, oriented to person and place, cooperative, and depressed at the time of testing. He cried episodically when he experienced difficulty, but he responded well to reassurance, and he was able to regain his composure. This case is presented to demonstrate the effect of a severe right-hemispheric lesion, which in this case was a massive occlusion of the right middle cerebral artery.

Case Example __35__ Age __49__ Sex __M__ Education __14__ Handedness __R__

General Tests:

Category (errors) __124__ Trail-making: Part A __180__ Part B __373__

TPT: Total time __30__ Location __0__ Memory __3__

Motor and Sensory Tests:

Finger-tapping	R __46__ L __30__	Fingertip	
Finger agnosia	R __0__ L __10__	number-writing	R __4__ L __12__

Supressions:

Tactile form

Visual	R __0__ L __0__	(time)	R __27__ L __38__
Tactile	R __0__ L __0__	(errors)	R __0__ L __3__
Auditory	R __0__ L __0__		

TPT: Time/Block R __1.4__ L __10.0__ Both __5.0__

Cognitive Tests:

Speech-Sounds Perception

(errors) __11__   Rhythm (errors) __13__

WAIS: (scaled score)

Information	13	Picture completion	4
Comprehension	14	Picture arrangement	2
Vocabulary	13	Object assembly	2
Similarities	11	Block design	2
Arithmetic	12	Digit symbol	3
Digit span	7		

VIQ __112__   PIQ __63__   FSIQ __90__

Aphasia: Homonymous heminopsia (left)
construction dyspraxia secondary
to visual defect, dyscalculia

Test results.   There is a striking difference between the right and
left cerebral hemispheres on every cognitive task administered. Note
that the highest nonverbal-scale subtests (DS, PC) are fully 1 standard
deviation below the lowest verbal-scale subtest (D) after correction is
made for age. The striking consistency of this performance level
difference is seen in the 49-point decrement of the performance IQ
below the verbal IQ. The verbal-comprehension factor (I, C, S, V)
shows mild inconsistency of performance but good cognitive preservation. There is an above-average fund of background information (I),
concepts, and ideas (V). Capacity for insight is commensurate with
overall verbal-ability level. The average-level verbal-abstraction score
on the S subtest is due to overlearned basics on the first five items
followed by spotty abstraction on the next several items, which
received partial credit. There were no frankly concrete responses until
the patient's ability ceiling was reached. There is significant inconsistency of performance level on the attentional factor (A, D) as well.
This suggests relatively well preserved concentration ability (A) with
short attention span (D). The results may be misleading in this case,
since this man previously worked in a quantitative technical field that
emphasizes a good deal of calculation. The relatively better performance on simple calculations such as those that are presented on the A
subtest probably reflects overlearning of such skills through massive
practice effect. The score on D seems to be a better index of his
attentional competency, since there is much less practice effect, since
novel learning is required, and since the task places no time pressure
on performance. The subtests of the perceptual-organization factor
show gross and generalized suppression of performance level. This
sort of performance decline is typical of acutely destructive, severe,
strongly lateralized lesions or recent onset lesions such as this man
had recently suffered at the time of testing.

The elevated Category Test score reflects largely random responding and very little ability to learn from experience across a variety of
principles. Simple motor speed on the Finger-tapping Test shows mild
slowing with the dominant right hand but moderate slowing with the
left. The left hand is 35 percent slower than the right. The patient was
unable to complete the TPT task with either hand, but second-trial
performance with the nondominant hand was very much poorer than
that on the first trial with the dominant hand. In the presence of
strongly lateralized right-hemispheric sensory disturbance such as this
man shows, it is reasonable to infer that the failure to complete the
task with the right hand was due to fatigue. This also seems to account

for the failure to make any progress on the final TPT trial, in which both hands were used.

The Sensory-Perceptual Examination reveals dense tactile sensory loss in the left upper extremity, mild binaural hearing loss, and dense left homonymous hemianopsia. There is left finger agnosia, agraphesthesia, and astereognosis with mild dextral impairment of tactile finger identification and graphesthesia. There was marked constructional dyspraxia in attempts to copy a Greek cross. Basic language skills were reasonably well preserved, although the patient called a clock a timer and then corrected himself spontaneously. The visual-field defect was seen in several items where he failed to read the left half of the stimulus array. The item "7 SIX 2" was first read as "6-2," and "see the black dog" was first read as "the dog." "Seven" was read as "even," and "he is a friendly animal, a famous winner of dog shows" was first read as "a friendly famous dog shows." The patient said that he had forgotten how to subtract on the item $85 - 27 = ?$. This probably reflects confusion of the spatial elements of the task rather than difficulty with the categorical structure of numbers or of the symbolic arithmetic operations per se. The patient read and copied the numbers correctly, and he recognized the operation as subtraction. His unwillingness or inability to attempt the task precludes detailed comment on the sort of difficulty he might display. Problems in carrying would be a likely component of errors made because of the spatial component involved with the task and the impairment of such skills with right-posterior lesions. This is borne out by the patient's error on the mental calculation $17 \times 3 = ?$. He gave his answer as 41 instead of 51. He was able to recall overlearned multiplication-table items without difficulty or error.

Seashore Rhythm Test performance is nearly random. The test is quite rapid, and it can easily confuse the patient with a short attention span, such as this man. Performance on the Speech-Sounds Perception Test, a left-temporal aural discrimination task, is only mildly impaired. This task is much slower, cues its items for the patient, and is mediated by his intact left cerebral hemisphere. It is reasonable that he should perform at a higher level on such a task, and he does so. The pattern of results is consistent with the laterality of the lesion and the patient's accessory psychiatric symptomology, particularly his depression.

Case 36

Background data. The patient is a 56-year-old, right-handed, married white male with 16 years of education. He works as an elementary-school teacher. The patient was experiencing a situational adjustment reaction in addition to the depressive phase of manic–depressive illness at the time of this examination. Referral was made for neuropsychological assessment to rule out an organic component to the syndrome.

Case Example _36_ Age _56_ Sex _M_ Education _16_ Handedness _R_

General Tests:

Category (errors) _90_ Trail-making: Part A _11_ Part B _80_

TPT: Total time _16.2_ Location _3_ Memory _7_

Motor and Sensory Tests:

Finger-tapping	R _52_ L _47_	Fingertip	
Finger agnosia	R _3_ L _4_	number-writing	R _0_ L _0_
Supressions:		Tactile form	
Visual	R _0_ L _2_	(time)	R _18_ L _20_
Tactile	R _0_ L _0_	(errors)	R _0_ L _0_
Auditory	R _2_ L _2_		

TPT: Time/Block R _.52_ L _.64_ Both _.46_

Cognitive Tests:

Speech-Sounds Perception

(errors) _8_   Rhythm (errors) _5_

WAIS: (scaled score)

Information	12	Picture completion	8
Comprehension	10	Picture arrangement	6
Vocabulary	11	Object assembly	7
Similarities	10	Block design	9
Arithmetic	8	Digit symbol	7
Digit span	10		

VIQ _105_   PIQ _100_   FSIQ _103_

Aphasia: None

Test results. The WAIS results show fairly consistent performance as reflected in the IQ scores and the subtest scatter. The verbal-
comprehension factor (I, C, S, V) shows no significant scatter and
suggests that the patient has always functioned near to his current
level. The long-term-memory items that are measured by many of the
items on these subtests show good preservation. The attentional factor
(A, D) shows mild decline on the concentration component (A), with
preservation of attention span (D). This is consistent with situational
anxiety. There is also mild impairment of foresight, planning, and
sequencing skill (PA) in comparison to performance on the remainder
of the perceptual-organization-factor subtests (BD, PA, OA), which
cluster near the mean for age. Cognitively this patient shows relatively
good performance for age.

Interpretation of the Halstead-Reitan Battery scores must be
made with caution, since the impairment index in this case appears to
be inflated by several borderline scores. Note that the TPT Location,
Seashore Rhythm, and Speech-Sounds Perception tests are each barely
into the impaired range. If one were to exclude those scores from the
index it would be within normal limits overall. This is one of the
features of an index based on cutoff scores that the interpreter of such
results must keep in mind. Borderline scores can over- or underestimate the degree of deficit greatly, as in this case. Level of performance
is the lowest level of inference, as Reitan has taught, and it is always
necessary to consider the means by which the subject arrived at a
given performance level; however, there are test patterns and specific
deficits which signal brain damage in this individual.

The Sensory–Perceptual Examination reveals inconsistent auditory suppressions in each ear with double simultaneous binaural
stimulation. The patient's response with monaural stimulation is
errorless. There are inconsistent left-visual suppressions with double
simultaneous stimulation above and at eye level. The binaural auditory
suppressions reflect bitemporal brain dysfunction with a probable
structural basis. The visual suppressions are also consistent with right-
temporal dysfunction. The Seashore Rhythm Test is a nonlateralized
temporal-lobe indicator and was performed at a marginally impaired
level. The performance on the Speech-Sounds Perception Test, a left-
temporal indicator, is also marginally impaired. Together these consistent results point to mild bitemporal-lobe disorder. There is mild
impairment of tactile finger recognition, with almost all errors confined
to the ring fingers of both hands. This is a common error, since the
ring and middle fingers are most often confused by normals without
neurological disorder. Graphesthesia and stereognosis are intact in

this individual. There was consistent right–left confusion, but examination for aphasic disturbance was noncontributory.

The patient's competence on motor tasks is generally intact. He shows normal tapping speed and an approximate 10 percent difference between the dominant and nondominant hands; however, there is a striking reversal of the normal practice effect from the first to the second trial of the Tactual Performance Test. The patient is able to complete the task with each hand, but the dominant left hand does not benefit from transfer of the performance experience of the right hand on the first trial. Note that the time with both hands on the third trial is also moderately slowed. The incidental recall of the task is marginally impaired on one measure (TPT Location). This performance occurs in the absence of tactile or other associated sensory deficit. This is an isolated deficit without support from the history for an inference of head trauma or focal disease. It occurs on a task which is lengthly and taxing to a depressed individual who has poor concentration skills, which may offer an explanation.

He solves the TPT task more efficiently, but he does not make normal progress compared to his first-trial performance. Compare this performance with the very fast speed of Trails A and the good time on Trails B. If a premotor deficit with organization of a complex motor program and sequencing of it were to account for the deficit, it would have to be seen on the Trail-making Test as well as on the TPT. This is not the case here. It is more parsimonious and consistent to attribute the TPT reversal to a fatigue effect than to a focal lesion.

The Category Test results are well into the impaired range and also require explanation. The inefficiency of learning with a trial-and-error strategy is reflected in this score.

The results are consistent with mild cerebral dysfunction that is differentiable from the patient's psychiatric disorder. There is selective loss of adaptive ability as noted above, and there is some indication of structural temporal-lobe involvement bilaterally.

Case 37

Background data. The patient is a 61-year-old, right-handed, married white male. He has a high-school education and works as an accountant. The psychiatric clinical diagnosis at the time of the examination was paranoid schizophrenia. The question of a supra-marginal gyrus lesion of the dominant hemisphere was raised by the referring psychiatrist. The workup was done on a clinical basis to evaluate this clinical question.

Case Example 37   Age 61   Sex M   Education 12   Handedness R

General Tests:

    Category (errors) 104   Trail-making: Part A 36   Part B 67

    TPT: Total time 24.4   Location 2   Memory 7

Motor and Sensory Tests:

Finger-tapping	R 45 L 42	Fingertip		
Finger agnosia	R 3 L 3	number-writing	R 0	L 0
Supressions:		Tactile form		
Visual	R 2 L 0	(time)	R 18	L 16
Tactile	R 0 L 0	(errors)	R 0	L 0
Auditory	R 0 L 0			

    TPT: Time/Block   R 2.0   L .70   Both .74

Cognitive Tests:

    Speech-Sounds Perception

    (errors)   ⁻7   Rhythm (errors)   4

    WAIS: (scaled score)

Information	11	Picture completion	10
Comprehension	10	Picture arrangement	7
Vocabulary	11	Object assembly	10
Similarities	12	Block design	12
Arithmetic	12	Digit symbol	9
Digit span	7		

              VIQ 107   PIQ 114   FSIQ 111

Aphasia: Dysnomia

Test results.   The WAIS verbal-comprehension factor (I, C, S, V) shows good intellectual potential and cognitive preservation in an individual with high-average intelligence (I, V). Capacity for insight and social judgment (C) is adequate for ability level, and abstraction ability (S) suggests efficient conceptual skills. There is significant decline in attention span (D) compared to concentration ability (A), although the patient's work as an accountant adds a very great deal of practice effect to the calculation tasks of the A subtest. The attention and concentration skills are probably better estimated from D alone in this case. That mild level of impairment is consistent with expectation in a situationally anxious and depressed individual. The perceptual-organization factor (PC, BD, PA, OA) shows more impressive cognitive inefficiency, with an outstandingly low acore on PA. The patient's visuopractic skills are adequate for age, but he shows some mild difficulty with anticipation of the likely consequences of his actions.

The impairment index for the Halstead-Reitan Battery somewhat underestimates the level of dysfunction in this case. In addition to the items that are clearly in the impaired range (Category Test, TPT total time, TPT Location, Finger-tapping Test–rigbt hand) there are the Seashore Rhythm and Speech-Sounds Perception scores that verge on the brain-dysfunctional range. There is thus a more generalized quality to the impairment than the borderline impairment index would suggest.

The Sensory–Perceptual Examination is remarkable for two suppressions of the right upper visual quadrant, which indicates dysfunction in the temporal portion of the optic radiations of the left hemisphere. There was consistent confusion of the third and fourth fingers of each hand, but these errors are common in normals. Binaural hearing loss precluded examination for auditory suppression. Stereognosis and graphesthesia were within normal limits. The Aphsia Screening Test was remarkable for one naming error, in which the patient called a triangle a diamond.

Tapping speed was mildly slowed bimanually. The difference in tapping speed between the hands is within normal limits. The Tactual Performance Test, however, shows a consistently deviant performance. On the first trial with the dominant right hand the patient could complete only half of the task in the usual 10-minute time period. On the second trial he completes the test. The performance on the third trial is a bit slower than that on the second trial. The patient haphazardly works until he chances upon the solution principle, but he does not recognize it as such when he discovers it. The patient is disorganized, suggesting mild, generalized cerebral dysfunction that affects performance less dramatically when the test task is relatively brief. Those items that require sustained attention, effort, and concentration show reversion to a trial-and-error strategy and loss of an active problem-solving set. This may be related in part to the patient's psychotic disturbance. In regard to the referral question of a supramarginal gyrus lesion, these results do not provide supportive evidence. There is a patient in this case series who has such a lesion bilaterally on the basis of a head injury. The resultant syndrome of the dominant-hemisphere inferior parietal lobule (supramarginal and angular gyri) is alexia with agraphia. No such symptoms were noted in this individual.

Case 38

Background data.   The patient is a 26-year-old, right-handed, married black male with 12 years of education. He formerly worked as a job developer. The history is remarkable for a severe head injury which the patient suffered when he was thrown from his motorcycle while traveling at high speed. He was wearing a crash helmet. He struck the left side of his head when he hit the ground and suffered a depressed skull fracture with a contusion of the left inferior temporal gyrus and a massive subdural hematoma. The lesion was subtemporally decompressed, and the contusion was debrided. The acute subdural hematoma was evacuated of an estimated 100–120 cc of clotted blood in the site of the injury to the left hemisphere. Neurosurgical care was obtained on the day of injury. By the time of the neuropsychological examination the patient had spontaneously regained relatively intact speech function—the inferior angle of the blow to the head spared the perisylvian speech zone. There was an incomplete left homonymous hemianopsia, paresis of the third, fourth, and seventh cranial nerves on the left, and paraparesis which was improving with physical therapy. The patient was given the WAIS 7 months after his injury. That evaluation showed a verbal IQ of 82, a performance IQ of 68, and a full-scale IQ of 75. The results reported below were obtained in a followup evaluation of the patient's neuropsychological status as part of an assessment of his vocational rehabilitation potential 13 months after his injury.

Case Example __38__ Age __26__ Sex __M__ Education __12__ Handedness __R__

General Tests:

Category (errors) __58__ Trail-making: Part A __154__ Part B __184__

TPT: Total time __28.6__ Location __1__ Memory __6__

Motor and Sensory Tests:

Finger-tapping	R __59__ L __36__	Fingertip	
Finger agnosia	R __3__ L __3__	number-writing	R __0__ L __0__

Supressions:

Tactile form

			(time)	R __18__ L __18__
Visual	R __0__ L __0__	(errors)	R __0__ L __0__
Tactile	R __0__ L __0__		
Auditory	R __0__ L __0__		

TPT: Time/Block R __2.5__ L __2.1__ Both __.86__

Cognitive Tests:

Speech-Sounds Perception

(errors) __9__   Rhythm (errors) __12__

WAIS: (scaled score)

Information	__6__	Picture completion	__6__
Comprehension	__9__	Picture arrangement	__9__
Vocabulary	__8__	Object assembly	__4__
Similarities	__8__	Block design	__9__
Arithmetic	__12__	Digit symbol	__7__
Digit span	__9__		

VIQ __91__   PIQ __81__   FSIQ __86__

Aphasia: Dysnomia, dyslexia (related to visual deficit), dysarthria. Left Homonymous Hemianopsia

Test results.   The patient shows low–average ability in the verbal realm overall. The relatively higher V than I subtest pattern suggests a history of school difficulty in a man with access to a limited range of concepts and ideas that he can express verbally. Capacity for social judgment is remarkably good, and this was readily apparent in extended therapeutic contacts with the patient over a period of a year or more. The low score on S is consistent with the primary left-temporal site of the cerebral contusion, but the rapid neurosurgical care led to an excellent recovery of function in this area. Attention span (D) is intact as is the patient's concentration ability (A) (which underwent improvement during his rehabilitation course). Visual–motor coordination and spatial perception (DS, BD) are slightly impaired.

A remarkable feature of the WAIS results is the lower score on the performance scale as compared with the verbal scale. This is a very important clue to the mechanism of injury. It is also consistent with the presence of a left homonymous visual-field defect even though the gross-force head injury and subdural hematoma occurred on the left side of the head. The major damage indicated by these findings, however, is to the right side of the brain. In previous head-injury cases presented in this series a point has been made of the contrecoup injury mechanism, in which the major effect of injury is often in a mirror-opposite position from the primary site of the injury. This man's residual brain dysfunction occurred not so much from the direct blow and wound to his left temporal lobe as from the pressure caused by the massive blood clot between his skull and the left side of his brain. The subdural hematoma pressed the right side of his brain against the right inner table of his skull and caused the major symptoms of brain damage. The brain is able to compress to some degree, and there is a potential for partial sparing of function in a young person such as this if the direct pressure against an immovable obstacle such as the skull can be surgically removed. The pressure effect can cause ischemic effects and neuronal damage from the direct pressure effects themselves. There is edematous swelling of the brain as a whole after a severe injury such as this, which also increases the pressure effects and the level of generalized residual dysfunction.

The preservation of nonverbal abstraction noted on the BD subtest of the WAIS is seen in the remarkably mild level of impairment on the Category Test, which is just into the mildly impaired range of brain dysfunction. Given the severity of the injury, this is an amazingly good performance, graphically illustrating the principle of brain function plasticity and recovery potential of brain function in young persons such as this.

The Sensory–Perceptual Examination was remarkable for a left homonymous hemianopsia which presented an oblique loss of the visual field. The loss was greatest above eye level and least below eye level. This is consistent with an inference of greatest damage to right-temporal-lobe fibers of the optic radiation and less pressure on the right-parietal-lobe fibers, as would be expected from the massive hematoma in the left inferior temporal area of the brain. Note that there was no visual-field loss in the right homonymous visual hemifields, even though the primary injury was directly to the left side of the brain. The major deficit-producing lesion, however, was the displaced pressure effect transmitted through the brain substance rather than the direct lesion itself. There was some confusion of the ring finger of each hand with the middle finger, but this is a common error, even in normals. No disturbance of tactile sensation, graphesthesia, or stereognosis was found. Audition was intact, and there were no suppressions with double simultaneous auditory or tactile stimulation.

The Aphasia Screening Test was remarkable for word-finding difficulty and reading errors related to the visual-field defect. The patient was shown a picture of a square and asked to name it. He replied "Rect . . . tri . . . rectangle." He called a cross a "four-corner square" and a triangle a "point," after which he corrected himself. He read 7-SIX-2 as "6-2" at first because of the visual-field defect. He also read "he is a friendly animal, a famous winner of dog shows" as "friendly, famous," after which he was shown how to look at the rest of the array, whereupon he read the item correctly. He mispronounced "Episcopal" as "epitatal" and then as "episokiddle" in an attempt to correct his error.

Examination of motor performance shows a pronounced difference in speed of motor output on the Finger-tapping Test with the two hands. Speed with the dominant right hand is superior, while that with the left hand is 39 percent slower. This is four times the difference in speed that is normally expected between hands. It is another indication of the much greater dysfunction of the right hemisphere in this man due to the displaced pressure effects that compressed his right cerebral hemisphere against his right hemicranium. There is bimanual impairment of more complex motor problem solving on the Tactual Performance Test. The patient made modest progress from the first TPT trial to the second, but he continued to show marked impairment with inability to complete the task within the allotted time limits. Fifteen minutes were allowed with each hand individually as a testing-the-limits procedure, and this resulted in six blocks placed with the right hand and seven blocks placed with the left hand. Reitan (unpublished manuscript) has noted that patients accomplish in 15 minutes essentially what they can accomplish with unlimited time on any given trial.

This patient recovered his ability to walk with assistance, and he returned to his wife and family to be followed on an outpatient basis for additional physical therapy at a VA facility near his home. His case illustrates the plasticity of brain functions in the young and the recovery potential of young head-trauma victims as well as an unusual mechanism of head injury.

Case 39

Background data. The patient is a 54-year-old, right-handed, divorced white male with 10 years of education. He was medically disabled and unemployed at the time of this examination. The history is remarkable for a cerebrovascular accident in the distribution of the right posterior cerebral artery. A computer-tomographic brain scan confirmed the presence of low-density areas in the right medial occipital and right medial temporal areas. The lesion was associated with a left homonymous visual-field defect and short-term-memory difficulty. Neuropsychological evaluation was requested by the neurologist managing the case as an aid to assessment of the patient's residual cognitive strengths and deficits.

Case Example 39   Age 54   Sex M   Education 10   Handedness R

General Tests:

Category (errors) 119   Trail-making: Part A 121 Part B 513

TPT: Total time 30   Location 0   Memory 6

Motor and Sensory Tests:

Finger-tapping   R 20   L 19   Fingertip

Finger agnosia   R 0   L 0   number-writing   R 0   L 10

Supressions: Tactile form

Visual   R 0   L 0   (time)   R 19   L 22

Tactile   R 0   L 0   (errors) R 0   L 0

Auditory R 0   L 0

TPT: Time/Block R 2.5 L 3.3 Both 2.0

Cognitive Tests:

Speech-Sounds Perception

(errors)   _16_   Rhythm (errors)   _10_

WAIS: (scaled score)

Information   9   Picture completion   6

Comprehension   9   Picture arrangement   7

Vocabulary   13   Object assembly   6

Similarities   11   Block design   4

Arithmetic   10   Digit symbol   6

Digit span   10

VIQ 104   PIQ 84   FSIQ 95

Aphasia: Left-right confusion, dyscalculia

Test results. There is a 20-point discrepancy between the patient's verbal and performance IQ scores that highlights his right-
hemispheric cognitive dysfunction. The performance IQ score below
the average level should suggest to the observant examiner that there
may be nonverbal cognitive loss in the presence of average-level left-
hemisphere verbal functioning. A similar difference between the scores
would probably be of less clinical significance in most cases if both of
these scores were 15 IQ points higher. It is not so much the absolute
level of performance as the range of adaptive abilities affected that
should be noted. An average score in a very superior subject indicates
probable deficit, whereas it does not suggest this if all scores cluster
at an average level. In this individual subaverage scores suggest
impairment of basic adaptive abilities and require explanation.

The verbal-comprehension factor (I, C, S, V) still shows significant subtest scatter after age correction. The range of concepts and
ideas that this man has mastered from personal experience and training
(V) is greater than his fund of formal background information (I)
because the patient is undereducated for his ability level. Capacity for
insight and practical social judgment is barely adequate for ability
level, but the patient should be able to manage his personal affairs
with commonsense efficiency. His abstraction and conceptualization
capacity (S) is consistent with the findings on V that suggest high-
average native ability. Attentional-factor subtests (A, D) show intact

concentration ability (A) and attention span (D). Note that there is suppression of the perceptual-organization-factor subtests (PC, BD, PA, OA), but there is relative sparing of PA and OA. The patient's approach to OA was a piecemeal strategy in which he analyzed the internal details of the figures without an overall plan of what the final figure would be until he had almost completed it. This suggests left-hemispheric information processing to compensate for the right-hemispheric dysfunction. The sparing of PA relative to BD is consistent with the more posterior location of the primary occipital lesion of the cerebral cortex. Recall that PA is sensitive to right-anteriotemporal functioning, while BD is sensitive to right-parietal functioning. If PA is higher than BD, a more posterior lesion is suggested; if the reverse is true, a more anterior lesion is likely. There is also infarction in the right temporal lobe, but this is in the medial portion of the lobe, where there is a primary effect on the memory functions of the hippocampus and other adjacent structures. There is thus sparing of the foresight and planning functions that are dependent upon the right-anteriotemporal-convexity portion of the cortex.

The Aphasia Screening Test is remarkable for mild right–left confusion and a minor carrying error on mental calculation. As expected with a right-hemisphere lesion locus, speech functions are unaffected. Tbe Sensory-Perceptual Examination reveals the left homonymous visual-field defect as noted by the neurologist. There is right-side hearing loss, so that testing for auditory suppression could not be done. Tactile sensation is intact, and there is no suppression with double simultaneous tactile stimulation. There is dysgraphesthesia of the left hand only. Stereognosis is intact bimanually.

Motor examination shows bimanual slowing on the Finger-tapping test, a simple motor-speed measure. There is inefficient visual search and slowed motor output on both parts of the Trail-making Test. These motor deficits are present on more complex tasks as well, such as the Tactual Performance Test, where the level of performance remains quite poor throughout the task. The performance on tapping appears to be due to lowered energy level, since there is no lateralized motor deficit and since the motor portions of the cortex are not affected in this individual. The poor performance on the TPT and the Trail-making Test are consistent wiht a trial-and-error approach to the task, which appears to be independent of visual cueing. The Trail-making Test is a visually guided task, while TPT is not. A similar pattern of trial-and-error responding characterized the performance on the Category Test. A variety of other indicators show moderate deficit but are noncontributory to a focal analysis of the lesion.

Case 40

Background data. The patient is a 33-year-old, right-handed, married Filipino-American male who is employed as an Army clerk. He has a high-school education. His medical history is remarkable for neurosurgical removal of a third ventricular craniopharyngioma by means of a transcallosal approach reached via right-frontal craniotomy. The operative report records the neurosurgeon's impression that "the tumor was large, certainly bigger than a hen's egg." The current set of test results were obtained on a preoperative basis.

Case Example 40 Age 33 Sex M Education 12 Handedness R

General Tests:

Category (errors) 61 Trail-making: Part A 36 Part B 95

TPT: Total time 26.6 Location 5 Memory 8

Motor and Sensory Tests:

Finger-tapping R 44 L 38   Fingertip

Finger agnosia R 1 L 1   number-writing R 2 L 6

Supressions: Tactile form

Visual   R 0 L 0   (time)   R 18 L 20

Tactile R 0 L 0   (errors) R 0 L 0

Auditory R 0 L 0

TPT: Time/Block R 1.4 L 1.0 Both .26

Cognitive Tests:

Speech-Sounds Perception

(errors) 10   Rhythm (errors) 14

WAIS: (scaled score)

Information	6	Picture completion	10
Comprehension	9	Picture arrangement	7
Vocabulary	9	Object assembly	9
Similarities	7	Block design	5
Arithmetic	8	Digit symbol	12
Digit span	9		

VIQ 87 PIQ 91 FSIQ 88

Aphasia: Mild construction dyspraxia.

Test results. The WAIS results show a low-average level of performance overall, but the patient learned English as a second language in school as a child. He speaks Tagalog as his first language, but he is now very fluent and articulate in English, and he evidences excellent English comprehension. His relatively lower scores on the verbal scale thus reflect a somewhat lower level of performance than his estimated average native-ability level because of cultural-item content bias and lesser exposure to this information than a native-born American. This is not uncommonly seen in a public hospital population which has a good many persons who have experienced cultural disadvantagement. The relative subtest patterns are still valid, but the level of performance is doubtless suppressed to some degree in this individual. It is wise to keep in mind such bias that is inherent in the test item content for a multicultural and multilingual patient such as this man. One does not want to attribute to organic deficit performance decrement associated with such cultural factors.

Consideration of the verbal-comprehension factor (I, C, S, V) shows a relative lack of Americanized formal background information (I) but good ability to think and conceptualize in English (V). There is also appreciation of conventional Western cultural proverbs, platitudes, and social conventions as well as adequate intellectual capacity for putting these principles to effective practical use (C). The attentional-factor subtests (A, D) show adequate concentration ability (A) and attention span (D) for measured ability level and are comparable with each other. The perceptual-organization factor (PC, BD, PA, OA), in contrast, shows outstanding deficit on the PA and BD subtests. There is not a significant difference between these subtests, which are sensitive to anterior (PA) and posterior (BD) right-hemisphere functioning. There is thus reason to suspect serious right-hemisphere decline from an average level, as suggested by PC, which is relatively insensitive to the effects of cerebral dysfunction. The possibility of cultural bias must be kept in mind with the PA items, but the performance on C suggests that an average score could be expected from this individual.

Motor examination shows tapping speed which is bimanually slowed to a mild degree. The expected approximate 10 percent superiority of speed with the dominant hand is maintained. The patient was allowed to complete the Tactual Performance Test with each hand individually, and each unimanual performance took approximately twice the normal time limit. Performance on the final TPT trial was excellent, since the patient was able to anchor each identified space with one hand while he used the other hand to search for the matching block. Sensory examination was remarkable for right-side dysgraphesthesia and for bilateral hearing loss with right greater than left. The remaining sensory findings were within normal limits. The TPT performance decrement in the absence of sensory disturbance is consistent with bilateral premotor-area dysfunction. There were no frank aphasic errors, but spelling difficulty and aural discrimination errors were made ("sqare" for "square," "shall" for "shouted"), which could be culturally/linguistically based. A carrying error on the written subtraction problem $85 - 27 = ?$ resulted in the response 48 instead of 58. The categorical structure of number and symbolic arithmetic operations dependent upon tertiary parietal functioning of the left hemisphere were intact. The more complex mental calculation $17 \times 3 = ?$ was correctly answered as 51. There was also mild construction dyspraxia in an attempt to copy a Greek cross.

Results of the Finger-tapping, TPT, and Category tests in combination suggest a forebrain-dysfunction syndrome with sparing of posterior-hemispheric function. The prefrontal (Category), premotor (TPT), and sensorimotor (Finger-tapping) areas are involved. There is also evidence for anteriotemporal dysfunction from the Seashore Rhythm Test and Speech-Sounds Perception Test performances. The Seashore Rhythm Test, a nonlateralized temporal-lobe indicator, shows a performance level that approaches the random level (13 errors made; 15 errors is the chance level). The Speech-Sounds Perception Test, a left-temporal indicator, is also mildly impaired. The neuropsychometric data are consistent with the known lesion locus, and the effects are bilateral, as would be expected with a midline lesion which exerted pressure effects once it achieved large size in the small third ventricular space.

Case 41

Background data. This patient is a 23-year-old male with 15 years of education who was attending college at the time of the neuropsychological testing. The patient was self-referred because of development of vague problems which appeared to be interfering with his college performance. After the neuropsychological examination was completed, the patient was referred to a neurologist, who concurred with the general conclusions. Attempts were made to control the patient's condition without surgery, although surgery was later found to be necessary.

Case Example __41__ Age __23__ Sex __M__ Education __15__ Handedness __R__

General Tests:

Category (errors) __−__ Trail-making: Part A __38__ Part B __72__

TPT: Total time __8.3__ Location __5__ Memory __8__

Motor and Sensory Tests:

Finger-tapping	R __49__	L __44__	Fingertip
Finger agnosia	R __0__	L __0__	number-writing R __0__ L __0__

Supressions:

Tactile form

Visual	R __0__	L __0__	(time) R __12__ L __14__
Tactile	R __0__	L __0__	(errors) R __0__ L __0__
Auditory	R __0__	L __0__	

TPT: Time/Block R __.5__ L __.25__ Both __.08__

Cognitive Tests:

Speech-Sounds Perception

(errors) __14__   Rhythm (errors) __8__

WAIS: (scaled score)

Information	__10__	Picture completion	__8__
Comprehension	__14__	Picture arrangement	__13__
Vocabulary	__11__	Object assembly	__12__
Similarities	__12__	Block design	__11__
Arithmetic	__7__	Digit symbol	__10__
Digit span	__11__		

VIQ __105__   PIQ __104__   FSIQ __105__

Aphasia: Spelling (square, triangle, clock);
dyscalculia; right-left confusion

Test results. On the whole, the general measures of brain damage were performed well. Brain-damaged performance occurred on only two of the six tests given that make up the impairment index. The Speech and Rhythm tests contribute to an Impairment Index of 0.3. The Location score was just within the normal range at 5; however, it would appear to be impaired when compared with the Memory score of 8. As the Category Test was not given, the impairment index must be loosely interpreted.

Significant neuropsychological deficits existed in three major groupings. Auditory-perceptual problems were suggested by the Speech-Sounds and Rhythm deficits. Tactile perceptual problems were demonstrated by a relative deficit on the right-hand trial of the TPT. Concomitant spatial difficulties related to tactile perception were indicated by the relative Location score deficit. Finally, dysphasic symptoms occurred which seem related to the auditory and tactile perceptual problems. The spelling dyspraxia indicates an inability to sound out complex words; this is likely due to phonetic problems as a result of the deficits in phonetic hearing on the Speech test. The tactile-perceptual deficits interfere with fine motor control and distinguishing of body sides and parts, which accounts for the dysgraphia and ideational dyspraxia. Finally, the dyscalculia is a manifestation of subtle spatial difficulties which often accompany tertiary temporal–parietal–occipital injuries.

Certain strengths are important to note. No deficit was seen on the Trail-making Test, which indicates a lack of serious or diffuse damage. Also no lateralized or level-of-performance deficits are seen on the simple motor and sensory measures. This result argues strongly against injury to the motor and sensory strip.

A highly localized yet mild lesion seems to be represented in this profile. There are simple auditory perceptual deficits which implicate the left-temporal-lobe or the immediate surrounding areas (Speech and Rhythm test deficits). These deficits are accompanied by mild dysphasic signs that localize to the same general area (spelling dyspraxia and dysgraphia). The only other deficits are the right-hand trial and the Location score of the TPT, which may indicate a tertiary temporoparietooccipital-area involvement. Together these two foci (secondary temporal lobe and the tertiary juncture), since they are adjacent, suggest a highly localized lesion.

The lesion does not have widespread effects. Consequently, the Trail-making Test is performed well within normal limits, and a relatively low impairment index of 0.3 is earned. A localized lesion with a relatively mild overall profile suggests three etiological possibilities. An old trauma in which the acute coup and milder contrecoup deficits have disappeared is a distinct possibility. Two features of the present profile, however, do not fit such an interpretation. First, the presence of deficits such as the dysphasic symptoms are inconsistent with the hypothesis of a chronic problem in such a mild injury. Second, the present lesion is highly localized, a finding which is uncommon in trauma injuries where a blow to the head more diffusely affects the site of injury.

The second possibility is an extrinsic tumor. Such a lesion creates a localized profile affecting the area of the brain directly below the tumor. Again, two aspects of the present profile make this possibility unlikely. An impairment index of 0.3 is too low for an extrinsic tumor, which typically yields an index in the range of 0.5–0.6. Also, the young age of the patient argues against the possibility of a neoplasm. These two considerations, however, only decrease the likelihood of an extrinsic tumor and do not completely rule out such an eventuality.

Given the age of the person and the location and the severity of the lesion, perhaps the most likely etiology is a congenital vascular anomaly. This lesion is a result of the blood vessels tangling together as they are formed, which results in a strained vascularity that can develop symptoms early in life. Neuropsychologically, the symptoms appear much as an aneurysm with a highly localized and mild yet acute picture.

Case 42

Background data. The patient was a 16-year-old male in a special-education program who was evaluated for vocational rehabilitation. The patient's history indicated a lifelong pattern of dysfunction.

Case Example __42__ Age __16__ Sex __M__ Education __10__ Handedness __R__

General Tests:

Category (errors)__58__ Trail-making: Part A __58__ Part B __125__

TPT: Total time _____ Location __0__ Memory __8__

Motor and Sensory Tests:

Finger-tapping	R __46__ L __45__	Fingertip	
Finger agnosia	R __0__ L __0__	number-writing	R __4__ L __5__

Supressions:

Tactile form

Visual	R __0__ L __0__	(time)	R __14__ L __16__
Tactile	R __0__ L __0__	(errors)	R __0__ L __0__
Auditory	R __0__ L __0__		

TPT: Time/Block R __.61__ L __.55__ Both __.41__

Cognitive Tests:

Speech-Sounds Perception

(errors) __4__   Rhythm (errors) __6__

WAIS: (scaled score)

Information	__3__	Picture completion	__7__
Comprehension	__7__	Picture arrangement	__10__
Vocabulary	__5__	Object assembly	__6__
Similarities	__6__	Block design	__6__
Arithmetic	__7__	Digit symbol	__9__
Digit span	__5__		

VIQ __79__   PIQ __86__   FSIQ __81__

Aphasia:

Naming (cross, triangle); spelling (triangle); reading (#16); body positioning (#31,32)

Test results.   The full-scale IQ indicates a dull-normal to border-line level of intelligence. Some variation between the VIQ and the PIQ may represent the effects of a brain lesion, in which case a higher potential level of intelligence may have existed. An impairment index of 0.7 is earned, although this estimate may be somewhat elevated. In looking at the individual scores making up this index one can determine that only mild deficit is present on four of the five measures. The TPT Location measure is the only severely disrupted score. The Category Test, the TPT total time, and the Finger-tapping and Rhythm tests all fall just within the brain-damaged range of performance. Despite the severe numerical rating, then, the impairment index actually represents only moderate impairment.

Basic sensory measures, including the Finger Agnosia and suppression tests, show no neuropsychological deficit. Complex sensory disruption is seen on the Fingertip Number-writing Test, although no significant lateralizing signs are present. Some motor dysfunction is present, although inconsistent lateralizing indications are provided. The Finger-tapping and Grip Strength tests demonstrate right-body deficits in motor speed and strength, which suggests left hemisphere dysfunction; however the TPT left-hand trial, in comparison with the right-hand measure, suggests right-hemisphere injury. The motor and sensory results together therefore do not provide consistently lateralized deficits. The indications include either no brain-related dysfunction or diffuse, nonlateralized injury.

Considerable cognitive deficits are also apparent on both the left- and the right-hemisphere tasks. Naming, reading, and spelling problems are largely indicative of left-hemisphere dysfunction. This focus is supported by the VIQ–PIQ difference and the deficit on Trails B; however, there is no difficulty present on the Speech Test.

Right-hemisphere dysfunction is indicated by the Rhythm Test deficit and the spatial problems on BD and OA. Likewise, the deficit on the TPT Location score in relation to the Memory scale suggests spatial difficulties in support of the BD and OA deficits and right-hemisphere dysfunction.

The relation between Trails A and Trails B suggests damage to both hemispheres, since each is approximately equally impaired. The errors on the Aphasia Test that involve body positioning also do not suggest any specific lateralized lesion. In all, the data is consistent with a diagnosis of diffuse brain damage.

Case 43

Background data. This 18-year-old male was referred for a neuropsychological examination in an attempt to identify his current level of neuropsychological skills. As with Case 42, the patient had evidenced a lifelong pattern of neuropsychological dysfunction stemming from an unknown cause.

Case Example 43 Age 18 Sex M Education SEd8 Handedness R

General Tests:

Category (errors) 127 Trail-making: Part A 240 Part B 300 disc.

TPT: Total time _____ Location 0 Memory 8

Motor and Sensory Tests:

Finger-tapping R 38.2 L 37.8 Fingertip

Finger agnosia R 6 L 0 number-writing R 1 L 1

Supressions: Tactile form

Visual R 0 L 0 (time) R 18 L 20

Tactile R 0 L 0 (errors) R 0 L 0

Auditory R 0 L 0

TPT: Time/Block R .61 L 2.5 Both .98

Cognitive Tests:

Speech-Sounds Perception

(errors) 12 Rhythm (errors) 9

WAIS: (scaled score)

Information	2	Picture completion	6
Comprehension	2	Picture arrangement	3
Vocabulary	1	Object assembly	6
Similarities	6	Block design	6
Arithmetic	2	Digit symbol	7
Digit span	4		

VIQ 60 PIQ 72 FSIQ 63

Aphasia: Spelling & drawing (square, cross,
triangle); naming (triangle; reading
(letters, numbers, words); pronunciation
(#19,20; writing (#24); calculation (#24,
26); ideational dyspraxia (#32)

Test results. Mental-defective functioning is seen on both the full-scale IQ and the verbal IQ. The only deficit prominent on the performance section involves the Picture Arrangement subtest, where complex visual-analysis problem-solving skills are required and a large verbal component is tested.

The WAIS suggests a brain injury which probably occurred before school age. Congenital retardation is unlikely in view of the variability on the WAIS, which indicates discrete neuropsychological deficiencies due to brain damage. For the same reason the variability in the WAIS subtest performance makes a diffuse injury unlikely.

A 0.86 impairment index is earned, with the only good performance occurring on the TPT Memory score. Several measures of the index are severely impaired. The Category Test and the TPT total time and Location measures demonstrate the severity of the 0.86 impairment rating, while only moderate disruption is seen on the Finger-tapping, Speech-Sounds, and Seashore Rhythm tests. The high impairment rating and the three measures which show extreme dysfunction indicate a highly destructive lesion. The variability in performance of the individual measures suggests either a focal lesion or a diffuse lesion in which certain areas of involvement are more severely affected.

Motor and sensory dysfunction is seen with conflicting lateralizing indications. The Finger-tapping and Finger Agnosia measures both indicate lateralized involvement of the left hemisphere. The TPT and one auditory suppression, however, demonstrate right-hemisphere dysfunction. The Grip Strength Test and the Fingertip Number-writing Test also show mild deficit. The Grip Strength results support weakly the right hemisphere dysfunction, while the Fingertip Number-writing results do not lateralize.

No strong lateralized deficits arise from the cognitive test comparisons. The Trail-making Tests are severely disrupted, and it is difficult to determine which is more severely impaired. The Trails A score almost equals the Trails B score, although part B was discontinued because the person was unable to understand the test or became too confused to maintain the solution plan. The Speech and Rhythm tests are only moderately disrupted, however, indicating no particular lateralized deficit, although the Rhythm test may be slightly more impaired.

Severe dysphasia is present, which implicates the left hemisphere more than the right hemisphere, although both hemispheres are probably involved in the deficit. The wide-ranging nature of the deficits manifest on the Aphasia Test point strongly to left-hemisphere dysfunction. Naming deficits in combination with severe spelling problems and writing, reading, and pronunciation difficulties are largely indicative of left parietal-lobe dysfunction. The drawing, calculation, and ideational dyspraxia signs may be indicative of either left- or right-hemisphere injury.

Brain-damaged performance is evident on the entire neuropsychological profile, although the question of congenital retardation versus acquired brain lesion is difficult to answer. The mental-defective range of functioning seen on the WAIS implies that lowered neuropsychological performance should be expected. In fact, the severely affected tests include those measures which entail complex cognitive tasks (Category, TPT). Tests such as Speech and Rhythm that do not require problem-solving skills but instead test basic perceptual abilities are not as severely disrupted.

While mental retardation can account for several other deficits, at least those involving complex cognitive abilities, there are several other deficits which are less attributable to the low intellectual level of congenital mental retardation. For example, the motor and sensory deficits (especially the auditory suppression) suggest an acquired lesion and one that involves tissue destruction. The extensive dysphasia supports this contention in suggesting specific neuropsychological deficits rather than the general lowered level of intellectual function concomitant with mental retardation.

Are there indications, then, of a localized brain lesion? The motor/sensory findings suggest specific areas of dysfunction, although both the right and left hemispheres are implicated. Likewise, the cognitive-test comparisons do not suggest any specific area of impairment. The dysphasia demonstrates damage to the temporal-parietal area of the left hemisphere, although this confined area of damage is not suggested by other deficits. If this area were acutely and exclusively dysfunctional, the TPT and Fingertip Number-writing Test should show accompanying deficits.

As the deficit picture stands, there are indications of dysfunction all over the brain. The motor/sensory strip and left temporal-parietal area are mentioned above. The left frontal lobe is suggested by the severe Category Test deficit. Right temporal lobe involvement is suggested by the auditory suppression, the Rhythm and Picture Arrangement deficits. The conclusion must be that diffuse brain damage exists with a spotty deficit pattern that indicates an old and static injury, probably dating from birth.

Case 44

Background data. This is a 38-year-old male who recently showed increasing signs of anxiety marked by "memory problems" and several vague complaints about headaches and "pressure on the brain." The patient was referred to determine if any signs of an organic lesion existed.

Case Example __44__ Age __38__ Sex __M__ Education __14__ Handedness __R__

General Tests:

Category (errors) __48__ Trail-making: Part A __27__ Part B __50__

TPT: Total time _____ Location __7__ Memory __10__

Motor and Sensory Tests:

Finger-tapping   R__56__ L __52__   Fingertip

Finger agnosia   R __0__ L __0__   number-writing R __0__ L __0__

Supressions: Tactile form

Visual   R __0__ L __0__   (time)   R __12__ L __14__

Tactile   R __0__ L __0__   (errors)   R __0__ L __0__

Auditory   R __0__ L __0__

TPT: Time/Block   R __.35__ L __.30__ Both __.10__

Cognitive Tests:

Speech-Sounds Perception

(errors) __5__   Rhythm (errors) __2__

WAIS: (scaled score)

Information __9__   Picture completion __14__

Comprehension __14__   Picture arrangement __10__

Vocabulary __13__   Object assembly __12__

Similarities __9__   Block design __10__

Arithmetic __7__   Digit symbol __11__

Digit span __12__

VIQ __104__   PIQ __114__   FSIQ __109__

Aphasia: None

Test results.   Overall, a normal intellectual level of functioning is suggested by the WAIS. A 10-point difference between the VIQ and the PIQ scores alerts one to the possibility of a brain-related deficit in verbal functions. Generally, bright-normal scores are seen on the performance subtests, with little variation between the individual measures. The verbal subtests, however, demonstrate bright-normal scores on the better-performed measures, while three subtests show deficiencies at least three scale score points below the mean performance of the bright-normal verbal subtests.

An impairment index of 0.0 is earned. None of the impairment-index measures fall into the brain-damaged range. Such a rating argues strongly against the likelihood of a brain lesion.

Motor and sensory tests demonstrate no brain-related deficits. The Finger-tapping Test shows motor speed to be well within normal limits of expected performance. Likewise, sensory abilities are adequately demonstrated. The Finger Agnosia, Fingertip Number-writing, and suppression tests show no errors on either hand. The TPT overall scores are within normal limits, as are the ratios among the right-hand, left-hand, and both-hands trials. The left-hand trial is not quite as quickly performed as would be expected given the right-hand score; however, the ratio does not seem to be clinically significant.

Other than the WAIS deficits, no cognitive dysfunction is seen. The general tests on the impairment index as well as the Trail-Making test (parts A and B) are adequately performed without exception. No dysphasia is present on either the left- or right-hemisphere tasks.

Clear deficits on the WAIS are indicators of brain damage. There are several important points which argue against a brain injury, however. First, within the WAIS results themselves the generally sensitive subtests (Digit Symbol, Digit Span) are not dysfunctional. In a lesion which is as severe as the verbal deficits suggest it is uncommon for the generally sensitive tests to be so well performed unless the injury is chronic with much of the original dysfunction recovered. Despite the large VIQ–PIQ difference, a chronic injury is a distinct possibility, and other parts of the profile must be examined to determine this person's neuropsychological status.

In looking at the remaining neuropsychological tests it becomes apparent that a significant brain lesion does not exist. The 0.0 impairment index indicates the unlikeliness of a brain injury. Combine this result with the lack of any motor or sensory dysfunction and the possibility of a cerebral lesion becomes even more remote. The most likely diagnosis, therefore, is normal.

Case 45

Background data. This 54-year-old right-handed man was a truck driver who suffered a severe head injury 18 months prior to the testing. Neuropsychological testing was requested to evaluate how much chronic loss there was in the case and—for legal purposes—the degree that this was consistent with the patient's history of head trauma.

Case Example __45__ Age __54__ Sex __M__ Education __11__ Handedness __R__

General Tests:

    Category (errors) __65__ Trail-making: Part A __54"__ Part B __107"__

    TPT: Total time _____ Location __4__ Memory __6__
                 __24'49"__

Motor and Sensory Tests:

Finger-tapping	R __51.8__ L __43.4__	Fingertip
Finger agnosia	R __0__ L __0__	number-writing R __0__ L __0__

    Supressions: Tactile form

        Visual   R __0__   L __0__   (time)   R __18__ L __20__

        Tactile   R __0__   L __0__   (errors)   R __1__   L __0__

        Auditory   R __0__   L __0__

    TPT: Time/Block   R __3.33__ L __.95__   Both __.53__

Cognitive Tests:

    Speech-Sounds Perception

     (errors)   __15__   Rhythm (errors)   __6__

    WAIS: (scaled score)

Information	__9__	Picture completion	__11__
Comprehension	__10__	Picture arrangement	__6__
Vocabulary	__12__	Object assembly	__10__
Similarities	__11__	Block design	__9__
Arithmetic	__10__	Digit symbol	__9__
Digit span	__11__		

         VIQ __105__   PIQ __105__   FSIQ __105__

Aphasia: Spelling (square, triangle); naming
      (cross); calculation (#26); drawing
      (key); ideational dyspraxia

Test results. Normal intellectual functioning is seen on all three IQ measures. No VIQ–PIQ difference exists; however, some variation on the individual subtests is present. The only obvious deficit occurs on PA. The generally sensitive tests, Digit Symbol and Digit Span, do not show deficits, which greatly lowers the likelihood of a brain lesion.

The impairment index of 0.85 is in direct contrast with the WAIS results. Such a high impairment rating is strongly indicative of brain injury. The rating may be unusually high, however, as a result of several measures that just reach the brain damaged range of performance. For example, the Rhythm test, the left-hand trial of the Finger-tapping Test, and the TPT Location measure all fall just within the brain-damaged range of performance. Also, the TPT total-time measure is the only test which is severely impaired. Such a rating suggests a mild-to-moderate brain dysfunction with wide-ranging effects that disrupt to a moderate degree a number of generally sensitive tests.

Except for the left-hand trial of the Finger-tapping Test and the right-hand trial of the TPT, no motor or sensory deficits are seen. The lack of sensory findings and the inconsistent lateralization suggested by the two motor deficits gives little credence to the findings in terms of their suggesting a particular lesion locus. The results may be the product of generalized dysfunction that causes spotty deficits.

Both left- and right-hemisphere deficits are seen on the neuropsychological profile. Outstanding left-hemisphere deficits are encountered on the TPT and the Aphasia-Test. Parietal-type symptoms include tactual–perceptual and ideational dyspraxia signs. These deficits are generally associated with the parietal lobe, although other deficits occur that indicate other parts of the left hemisphere. For example, the Speech Test deficit implicates the left temporal lobe. A lesser deficit on the Rhythm Test may be associated with the anterior left hemisphere, independent involvement of the right hemisphere, or general disruption due to brain damage.

Apart from the left-hand-trial Finger-tapping Test deficit, relatively few right-hemisphere indications are seen. Trails A suggests right-hemisphere involvement, although it is not impaired relative to Trails B. The absolute impairment in the absence of relative impairment lessens the likelihood that lateralized damage is present.

Certain strengths are apparent that need to be recognized in the overall interpretation of the profile. First, the WAIS shows little deficit. This result is unlikely unless the lesion is highly circumscribed or chronic in nature, thereby manifesting no acute signs.

The deficit pattern immediately suggests severe brain injury with the 0.86 impairment index. Overall, the deficits present are not of a severe nature, although at least mildly deficient performance is seen throughout a wide variety of tests. The conclusion of brain damage is therefore inescapable.

The present profile suggests that predominantly the left hemisphere is involved, with little or no indications of right-hemisphere injury. The TPT, Speech, and dysphasia results line up on the left-hemisphere side of the ledger, while the Finger-tapping Test deficit is the only strong indication of right-hemisphere dysfunction. Since no corroboratory evidence is present to support the Finger-tapping Test result, right-hemisphere damage largely can be ruled out.

The left-hemisphere results show further indications that the lesion is confined to the posterior half of the left hemisphere. The dysphasia indicates parietal-lobe dysfunction. This lesion locus is supported by the TPT deficit in the absence of a right-hand Tapping deficit. Furthermore, the injury is not confined to this area, since a Speech Test deficit indicates the left temporal lobe; the anterior temporal lobe may also be implicated by the Rhythm Test deficit. The anterior parietal lobe and the frontal lobe of the left hemisphere are apparently not involved, since no simple sensory signs are present and since the Category Test is not severely impaired.

The test pattern is therefore not indicative of a diffuse injury, although neither is a localized lesion indicated. The results still demonstrate the spotty deficit pattern characteristic of a diffuse lesion even though the area of dysfunction is relatively circumscribed (posterior aspect of the left hemisphere). The most likely explanation of the test results given this pattern of deficits is an old trauma. The relatively circumscribed area of involvement is explained in the nature of a deficit acquired by traumatic injury. Also, the spotty area of deficit arises from the process of recovery inherent in a traumatic injury. Once the lesion is acquired and the deficits are incurred, the person begins to recover from the acute effects. The skills that are used the most and are the most overlearned recover the quickest, thereby leaving a spotty deficit pattern. The WAIS skills have been recovered in this person, while the dysphasia signs remain as either permanent deficits or ones that have not yet recovered.

Case 46

Background data.   This is a 49-year-old male with a history of severe trauma apparently to the frontal lobes of the brain. The patient, after recovery from the trauma, continued to show problems in his work as a shop foreman. He was referred for evaluation of any residual deficits.

Case Example __46__ Age __49__ Sex __M__   Education __12__ Handedness __R__

General Tests:

Category (errors)__112__ Trail-making: Part A __56"__ Part B __98"__

TPT: Total time __14'50"__ Location __2__ Memory __6__

Motor and Sensory Tests:

			Fingertip		
Finger-tapping	R __51__	L __52__	number-writing	R __3__	L __1__
Finger agnosia	R __0__	L __0__			

Supressions:

Tactile form

			(time)	R __10__	L __9__
Visual	R __0__	L __0__	(errors)	R __0__	L __0__
Tactile	R __0__	L __0__			
Auditory	R __0__	L __0__			

TPT: Time/Block R __.57__ L __.71__ Both __.21__

Cognitive Tests:

Speech-Sounds Perception

(errors) __5__   Rhythm (errors)   __3__

WAIS: (scaled score)

Information	8	Picture completion	8
Comprehension	7	Picture arrangement	11
Vocabulary	11	Object assembly	9
Similarities	7	Block design	5
Arithmetic	9	Digit symbol	8
Digit span	9		

VIQ __93__   PIQ __100__   FSIQ __96__

Aphasia: None

Test data. The full-scale IQ falls within the range of normal intelligence, as do the VIQ and the PIQ. The VIQ–PIQ difference of seven points favors the performance subtests and may represent slight loss of verbal ability as a result of brain dysfunction. The premorbid level of function is best estimated in the normal range.

Both right- and left-hemisphere deficits are suggested by the WAIS. The C and S subtests show scores that approach significantly deviant ranges and that may relate to brain-dysfunction deficiencies. These deficits indicate left-hemisphere dysfunction probably related to abstract verbal-conceptual functioning. More basic verbal abilities, such as receptive language understanding and language expression seen in V and I, remain intact. It is only the more complicated verbal abilities requiring conceptual thinking that are impaired. The other deficit occurs on BD and represents dysfunction in spatial ability. This deficit is more prominent than the verbal problems.

A low impairment index of 0.43 is seen, with only three of the seven tests on the index being disrupted. The Category Test is severely disrupted, as is the TPT Location measure. The TPT Memory measure is only slightly dysfunctional, and the TPT total time approaches the brain-damaged range of performance, although it is less than the cutoff level and is therefore not included in the rating. With severe impairment on two of the measures and the TPT total-time measure approaching the cutoff level, the brain dysfunction may be more severe than it appears from the numerical value. The severity of the disorder must be gleaned from a profile analysis of the entire set of results.

Motor and sensory measures remain relatively intact, with no errors on the Finger Agnosia Test and no suppressions; the Fingertip Number-writing Test, however, shows slight dysfunction favoring the right hand. Supporting lateralized deficits are apparent on both the Finger-tapping and Grip Strength tests. While both motor measures show absolute levels of performance within normal limits, a relative deficit exists. The right-hand-trial values are less than those for the left-hand trials, and this occurs in a right-hand-dominant person. Even though the absolute levels of function are at normal levels of performance, a deficit is strongly indicated in the left hemisphere. Curiously, however, the opposite lateralization is suggested by the TPT performance—the left-hand trial is more poorly performed than the right-hand trial.

Despite the severe impairment on some of the general measures, relatively few deficits are manifested on the neuropsychological profile as a whole. The right hemisphere is implicated largely by the lateralized TPT deficit on the left-hand trial and by the BD deficit. This deficit complex suggests basic spatial and tactual–perceptual difficulties, which may be associated with either the parietal or frontal lobes of the right hemisphere. No construction dyspraxia or left-hand sensory deficits are apparent, however, Likewise, the Rhythm Test is not impaired.

Left-hemisphere tasks that are deficient include the right-hand trial of the Finger-tapping and Fingertip Number-writing tests. This combination of deficits implicates the left-hemisphere motor/sensory strip. Other deficits on the WAIS occur, as mentioned above, although no dysphasia signs or deficits on the Speech-Sounds Test are seen. Both parts of the Trail-making Test are approximately equally impaired, thereby indicating no strong lateralization of deficit.

The borderline impairment index and the lack of dysphasia signs do not indicate the presence of a brain injury; however, the severe dysfunction seen on the Category and the TPT Location measures contradicts these results. The profile must be analyzed as a whole to determine if an identifiable deficit pattern is present.

The most striking deficit is the severe disruption of the Category Test, which often can indicate left-frontal-lobe dysfunction. This postulate is especially likely in this profile, where few other neuropsychological deficits are present. The most outstanding deficit beyond the Category score is the problem in motor speed. The problem on the Fingertip Number-writing Test, which occurs in the absence of other corroboratory sensory findings, can also be explained by a frontal-lobe dysfunction. Complex sensory deficits are common in prefrontal-lobe disruption, where the Category Test deficits are also placed.

The more posterior aspects of the left hemisphere, including the temporal lobe, must also be intact, since an excellent performance on the Speech-Sounds Test is inconsistent with a lesion in this area. The WAIS deficits on the Comprehension and Similarities subtests therefore must not be related to simple receptive language dysfunctions of the left temporal lobe; instead, the deficits arise as a result of the disruption of abstract verbal-conceptual abilities associated with left-prefrontal dysfunction.

The right-hemisphere deficits still remain, however, and do not fit well with the postulation of a left-frontal-lobe disorder. The deficits in the TPT left-hand trial and the Block Design Test also do not suggest an immediate lesion locus other than a general right-hemisphere involvement; however, it is unlikely that these deficits could arise as a result of right-parietal-lobe disruption, since no construction dyspraxia is present. Therefore, by the process of elimination the results may be related to anterior-hemisphere dysfunction. This postulate is not supported, however, by the fact that the Rhythm Test is adequately performed. This result may be explained if the right temporal lobe is assumed to have remained intact.

The picture, then, stands of a bilateral frontal-lobe dysfunction that leads to a mild disorder according to the impairment index and the overall lack of wide-ranging deficits. The lack of generalized effects on more of the sensitive measures and the lack of any dysphasic symptoms make an acute injury unlikely. These three facts (a bilateral, mild, and chronic deficit pattern) are consistent with substantial recovery from a trauma that caused residual effects associated with frontal-lobe function.

Case 47

Background data.   This 17-year-old male with 11 years of special
education was reportedly normal until meningitis was diagnosed at age
8 months. After that time the patient developed slowly and was placed
in a special-education program in school. The evaluation was done at
the request of the Social Security Department for determination of
eligibility for disability payments.

Case Example __47__ Age __17__ Sex __M__ Education __11__ Handedness __R__

General Tests:

Category (errors) __115__ Trail-making: Part A __60"__ Part B __249"__

TPT: Total time __30'__ Location __1__ Memory __3__

Motor and Sensory Tests:

Finger-tapping   R __49__   L __47__   Fingertip

Finger agnosia   R __*__   L __*__   number-writing   R __8__   L __10__

Supressions: Tactile form

    Visual   R __0__   L __2__   (time)   R __*__   L __*__

    Tactile   R __0__   L __0__   (errors)   R __*__   L __*__

    Auditory   R __0__   L __0__

TPT: Time/Block   R __2.5__   L __2.5__   Both __1.7__

Cognitive Tests:

Speech-Sounds Perception

   (errors)   __38__   Rhythm (errors)   __16__

WAIS: (scaled score)

Information	4	Picture completion	8
Comprehension	5	Picture arrangement	4
Vocabulary	2	Object assembly	4
Similarities	6	Block design	6
Arithmetic	4	Digit symbol	5
Digit span	4		

VIQ __71__   PIQ __72__   FSIQ __69__

Aphasia: Naming (square, cross, fork); spelling
(square, cross, triangle); drawing
(numbers, letters, words); pronunciation;
calculation (#25,26); right-left confusion;
ideational dyspraxia; construction dyspraxia

Test results. Borderline to mental-defective functioning is indicated by the WAIS IQs. The verbal and performance sections show no significant difference in function on overall measures. The VIQ is 71, 1 point lower than the PIQ of 72. The premorbid level of function may have been higher, since one subtest (PC) is performed in the average range of function. However, the relative invariance of the WAIS profiles suggests that intellectual functions have never been more highly developed.

Despite the otherwise uniform level of performance, two subtests (V and PC) are significantly different from the rest of the profile. This pattern of results represents a deficit in long-term-memory storage and/or acquisition versus good ability in an immediate-adaptive task. This result is usual in adult brain damage, since long-term-memory tasks such as Vocabulary are usually insensitive to brain damage, while immediate-adaptive tasks such as Picture Arrangement are disrupted.

A severely impaired rating of 1.0 is earned on the impairment index. All seven tests fall into the brain-damaged range, with severe impairment seen on six of the measures. The only measure that does not show severe impairment is the Finger-tapping Test, where a relatively mild and unilateral deficit is manifested.

Motor/sensory deficits do not suggest a strongly lateralized dysfunction, although lateralized deficits do occur. Two left-eye visual suppressions occur, suggesting dysfunction of the right cerebral hemisphere. This postulate is not supported by the other motor/sensory results. The deficit on the Fingertip Number-writing Test is bilateral without significantly different performance on either hand, although the right-hand test is more poorly performed. The person was unable to do the Finger Agnosia Test. The Finger-tapping test deficit suggests a slight left-hemisphere motor/sensory deficit.

Cognitive dysfunction is seen throughout the neuropsychological profile on tasks associated with both the right and left cerebral hemispheres. In the left hemisphere, severe dysfunction is suggested by extensive dysphasia. The naming, spelling, and reading items show severe dysfunction. Pronunciation and calculation deficits occur concomitantly, which supports the indication of left-hemisphere dysfunction. Consistent with the extensive dysphasia, a severely deficient performance occurs on the Speech-Sounds Test. The Vocabulary and Trails B deficiencies are also consistent with a severe left-hemisphere disorder.

Spatial difficulties on the Aphasia Test drawing items that are most associated with right-hemisphere dysfunction (cross, key) are evident. Likewise, the TPT performance demonstrates an inability to learn from experience, a deficit that is related to either left-frontal-lobe or severe right-hemisphere spatial difficulties. The Trails A and Rhythm deficits are also associated with right-hemisphere dysfunction.

Severe dysfunction is seen throughout the entire neuropsychological profile. Such diffuse and severe deficiencies on all of the tests in a person of this age immediately suggests one of two etiological possibilities: First, the deficit pattern may reflect a recent trauma that is exerting uniform disruptive effects on the brain as a whole. Second, an early brain injury that caused general dysfunction and affected the person's ability to develop neuropsychological skills is also a possibility.

The possibility of an acute trauma to the brain fits the generalized dysfunction. All general tests are disrupted, and motor and sensory dysfunction is also present. No localized deficit patterns are seen, however, in either the motor/sensory or cognitive measures. An area of more focal involvement is usually expected in a traumatic injury, even a very severe trauma. For this reason the second possibility seems a more likely explanation.

Closer analysis of the test pattern confirms the impression of an early brain disorder. The lesser dysfunction seen on the motor tasks is not characteristic of an acute injury unless it is far removed from the motor/sensory strip. The present deficit profile suggests no localized, circumscribed lesion. Also, the relative lack of WAIS variability is not indicative of an acute lesion. A chronic injury occurring early in life is further indicated by the relative deficit in stored-memory tasks and other traditional "hold" tests, while more immediate-adaptive tasks are better performed. Finally, the uniform deficit on the TPT and the severe problems with the Category Test indicate an inability to learn from experience. Such a diffculty with tasks that require hypothesis formation and validation may explain the uniform deficit on the WAIS. An early injury disrupts the ability to acquire new information through experience.

The present results, while showing uniform disruption and without indication of localized disorder, still provide considerable information relevant to the diagnosis of the brain disorder. While the actual cause cannot be determined exclusively from the neuropsychological results, the testing provides unique information regarding prognosis and allows rehabilitative-health professionals to make accurate decisions about the kind of lifestyle this person is prepared to assume.

Case 48

Background data.   This is a 27-year-old policeman with 14 years of education. During a gunfight the patient was shot through a frontal lobes, the entrance wound lying near the left frontal/temporal area. The testing was done as part of a Social Security evaluation 18 months after the gunfight.

Case Example __48__ Age __27__ Sex __M__   Education __14__ Handedness __R__

General Tests:

Category (errors) _____ Trail-making: Part A _25"_ Part B _57"_

TPT: Total time _11' 38"_ Location __2__ Memory __7__

Motor and Sensory Tests:

Finger-tapping   R _44_ L _37_   Fingertip
Finger agnosia   R _2_   L _2_   number-writing R _0_ L _2_

Supressions: Tactile form

   Visual   R _0_   L _0_   (time)   R _20_ L _18_

   Tactile   R _0_   L _0_   (errors)   R _1_   L _1_

   Auditory   R _2_   L _0_

TPT: Time/Block   R _.43_ L _.55_ Both _.19_

Cognitive Tests:

Speech-Sounds Perception

  (errors)   _10_   Rhythm (errors)   _5_

WAIS: (scaled score)

Information	9	Picture completion	6
Comprehension	14	Picture arrangement	12
Vocabulary	8	Object assembly	15
Similarities	10	Block design	10
Arithmetic	10	Digit symbol	8
Digit span	12		

     VIQ _102_   PIQ _102_   FSIQ _102_

Aphasia: Reading

Test results. A rather peculiar scatter on the WAIS shows limited areas of deficit as well as strength. Scores on C and OA suggest a premorbid level of functioning that would have been well above average. The I, V, and possibly S and A subtest scores indicate either a poor educational history or some loss of verbal functions due to brain dysfunction. An extremely poor PC score is indicative of visual-analysis difficulties in which the person is unable to scan an unfamiliar picture and identify relevant details. Further visual-perceptual problems are evident from the BD performance. Because the OA score is so high and none of the construction items on the Aphasia Test were poorly performed, it is likely that spatial skills are intact. In that case the BD deficit reflects an inability to organize a spatial strategy for solving the problem rather than a basic spatial disability. Some problem on the Digit Symbol subtest is present, which would be expected if a brain dysfunction is postulated.

The postulate of brain damage, made from the erratic WAIS profile, is further corroborated by the performance on the tests sensitive to brain damage in general. The Digit Symbol subtest was already mentioned, and the TPT Location score and the absolute and relative levels of the Finger-tapping Test are also examples. Several generally sensitive tests, however, were not performed in the brain-damaged range. For example, the Trail-making Tests and the TPT total-time and Memory scores were well within normal limits. These findings suggest a mild or very circumscribed lesion.

Two different sets of brain-related deficits line themselves up. One set is associated with right-hemisphere function and includes motor and sensory deficits along with some cognitive deficits. A bilateral motor-speed deficit is evident on the Finger-tapping Test, which is somewhat worse for the left hand than the right. Mild, complex sensory deficits show up on the Fingertip Number-writing Test and the left-hand trial (relative to the right) on the TPT. Deficits for Finger Agnosia fail to lateralize and are most likely unrelated to the other sensory deficits. Right-hemisphere cognitive deficits consist predominantly of the WAIS performance subtests, which again involve visual-integrative abilities. The poor TPT Location score falls under this category as well. The person is unable to reconstruct a complex spatial configuration even though the necessary information is within memory.

The second set of deficits involves left-hemisphere indicators, including four very specific deficits. The most prominent is the presence of right-ear auditory suppressions, indicating a destructive left-temporal-lobe lesion. The other three deficits are cognitive problems and include the Speech-Sounds Perception Test, the Vocabulary subtest of the WAIS, and a slight dyslexic error on the Aphasia Test. The Category test was not given.

There is clearly bilateral involvement, with serious impairment in the left hemisphere being indicated by the auditory suppressions. The left-hemisphere damage, while serious, also appears to be highly localized. The Trail-making Test part B is adequately performed, which, as a general indicator of left-hemisphere damage, involves basic verbal abilities and which along with the auditory suppression suggests highly specific left-temporal-lobe dysfunction. Thus a very serious injury is indicated that involves only a very small portion of the brain, so that some general left-hemisphere indicators remain intact.

The right-hemisphere motor strip is implicated by the left-hand Finger-tapping deficit. Sensory deficits are seen, but the lack of simple sensory problems tends to argue against a parietal-lobe lesion. Complex sensory deficits can occur in frontal-lobe damage, and the other cognitive right-hemisphere deficits in this case support such a hypothesis. The cognitive deficits include the left-hand TPT score and Block Design, which are associated with both posterior and anterior right-hemisphere dysfunction. In this case, however, they would appear to indicate an anterior focus. No construction dyspraxia or simple sensory deficit occurs, which would be expected in spatial and tactual-perceptual problems that accompany posterior-right-hemisphere injuries. Also, the excellent performance on Trails A is uncommon in significantly disruptive posterior-right-hemisphere injuries, whereas such performance is not uncommon with right-frontal damage. Finally, the Picture Completion deficit is a rare occurrence but also one that argues for a frontal-lobe lesion as opposed to a more posterior placement. This deficit results from the disruption of the ability to actively search unfamiliar and complex visual configurations for relevant detail, a frontal-lobe skill.

Case 49

Background data. This 57-year-old male came to the psychiatric clinic at the request of his employer, who felt the patient was having a "nervous breakdown" secondary to additional stress at work over the past 4 months. The patient himself complained of a feeling of headache, dizziness, and a loss of ability to concentrate. As routine procedure in cases of this type, both neuropsychological and neurological examination were scheduled. Both suggested essentially identical conclusions.

Case Example 49   Age 57   Sex M   Education 12   Handedness R

General Tests:

    Category (errors) 104   Trail-making: Part A 75" Part B 330"

    TPT: Total time 28' 30" Location 1   Memory 2

Motor and Sensory Tests:

    Finger-tapping   R 42   L 32   Fingertip

    Finger agnosia   R 0   L 10   number-writing R 7   L 9

    Supressions: Tactile form

        Visual   R 0   L 0   (time)   R 14 L 18

        Tactile   R 0   L 0   (errors)   R 0   L 0

        Auditory R 0   L 0

    TPT: Time/Block R 10.0 L .85 Both 3.3

Cognitive Tests:

    Speech-Sounds Perception

      (errors)   9   Rhythm (errors)   13

    WAIS: (scaled score)

Information	12	Picture completion	6
Comprehension	6	Picture arrangement	8
Vocabulary	6	Object assembly	5
Similarities	7	Block design	4
Arithmetic	7	Digit symbol	4
Digit span	11		

        VIQ 93   PIQ 87   FSIQ 90

Aphasia: Drawing (all figures), naming,
      reading, pronunciation, calculation

Test results. Overall intellectual measures place this person in the low range of normal on all three IQ scores. While little difference is evident on the VIQ and the PIQ, it is apparent from looking at the individual subtest scores that considerable variation occurs. High scores on the I and Digit Span subtests suggest above-average premorbid functioning. The unusually low scores, by comparison, on the other verbal subtests and most of the performance subtests likely indicates brain-related deficits. The concomitant deficit on C and S in view of the otherwise excellent verbal skills demonstrated on the I subtest suggests a verbal-conceptual difficulty. The deficit on A is likely to indicate either a problem with arithmetic operations or a problem-solving difficulty in working with complex verbal information.

Generalized decrement is seen on the performance subtests. Only the PA score is normal (with age corrections). This general decline on performance subtests is likely the result of brain dysfunction, since the PA and the verbal subtest scores indicate that a higher level of function would be expected. This decline is either the result of a diffuse right-hemisphere lesion or a general reaction to a severe brain lesion.

An impairment index of 1.0 signifies a severely disrupted profile indicative of a severe brain lesion. The Category Test and the TPT measures are greatly disrupted. Moderate deficits are apparent on the Finger-tapping and Seashore Rhythm tests, while only mild disruption occurs on the Speech-Sounds Test.

Both right- and left-hemisphere measures are disrupted; however, the left-hemisphere tasks appear to show greater dysfunction. First, the severe Category Test deficit is oftentimes indicative of left-frontal-lobe disruption. The TPT right-hand and both-hands trials are extremely deficient in comparison with the excellent performance on the left-hand trials; this result is indicative of either tertiary-left-parietal-lobe dysfunction or left-prefrontal-lobe injury. The motor coordination problems evident in the both-hands score is more often the result of frontal-lobe dysfunction. Incidental spatial memory, as signified by the Memory and Location scores, is also deficient and is consistent with a left-hemisphere injury in view of the right-hand versus left-hand performance differential.

Sensory symptoms are also present. Finger Agnosia and Fingertip Number-writing Test deficits indicate left-parietal-lobe involvement. Bilateral Fingertip Test deficits most likely result from injuries to the left hemisphere. Deficits on fingertip number writing may indicate either prefrontal-lobe or tertiary-parietal-lobe dysfunctions, unlike the Finger Agnosia deficits, which suggest anterior-parietal-lobe damage.

Several test comparisons are useful. Trails B is more seriously impaired than Trails A and indicates left-hemisphere dysfunction. In fact, the severe deficit on the Trails B performance may signify a deficit in cognitive flexibility in which the person is unable to switch between the two cognitive sets (number and letter alternation). This fact would specify a left-prefrontal-lobe lesion. Comparison of Speech and Rhythm performances suggests either bilateral damage or more anterior than posterior left-hemisphere damage, since a greater deficit occurs on the Rhythm Test. When the balance of the evidence suggests a left-hemisphere injury, Rhythm problems often localize to the more anterior portions of the left hemisphere.

Finally, comparison of the dysphasia signs with the good performances on the Aphasia Test yields some useful information. Naming, pronouncing, and reading aloud are expressive language tasks. When these signs occur in the absence of receptive language deficits (such as spelling dyspraxia and dysgraphia), anterior-left-hemisphere dysfunction is indicated. Calculation problems also occur; they do not indicate a specific locus by themselves but are consistent with the anterior locus of injury suggested by the other deficits. The drawing difficulties are usually indicative of parietal-lobe involvement when basic spatial abilities are affected. In this case all figures are poorly drawn, indicating either severe spatial deficit or difficulty regulating behavior sufficiently to complete the task adequately. This latter problem is often seen in prefrontal-lobe dysfunction of either hemisphere. The person is unable to verbally regulate behavior (in left-prefrontal-lobe damage) in order to follow the instructions properly, or spatial thinking (in right-prefrontal-lobe damage) is unable to guide the person's actions, such that geometric configurations cannot be concocted.

The first question is one of whether these deficits indicate unilateral or bilateral damage. Several right-hemisphere tasks are disrupted, but the left-hemisphere deficits are more severe. In looking more closely at the right-hemisphere tasks, damage seems unlikely. The construction dyspraxia on all figures of the Aphasia Test, the left-hand motor-speed deficit, and the general decline on the performance subtests, if indicative of right-hemisphere damage, would indicate severe involvement of the right parietal lobe. The lack of finger dysgnosia and the excellent performance of the left-hand trial of the TPT argue strongly against this postulate.

The existing right-hemisphere deficits must be alternatively explained, however, before one discards the postulate of right-hemisphere damage. In view of the overwhelming evidence for a left-hemisphere lesion, the right-hemisphere tasks that are deficient can likely be accounted for as secondary deficits. The performance tests of the WAIS are immediate-adaptive tasks and therefore are generally sensitive to certain kinds of brain damage. In severe left-prefrontal-lobe injuries motor-coordination and problem-solving skills are deficient and can account for the deficits seen in this case on the WAIS performance subtests. The construction dyspraxia can be accounted for in the same manner, since it does not seem to represent severe spatial deficit. The Finger-tapping deficit with the left hand relative to the right hand is not easily attributed to left-hemisphere injury. While bilateral motor and sensory disruption can often occur in dominant-left-hemisphere injuries, it is usual for the body side contralateral to the injury to be more impaired than the ipsilateral body side. Despite this one inconsistency, the right-hemisphere results that show deficiency seem best explained as secondary deficits.

Furthermore, the deficits indicate a localized lesion within the left hemisphere. The severe Category Test deficit draws attention to the possibility of a prefrontal-lobe injury. This possibility is strengthened by the particular complex of Aphasia Test deficits, the Rhythm Test deficit (in the absence of a right-hemisphere lesion), and the TPT dysfunction. The TPT can, of course, localize to the posterior parietal lobe. In the absence of other strong posterior or parietal-lobe indicators, such a severe TPT deficit is unlikely to be associated with this area. The WAIS deficits on the verbal-abstraction tests (C, S) also support a prefrontal-lobe dysfunction. In view of the widespread effects across many tests and the severity of effects on the individual tests, a prefrontal-lobe lesion of considerable disruption is apparent.

The severity of the lesion is further indicated by the anterior-parietal-lobe and posterior-frontal-lobe involvement, which is confirmed by the Finger Agnosia and Finger-tapping Test deficits. Likewise, the Speech Test deficit hints at very slight left-temporal-lobe dysfunction. The lesion, then, is not only causing severe disruption in the prefrontal lobes but is exerting mild effects as far back as the motor/sensory strip and possibly to the secondary areas of the temporal lobe.

The general activity, as well as the dysgraphia signs and the extreme lateralized indications of some test comparisons signifies an acute lesion. The most likely process alternatives of such an acute and severe neuropsychological profile include vascular hemorrhage and fast-growing tumor. Distinguishing between these two alternatives on the basis of the neuropsychological results is difficult and is best done in conjunction with a thorough medical history. Given the history, a tumor seems likely, since tumors will generally appear more gradually with a longer history of medical symptomatology such as headache, dizziness, neck stiffness, and other signs associated with increased intracranial pressure.

Case 50

Background data. This 28-year-old male was diagnosed as having a tumor of the left parietal area, an unusual finding in an individual this age. Baseline testing was performed to evaluate function prior to surgery.

Case Example 50   Age 28   Sex M   Education 12   Handedness R

General Tests:

Category (errors) 77   Trail-making: Part A 60" Part B 132"

TPT: Total time 16'15" Location 7   Memory 8

Motor and Sensory Tests:

Finger-tapping   R 44   L 40.4   Fingertip
Finger agnosia   R 3   L 1   number-writing R 2   L 0

Supressions: Tactile form

Visual   R 0   L 0   (time)   R 25   L 20

Tactile   R 1   L 0   (errors)   R 2   L 0

Auditory   R 3   L 0

TPT: Time/Block R .6   L .6   Both .42

Cognitive Tests:

Speech-Sounds Perception

(errors)   —   Rhythm (errors)   4

WAIS: (scaled score)

Information	8	Picture completion	11
Comprehension	7	Picture arrangement	7
Vocabulary	7	Object assembly	11
Similarities	8	Block design	11
Arithmetic	4	Digit symbol	7
Digit span	10		

VIQ 83   PIQ 97   FSIQ 88

Aphasia: Drawing (square, cross, Kay); naming
(cross, baby, fork); spelling (#6);
writing (#12, 20, 24); reading (#15, 16
30); pronunciation #19, 22); calculation
(#26); ideational dyspraxia (#28, 32)

Test results. The overall intellectual measure places this person just below the normal range of scores. This placement may be misleading in view of the 14-point difference between the VIQ and the PIQ. The PIQ score and individual subtest scores of 10 and 11 suggest a premorbid intellectual level well into the normal range of functioning.

General decline is seen on the verbal section, with three of the subtests falling at least three scaled score points below a normal level of function. The Arithmetic subtest shows definite brain-related dysfunction at a scaled score of only 4. Both C and V fall three scaled score points below the highest verbal subtest, Digit Span. These two deficits are also most likely brain-related problems. The I and S scores fall within the normal range of variation and may or may not be attributable to brain damage.

Two deficits also occur on the performance section (PA, Digit Symbol). Apart from the Digit Symbol subtest, which is generally sensitive to brain damage, all WAIS deficits seem to suggest complex verbal dysfunction. The more complex verbal tasks, such as explaining word meanings and interpreting social situations, are dysfunctional. The more basic verbal tasks, such as general-information store, immediate auditory memory, and recognizing verbal concepts, are well performed, as are most manual-manipulative tasks.

An impairment index of 0.5 is earned, with three of the six tests included being impaired. The TPT total-time, Category, and Finger-tapping Test measures are moderately dysfunctional. The Speech-Sounds Test is not available for inclusion into the index. No impairment is seen on the TPT Location and the Memory measures or the Rhythm Test.

Perhaps the most striking evidence is seen on the sensory measures. The Finger Agnosia and Fingertip Number-writing tests both demonstrate lateralized impairment to the right body side. This lateralization is supported by a right-sided tactile suppression. Generalized motor impairment occurs on the Finger-tapping measure without indication of lateralized deficit. Some right-hemisphere indications are seen on the TPT left-hand trial. Left lateralization is seen in the auditory suppressions.

More consistent lateralizing signs are seen in the cognitive testing. Trails B is relatively more impaired than Trails A, although both fall into the brain-damaged range. Left-hemisphere dysfunction is further indicated by the Aphasia Test results. Considerable dysphasia is present, with severe damage indicated by extensive word-finding problems as well as supporting evidence in the other dysphasic indications. Extensive writing, reading, and pronunciation problems support the dysnomia in the suggestion of severe left-hemisphere disruption. Spelling, calculation, and ideational dyspraxia problems further support this contention. Drawing problems are also present, although they largely involve the spatially difficult items. This deficit may be due either to spatial right-hemisphere problems or to left-hemisphere disruption of dominant-hand sensory/motor abilities and/ or left-parietal injury.

Certain strengths also bear pointing out in light of the specific deficits mentioned above. The WAIS performance section highlights strengths on spatial tasks, including BD and OA, and the PC subtest is well performed. The Seashore Rhythm Test also is adequately performed. The adequate spatial abilities on the WAIS contrast with the drawing difficulties and the TPT problems on the left-hand trial.

In view of the symptoms it appears that the left-hemisphere motor/sensory indicators point appropriately. Severe tissue-destruction has occured in the left temporal lobe, probably at a subcortical level.

Given left-hemisphere damage, the next question is whether the lesion is localized or diffuse. The sensory signs indicate anterior-parietal-lobe involvement. The Finger Agnosia and tactile-suppression deficits generally arise from direct disruption of the primary and secondary areas of the parietal lobe. Further parietal-lobe dysfunction is seen in the Fingertip Number-writing Test and the general overall deficit on the TPT. These two deficits are often associated with more posterior parietal-lobe disruption, however. The extensive dysphasia also supports posterior-parietal-lobe involvement. So far, then, the lesion appears to encompass the entire parietal lobe of the left hemisphere.

The temporal suppressions indicate the lack of intactness of the left temporal lobe. The lesion, then, involves the temporal-parietal area, with a localized pattern of deficits which nevertheless encompasses a large area of the cortex. Maximal involvement is indicated anteriorly by the suppressions and posteriorly by the extensive dysphasia. This is consistent with a logical etiologic alternative of a tumor as the history indicates, since the lesion involves a focal area of the brain with severe effects in a large area of the brain.

Case 51

Background data. This 30-year-old male with 18 years of education (M.A. degree) appeared at the clinic complaining of anxiety and headaches. A neuropsychological examination was employed to rule out a neurological disorder. (After testing was completed, the patient was sent to see a neurologist/neurosurgeon.)

Case Example __51__ Age __30__ Sex __M__ Education __18__ Handedness __R__

General Tests:

Category (errors) __15__ Trail-making: Part A __32"__ Part B __72"__

TPT: Total time __8'50"__ Location __5__ Memory __7__

Motor and Sensory Tests:

Finger-tapping R __43__ L __48__   Fingertip

Finger agnosia R __0__ L __0__   number-writing R __4__ L __6__

Supressions: Tactile form

Visual   R __0__ L __0__   (time)   R __28__ L __24__

Tactile   R __0__ L __0__   (errors) R __0__ L __0__

Auditory R __0__ L __0__

TPT: Time/Block R __.51__ L __.21__ Both __.16__

Cognitive Tests:

Speech-Sounds Perception

(errors) __7__   Rhythm (errors) __2__

WAIS: (scaled score)

Information __13__   Picture completion __10__

Comprehension __17__   Picture arrangement __9__

Vocabulary __16__   Object assembly __14__

Similarities __12__   Block design __10__

Arithmetic __15__   Digit symbol __13__

Digit span __17__

VIQ __129__   PIQ __108__   FSIQ __121__

Aphasia: Pronunciation (#19); calculation (#25, 26)

Test results.   Superior overall intellectual functioning is seen on the WAIS full-scale IQ. A 21 point difference between the VIQ and PIQ suggests the likelihood of brain related deficits, especially in the right hemisphere. There are deficits, however, on both the perform-ance and the verbal subtests. Very slight deficiencies are seen on I and S in relation to the mean level of performance on the verbal subtests. Deficits of similar severity are seen on PA, PC, and BD. Generally sensitive measures on the WAIS (Digit Symbol, Digit Span) are not dysfunctional.

The high scores on the performance subtests are not as elevated as the high verbal-subtest scores. Such an occurrence may be the result of general depression of the manual/spatial abilities or the fact that the premorbid PIQ was not as elevated as the VIQ. The latter explanation seems more likely in view of the educational skills. General depression is also unlikely when the generally sensitive subtests are not deficient.

Only one of seven tests on the impairment index showed impair-ment. The Finger-tapping Test shows a lateralized deficit of significant proportions for the right (dominant) hand. Both the TPT Location measures and the Speech-Sounds Test are marginally dysfunctional but do not fall into the brain-damaged range of performance. The Category Test is extremely well performed and appears to reflect the superior level of intelligence.

In support of the low impairment rating, there are few neuropsy-chological deficits. Simple sensory tasks are well performed. The motor-speed deficit of the right-hand Tapping trial was mentioned above. Complex sensory dysfunction is seen on the Fingertip Number-writing Test (without strong lateralized indications). Further sensory deficits may be indicated by the relatively poor performance on the right-hand trial of the TPT compared to the left-hand trial. Taken together these deficits suggest left-hemisphere dysfunction, in direct contradiction to the indications of the VIQ–PIQ difference.

Many of the higher-order cortical functions remain intact. The general tests, including the Category, Trail-making, and the overall TPT measures, are all adequately performed with no indications of brain-related deficits. The auditory-perceptual tests (Speech and Rhythm) are also within the normal range of performance, although the Speech-Sounds score is borderline. Despite the excellently per-formed general tests, there are some deficits on the cognitive tests that support the deficits seen on the WAIS. Three errors on the Aphasia Test provide definite indications of brain-related deficits. Poor performance on both the calculation tasks and on an item that requires pronunciation of a multisyllabic word comprise a deficit complex that is often associated with left-parietal-lobe or left-premotor-area dysfunction.

The interpretation of these test results must start with the basic question of whether there exists any brain damage. The low impairment index and the lack of deficit on the generally sensitive tests argue for an interpretation of normal neuropsychological status. When the deficits that are apparent are more closely examined, this interpretation is called into question, however. First, dominant-hand motor speed is worse than nondominant-hand speed, a result which is accompanied by confirmatory lateralized motor/sensory signs. This result is highly uncommon in a healthy brain. Add to this the fact that three dysphasic errors occur (a result which alone correctly classifies 78 percent of a brain-damaged population), and the interpretation of the brain-damaged performance is inescapable.

Taken together this particular deficit complex suggests not only brain damage but also a localized lesion. The most outstanding deficit is the motor-speed problem of the right hand, which suggests a posterior-frontal-lobe locus. This location is supported by the dysphasia in that sequential motor and mental manipulations are required, tasks performed in the premotor area.

Verbal deficits are recognized from the WAIS I, S, PA, and PC. These deficits do not seem to imply the same area of involvement as the Tapping result. In fact, temporal-lobe disruption is implicated. This location is not inconsistent with a posterior-frontal-lobe focus in that the lesion can be situated along the Sylvian fissure at the border of the anterior temporal lobe and the posterior frontal lobe.

Such a lesion site would be consistent with the deficits as well as the strengths of the neuropsychological profile. The Speech Test result is normal to borderline, which would be expected if one was postulating an anterior-temporal-lobe lesion. Likewise, simple sensory performance is adequate, since the anterior parietal lobe is uninvolved. Prefrontal-lobe functions are excellent, as indicated by the Category Test performance; posterior-parietal-lobe abilities also remain intact, with no gross dysphasia such as dysnomia, spelling dyspraxia, or dyslexia being present.

Etiological alternatives are rather limited given the discreteness of the lesion. Tumors and pinpoint open head traumas resulting in very localized lesions, such as seems indicated in this case, are unlikely given the lack of general disruption seen in the overall neuropsychological profile. The only likely alternative which conforms to both the highly circumscribed area of involvement and the lack of wide-ranging disruption of cortical functions is an aneurysm. This alternative fits nicely the only lesion site that seems probable: the Sylvian fissure in the region of the anterior-temporal/posterior-frontal juncture. Given the age of the person, a congenital vascular anomaly that has developed into an aneurysm is likely. The dysphasia and the sharp difference between the right- and left-hand Finger-tapping Test scores reveals the acuteness of the lesion. While this alternative is not the only explanation for the neuropsychological profile, it is the most likely etiology. Combined with a thorough medical history that corroborates such a diagnosis it would provide a reliably accurate diagnosis.

The present case shows the power of a comprehensive battery of tests over a mere screening battery. With a screening battery of the "most sensitive" tests (e.g., those measures included on the impairment index) this case would likely have been misdiagnosed. Neuropsychological functions should be viewed together so that a pattern of deficits can emerge. Such patterns are often crucial to identification of highly localized yet mild lesions, such as occurs in this case.

Case 52

Background data. This 30-year-old female was evaluated for residual deficits following right-frontal bleeding associated with an aneurysm of the anterior communicating artery. Testing took place 1 year after the initial hospitalization.

Case Example 52   Age 30   Sex F   Education 16   Handedness R

General Tests:

Category (errors) 80   Trail-making: Part A 42" Part B 46"

TPT: Total time 6'51" Location 10   Memory 10

Motor and Sensory Tests:

Finger-tapping	R 48	L 41	Fingertip		
Finger agnosia	R 0	L 0	number-writing	R 2	L 1

Supressions: Tactile form

Visual	R 0	L 0	(time)	R 19	L 29
Tactile	R 0	L 0	(errors)	R 0	L 0
Auditory	R 0	L 0			

TPT: Time/Block   R •38   L •19   Both •11

Cognitive Tests:

Speech-Sounds Perception

(errors)   4   Rhythm (errors)   12

WAIS: (scaled score)

Information	15	Picture completion	9
Comprehension	18	Picture arrangement	13
Vocabulary	12	Object assembly	17
Similarities	19	Block design	14
Arithmetic	7	Digit symbol	18
Digit span	18		

VIQ 133   PIQ 128   FSIQ 130

Aphasia: Drawing (mild, all figures), writing, calculation, ideational dyspraxia

Test results. The WAIS shows an interesting profile of strengths and weaknesses. The verbal skills are generally superior, although the V score is somewhat lowered, most likely because of lack of education. Attention and concentration abilities appear to be excellent, as demonstrated by the scores of the Digit Symbol and Digit Span subtests. Perceptual–motor skills on the WAIS show a wide variability, with indications of superior premorbid ability on the OA and Digit Symbol subtests. Deficient performance is most prominent on PC and PA, with a possible mild deficit on BD. It would appear that the patient has difficulty actively scanning complex visuospatial material both to ascertain the relevant details and, in the case of PA, to reintegrate them into a logical sequence. Good performance on OA argues against either a motor or spatial problem explaining the relative deficit on BD. The PC and PA deficits argue for a problem-solving difficulty to explain the BD problem. On the complex spatial designs the patient likely had difficulty deciding upon the relevant details for the solution and combining the various components of the problem into a solution. Perhaps the most striking deficit on the WAIS is the poor performance on A. Since verbal, attentional, and basic calculation skills seem to be intact, a less parsimonious explanation of the deficit is necessary. Investigation of individual-item performance reveals that errors are made only on those items requiring a thorough investigation of relevant aspects of the problem so that a step-by-step plan for the problem's solution can be devised. It would appear that the patient is unable to analyze a complex story problem. She apparently has difficulties with the sequential and spatial aspects of complex verbal constructions.

Of the tests generally sensitive to brain damage, the following are in the brain-damaged range: Tapping, Category, and Seashore Rhythm.

Performance on the Aphasia Test revealed a mild construction dyspraxia on all figures. The patient was unable to draw even the simplest figures accurately. While the overall gestalt of the figures was not entirely disrupted, as in posterior-right-hemisphere injuries, the figure was poorly integrated into a complete configuration. Problems writing the name of a visually presented object were also seen. Mental arithmetic in which complex calculation is called for also was poorly performed. Also, the patient had difficulty mentally visualizing a complex motor movement without actually executing the act (number 32 on the Aphasia Test).

A brain injury is evident from several errors on the Aphasia test and a lateralized motor deficit. All deficits are consistent with a right-hemisphere lesion: left-hand motor-speed problem, WAIS deficits, and the difficulties on the Aphasia Test. All of the cognitive tasks that were poorly performed require the ability to either sequentially or spatially organize a step-to-step plan to arrive at a solution. These abilities are most disrupted by right-frontal lesions. Such a localization is supported by the relative deficit on the Finger-tapping Test as compared to the TPT. Also important is the performance on the drawings on the Aphasia Test. In posterior lesions the figures, especially the cross, are often distorted in appearance as opposed to just poorly integrated or haphazardly put together, as is the present case.

The present case illustrates two important points. First, there are definite limitations to the diagnostic process with the Halstead-Reitan Test Battery. It is not always possible to identify accurately the exact location or the neurological process that accounts for the neuropsychological profile. Second, it is important to identify all deficits as well as strengths and search for the explanation that accounts for them most logically. As a related point, profile analysis is paramount to the process of deciding what is or is not a deficit. For example, on the WAIS a scaled score of 13 on PA is a deficit when compared with a premorbid level of perceptual–motor ability at a scaled score of 18 or 19. By the same token, however, if this is the only deficit of its kind in the entire profile, then it is unlikely that the deficit is brain related. Taking care to identify brain-related deficits and to integrate these deficits into a logical neuropsychological profile greatly strengthens the diagnostic power of the test battery.

Case 53

Background data. This 55-year-old patient was tested prior to surgery for a grade III astrocytoma in order to establish a behavioral baseline.

Case Example _53_ Age _55_ Sex _M_ Education _11_ Handedness _R_

General Tests:

Category (errors) _63_ Trail-making: Part A _66_ Part B _180_

TPT: Total time _24'6"_ Location _1_ Memory _3_

Motor and Sensory Tests:

Finger-tapping	R _22_	L _44_	Fingertip		
Finger agnosia	R _3_	L _0_	number-writing	R _18_	L _1_

Supressions:

Tactile form

Visual	R _0_	L _0_	(time)	R _20_	L _18_
Tactile	R _0_	L _0_	(errors)	R _0_	L _0_
Auditory	R _0_	L _0_			

TPT: Time/Block R _3.3_ L _.80_ Both _.61_

Cognitive Tests:

Speech-Sounds Perception

(errors) _21_   Rhythm (errors) _11_

WAIS: (scaled score)

Information	7	Picture completion	9
Comprehension	5	Picture arrangement	6
Vocabulary	6	Object assembly	5
Similarities	0	Block design	9
Arithmetic	6	Digit symbol	6
Digit span	6		

VIQ _72_   PIQ _93_   FSIQ _80_

Aphasia: Spelling (triangle), reading, pronunciation, calculation, drawing (key)

Test results. Intelligence testing reveals a borderline verbal IQ with general decrement on all verbal subtests. The S performance suggests a complete inability to assume a verbal abstract attitude. Performance on the perceptual–motor sections fell into the average range, and a 21-point difference exists between the verbal and performance IQs. This difference is quite large and may be indicative of a lateralized brain injury.

All tests generally sensitive to brain damage were impaired, yielding an impairment index of 1.0. The Category Test was only mildly impaired, which may be the result of a low verbal intelligence as much as the result of brain impairment. The Speecb-Sounds Test was relatively more impaired than the Seashore Rhythm Test, although both were performed in the brain-damaged range. All three TPT measures were well into the brain-damaged range, as was the Finger-tapping Test.

Several motor and sensory measures were impaired; taken together these deficits indicate a left-hemisphere injury. A severely lateralized motor-speed was seen on the Tapping test. Likewise, a lateralized sensory deficit occurs on the Finger Agnosia and Fingertip Number-writing tests. A lateralized deficit occurred on the Coin Recognition Test in both number of errors and time to complete the task.

Further cognitive deficits were found on the Trail-making and Aphasia tests. A relative deficit on the Trail-making Test part B occurred compared to part A, which is indicative of a left-hemisphere injury. Several dysphasia signs, including a spelling disability (spelling dyspraxia), poor calculation skills (dyscalculia), reading deficits (dyslexia), and pronunciation problems (dysarthria), support the hypothesis of a left-hemisphere injury. Certain cognitive strengths were found and include good spatial problem-solving skills on the BD subtest, good ability to visually scan and observe the relevant details of a picture on the PC subtest, and good ability to learn from experience on the TPT and to improve with each trial.

With the impairment index of 1.0 and clearly lateralized motor and sensory signs, the question of brain damage is easily answered in the affirmative. All cognitive deficits seem to lateralize to the left hemisphere, as do the motor and sensory signs. The exact location within the left hemisphere is not as clear, however; the overall pattern of deficits must be more closely examined.

The most striking deficit is the motor/sensory problem, which is moderate to severe. The motor/sensory strip (pre- and post-central gyri) appears to be the primary area of involvement. Other deficits suggest more wide-ranging areas of involvement that may not be as severely disrupted as the motor/sensory strip. For example, the severely disrupted performance on the right-hand trial and the Memory and Location measures of the TPT indicate a cognitive as well as pure motor/sensory component to the TPT deficit. Such a deficit would indicate tertiary parietal-lobe dysfunction. The Speech-Sounds Test deficit and the dyslexia indicate temporal and temporal–occipital involvement, while the spelling dyspraxia and the dysarthria suggest more anterior dysfunction, where verbal sequential deficits occur. Therefore the overall picture is one of a severe focal area of involvement with a surrounding area of somewhat lesser disruption.

The diagnosis most consistent with the age and neuropsychological profile is a fast-growing tumor. The focal and severe nature of the deficits suggests either a space-occupying lesion or a vascular injury that has severely disrupted a focal area of the brain, such as an aneurysm that has ruptured. The fact that a surrounding area of lesser deficit may exist argues for a space-occupying lesion, which has widespread effects through the pressure exerted as a result of the added mass in the brain.

Another hypothesis that cannot be ruled out completely on the basis of the test results alone is occlusion of the left middle cerebral artery. The present deficit pattern follows the middle-cerebral-artery distribution and is severe, as is usually the case with an occlusion. This possibility can be ruled out only on the basis of the detailed medical history, as presented.

Case 54

Background data. This 54-year-old patient was tested after surgeons removed a grade II astrocytoma from the posterior left parietal–occipital area of the brain. Testing was completed 6 months after the surgery.

Case Example 54   Age 54   Sex M   Education 14   Handedness R

General Tests:

Category (errors) 65   Trail-making: Part A 54"   Part B 107"

TPT: Total time 24'49" Location 4   Memory 6

Motor and Sensory Tests:

Finger-tapping   R 51   L 43

Finger agnosia   R 0   L 0

Fingertip number-writing   R 0   L 0

Supressions:

Visual   R 0   L 0

Tactile   R 0   L 0

Auditory R 0   L 0

Tactile form

(time)   R 20   L 18

(errors) R 0   L 0

TPT: Time/Block   R 1.67 L .95   Both .53

Cognitive Tests:

Speech-Sounds Perception

(errors)   15   Rhythm (errors)   6

WAIS: (scaled score)

Information	9	Picture completion	9
Comprehension	10	Picture arrangement	11
Vocabulary	12	Object assembly	10
Similarities	11	Block design	9
Arithmetic	10	Digit symbol	6
Digit span	11		

VIQ 105   PIQ 105   FSIQ 105

Aphasia: Spelling (square, triangle); naming (cross); calculation (#26); drawing (key); ideational dyspraxia (#32)

Test results. Normal intelligence is seen in the full-scale IQ, with general agreement from both VIQ and the PIQ. The overall mean of the verbal subtests excluding Information is approximately a scaled score of 11. The I score is slightly deviant from this mean at a score of 9. This difference may be the result of a brain-related deficit or may be just normal variation. A definite variation occurs between DS and the other performance subtests. This difference is more likely due to brain-related dysfunction. The overall lack of significant severe deficits on the WAIS indicates either a chronic lesion or a highly focal one in which no wide-ranging effects can be seen, if in fact a brain lesion exists at all.

An impairment index of 0.86 is earned, with only one measure being performed within the normal range. The TPT Memory score does not contribute to the impairment rating, although it borders on the brain-damaged range of performance. A generally moderate deficit is seen for the impairment index as a whole, which strongly suggests brain dysfunction.

No consistently lateralized motor or sensory deficits are seen. The only two deficits are found on the Finger-tapping Test and the TPT measure, and these two results indicate impairment in opposite hemispheres. The Finger-tapping Test shows a slight problem on the left-hand trial. The absolute score is just barely into the brain-damaged range for nondominant-hand motor speed. The left-hand score is slightly dysfunctional in a relative sense as well; compared to the right-hand trial a 14 percent difference is seen, where a 10 percent difference is normally expected. A more striking difference is seen on the TPT, where the right-hand trial is much worse than would be expected when compared to the left-hand trial. No other abnormalities are seen on the motor/sensory measures.

General cognitive disruption is seen on the Category Test and the TPT total-time and Location scores. Trails A and B scores show equal impairment, and both fall into the brain-damaged range. Indications of lateralized impairment are seen from the Speech-Sounds versus Rhythm tests. More impairment on the Speech-Sounds Test indicates left-hemisphere dysfunction that probably involves the secondary areas of the posterior left temporal lobe.

Extensive dysphasia is also present, confirming the left-hemisphere dysfunction postulated from the Speech/Rhythm comparison. Both spelling dyspraxia and dysnomia occur, a serious sign. Significant word-finding problems occur along with other verbal dysphasic errors on the Aphasia Test, including difficulties calculating, drawing, and mentally evaluating body positions.

Despite the relative lack of deficit on the WAIS, a brain injury is strongly indicated by the impairment index and the general disruption on the neuropsychological profile. In this case the motor/sensory results do not provide lateralizing indicators, although the profile pattern suggests left-hemisphere dysfunction and an absence of any significant right-hemisphere damage.

The extensive dysphasia is the best clue to the location of the injury. Dysnomia is almost always indicative of left-hemisphere dysfunction, although no specific locus is strongly indicated by this result alone. The result in combination with spelling dyspraxia, dyscalculia, and construction dyspraxia tends to implicate tertiary-parietal-lobe involvement.

In view of the amount of "left-hemisphere" dysphasia and the lack of lateralizing indications pointing to the right hemisphere, it appears that the left hemisphere exclusively is involved. The few right-hemisphere indicators seem to be secondary results of the left-hemisphere injury. The tertiary parietal-lobe injury indicated by the primary dysphasic signs is further supported by the other test results. The Speech-Sounds Test deficit implicates the secondary areas of the left temporal lobe, which in the posterior aspects of the temporal lobe are adjacent to the posterior tertiary areas indicated above. The lack of deficit on the Rhythm Test in comparison to the Speech-Sounds and Aphasia tests tends to argue for a more posterior placement of the lesion in the temporal and parietal lobes, as well.

Case 55

Background data. This 26-year-old patient was tested after a severe head trauma accompanied (at the time of testing) by significant hydrocephalus under partial control by a shunt placed surgically into the right lateral ventricle. Testing was to determine present level of functioning.

Case Example _55_ Age _26_ Sex _M_ Education _12_ Handedness _R_

General Tests:

Category (errors) _126_ Trail-making: Part A _4'21"_ Part B _10'_

TPT: Total time _30'_ Location _0_ Memory _3_

Motor and Sensory Tests:

Finger-tapping	R _17_ L _15_	Fingertip	
Finger agnosia	R _0_ L _0_	number-writing	R _7_ L _7_
Supressions:		Tactile form	
Visual	R _4_ L _3_	(time)	R _21_ L _21_
Tactile	R _3_ L _6_	(errors)	R _1_ L _1_
Auditory	R _2_ L _0_		

TPT: Time/Block R _10.0_ L _1.7_ Both _3.3_

Cognitive Tests:

Speech-Sounds Perception

(errors) _24_   Rhythm (errors) _11_

WAIS: (scaled score)

Information	_7_	Picture completion	_0_
Comprehension	_4_	Picture arrangement	_6_
Vocabulary	_4_	Object assembly	_1_
Similarities	_4_	Block design	_4_
Arithmetic	_6_	Digit symbol	_2_
Digit span	_5_		

VIQ _70_   PIQ _52_   FSIQ _60_

Aphasia: Drawing (cross, key); naming (cross, triangle); pronunciation; reading (letters, sentences); calculation; R-L confusion.

281

Test results. The overall earned IQ places this person in the mental-defective range of functioning. In examination of the VIQ–PIQ difference, however, it becomes clear that there is wide variability in skills. A 22-point difference berween the IQs suggests that a brain injury is likely. Such large differences are usually the result of acquired deficit rather than congenital retardation. Looking at individual subtest scores often provides evidence for determining whether the deficits are acquired or inborn. In this case the I, PA, and A scores are significantly different from the other scores, suggesting that this person had a higher premorbid level of functioning and then acquired these deficits. His I and A performances indicate that he can do simple tasks that require merely long-term memory or simple verbal understanding and arithmetic addition. Other tasks (C, V, S, and Digit Span) that necessitate immediate-adaptive abilities are too difficult. On these tests he must think, devise elaborate verbal explanations, or sustain his attention and concentration. Likewise, on the performance subtests he must actively search a complex visual configuration (PC), recognize and then construct objects (OA), and maintain a sustained effort at matching numbers with the proper symbols (Digit Symbol). Deficits are manifested on tasks requiring adaptive and novel responses. It should be noted, however, that the patient is probably showing generalized deficit on the WAIS and just performs worse on the immediate-adaptive tests.

All of the seven tests of the impairment index were given, and a rating of 1.0 confirms the generalized and severe disruption seen on the WAIS. All tests of the index were severely impaired and fell well into the brain-damaged range. In fact, all tests given except the Finger Agnosia measure were severely disrupted.

Such generalized impairment results in decrements on both left- and right-hemisphere measures. Motor and sensory deficits are evident; the Finger-tapping test indicating bilateral impairment, with the dominant hand (and therefore left hemisphere) being more severely disrupted in both motor speed and strength. The Fingertip Number-writing score was bilaterally impaired, with no indication of one side being worse than the other. Dominant-hemisphere injuries often result in bilateral impairment of this test owing to the coordinating functions of this hemisphere that necessitate bilateral sensory representation. Suppressions occurred in all modalities, with only the auditory measure indicating lateralized injury (left hemisphere). As mentioned, Finger Agnosia was unimpaired, which is an unusual finding given the severe sensory problems indicated by the suppressions.

Cognitive functions were severely disrupted, and again the left-hemisphere tasks seem slightly worse, although impairment of both right- and left-hemisphere tests is obvious. Trails B is significantly more impaired than Trails A, and the Speech-Sounds Test is more impaired than Rhythm. Likewise, the right-hand (left-hemisphere) trial of the TPT is much worse than the left-hand (right-hemisphere) trial. Finally, bilateral impairment on the Aphasia Test is seen. Right-hemipshere dysfunction is indicated by the construction dyspraxia occurring on the drawings of the Greek cross and the key. Left-hemisphere damage is suggested by naming, pronunciation, and reading problems. The calculation and right–left-orientation problems corroborate the other dysphasia signs.

Brain damage is obvious from the severe performance decrements seen on almost every test. Since the deficit profile is one of generalized impairment, there are no indications of focal lesions. Both left- and right-hemisphere tasks are uniformly disrupted, which strongly suggests bilateral and diffuse impairment. As a result, localized disorders such as cerebrovascular accidents and space-occupying lesions are ruled out as possible etiologies.

Case 56

Background data.   This 45-year-old man suffered a major occlusion of the left internal carotid artery 11 months prior to the testing. Testing was requested to evaluate the patient's level of disability. The patient is reported to have previously had low normal intelligence.

Case Example 56 Age 45 Sex M Education 11 Handedness R

General Tests:

Category (errors) 63 Trail-making: Part A 66" Part B 180"

TPT: Total time 20'54" Location 1 Memory 3

Motor and Sensory Tests:

Finger-tapping R 22 L 44 Fingertip
Finger agnosia R 3 L 0 number-writing R 10 L 4

Supressions: Tactile form
                                    (time) R 25 L 18
Visual R 0 L 0
                                    (errors) R 2 L 1
Tactile R 0 L 0

Auditory R 0 L 0

TPT: Time/Block R 2.7 L .78 Both .51

Cognitive Tests:

Speech-Sounds Perception
(errors) 21 Rhythm (errors) 11

WAIS: (scaled score)

Information 7 Picture completion 7
Comprehension 5 Picture arrangement 9
Vocabulary 6 Object assembly 9
Similarities 0 Block design 6
Arithmetic 6 Digit symbol 5
Digit span 6

VIQ 72 PIQ 93 FSIQ 80

Aphasia: Spelling (triangle), reading,
pronunciation, calculation,
drawing (key)

285

Test results.   Dull-normal intelligence is seen in the full-scale IQ; however, this score may be misleading in view of the variation within the WAIS scores. The PIQ suggests a low average intellectual level of functioning, despite apparent deficits on two performance subtests (BD, Digit Symbol). Rather generalized decrement is seen on the verbal section, but low normal premorbid verbal abilities are suggested by the PIQ and the patient's history.

The generally sensitive WAIS subtests are disrupted, suggesting a brain-related deficit that is responsible for the poor WAIS performance. The BD score alerts one to a possible spatial deficit resulting from damage to either of the parietal lobes. Verbal disruption is most notable on the WAIS. The VIQ is more than 20 points below the PIQ, and generalized decrement is apparent on each of the verbal subtests. The S score is most striking, where no points were obtained (scaled score of zero). The WAIS, then, suggests a severe and probably acute lesion as demonstrated by the large discrepancy between verbal and performance abilities.

An impairment index of 1.0 is earned. All tests are disrupted, with severely dysfunctional performance on all but two of the measures (Category and Rhythm). Such an impairment rating corroborates the severe disruption seen on the WAIS.

Most deficits suggest a left-hemisphere lesion; the relative deficit on Trails B compared to Trails A, Speech-Sounds compared to Rhythm, and right-hand motor/sensory performance compared to left-hand performance all suggest left-hemisphere dysfunction. Both motor/sensory and cognitive disruption is evident. Right-hand motor-speed deficits occur on the Finger-tapping test. Lateralized sensory deficits also implicating the left hemisphere are seen on both the sensory tests. Right-hand deficits occur on the Finger Agnosia and Fingertip Number-writing tests; however, no suppressions occur. Severe discrepancies between the right- and left-hand trails of the TPT indicate motor/sensory disruption as well as a cognitive component to the deficit.

Left-hemisphere cognitive disruption is seen on several tests. The Speech-Sounds Test is quite poorly performed, indicating severe disruption of phonemic understanding. Several dysphasia signs occur on the Aphasia Test, indicating left-hemisphere dysfunction. Spelling, reading, and pronouncing difficulties are the most prominent left-hemisphere indicators. Calculation problems are evident that probably also can be associated with left-hemisphere dysfunction. Drawing problems are evident on only one item, the key. This item is often drawn without sufficient detail in left-hemisphere-damaged subjects. Where the spatial features of the key are generally preserved and the item lacks detail, a left-hemisphere injury is indicated. In this case, then, the drawing difficulty probably indicates left-hemisphere damage, as well.

Certain right-hemisphere tasks are also poorly performed. The Trails A score is well into the brain-damaged range. This deficit is likely the result of the generalized disruption of the left hemisphere. The Trails B test is much more dysfunctional than Trails A, which usually implies a lateralized lesion to the left hemisphere. Likewise, the Rhythm Test is well into the brain-damaged range, although it is better performed than the Speech-Sounds Test, again indicating a left-hemisphere lesion. Finally, the BD subtest is more poorly performed than most of the other performance subtests. This result usually indicates a right-hemisphere lesion; however, when it is accompanied by a complex of deficits strongly indicating the left hemisphere over the right then the result is attributed to mild spatial problems, which can occur in the left parietal lobe. This interpretation is supported by the severe right-hand TPT deficit in this case, which also implies left-parietal spatial dysfunction.

It would appear that all deficits are consistent with a left-hemisphere lesion. It is apparent that the motor/sensory strip is involved by the Finger-tapping, Finger Agnosia, and Fingertip Number-writing deficits. Further areas of involvement can be isolated by looking at the Speech-Sounds and Aphasia deficits. A severe deficit on the Speech-Sounds Test suggests secondary left-temporal-area involvement. Further temporal-lobe as well as tertiary-area parietal-lobe involvement is indicated by the extensive dysphasia present. It would appear, in fact, that the entire left hemisphere, except for the middle and anterior portions of the frontal lobe, is involved. The Category Test is not disrupted severely enough to infer frontal-lobe involvement beyond the motor strip.

Such a deficit complex follows the distribution of the left middle cerebral artery and therefore leads to the most probable etiological alternative. In light of the severity, as indicated by the 1.0 impairment index, an infarction or a hemorrhage of the internal carotid or middle cerebral artery is most likely the cause of the disorder. These two possibilities may be distinguished in this case on the basis of lack of suppressions. A hemorrhage, especially one involving the entire area of distribution of the middle cerebral artery, is a very debilitating disorder and one that usually results in tissue destruction of either the auditory or tactile primary areas. Since infarctions are usually not as severe (assuming that the occlusion of the artery is not permanent), suppressions are less frequently seen. Thus an infarction is a more likely explanation in the present case, where no suppressions occur.

Case 57

Background data. This 31-year-old female was injured in an automobile accident in which her frontal lobes severely impacted on the front windshield while she was a passenger in the right front seat. She was unconcious for 7 days following the accident. Testing was done 39 days after the accident, just before the patient was to return home.

Case Example __57__ Age __31__ Sex __F__ Education __12__ Handedness __R__

General Tests:

    Category (errors) __93__ Trail-making: Part A __21__ Part B __124__

    TPT: Total time __10'38__ Location __4__ Memory __9__

Motor and Sensory Tests:

Finger-tapping	R __54.6__ L __47.2__	Fingertip	
Finger agnosia	R __0__ L __0__	number-writing	R __4__ L __3__

Supressions:		Tactile form	
		(time)	R __14__ L __16__
Visual	R __0__ L __0__		
Tactile	R __0__ L __0__	(errors)	R __0__ L __0__
Auditory	R __0__ L __0__		

    TPT: Time/Block R __.63__ L __.16__ Both __.24__

Cognitive Tests:

    Speech-Sounds Perception
      (errors) __13__   Rhythm (errors) __14__

    WAIS: (scaled score)

Information	__14__	Picture completion	__12__
Comprehension	__18__	Picture arrangement	__12__
Vocabulary	__16__	Object assembly	__8__
Similarities	__13__	Block design	__7__
Arithmetic	__9__	Digit symbol	__8__
Digit span	__10__		

        VIQ __119__   PIQ __97__   FSIQ __110__

Aphasia: Reading (#13), pronunciaiton (#20), drawing (key)

Test results.   Bright-normal intellectual functioning is seen in the full-scale IQ, although variation in the VIQ and the PIQ scores suggests that premorbid levels of functioning may be underestimated by the full-scale IQ. A VIQ of 119 arises from a verbal section in which considerable intertest scatter exists. Ths scatter suggests that even the VIQ may underestimate premorbid ability. Superior verbal abilities are indicated by the C and V scores. A similar level of premorbid performance is also reflected in the PC and PA subtests.

WAIS deficits are more prominent on the performance subtests, although verbal deficits do also occur. The BD, OA, and Digit Symbol subtests all fall at least four scale score points below the high performance-subtest scores. These deficits appear to represent spatial deficiencies as well as general impairment (manifested on the Digit Symbol subtest). General impairment is also seen on the Digit Span subtest of the verbal section. Verbal-subtest deficit is also seen on A and perhaps on S, although to a lesser extent. The more prominent deficits on the performance section argue for a right-hemisphere lesion, although slight deficits on the verbal subtests also indicate left-hemisphere dysfunction.

An impairment index of 0.57 is obtained, with brain-damaged performance on four of the seven tests making up the impairment index. Mild-to-moderate impairment is seen on the Category Test, the Location score of the TPT, and the Speech-Sounds and Rhythm tests. The other two TPT measures and the Finger-tapping Test scores for both hands are well within normal limits. A middle-range rating and only mild-to-moderate impairment on the contributing tests suggests a moderate lesion without severe focal effects.

Impairment is seen on both left- and right-hemisphere tasks without strong motor/sensory indications. Errors do occur on the Fingertip Number-writing Test, although bilateral impairment is seen without strong lateralizing indications on the other motor or sensory tasks (Tapping, Finger Agnosia, and suppressions). A slight left-hand deficit on the Finger-tapping Test is apparent, although this result is too weak to suggest an exclusively lateralized lesion and is not, in fact, corroborated by the other motor/sensory results. Lateralized impairment is evidenced on the right-hand trial of the TPT. In view of the overall lack of other motor and sensory impairment this deficit is probably more related to spatial- and tactual-perceptual difficulties, however.

As with the WAIS, cognitive impairment on the other neuropsychological measures suggests both left- and right-hemisphere involvement. In comparison of Trails B with Trails A a left-hemisphere dysfunction is suggested. This result is contradicted by the Speech/Rhythm comparison, which indicates right-hemisphere dysfunction (bilateral deficit is also a possibility).

The Aphasia Test showed three errors, two of which lateralize strongly to the left hemisphere (the other error can lateralize to either hemisphere). The first two were a reading deficit and a pronunciation deficit, which probably relate to the posterior aspects of the left hemisphere. The other deficit involves poor drawing of the key and may represent either spatial difficulties associated with the right hemisphere or the result of poor drawing skills, which relates to left-hemisphere abilities. Without qualitative analysis of the actual drawing it is difficult to determine which hemisphere is responsible for the deficit.

A brain injury is apparent from the 0.57 impairment rating and the three errors on the Aphasia Test as well as numerous cognitive deficits. The individual results do not reveal any severe deficits and would appear to be consistent with a 0.57 impairment rating. The lesion is likely of moderate severity and without clearly focal lines of demarcation.

The motor and sensory results do not signify any strongly focal or lateralized areas of involvement. The cognitive deficits are also in agreement with the impairment index in not specifying a focal lesion. Both the motor/sensory and cognitive results indicate bilateral impairment.

In the left hemisphere the results seem to indicate a more circumscribed area of involvement confined generally to the posterior regions. The frontal lobe of the left hemisphere seems less intact, as indicated by the Category Test and Trails B as well as the TPT performance in the absence of sensory signs. The Speech Test deficit suggests mild involvement of the left temporal lobe. A slight deficit on Similarities and the deficits on Arithmetic and Digit Span also indicate this general area of dysfunction.

Right-hemisphere deficits do not suggest such a circumscribed area of involvement in the right hemisphere. A slight Finger-tapping Test deficit coupled with a definite Rhythm Test deficit suggest right-anterior-hemisphere involvement. The right-posterior-hemisphere region is implicated by the spatial deficits, including the drawing difficulties and the WAIS performance-subtest deficits. It can be seen that a rather diffuse and mild-to-moderate lesion is suggested by the right-hemisphere deficits.

This pattern of moderate overall disruption seen on the neuro-psychological profile with a circumscribed lesion in one hemisphere and a more diffuse lesion in the other hemisphere leads to one etiological conclusion. A trauma is the only likely explanation for the test pattern. The dysphasia results and the 22-point difference between VIQ and PIQ suggest a fairly acute injury in which the immediate disruptive effects of the lesion are still visible.

In light of the overall lack of severity of the neuropsychological disruption and the acute effects from which the patient is likely to recover, a good prognosis can be predicted. Mainly immediate-adaptive functioning has been affected on the neuropsychological profile. This fact is a good prognostic indication, since it implies recoverable functions in a moderate injury where more "crystalized" abilities remain intact.

Case 58

Background data. This 45-year-old male was tested toward the end of a hospitalization for multiple sclerosis (MS). This was the patient's fifth hospitalization for this disorder. Although he was originally admitted for an exacerbation of the disease process, most of the acute signs had disappeared by the time of testing.

Case Example __58__ Age __45__ Sex __M__ Education __12__ Handedness __R__

General Tests:

Category (errors) __50__ Trail-making: Part A __19"__ Part B __85"__

TPT: Total time __16'12"__ Location __2__ Memory __6__

Motor and Sensory Tests:

Finger-tapping   R __63.2__ L __46.4__   Fingertip

Finger agnosia   R __-__ L __-__   number-writing   R __1__ L __2__

Supressions: Tactile form

    Visual   R __0__ L __0__   (time)   R __12__ L __12__

    Tactile   R __0__ L __0__   (errors)   R __0__ L __0__

    Auditory   R __1__ L __2__

TPT: Time/Block   R __.89__ L __.59__ Both __50__

Cognitive Tests:

Speech-Sounds Perception

    (errors)   __15__   Rhythm (errors)   __3__

WAIS: (scaled score)

Information   __8__   Picture completion   __12__

Comprehension   __11__   Picture arrangement   __11__

Vocabulary   __9__   Object assembly   __7__

Similarities   __11__   Block design   __6__

Arithmetic   __6__   Digit symbol   __7__

Digit span   __9__

VIQ __96__   PIQ __103__   FSIQ __99__

Aphasia: Reading, calculation, ideomotor apraxia

Test results. The WAIS differential favors the performance subtests slightly, which seems to be the result of large age corrections which appear to be unwarranted in this particular case. The performance section yields apparent decrements on PC, OA, and BD when compared to the other subtest scores in the section. Such large differences within the performance section lead to a firm hypothesis of brain dysfunction. The results could be due to spatial/visual analysis deficits or to motor problems, which can result from a focal lesion or MS.

The verbal section shows decrement on the A and perhaps the I subtests. Given the VIQ–PIQ difference, the verbal section does not indicate as much left-hemisphere dysfunction as would be expected, especially since A may be dysfunctional in right-hemisphere injuries as well as left-hemisphere injuries. The VIQ–PIQ difference appears to be misleading in this case, and the balance of evidence suggests a right-hemisphere lesion, if any.

The impairment index equals 0.5 and is suggestive of a mild brain impairment. Performances on the TPT total-time and Location scores and the Speech-Sounds Perception test contribute to the 0.5 index. The Finger-tapping Test, while within normal absolute levels, shows a relative deficit for the left hand. Suppressions in the left visual field and bilaterally in the ears tend to confirm the indications of brain impairment.

The results fall into two basic categories, with some conflicting strengths and weaknesses. The first category represents right-hemisphere deficits and includes predominantly motor and sensory problems. The visual suppression in the left visual field stands out as the most important deficit in the right hemisphere. The slight deficit in left-hand motor speed (Finger-tapping Test) accompanies the suppression in indicating right-hemisphere motor/sensory impairment. Unfortunately, the Finger Agnosia and Grip Strength tests were not given. The Fingertip Number-writing Test was mildly impaired but not lateralized. Mild spatial/motor deficits on the WAIS also implicate right-hemisphere involvement, as does the Location score of the TPT.

Several right-hemisphere strengths need to' be brought to light in discussing the test pattern. The excellent pattern of scores on Trials A, PA, and Rhythm argues strongly against significant right-hemisphere cortical involvement. These three tests together are highly unlikely to be performed so well in cases with significant massive involvement of cortical tissue of the right hemisphere. Likewise, the TPT falls just barely into the brain-damaged range and does not show a lateralized deficit on either hand. It is likely that the TPT deficit results from generalized motor/sensory and mild spatial dysfunction rather than a focal right-hemisphere lesion.

The second set of deficits corresponds to the left hemisphere, and the deficits are cognitive and sensory in nature. The Speech-Sounds Test demonstrates some problems in discriminating basic speech sounds, which represents left-temporal-lobe dysfunction. Mild dysphasia signs occur and include reading, calculating, and ideomotor apraxia difficulties. Again, suppressions occur, this time in the auditory modality.

This deficit complex does not appear to represent any specific focal lesion. The auditory suppression and the Speech-Sounds Test deficits localize to the left temporal lobe; however, the dyscalculia and ideomotor apraxia do not fit such an interpretation. Certain strengths also occur, as in the right-hemisphere pattern, which confuse the picture and argue strongly against a significant focal lesion. The Trails B performance is highly unlikely given a left-temporal-lobe lesion in which suppressions occur. Likewise, the Finger-tapping Test performance argues for a relatively intact left hemisphere.

The results are quite conflicting and do not appear to make sense in terms of cortical impairment. The left hemisphere appears to be severely disrupted, as indicated by the auditory suppressions. Likewise, suppressions occur in the right hemisphere. In each case, however, certain tests are excellently performed, which discounts the possibility of a cortical injury consistent with the severity suggested by the suppressions. Whenever severely conflicting results occur, a psychiatric diagnosis must be entertained. Such an explanation does not appear appropriate in this case given the motor and sensory problems and excellent performance on certain immediate-adaptive abilities (Trails, Rhythm, and Digit Span), that require sustained concentration and abilities such as are impaired in psychiatric conditions.

A subcortical disorder must also be considered when conflicting results occur, especially since in the present case appropriate cognitive deficits do not accompany the manifested motor/sensory problems. In the present case right-hemisphere deficits include prominent motor and sensory problems accompanied by mild cognitive deficits. given the right-hemisphere cognitive strengths in PC, PA, Trails A, and Rhythm, the cognitive deficits that are extant seem to arise from diffuse and spotty lesions characteristic of subcortical disorders. Likewise, in the left hemisphere severe sensory problems are not accompanied by severe cognitive problems, and the same spotty cognitive deficits are apparent. A subcortical disorder would appear the most likely explanation, and two alternatives present themselves: Parkinson's disease and multiple sclerosis.

Parkinson's disease is basically a motor disorder resulting from disruption of the basal ganglia. As such, the present results do not appear to be the result of Parkinson's disease. The Finger-tapping Test score is too high, and no other indications of motor problems such as dysgraphia are present. The motor symptoms of the disease process can be largely eliminated by medication, however, and for this reason the diagnosis can not be completely ruled out.

The typical performance profile for multiple sclerosis includes motor and sensory deficits (often inconsistent) and mild cognitive deficits. The present case follows this pattern, although auditory problems occur and the VIQ is less than the PIQ, which is uncommon in MS. As mentioned above, the scores on WAIS performance are inflated by age corrections. This phenomenon may tend to artificially inflate the PIQ. In actuality, there are significant deficits on this section that are being masked by the age correction, causing the PIQ to be larger than the VIQ. Also, while auditory suppressions are uncommon in MS, they do occur and cannot otherwise be logically explained in the present case.

In summary, the present results seem to arise from a subcortical disorder, most probably multiple sclerosis. The most prominent symptoms are the visual and auditory suppressions, which represent lower-brain lesions. Cognitive deficits also occur and include mild verbal, left-hemisphere problems and mild spatial, right-hemisphere problems. As diffuse, spotty deficits, the cortical indications are consistent with a subcortical disorder such as multiple sclerosis that attacks tissue in no uniform or focal manner.

This profile clearly shows the inconsistent and oftentimes confusing picture typical of diffuse, degenerative noncortical disease processes. When motor and sensory signs are inconsistent with cognitive deficits and suppressions occur in an otherwise mild-looking pattern, a subcortical disorder should be suspected and a thorough medical history must be obtained. Multiple sclerosis typically reveals itself by motor and sensory symptoms, such as visual difficulties, that may occur and then remit. Parkinson's disease is often indentifiable by a resting tremor in the hand that is often unilateral, by a fixed facial expression, and by decreased overall movement with stooped gait.

Case 59

Background data. This 21-year-old male, enrolled in college, had complained of recent difficulties in his schoolwork accompanied by headache, "blurred" vision, and anxiety. A neuropsychological examination was requested to determine if a neuropsychological difficulty might be related to his problems.

Case Example 59 Age 21 Sex M Education 13 Handedness R

General Tests:

Category (errors) 44 Trail-making: Part A 20" Part B 44"

TPT: Total time 2'10" Location 9 Memory 10

Motor and Sensory Tests:

Finger-tapping R 56 L 53 Fingertip
Finger agnosia R 0 L 0 number-writing R 0 L 1

Supressions: Tactile form

Visual R 0 L 0 (time) R 16 L 16
Tactile R 0 L 0 (errors) R 0 L 0

Auditory R 0 L 0

TPT: Time/Block R .6 L .4 Both .22

Cognitive Tests:

Speech-Sounds Perception
(errors) 8 Rhythm (errors) 4

WAIS: (scaled score)

Information 13 Picture completion 15
Comprehension 17 Picture arrangement 14
Vocabulary 11 Object assembly 11
Similarities 13 Block design 12
Arithmetic 14 Digit symbol 15
Digit span 16

VIQ 120 PIQ 121 FSIQ 122

Aphasia: Reading (#16), drawing (key)

Test results. A superior level of functioning is seen on the WAIS, with no appreciable difference between the verbal and performance subtests. Some interest scatter is evident. The V score is below the overall mean of the other verbal subtests by three scaled score points. Similarly, OA is three scaled score points below the mean for other performance subtests. The likelihood of these being brain-related deficits is not great for three reasons. First, the generally sensitive subtests are excellently performed (in fact, above the overall mean scaled score of 14). Second, the particular pattern of deficits (V, OA) points to no specific known lesion. Finally, the other tests of the WAIS do not corroborate the notion of a brain injury that could result in such a deficit complex. That is, if V is deficient, then a verbal problem would be present that would most likely cause disruption on other WAIS verbal subtests. A deficit on OA indicates a spatial problem in which BD would be expected to show the inadequacy. It is unlikely, then, that the deficits on the WAIS are manifestations of brain damage.

An impairment index of 0.14 confirms the impressions from the WAIS that a brain injury is unlikely. The Speech-Sounds Test is the only measure of the index which is deficient, and even this deficit falls just barely into the brain-damaged range.

Simple motor and sensory measures are all excellently performed. The Finger-tapping Test does show a slightly discrepant ratio between the two hands. The left hand is slightly fast in comparison to the 10 percent differential usually expected. This ratio is not clinically discrepant, however, and both measures (right and left hands) are within the normal range of scores. Despite the excellent simple motor and sensory functions, one complex sensory error occurs on the left-hand trial of the Fingertip Number-writing Test. In view of the otherwise excellent performance on the motor/sensory measures and the fact that only one error occurs in 20 trials, this result is probably within normal limits of function.

Cognitive measures are also performed adequately, on the whole. The Category Test is well within normal limits. The Trail-making Test is also well within normal limits, and the ratio between the two parts of the test is not discrepant.

Certain deficits, however, are evident on the Speech-Sounds and Aphasia tests. The Speech-Sounds Test, as mentioned above, falls just barely into the brain-damaged range. The two errors on the Aphasia Test consist of reading and drawing tasks. Other, more traditional pathognomic signs of the Aphasia Test, such as dysnomia, spelling dyspraxia, and dysarthria, do not show up in the current test protocol.

Only four results seem pertinent to determining whether or not the present pattern of results indicates a brain lesion. Three neuropsychological deficits exist—the Speech-Sounds Test deficit and the two errors on the Aphasia Test. A brain lesion that would account for or result in these deficits cannot be defensibly defined. The Speech-Sounds Test deficit and the reading and drawing deficits argue for both a secondary temporal and tertiary parietal injury in the left hemisphere. Such a lesion focus would cause other deficits, such as more extensive dysphasia and sensory signs, that are not present in this profile.

This neuropsychological profile does not seem to be the result of a brain lesion. Even though two errors occur on the Aphasia Test, a result typically thought to signify brain damage 86 percent of the time, the overall profile is not consistent with any known brain lesion. The low impairment index, the lack of any lateralized or strongly focal deficit complexes, and the lack of any indications of a subcortical or psychiatric disorder suggest that the present neuropsychological profile represents a neurologically normal subject.

Case 60

Background data. This patient had a meningioma that, it was estimated, had been slowly growing over a period of at least 1 year. For most of this time the patient reported that no symptoms were present. He eventually came to a medical center to be treated for headaches. The neuropsychological examination was done as part of the patient's evaluation at that time.

Case Example __60__ Age __49__ Sex __M__ Education __14__ Handedness __R__

General Tests:

Category (errors) __56__ Trail-making: Part A __45"__ Part B __78"__

TPT: Total time __13'29"__ Location __1__ Memory __6__

Motor and Sensory Tests:

Finger-tapping   R __54.6__ L __50.4__   Fingertip

Finger agnosia   R __0__   L __0__   number-writing   R __12__ L __6__

Supressions: Tactile form

   Visual   R __0__ L __0__   (time)   R __28__ L __20__

   Tactile   R __0__ L __0__   (errors)   R __0__ L __0__

   Auditory   R __0__ L __0__

TPT: Time/Block   R __.70__ L __.28__ Both __.39__

Cognitive Tests:

Speech-Sounds Perception

(errors) __9__   Rhythm (errors) __7__

WAIS: (scaled score)

Information __11__   Picture completion __9__

Comprehension __9__   Picture arrangement __9__

Vocabulary __16__   Object assembly __14__

Similarities __12__   Block design __9__

Arithmetic __9__   Digit symbol __13__

Digit span __8__

VIQ __107__   PIQ __117__   FSIQ __112__

Aphasia: Drawing (all figures), naming, body positioning (#13,32)

Test results.   Above-average performance on the WAIS is seen overall, with somewhat better scores on the performance subtests. There is variation within both the verbal and performance parts of the test, and such variation is suggestive of brain damage. Performance deficits are seen on BD, PC, and PA, indicating visuospatial as well as verbal deficits. Verbal deficits are seen on A and C, suggesting left-hemisphere deficits that relate to verbal problems. A deficit on Digit Span is probably related to the general sensitivity of this subtest to brain damage overall. In total, the WAIS indicates brain damage, as demonstrated by the variability of the scores in which some subtests suggest superior premorbid ability while other subtests reveal only average performance. The pattern of results, however, does not readily specify a unilateral lesion, since both verbal and performance deficits occur.

An impairment index of 0.57 corroborates the WAIS findings and the indications of a brain injury. Both auditory perceptual measures (Speech-Sounds and Rhythm), the Category Test, and the TPT Location score contribute to the impairment rating; however, of these, only the TPT Location score is severely disrupted. The other measures show only mild impairment.

Simple motor and sensory impairment is not seen; however, complex sensory disruption is evident. The Fingertip Number-writing Test and the TPT show impairment on the right-hand trials, while the left-hand trials remain intact. Further left-hemisphere indications are seen from the Aphasia Test. All drawing items are impaired, which is often an indication of left-parietal-lobe rather than right-parietal-lobe dysfunction. When all drawings are impaired, the likelihood of motor and sensory disruption of the dominant hand is great. A spatial deficit is an unlikely etiology in the impairment of drawing of simple spatial configurations such as a square or a triangle. The impairment of complex sensory functions of the dominant hand, as seen from the deficits on Fingertip Number-writing and TPT, is therefore a more likely explanation for the drawing deficit.

The other deficits on the Aphasia Test also indicate left-hemisphere injury. Misnaming objects is a common verbal deficit associated with left-hemisphere damage. Likewise, body-positioning tasks that involve right–left discrimination and mental kinesthetic/proprioceptive abilities are often associated with the left hemisphere.

Other results occur that do not lateralize or suggest right-hemisphere dysfunction. for example, neither the Speech-Sounds nor the Rhythm Test is more impaired than the other; therefore no lateralized lesion is immediately suggested. Trails A, however, is more impaired than Trails B, indicating right-hemisphere dysfunction.

Several strengths occur in the record which bear pointing out. Basic motor and sensory abilities remain adequate, indicating an intact motor/sensory strip. Also, complex verbal abilities are well preserved even though some spotty verbal deficits appear, such as naming or word-finding difficulties and a poor score on the Comprehension subtest and the Speech-Sounds Test.

In view of the extensive dysphasia a brain injury is evident; however, the lateralization is in question. The WAIS VIQ–PIQ difference suggest a left-hemisphere lateralization, although deficits are seen on some performance subtests, which confuses the picture. The appearance of complex sensory deficits strongly argues for a left-hemisphere focus. The dysphasic signs are consistent with a left-hemisphere injury as well; however, some results, remain to be explained.

The WAIS performance deficits suggest some spatial difficulties that can be explained if the left-hemisphere injury involves the left parietal lobe. This focus seems likely in view of the complex sensory deficits and the dysphasia. The Aphasia Test errors occur on items typically associated with tactual-perceptual abilities or left-parietal-lobe functions. The drawing and body-positioning items rely heavily on tactile sensory information of the dominant hand, which the left parietal lobe provides.

The left-parietal-lobe focus is consistent with the other neuropsychological results. The WAIS deficit seen on the Arithmetic subtest, the TPT Location deficit, and the Block Design deficit all suggest some spatial difficulty, which is often seen in left-parietal-lobe injuries. Only slight verbal problems are seen (Comprehension subtest and naming on the Aphasia test), which again suggests a left-hemisphere lesion that does not involve the temporal or tertiary parietal areas (the predominant verbal regions) as much as the Parietal "spatial" areas.

The lesion seems to be somewhat focal, as indicated by the disruption of parietal spatial functions in the absence of considerable verbal problems, which are associated with the tertiary parietal area. Minor verbal difficulties are apparent, however, which argues against a highly focal lesion. Two verbal deficits, the Comprehension subtest and the naming problem, are probably associated with the disruption of the tertiary parietal-lobe region; however, the speech-sounds discrimination deficit is more likely related to secondary left-temporal-lobe disruption. The deficit demonstrates an area of dysfunction that is somewhat removed from the highly focal area responsible for the spatial and the other two verbal deficits.

Given the low impairment rating and the fairly limited locus of the lesion, the pattern is typical of an extrinsic tumor.

Case 61

Background data. This patient is a 30-year-old male diagnosed as having chronic undifferentiated schizophrenia. At the time of testing the patient was undergoing his fifth psychiatric hospitalization in an inpatient setting. The neuropsychological examination was performed along with an EEG and CT scan to evaluate the possible role of organic factors in the patient's poor response to treatment. All procedures led to the same conclusion.

Case Example _61_ Age _30_ Sex _M_ Education _12_ Handedness _R_

General Tests:

Category (errors) _40_ Trail-making: Part A _60"_ Part B _105"_

TPT: Total time _20'_ Location _5_ Memory _7_

Motor and Sensory Tests:

Finger-tapping   R _62_   L _57_   Fingertip

Finger agnosia   R _0_   L _0_   number-writing   R _9_   L _3_

Supressions: Tactile form

Visual   R _0_   L _0_   (time)   R _16_   L _14_

Tactile   R _0_   L _0_   (errors)   R _0_   L _0_

Auditory   R _0_   L _0_

TPT: Time/Block   R _•75_   L _•78_   Both _•50_

Cognitive Tests:

Speech-Sounds Perception

(errors)   _5_   Rhythm (errors)   _4_

WAIS: (scaled score)

Information	10	Picture completion	9
Comprehension	11	Picture arrangement	11
Vocabulary	9	Object assembly	11
Similarities	13	Block design	12
Arithmetic	9	Digit symbol	11
Digit span	10		

VIQ _101_   PIQ _106_   FSIQ _103_

Aphasia: Pronunciation, calculation (#25,26), body positioning (#31,31)

Test results.   Overall intelligence as seen on the WAIS is normal, with little diffference between the VIQ and the PIQ. There is also little variation between the performance of the individual subtests. Some slight discrepancy is seen between V and A from the high score on the verbal section (S). This disparity may represent some brain-related deficit, although two things argue against this hypothesis. First, the average of the other verbal subtests (those assumed to be adequately performed) is less than three scaled score points above the "deficient" subtests, which argues against a brain-related-deficit explanation of the lower scores on V and A. Second, the WAIS pattern of deficits suggests no particular identifiable-brain-lesion set of results.

A relatively low impairment index of 0.14 is earned, with the only brain-damaged performance occurring on TPT total time. All tests were given, and no strong indication of brain damage is seen.

Despite the lack of indications on the WAIS and the overall impairment measures, several neuropsychological deficits appear. Some motor/sensory measures are poorly performed. The Fingertip Number-writing Test indicates lateralized impairment, with more errors occurring on the right body side. The TPT impairment on the left body side contradicts the Fingertip Number-writing results, however. No spatial deficits occur in the profile, indicating that the TPT deficit is likely the result of motor or sensory problems (unless the patient is psychotic, in which case the deficit may result from psychiatric etiology); if it is brain related, then the motor/sensory results indicate either bilateral involvement or inconsistently lateralized results.

Several cognitive deficits arise in the profile and—like the motor/ sensory indicators—are somewhat inconsistent. Several dysphasia signs occur and make a brain lesion a likely possibility. The deficits fall into three categories. Pronunciation problems are evident in the person's inability to adequately repeat "Methodist Episcopal." Calculation difficulties are evident on two arithmetic problems involving subtraction and multiplication. Finally, body-positioning errors are made to both written and verbal commands. These dysphasia errors all point to a left-parietal-lobe focus. Other problems are noted on the Trail-making Tests. Both parts are performed in the brain-damaged range, with neither being significantly more impaired than the other. No localized or lateralized injury is indicated.

Several strengths are seen. Both auditory-perceptual tasks (Speech-Sounds and Rhythm) are adequately performed, suggesting an intact left temporal lobe. Motor and sensory tasks associated with the function of the primary areas of the frontal and parietal areas are well performed. Both the Finger-tapping and Finger Agnosia tests are excellently done and suggest an intact motor/sensory strip. The lack of spatial deficits on the WAIS performance section and Aphasia Test drawing items indicates an intact right posterior parietal lobe and argues against a serious lesion in the left posterior parietal lobe.

The determination of whether or not the present test pattern represents a brain lesion is a difficult task. The impairment index of 0.14 and the generally good performance of those tests that are most sensitive to brain injury suggest that a brain lesion is unlikely; however, the number or errors on the Aphasia Test argues strongly for a brain lesion.

When a few signs strongly argue for the possibility of a brain lesion in the absence of general impairment, a highly local area of damage is implicated. Does the present pattern of results resemble a focal brain lesion? A left-parietal-lobe lesion may be responsible for the dysphasia, the Fingertip Number-writing problem, and the overall TPT deficit; however, two other results do not conform to this interpretation. First, no finger agnosia is present which result is unexpected if this deficit complex represents anterior-parietal-lobe disruption. Second, confirmatory deficits associated with the left posterior parietal lobe, such as right-hand TPT problems, spelling dyspraxia, dysnomia, and spatial problems, are not present. The lateralized TPT deficit indicating right-hemisphere localization is also in contradiction to a focal lesion in the left parietal lobe. It would seem unlikely, then, that the current results represent a brain lesion.

Case 62

Background data. This 22-year-old male has a history of repeated hospitalization in adolescence for behavioral and psychiatric disorders. The current admission was accompanied by paranoid delusions (mostly of thought control) and auditory hallucinations (voices instructing him on how to behave). The patient showed marked ambivalence and a very flat affect. Neuropsychological testing was used to investigate the possiblity of an organic cause.

Case Example 62 Age 22 Sex M Education 10 Handedness R

General Tests:

Category (errors) 52 Trail-making: Part A 53" Part B 69"

TPT: Total time 12'16" Location 7 Memory 9

Motor and Sensory Tests:

Finger-tapping R 47.2 L 42.8 Fingertip

Finger agnosia R 0 L 0 number-writing R 0 L 0

Supressions: Tactile form

Visual R 0 L 0 (time) R 20 L 16

Tactile R 1 L 0 (errors) R 0 L 0

Auditory R 0 L 0

TPT: Time/Block R .60 L .33 Both .29

Cognitive Tests:

Speech-Sounds Perception

(errors) 9 Rhythm (errors) 15

WAIS: (scaled score)

Information	5	Picture completion	4
Comprehension	5	Picture arrangement	10
Vocabulary	7	Object assembly	12
Similarities	10	Block design	2
Arithmetic	12	Digit symbol	11
Digit span	5		

VIQ 85 PIQ 85 FSIQ 84

Aphasia: Writing (#210)

Test results.   General intelligence scores indicate a dull-normal
level of functioning with no difference between overall verbal and
performance levels. Individual-subtest comparisons, however, suggest
by their large discrepancies the possiblity of brain-related deficits.
Average and above-average scores on verbal and performance subtests
indicate normal premorbid levels of function. The pattern of verbal
deficits is somewhat inconsistent with typical verbal problems seen
arising from left-hemisphere damage. Deficits on I, C, V, and Digit
Span are uncommon with such good scores on S and A. Likewise,
such a severe BD deficit is highly unlikely to occur with such a high
score on OA, a test requiring much the same skills as the BD subtest.
Such a severe deficit is also unlikely to occur without some deficit on
Digit Symbol, the subtest on the WAIS most sensitive to brain damage
in general. The WAIS results, then, are tentative and need to be
checked against further, more conclusive indications of brain dysfunction.

An impairment index of 0.57 provides some substantiation for the
postulate of brain-related deficits. This substantiation also becomes
tentative, however, when a closer look at the tests is taken. The only
test of the rating that falls well into the brain-damaged range is the
Seashore Rhythm Test. The Category, Finger-tapping, and, to a lesser
extent, Speech-Sounds tests all yield scores just above the cutoff
between normal and brain-damaged performance.

From the neuropsychological profile as a whole both motor/
sensory and cognitive deficits are apparent. A severe lateralized left-
parietal-lobe lesion is indicated by the tactile suppression. No other
sensory signs accompany this result, and no lateralized motor dysfunction is strongly suggested. General and slight decline is evident
on the Finger-tapping Test, but no lateralized injury is indicated.

Several cognitive deficits occur. Trails A is well into the brain-
damaged range, but Trails B is excellently performed. It is unusual to
perform this poorly on Trails A and yet do so well on Trails B, which
requires the same skills plus added verbal skills. Both auditory
perceptual tests are performed in the brain-damaged range, Rhythm
being more poorly performed than Speech-Sounds. One error occurs
on the Aphasia Test on the item involving writing the word "square".

Excellent performances occur on the Aphasia Test overall and
the TPT Memory, Location, and relative-hand performances. Also,
the lack of sensory signs (except for the one suppression) is a
significant strength. Based upon these results a parietal-lobe injury of
either hemisphere is unlikely.

The 0.57 impairment index, along with the tactile suppression, the erratic WAIS profile, and the numerous cognitive deficits suggests a brain lesion. With a closer look at the deficit pattern, however, several inconsistencies are seen that call into question the hypothesis that these deficits are brain related.

If a brain lesion does exist, then an indentifiable pattern of deficits should occur. The most prominent sign, the tactile suppression in this case, is always a reasonable place to begin the analysis. A deficit as severe as a suppression should almost always have accompanying deficits. In the present case no finger agnosia is seen, which is inconsistent with the type of lesion suggested by the suppression. Other parietal signs are lacking—no TPT deficit, no Fintertip Number-writing deficit, no appreciable dysphasia. In view of these results another explanation for the suppression must be sought that better fits the available data.

Either a subcortical disorder or a psychiatric diagnosis can be invoked to explain the occurrence of a suppression in the absence of other signs of cortical dysfunction. A subcortical disorder is unlikely in light of the lack of lateralized motor or sensory signs and the numerous other cognitive deficits (Category, Trails A, WAIS, Speech-Sounds, Rhythm), which would indicate cortical dysfunction if there were brain damage at all. The likelihood of a psychiatric disorder that could cause these deficits must be entertained.

Those tests involving complex behavior, sustained concentration, and/or higher cognitive functions are most likely to be impaired in neuropsychological deficit patterns attributed to psychiatric etiology. In this case those tests (e.g., Category, Rhythm, and Digit Span) are impaired. Other tests also involving these skills (e.g., Arithmetic and Digit Symbol) are adequately performed. Such inconsistency in performance is also characteristic of psychiatric neuropsychological profiles. The patient is unable or unwilling to maintain his attention to a task. Consequently, some items may demonstrate patient capabilities found deficient in other items of the same genre and difficulty. This apparent contradiction in performance levels is an indication of the patient's inability or lack of desire to sustain his level of performance.

The tactile suppression in the present case is another indication of the person's inability to attend to task. The severe BD deficit occurring in conjunction with excellent OA performance is also due to a psychiatric deficit. Qualitative analysis of test performance is enlightening at this point. The patient became quite frustrated with the test and refused to or was unable to apply himself because of his psychiatric disability. Thus the score reflects the obstacle to performing, which is the nature of a psychiatric disorder. Another example of the psychiatric disorder interfering with performance is the discrepancy between Trails A and Trails B. With psychiatric patients it is common to find improved performance once they have become exposed to a situation and the "shock" of something new has worn off. Both parts of the Trail-making Test are similar in format which allows psychiatric patients to accomodate to the situation by the time they take the second Trail-making Test. Thus psychiatric patients may do better the second time around because performance is not limited by a basic brain deficit but by psychological reaction to the test solution.

The current results seem to be best accounted for by a psychiatric etiology. The pattern of test results does not look like an identifiable cortical or subcortical lesion, and the history is consistent with a chronic psychiatric disorder.

This case points out the importance of integrating the entire profile before making the decision about whether or not brain damage exists. In the present profile a 0.57 impairment rating, a tactile suppression, an erratic WAIS profile, and numerous deficits on the neuropsychological tests represent compelling evidence for a brain lesion. Only on examination of how the entire deficit profile fits together does it become obvious that a brain lesion cannot explain the particular configuration of results.

Case 63

Background data.   This 19-year-old male had recently finished his first year of college but was finding that it took too much concentration. He also complained of a large number of usually vague physiological complaints. As a result, he was referred for neuropsychological and neurological evaluation.

Case Example 63   Age 19   Sex M   Education 13   Handedness R

General Tests:

   Category (errors) 32   Trail-making: Part A 35   Part B 77

   TPT: Total time 7'31" Location 10 Memory 10

Motor and Sensory Tests:

   Finger-tapping   R 51 L 53   Fingertip
   Finger agnosia   R 1 L 1   number-writing R 2   L 0

   Supressions: Tactile form
                                                             21   16
      Visual   R 0   L 0   (time)   R _____ L _____
      Tactile   R 0   L 0   (errors)   R 0   L 0
      Auditory   R 0   L 0

   TPT: Time/Block R .5 L .17 Both .10

Cognitive Tests:

   Speech-Sounds Perception

      (errors)   4   Rhythm (errors)   3

   WAIS: (scaled score)

      Information   11   Picture completion   13
      Comprehension   12   Picture arrangement   14
      Vocabulary   9   Object assembly   17
      Similarities   14   Block design   17
      Arithmetic   10   Digit symbol   11
      Digit span   7

            VIQ 106   PIQ 130   FSIQ 117

Aphasia: Spelling (square, triangle), reading,
           pronunciation, calculation

Test results. On the WAIS there was a 24-point difference between the verbal and performance IQs, a finding highly suggestive of a left-hemisphere dysfunction because of the lower verbal score. There were specific deficits of importance on Digit Span, which was reflected in poor performance on both digits forward and digits backwards. Verbal deficits may be due to cultural or school problems, but this does not seem to be the case presently.

The tests most sensitive to brain damage were relatively normal. The Category Test was performed with only 32 errors, well within normal limits. TPT was also excellent, as were the Memory and Location scores. The Rhythm and Speech-Sounds tests were normal, as was the overall level of the Finger-tapping Test (both hands greater that 50 taps per 10-second period). Thus the impairment index for this patient would be zero, typically interpreted as indicating no brain damage.

Despite the zero impairment index, several aspects of the test performance suggest some lateralized brain dysfunction. Although the Finger-tapping scores are at normal levels, the dominant-right-hand score is less than the nondominant-hand score, an unusual finding in normal individuals without a peripheral hand injury of some kind. On the TPT the right hand is quite slow compared to the left hand, which is almost 70 percent faster. There was a slight deficit on the Fingertip Number-writing Test, with two errors for the right hand and none for the left. Time to identify the shapes on the Tactile From Recognition Test was longer for the right hand than for the left. Most damaging was the patient's performance on the Aphasia Examination: the patient could not spell square or triangle, showed reading dysfunction, and had difficulty pronouncing "Massachusetts."

One is immediately struck by the seeming contradictions in the patient's test scores. On one hand, we have a young man who has recently completed his first year of college (with great difficulty) who has a zero impairment index. On the other hand, we have mild but clear signs of left-hemisphere dysfunction with numerous errors on the Aphasia Examination, mild motor deficits in the right hand, and mild sensory deficits on TPT and Fingertip Number-writing. There is significant loss on Digit Span, and verbal skills in general are well depressed below performance skills.

One possible hypothesis is that we are dealing with a schizophrenic or preschizophrenic individual. Several points argue against such an interpretation. First, the tests normally impaired in schizophrenia (e.g., Category Test) are performed quite well. Second, there is no suggestion of a chronic history usually associated with neuropsychological deficits. Finally, the deficits have a strong focal center, an unusual finding in schizophrenia which now can be rejected as the cause of the neuropsychological test results.

Assuming that there is a brain injury, several points must be examined. The very low impairment index argues against an acute or spreading nature of the symptoms. Focal point an examination of the scores suggests a focus in the parietal lobe. The signs for this include the greater impairment on the TPT as compared to Tapping, the good Category Test (incompatible with a frontal lesion), the good Speech-Sounds Test (imcompatible with a temporal focus), the mild sensory signs, and the obvious aphasia symptoms, particularly in the area of spelling and reading, functions associated with the tertiary parietal areas.

Several possible disorders can account for these deficits. First, there could be a congenital vascular anomaly that is exerting pressure on the brain and that may even have bled in the past, causing some minor tissue destruction. This minor tissue destruction would help account for the serious symptoms within a general pattern of an intact and superior brain. Such vascular anomalies often present as static (chronic) lesions and even in more serious forms will not present an impairment index greater than 0.6. In these disorders the patient is often brought in for headaches or for seizures. These disorders can sound very psychogenic since the vascular problem is often exacerbated by stress, which causes high blood pressure, with treatment aimed at the stress rather than at the brain disorder.

A second possibility in this case is a head trauma that has caused a significant contusion or minor laceration of the brain in the parietal lobe. In either case there can be bleeding and destruction of brain tissue, leading to the longlasting deficits seen even when most functions have recovered from the general trauma. It is not unusual to see such effects following an injury in an automobile or motorcycle or as the result of a sports accident in a man of this age.

This case illustrates the weakness of summary measures such as the impairment index. The patient has a significant and important deficit despite the fact that many global tests are performed without trouble. Had this patient just been given a screening battery of one test, such as the Bender-Gestalt or Category Test, no deficit would have been indentified. The patient would have been treated simply for his referral problem (psychogenic headaches secondary to stress and pressure of his first year of college). The case also illustrates the power of neuropsychological tests to identify subtle conditions that may have been missed by a routine neurological examination (as was the case with this subject).

Case 64

Background data. This 44-year-old male college graduate was tested to evaluate deficits associated with a diagnosis of multiple sclerosis. As the reader will see, however, the interpretation was done blindly by the evaluator, who did not know the patient's history.

Case Example 64   Age 44   Sex M   Education 16   Handedness R

General Tests:

Category (errors) 30   Trail-making: Part A 55   Part B 101

TPT: Total time 25'24"   Location 7   Memory 9

Motor and Sensory Tests:

Finger-tapping   R 43   L 35.2   Fingertip

Finger agnosia   R 2   L 2   number-writing   R 1   L 0

Supressions: Tactile form

Visual   R 0   L 2   (time)   R 16   L 18

Tactile   R 2   L 0   (errors)   R 0   L 0

Auditory   R 0   L 0

TPT: Time/Block   R .96   L 1.00   Both .56

Cognitive Tests:

Speech-Sounds Perception

(errors)   2   Rhythm (errors)   2

WAIS: (scaled score)

Information   12   Picture completion   9

Comprehension   14   Picture arrangement   9

Vocabulary   17   Object assembly   11

Similarities   10   Block design   11

Arithmetic   13   Digit symbol   12

Digit span   12

VIQ 118   PIQ 108   FSIQ 114

Aphasia: None

Test results.   Intelligence testing revealed bright-normal overall psychometric ability with somewhat better verbal than perceptual-motor performance. A 10-point difference separated the verbal and performance IQs. Relatively little intratest scatter characterized the profile. A very high score of 17 was earned on V, while the only significant deficit occurred on S, with a scaled score of 10. PC and PA were slightly low at a score of 9; however, the other performance scores averaged around 11, so that a 9 is not significantly different.

Tests of general neuropsychological impairment show rather inconsistent performance; some tests of more basic sensori-motor skills are impaired, while other tests of higher cognitive functions are unimpaired. For example, general tests of the impairment index, such as Category, Speech-Sounds, Rhythm, are within normal limits. Other general tests, such as the TPT and the Trail-making Test, are poorly performed. The impairment index is 0.3 overall, with the TPT total time and Finger-tapping measures contributing to the index.

Motor and sensory problems predominate in this record. Tapping performance showed a generalized decline, with the left hand being significantly more impaired than the right hand. Confusing sensory signs were also present. Visual and tactile suppressions occurred in the left and right sensory fields, respectively. Bilateral finger agnosia deficits and a right-hand Fingertip Number-writing deficit implicate left-hemisphere sensory-perceptual problems.

In addition to the complicated set of simple motor and sensory results, there are indications of motor and sensory problems that affect the higher cognitive abilities. An overall performance deficiency on the TPT as well as poorer performance with the left hand than the right suggest a motor/sensory problem underlying the TPT deficit. Also, poor performance on the Trail-making Test, with neither part A nor part B worse than the other, and no concomitant cognitive deficits on the rest of the test battery suggest again that basic motor/sensory skills are lacking rather than the higher cognitive components of the ability.

All higher cognitive abilities of the battery were performed excellently. The Speech-Sounds and Rhythm tests were well within normal limits. No acute aphasia signs were seen, and an excellent score on the Category Test was obtained. Certain strengths were noted on the achievement testing, with excellent academic preparedness apparent.

One is immediately struck by the lack of general cognitive impairment in the face of the severe motor and sensory disruption. The complicated and conflicting set of motor and sensory deficits is also an unusual finding that needs to be considered in deciding upon how to explain this particular set of results.

Despite a low impairment index and overall excellent performance on the measures generally sensitive to brain damage, the occurrence of suppressions determined to be valid clearly argues for the presence of brain damage, especially when the suppressions occur in two different modalities. The presence of brain damage is further supported by the consistent pattern of motor and sensory deficits. Had the deficits been random without pattern or consistency as to level of performance, a psychiatric disorder might have been postulated to account for the neuropsychological deficiencies.

In deciding upon etiology, it is important to focus upon two aspects of the test profile: (1) motor and sensory deficits occur in the absence of higher cognitive problems, and (2) motor and sensory deficits occur bilaterally in an otherwise excellent neuropsychological profile. Since the cortex would appear to be in excellent condition, judging just from the higher cognitive performance, the motor and sensory deficits must be the result of noncortical damage. Once a subcortical disorder has been decided upon, the options are narrowly limited.

The two most common subcortical disorders are Parkinson's disease and multiple sclerosis. Two cardinal signs of Parkinson's that usually show up on neuropsycological testing are micrographia (small writing) and tremor (seen also in the patient's writing or drawing). Neither of these two symptoms is present in the current case.

Multiple sclerosis is a demyelinating disease that often attacks the brain subcortically initially and that affects only the cortex in the latter stages. Consequently, motor and sensory deficits are usually prominent in such profiles, and visual difficulties are usually seen, if only transitorily at some point during the course of the disease (often in the form of visual suppressions or scotomata). Since the present case is clearly subcortical with visual suppressions and no evidence of serious cortical involvement, multiple sclerosis is the most likely diagnosis.

Case 65

Background data. This 29-year-old male with a 12th-grade education was admitted to a psychiatric ward for the third time in his life. He was referred for psychological testing to rule out an organic basis of his disorder.

Case Example _65_ Age _29_ Sex _M_ Education _12_ Handedness _L_

General Tests:

Category (errors) _32_ Trail-making: Part A _21"_ Part B _79"_

TPT: Total time _3' 37"_ Location _4_ Memory _9_

Motor and Sensory Tests:

Finger-tapping	R _52_	L _63_	Fingertip		
Finger agnosia	R _0_	L _0_	number-writing	R _0_	L _2_

Supressions:

Tactile form

Visual	R _0_	L _0_	(time)	R _7_	L _9_
Tactile	R _0_	L _0_	(errors)	R _0_	L _0_
Auditory	R _0_	L _0_			

TPT: Time/Block R _•34_ L _•65_ Both _•37_

Cognitive Tests:

Speech-Sounds Perception

(errors) ___3___   Rhythm (errors)   _5_

WAIS: (scaled score)

Information	_13_	Picture completion	_14_
Comprehension	_14_	Picture arrangement	_14_
Vocabulary	_11_	Object assembly	_17_
Similarities	_13_	Block design	_14_
Arithmetic	_13_	Digit symbol	_10_
Digit span	_10_		

VIQ _116_   PIQ _126_   FSIQ _122_

Aphasia: Ideational dyspraxia (#32)

Test results.   Superior intellectual functioning is seen on the full-scale IQ and the performance IQ. The VIQ, however, is 10 points lower indicating that verbal abilities are not as highly developed or have been disrupted through brain injury. Premorbid level of function cannot be estimated as being higher for verbal abilities, however, since little variability is evident in the intertest scatter on the verbal section. If brain-related deficits are present on the verbal section, they represent a global dysfunction affecting the entire section equally.

Individual subtest deviations occur on both the performance and the verbal sections. The two most sensitive measures to brain injury (Digit Span, Digit Symbol) are the lowest scores on the WAIS. Their scores fall at least three scaled score points below the overall mean level of performance on the WAIS, thereby indicating brain-related dysfunction. V and OA are also deviant from the mean level of performance. V may represent a brain-related deficit, although the dysfunction does not quite reach statistically significant proportions. OA is excellently performed at a scaled score of 17 and represents a marked and unusual deviancy from the rest of the WAIS profile.

One of the seven measures of the impairment index is disrupted, which yields a rating of 0.14. TPT Location is the only dysfunctional measure of the index. The Rhythm Test approaches the cutoff score, and the ratio between the right- and left-hand trials of the Finger-tapping test is deviant, although the absolute levels are within normal limits. These two results may indicate that the rating is underinflated, although this interpretation must depend upon corroboratory findings throughout the rest of the neuropsychological test profile.

Apart from the Finger-tapping Test discrepancy between the two hands, little motor/ sensory disruption is seen. No sensory signs are present on the Finger Agnosia or suppression tests. There is agreement between the TPT, and Fingertip Number-writing tests on a right-hemisphere motor/sensory deficit, in contradiction to the Finger-tapping Test results. Both tests manifest deficiencies on the left-hand trials, although mild. The fact that the Finger-tapping test, a more reliable measure of basic motor skills, disagrees with this interpretation and that no sensory findings accompany these mild deficits make their appearance more coincidental than indicative of any brain-related deficits. This deficit complex must be compared with the other findings before being totally ignored, however.

Cognitive deficits are few, apart from the WAIS, TPT, and mild Rhythm deficits mentioned above. The Category Test, the most generally sensitive measure to brain injury, is adequately performed. The only dysphasia error occurs on item 32, an ideational dyspraxia sign. While both parts of the Trail-making test are within normal absolute limits, part B is more poorly performed than part A. This result may be interpreted as representing brain-related dysfunction if it fits into a known deficit pattern representing a specific brain lesion.

While the impairment index indicates little likelihood of a brain disorder, there are several deficits on the profile that need to be accounted for. First, there is the right-hemisphere motor/sensory complex, a pattern which may represent localized brain dysfunction. Then, the WAIS deficits and the TPT and Aphasia Test deficits must be explained before a brain lesion can be ruled out.

If the motor/sensory deficit complex represents a right-hemisphere dysfunction, then the lesion must be located predominantly in the parietal lobe. A lesion in this region of the brain should manifest spatial difficulties in the BD and the Aphasia Test drawing items. The present profile does not show such deficits. In view of this fact and the inconsistencies evident from the contradictory Finger-tapping Test results and the lack of simple sensory signs, these results appear not to be indicative of a brain dysfunction.

On a closer inspection the TPT represents an unusual pattern of performance. Not only is no improvement seen across trials, the performance actually becomes worse the more experience the person has with the test. This pattern of performance is sometimes seen in psychiatric patients who become frustrated and whose performance therefore deteriorates as the test procedes.

The TPT results, then, suggest a psychiatric explanation of the test profile, a hypothesis which is supported by the incongruity of the test results as a whole. On the one hand, contradictory lateralized motor/sensory deficits are present. Likewise, cognitive test performances are also inconsistent. The Trail-making Test comparison indicates left-hemisphere dysfunction, while the Speech/Rhythm test comparison indicates right-hemisphere dysfunction. Neither comparison is followed by the appropriate concomitant deficits. For example, no significant dysphasia occurs to support the left-hemisphere contention; conversely, no strong right-hemisphere indicators are present to corroborate the right-hemisphere hypothesis. The psychiatric explanation appears most fitting in view of the overall inconsistency of the test results and the lack of ability to improve performance with experience. A psychiatric contention is further supported by the fact that most deficits occur on either complex tests or on tasks demanding sustained attention and concentration. For example, the WAIS deficits on Digit Span and Digit Symbol tests require both immediate attention and sustained concentration. Likewise, the TPT is a complex task, which may explain the emotional reaction so often seen to this task. Selected deficits also occur that do not seem to fit into the profile to be explained by any specific lesion. For example, the TPT Location and the ideational dyspraxia problems represent no specific dysfunction. The errors seem more related to a problem with attending to task requirements. In the case of the TPT location deficit a subject is tested on incidental memory, a task for which the person is unprepared and must rely on ability to draw from past experience. Likewise, the Aphasia Test task requires the person to act cognitively on the information before responding. In the present case the person responded in a reactive fashion because he was not sufficiently focused on the task to think about his response before acting.

In summary, the results are best explained by a psyciatric etiology, a fact well supported by a chronic MMPI profile. The neuropsychological results present in this case usually arise as a result of a psychiatric etiology of a chronic nature. The history must bear out the chronic nature of the pathology before this diagnosis can be made.

Case 66

Background data. This 48-year-old male was injured in an automobile accident when his truck "spun off" an interstate highway in icy conditions. The patient struck his head in the cab and was unconscious for 18 hours. The testing occurred some 4 months after the accident.

Case Example __66__ Age __48__ Sex __M__ Education __12__ Handedness __R__

General Tests:

    Category (errors) __—__ Trail-making: Part A __59"__ Part B __96"__

    TPT: Total time __10'35"__ Location __5__ Memory __8__

Motor and Sensory Tests:

    Finger-tapping   R __51.8__ L __41.8__   Fingertip

    Finger agnosia   R __0__   L __0__   number-writing   R __2__   L __5__

    Supressions: Tactile form

        Visual   R __0__   L __0__   (time)   R __14__   L __15__

        Tactile   R __0__   L __0__   (errors)   R __0__   L __0__

        Auditory   R __0__   L __0__

    TPT: Time/Block   R __.42__ L __.39__ Both __.25__

Cognitive Tests:

    Speech-Sounds Perception

        (errors)   __8__   Rhythm (errors)   __2__

    WAIS: (scaled score)

Information	__11__	Picture completion	__7__
Comprehension	__13__	Picture arrangement	__12__
Vocabulary	__12__	Object assembly	__10__
Similarities	__13__	Block design	__6__
Arithmetic	__7__	Digit symbol	__10__
Digit span	__13__		

             VIQ __111__   PIQ __105__   FSIQ __109__

Aphasia: Drawing (square), naming (cross), reading

Test results.   Intelligence testing reveals verbal abilities to be slightly above average and manual-manipulative skills to be essentially normal. Some unusual inconsistencies among the subtest scores occur that alert us to the possibility of brain-related deficits. The A, PC, and BD subtests are unusually low when compared to the average or above-average scores on the Digit Span and Digit Symbol measures. Given this WAIS profile, it might be hypothesized that a spatial deficit is operating to account for these inconsistencies. This postulate must be further substantiated by the rest of the data, however.

Some generally sensitive neuropsychological tests are impaired, substantiating the suspicion of brain-related dysfunction. Both parts of the Trail-making Test fall into the brain-damaged range. While the impairment index is only 0.33, it seems to be suggestive of brain impairment given the overall pattern of deficits.

The neuropsychological deficits fall into basically two categories. The first set of deficits is the larger category and represents right-hemisphere dysfunction. Within this set both motor/sensory and cognitive impairments are apparent. The difference between the right and left hands on the Finger-tapping Test is perhaps worse than the rest. The left-hand trial is the worst by 20 percent and indicates dysfunction in the posterior-right-frontal-lobe area. No simple sensory deficits accompany the motor problems; however, complex sensory difficulties are apparent. The Fingertip Number-writing Test manifests a lateralized deficit, indicating right-hemisphere dysfunction. This indication is further supported by a relative deficit on the left-hand trial of the TPT, even though the overall time to complete the test is within normal limits.

Almost all cognitive measures that are highly related to right-hemisphere function are impaired. Trails A was already mentioned, and construction dyspraxia was evident on the Aphasia Test item requiring the patient to draw a square. WAIS deficits, especially on BD, also occurred, which demonstrates the visuospatial deficits associated with right-hemisphere damage. The Arithmetic subtest can be related to either right- or left-hemisphere damage. Since gross verbal functioning seems to be largely intact in this case, the Arithmetic score probably confirms the right hemisphere deficit.

The second category of deficits is a rather small one and represents mild damage to the left hemisphere. Very mild deficits occurred on the Trails B and the Speech-Sounds tests, which fell just within the brain-damaged range of scores. Subtle problems in phonemic discrimination and verbal symbol processing are indicated. Other language deficits occurred on the Aphasia Test and include a mild naming problem when the patient was presented with a picture of a cross and a slight problem in reading ''see the black dog.''

Thus despite the low impairment index the overall pattern of results clearly indicates brain damage. The right hemisphere is more impaired than the left and seems to show a diffuse area of dysfunction. The right-hemisphere motor/sensory strip is implicated by the Finger-tapping deficit, while the appearance of construction dyspraxia suggests posterior-parietal involvement. The area of dysfunction in the right hemisphere, then, is rather widespread and does not appear to be too severe given the low impairment index and borderline performance with several of the deficits.

The left-hemisphere deficits seem to suggest a more circumscribed area of involvement. The deficits all involve verbal abilities, which represent left-temporal-lobe function. Again, however, the deficits are mild in nature and do not suggest a severe focal lesion, such as a tumor.

The picture of a mild bilateral deficit that is diffuse in one hemisphere and more focal in the other is a rather typical profile associated with a closed head trauma that has resulted in a concussion/contusion injury. The coup effects result from the impact and represent the left-hemisphere deficits in this case. Deficits are focal, owing to the injury received locally from the impact. The contrecoup effects are more diffuse because after impact the brain and skull separate opposite the site of impact, causing general injury to the brain and meninges on that side. The brain is also thrown against the rough edges of the skull, causing general injury to the contrecoup side. The severity of impairment is related to the severity of the trauma.

The chronicity of the injury is difficult to glean from the test results. The present profile could represent the mild residual effect from a serious injury that has subsequently yielded to significant spontaneous recovery of function. With traumatic lesions the brain temporarily loses many functions as a result of edema (swelling) and bruising, which gradually diminish with resultant restoration of many lost functions. This process makes it especially difficult to determine whether a given profile occurs as a result of temporary or permanent loss of function. The present mildly dysfunctional profile could just as well represent the original losses before spontaneous recovery occurred. Fortunely, traumatic injuries are usually easy to document through a thorough medical history, and the chronicity of the present injury need not be judged from the neuropsychological test results alone.

Case 67

Background data. This 20-year-old female was tested after a right frontal congenital arteriovenous malformation was indentified by angiogram in order to provide a baseline level of skills prior to surgery.

Case Example 67 Age 20 Sex F Education 11 Handedness R

General Tests:

Category (errors) 69 Trail-making: Part A 71" Part B 180"

TPT: Total time 22'05" Location 1 Memory 4

Motor and Sensory Tests:

Finger-tapping   R 41.4 L 12.2   Fingertip
Finger agnosia   R 0   L 0   number-writing R 12 L 12

Supressions: Tactile form

Visual   R 0   L 0   (time)   R 16 L 14

Tactile   R 0   L 0   (errors)   R 0   L 0

Auditory   R 0   L 0

TPT: Time/Block R .60 L 10.0 Both .61

Cognitive Tests:

Speech-Sounds Perception

(errors)   6   Rhythm (errors)   1

WAIS: (scaled score)

Information   9   Picture completion   7

Comprehension   10   Picture arrangement   11

Vocabulary   8   Object assembly   11

Similarities   12   Block design   7

Arithmetic   12   Digit symbol   8

Digit span   12

VIQ 103   PIQ 91   FSIQ 98

Aphasia: Spelling (cross), calculation (#26), ideational dyspraxia (#32)

Test results. Normal overall intellectual functions are seen in the full-scale IQ; some discrepancy occurs between the verbal and performance sections, however, with deficient functioning most noticeable on the performance subtests. Deficits on BD and PC appear to represent some form of spatial disability; however, OA is adequately performed, perhaps as a result of the above-average verbal abilities compensating for the spatial problems. A test generally sensitive to brain injury, the Digit Symbol subtest, was also disrupted. Some decrement was also seen on two verbal subtests (I, V). These results may reflect either long-term-memory-retrieval problems or just past academic problems that prohibited initial acquisition of the information.

A moderate impairment index of 0.7 is seen. Deficient performance occurs on the Category Test, the three TPT measures, and the nondominant-hand trial of the Finger-tapping Test. Both auditory-perceptual measures, Speech-Sounds and Rhythm, are adequately performed.

Consistent with the VIQ–PIQ difference, practically all deficits indicate right-hemisphere dysfunction. The outstanding features of the profile include the Finger-tapping Test, the left-hand trials, and the TPT (also the nondominant-left-hand trial). Marked discrepancies between the two hands indicate definite involvement of the right-hemisphere motor strip.

Secondary deficits are numerous and also indicate right-hemisphere dysfunction. The WAIS performance section deficits were mentioned as being indicative of spatial deficit. This postulate is corroborated by poor performance on Trails A and TPT Location; however, no construction dyspraxia occurs. Other strengths of the right hemisphere include good scores on the Seashore Rhythm and PA measures, as well as sensory functions of the left body side.

Some deficits occur that are typically associated with left-hemisphere function. These deficits include mildly deficient functioning on I and V, in spelling the word cross, and on Trails B. Numerous strengths of the left hemisphere, however, argue strongly against a lesion in this hemisphere. No motor or sensory problems are seen, and the right-hand trial of the TPT is adequately performed. Furthermore, excellent performance on Speech-Sounds and Rhythm and lack of dysnomia, dyslexia, dysarthria, and dysgraphia also argue against a left-hemisphere lesion. The left-hemisphere deficits that are present, then, probably arise secondarily from the moderate-to-severe right-hemisphere dysfunction.

Finally, deficits are evident that do not lateralize strongly to either hemisphere. Bilateral deficit on the Fingertip Number-writing Test occurs in the absence of sensory deficit from either hemisphere. the most likely explanation of this problem is a spatial-perceptual deficit that makes it difficult to integrate individual tactual sensations into a gestalt. Therefore the person is unable to recognize which number is being written on either hand. Calculation problems are seen when the task involves multiplication in which carrying of a remainder is necessary. Such a deficit is often closely aligned with spatial difficulties. Finally, ideational dyspraxia also seems to be associated with right-hemisphere dysfunction in this particular case. The deficit arises from spatial-thinking difficulties in which the person is unable to visualize the motor act without gaining the kinesthetic feedback received from actually engaging in the action. Thus in looking at the test deficits that do not lateralize inherently it can be seen that they do lateralize to the right hemisphere in this case.

The left-hand motor problems direct our attention to the right frontal lobe by their severity and marked difference from the rest of the profile. The remaining problem is to decide whether the rest of the deficits indicate posterior or anterior spatial difficulties. The lack of construction dyspraxia and the unusual WAIS pattern of deficits argues for an anterior focus. The lack of lateralized sensory deficits indicates intactness of the right parietal lobe. Moreover, the good performance on the Rhythm and PA measures is unlikely unless the right temporal lobe is intact. By the process of elimination the spatial difficulties can be attributed to the frontal lobe.

Closer examination of these deficits bears out this hypothesis. Poor performance on the TPT can result from either basic spatial and tactual perceptual deficits, which result from posterior-right-hemisphere lesions, or from frontal-lobe deficits, which cause a poor ability to organize a problem-solving strategy with which to approach spatial tasks. In the first case, TPT deficits would be expected to occur, with basic spatial and tactual-perceptual difficulties represented by deficits on BD, drawing tasks, and right-hemisphere sensory measures such as Finger Agnosia and Fingertip Number-writing (on the left hand). In the present case, however, the TPT deficits accompany deficits that are more indicative of frontal-lobe dysfunction. For examble, a PC and Trails A deficit complex indicates a problem with purposeful visual scanning that is generally associated with right-frontal-lobe functions. Likewise, the visual imaging associated with the successful performance of the ideational dyspraxia item on the Aphasia Test is dependent upon frontal-lobe function. When the frontal lobe is dysfunctional (especially the right frontal lobe), visual imaging, which as such is a significant part of this task, is not possible.

Case 68

Background data.   This 55-year-old male was identified by CT scan to have a right temporal tumor (later identified as a slow-growing grade I astrocytoma).

Case Example 68 Age 55 Sex M   Education 16 Handedness R

General Tests:

Category (errors) 45 Trail-making: Part A 34" Part B 58"

TPT: Total time 12'55"Location 7   Memory 9

Motor and Sensory Tests:

Finger-tapping	R 51.6 L 47	Fingertip	
Finger agnosia	R 0 L 0	number-writing R 2 L 0	

Supressions:

Tactile form

Visual	R 0 L 0	(time)	R 8	L 8
Tactile	R 0 L 0	(errors)	R 0	L 0
Auditory	R 0 L 0			

TPT: Time/Block R .35 L .54 Both .40

Cognitive Tests:

Speech-Sounds Perception

(errors) 4   Rhythm (errors) 10

WAIS: (scaled score)

Information	16	Picture completion	11
Comprehension	17	Picture arrangement	10
Vocabulary	15	Object assembly	13
Similarities	14	Block design	12
Arithmetic	9	Digit symbol	11
Digit span	10		

VIQ 125   PIQ 126   FSIQ 127

Aphasia: None

Test results. Intelligence quotients are in general agreement concerning the level of function. All three measures place this person in the superior range of performance. While there is no significant difference between the VIQ and PIQ, however, two deficits occur on the verbal section, with one inconsistency on the performance section. These deficits suggest the possibility of brain-related dysfunction by their discrepancy from the rest of the profile.

The two verbal deficits occur on the Arithmetic and Digit Span subtests. Basic verbal skills appear intact from the superior level of performance on the other verbal subtests. Thus verbal dysfunction cannot explain the Arithmetic and Digit Span deficits. Spatial and/or sequencing difficulties may be responsible for this particular deficit complex. This contention is weakly supported by one comparison from the performance section. While the PA score is not sufficiently deviant from the overall performance-section mean level of scores, it is three scaled score points below OA and two points below BD— discrepant because BD and OA tasks better represent spatial skills while the PA task requires more sequencing skills. In this case, then, a sequencing deficit is suggested.

With a 0.14 rating, very little dysfunction is seen on the impairment index. The Rhythm Test is the only impairment index measure that is disrupted. The Category Test approaches the brain-damaged cutoff score. A subject with such a high level of performance on the WAIS, however, is expected to do better on the Category Test, a task that is highly correlated with intelligence. Therefore such a high error score on the Category Test, even though it does not reach the brain-damaged range of performance, may be considered dysfunctional and perhaps indicative of a brain-related deficit.

Motor/sensory dysfunction is seen on two measures, the TPT and the Fingertip Number-writing Test. Conflicting lateralization is indicated by these two results, however. The Fingertip Number-writing deficit is mild and indicative of left-hemisphere dysfunction. The TPT deficit is seen in the more poorly performed left-hand trial and is a firmer indication of brain injury than the Fingertip Number-writing deficit. No other motor/sensory indications are present, however, that support the TPT deficit in indicating right-hemisphere injury.

Apart from the WAIS deficits, there are few cognitive indications of brain damage. The Trial-making Test is within absolute levels of normal performance on both parts; however, the ratio between the two parts is discrepant. Trails A is near the cutoff for brain-damaged performance, while Trails B is excellently performed. This discrepancy may indicate a slight right-hemisphere dysfunction. A right-hemisphere indication is present in the Speech/Rhythm comparison, where Speech Sounds is excellently performed while Rhythm falls into the brain-damaged range of performance.

Apart from the mild Fingertip Number-writing deficit, no left-hemisphere indications are present. No errors are seen on the Aphasia Test.

Despite the low impairment rating and the lack of dysphasia, brain injury seems to be present. The lateralized indications of brain-related dysfunction and the unusual performance on some of the neuropsychological tests, in view of the superior intellectual ability, argue strongly for a brain injury. Even though many of the tests are only mildly impaired, some not even impaired, some not even reaching the brain-damaged cutoffs, the consistency of the deficits in indicating a certain brain area makes the deficits more decisively indicative of brain-related impairment. The discrepancy in the full-scale IQ and the Category Test score also argue strongly for the presence of a brain injury.

The deficit complex consisting of Trails A, TPT left-hand trial, Arithmetic and Digit Span subtests, and the Rhythm Test suggests problems with tasks involving sequencing and complex visual and spatial analysis. The sequencing deficits imply anterior-right-hemisphere injury. The presence of visual and spatial deficits occur in the absence of indications of basic spatial disabilities (deficits on BD or the drawing items on the Aphasia Test) supports the contention of anterior-right-hemisphere dysfunction. The slight dysfunction on PA corroborates this hypothesis.

The next question is whether the lesion is placed frontally or in the anterior temporal region. The lack of motor deficits makes a frontal placement unlikely. Also, the Rhythm Test deficit argues for a temporal-lobe focus. Since the TPT deficit occurs in the absence of motor or sensory dysfunction, it too is consistent with a temporal-lobe focus. The deficit must be the result of higher cognitive difficulties, since there seems to be no motor or sensory basis for the deficit. Therefore the posterior-frontal-lobe focus (motor) and the anterior-parietal-lobe focus (sensory) are excluded. The posterior parietal lobe is not in question, since no basic spatial deficits are present to otherwise implicate this brain area. Likewise, the anterior frontal lobe does not seem to be involved, since a TPT deficit that localized to this region is usually expected to be accompanied by either bilateral or left-body deficits on the Fingertip Number-writing Test.

The right temporal lobe seems to be the most likely locus of the lesion; however, the rather mild deficit makes the process of diagnosis difficult. The lesion etiology must be a process that can cause a mild yet localized deficit pattern. While it is close to the motor strip, there is no motor-speed deficit. This resslt could occur either in a lesion that is highly circumscribed in its effects or one that is chronic and static so that the motor deficit may have recovered. Two etiologies satisfy these conditions (mild and without wide-ranging effects)—an aneurysm in a temporal branch of the right middle cerebral artery, or a slow growing tumor. Both possibilities explain the results equally well, and the neuropsychological results alone cannot distinguish between the two alternatives. Neurological diagnostic procedures and a medical history are needed for the final diagnosis.

Case 69

Background data.   This 63-year-old male with a 10th-grade education was referred for neuropsychological (as well as neurological)
examination with a history of a 5-year declining course in intellectual
abilities.

Case Example _69_   Age _63_   Sex _M_   Education _10_   Handedness _R_

General Tests:

Category (errors) _117_   Trail-making: Part A _32"_   Part B _480"_

TPT: Total time _30'_   Location _0_   Memory _3_

Motor and Sensory Tests:

Finger-tapping   R _51.2_ L _39.6_   Fingertip

Finger agnosia   R _0_   L _3_   number-writing   R _5_   L _6_

Supressions: Tactile form

   Visual   R _2_   L _0_   (time)   R _20_   L _22_

   Tactile   R _0_   L _0_   (errors)   R _0_   L _0_

   Auditory   R _0_   L _0_

TPT: Time/Block   R _3.3_   L _10.0_ Both _10.0_

Cognitive Tests:

Speech-Sounds Perception

  (errors)   _14_   Rhythm (errors)   _--_

WAIS: (scaled score)

Information	_6_	Picture completion	_5_	(6)
Comprehension	_9_	Picture arrangement	_9_	(12-13)
Vocabulary	_7_	Object assembly	_4_	(5-7)
Similarities	_9_	Block design	_6_	(7-8)
Arithmetic	_9_	Digit symbol	_7_	(10-11)
Digit span	_10_			

VIQ _94_   PIQ _92_   FSIQ _93_

Aphasia: Pronunciation, reading (#21),
calculation (#26)

Test results. Normal intellectual functioning is seen on the WAIS full-scale IQ with no significant difference between the verbal and performance IQs; however, interest scatter is evident on both verbal and performance sections. Approximately equal impairment is seen on the verbal and performance subtests.

Essential deficits occur on only two verbal subtests (I,V). With age corrections, deficits appear on three of the performance subtests (PC, OA, BD). In view of the PA score the Digit Symbol may also represent brain-related deficit, although this result is not as clear as the other performance deficits.

Overall the WAIS appears to yield a brain-damaged profile, although the two most sensitive subtests (Digit Symbol and Digit Span) show no impairment. No immediate localized lesion is suggested by the pattern of results, although impairment is obvious. The profile pattern may reflect either general impairment or some localized deficit that will be revealed in the other test deficits.

Impairment is seen on all six of the impairment index tests given, which yields a 1.0 rating. The Rhythm Test is not available for inclusion in the impairment index. Otherwise, severe impairment is seen on the Category Test and all three measures of the TPT. Moderate impairment is obvious on the Speech-Sounds Test and the left-hand trial of the Finger-tapping Test.

Motor and sensory measures yield conflicting results regarding the laterality of the lesion. The Finger-tapping Test suggests lateralized impairment to the opposite hemisphere. The Finger Agnosia and TPT results support the Tapping results in indicating right-hemisphere involvement. Fairly strong lateralization is indicated by the visual suppressions seen in the right visual field. This result, then, conflicts with Finger-tapping Test suggesting left hemisphere involvement.

Several cognitive tests are deficient. The severe Category Test deficit appears to represent more than the mild-to-moderate Category deficits that occur as a general reaction to brain injury. Deficits this severe usually indicate problem-solving difficulties in which the problem situation is not properly evaluated so that the appropriate intellectual operation can be applied or in which the person is unable to switch operations in the face of changing task requirements or reinforcements. A severe deficit is seen on Trails B in relation to Trails A. Such a large difference and the severity of the deficit on part B often indicate difficulty with the aspect of the test that requires cognitive flexibility. Like the Category deficit, this problem arises from difficulties with evaluating the problem situation and switching operations (switching between numbers and letters in the sequence).

Language deficits are also manifested in the profile on the Speech-Sounds and Aphasia tests. Some receptive language problems are indicated by the trouble discriminating speech sounds. Expressive language difficulties are indicated by the dysphasia signs. Trouble pronouncing and reading are the two language signs on the Aphasia Test. Also on the Aphasia Test there is trouble calculating a complex multiplication problem in which mental arithmetic is required.

This profile represents obvious brain damage with an impairment index of 1.0 and severe motor/sensory and cognitive deterioration. The pattern of deficits does not readily yield to attempts at localizing the lesion. The motor and sensory signs, usually useful in lateralization of a lesion, reveal conflicting indications of which hemisphere is involved. It must be concluded from the Tapping, Finger Agnosia, and TPT deficits versus visual suppression results that both hemispheres of the brain are involved.

Do the present results represent focal lesions, or are they the result of diffuse damage? The right-hemisphere lesion appears to involve the entire parietal lobe and at least the posterior frontal lobe, as evidenced by the Tapping, Finger Agnosia, and TPT measures. The WAIS results confirm the parietal focus with the BD deficit. Since the more severe deficits may also occur on PC and OA, a more anterior lesion locus may also be indicated by the greater deficit in complex visual-analysis tasks (as opposed to the more pure basic spatial skills tested by BD). For the left hemisphere the temporal lobe is indicated by the Speech-Sounds Test deficit. The left frontal lobe, however, is perhaps the most severely disrupted area of the left hemisphere. The severe deficits on the Category and Trails B tests indicate deficits in frontal-executive functions. Expressive language deficits support a left-frontal locus of injury.

The lesion, then, appears to be diffusely affecting the brain. A left-frontal-lobe focus appears that may represent more severe effects of the lesion in this region of the brain. The visual suppressions would normally indicate tissue-destructive damage of the occipital lobe. In this case, however, no compelling evidence for damage to this area of the brain exists other than the suppressions themselves. Alternate explanations for the result are needed, since it is unlikely that a tissue-destructive lesion could occur without giving rise to deficits accompanying the visual suppressions. In view of the frontal-lobe focus of injury it is possible that injury to the visual tracts could be responsible for the visual suppressions.

The most common diffuse process present in people of this age is an Alzheimer-like organic brain syndrome. This particular case, with its frontal lobe focus, argues for a form of this disease process known as Pick's disease. Early forms of Pick's disease often show diffuse deficits with a frontal-lobe and sometimes temporal-lobe focus. Suppressions are also common in these diseases, although they do not represent the same type of damage from suppressions seen in tissue-destructive lesions such as tumors. Pick's disease causes its effects in a diffuse, sometimes almost random pattern of areas throughout the brain (apart form the concentration in the frontal and temporal lobes early in the disease process). The disease is progressive and in its later stages causes severe intellectual deterioration because of the involvement of the entire cortical surface. The present case, then, seems to fit a diagnosis of early Pick's disease rather well in view of the diffuse deficits with a stronger frontal-lobe locus and the suppression that otherwise seems unexplainable. This case consequently also represents a recent onset of the disease process, since the anterior focus is still noticeable and since relatively little WAIS deterioration is seen.

The process of putting together the test results into a single cohesive unit is well represented in this case. The suppressions, a result usually crucial to the interpretation of a profile, took a secondary role in the interpretation of this case. It is necessary to interpret each result in light of the rest of the profile. Consequently, the suppressions were in this case a minor part of interpretation, since they did not fit well with the rest of the profile in determining the type and location of the lesion.

Case 70

Background data. This 24-year-old female was seriously injured while performing as a cheerleader at a basketball game. She did a somersault into the air, landing with her right parietal/occipital area forced into the sharp corner of the official scorer's table. She broke the skull in this area, necessitating surgery to halt bleeding and remove bone fragments. Testing occurred some 8 months later, after extensive surgery.

Case Example __70__ Age __24__ Sex __F__ Education __12__ Handedness __R__

General Tests:

Category (errors) _____ Trail-making: Part A __20"__ Part B __66"__

TPT: Total time __17'50"__ Location __9__ Memory __10__

Motor and Sensory Tests:

Finger-tapping	R __54__	L __43__	Fingertip		
Finger agnosia	R __0__	L __0__	number-writing	R __9__	L __8__
Supressions:			Tactile form		
Visual	R __0__	L __0__	(time)	R __10__	L __18__
Tactile	R __0__	L __1__	(errors)	R __0__	L __0__
Auditory	R __0__	L __0__			

TPT: Time/Block R __.73__ L __.51__ Both __.54__

Cognitive Tests:

Speech-Sounds Perception

(errors) __3__   Rhythm (errors) __5__

WAIS: (scaled score)

Information	__10__	Picture completion	__10__
Comprehension	__13__	Picture arrangement	__13__
Vocabulary	__10__	Object assembly	__14__
Similarities	__13__	Block design	__9__
Arithmetic	__12__	Digit symbol	__11__
Digit span	__10__		

VIQ __108__   PIQ __108__   FSIQ __109__

Aphasia: Drawing (square, cross, key); writing (clock, square); calculation; R-L confusion

Test results. Intelligence testing revealed an average overall level of performance with no outstanding areas of strength or deficit. The worst score was obtained on BD which may indicate a brain-related deficit if supported by similar deficits. As it stands, with very little intratest scatter and no significant difference between the verbal and performance IQs the WAIS yields little important neuropsychological information.

Selective deficits are seen on those tests making up the impairment index. Both parts of the Trail-making Test are adequately performed, as is the Speech-Sounds Perception Test and the Memory and Location scores of the TPT. A 0.5 impairment index is earned by poor scores on the Finger-tapping, Seashore Rhythm, and TPT total-time measures. (The Category Test was not given; thus the index is based on only six tests.) Such an index is generally indicative of brain damage.

The most striking areas of deficit occur with spatial and motor/sensory tasks. Tbe patient manifests considerable construction dyspraxia, having difficulty with even simple drawings on the Aphasia Test. Other deficits on the Aphasia Test include left–right disorientation, dyscalculia, and dysgraphia; all are measures of spatial and/or motor-sensory ability. The TPT test, a measure of spatial problem-solving skills through motor and sensory means, was this patient's second-worst performance. The pattern of deficit on the TPT test indicates poor spatial ability; hence the overall poor performance with no indication of one hand being worse than the other. Also, no improvement occurs on the third trial, which suggests that the added task of coordinating both hands is not well performed. A lateralized motor-speed deficit is seen on the Finger-tapping Test, with the left-hand trial being more poorly performed. As a pathognomonic sign a left-sided tactile suppression is highly indicative of brain damage and if valid almost always indicates a destructive right-parietal lesion. Borderline performance on the Rhythm Test also indicates right-hemisphere dysfunction. Poor performance also occurred on the Fingertip Number-writing Test, with neither hand being worse than the other. No errors were made on the Finger Agnosia test.

With four different types of errors on the Aphasia Test and a valid suppression, the question is one not of whether there is brain damage but rather of where the damage is located. Of all the deficits only two may be even initially considered to fall into the left-hemisphere category—the TPT deficit on the both-hands trial and bilateral deficits on Fingertip Number-writing. Furthermore, two excellent performances on the Trail-making Test part B and the Speech-Sounds Test argue strongly against any significant left-hemisphere injury. Left-body-sided motor and sensory problems and complex spatial cognitive deficits indicate a right-hemisphere dysfunction.

The area of damage is somewhat difficult to pinpoint. There is indication of primary parietal area involvement in the lowered Tapping score as well as tertiary area involvement suggested by the construction dyspraxia. The Rhythm deficit, the tactile suppression, and the lack of problems on Finger Agnosia and Trail-making part A must be accounted for, however. It would seem that there are wide-ranging deficits of mild-to-moderate severity involving a large portion of the right posterior hemisphere with a primary focus in the parietal lobe.

Whenever a suppression occurs, an infiltrating tumor must be considered a possibility. In this case such diagnosis is unlikely considering the overall mild-to-moderate severity of the neuropsychological disruption. Other destructive lesions must be ruled out, such as cerebrovascular diseases leading to neuronal death. Again, such lesions as infarctions and blood-vessel ruptures cause much more severe deficit patterns and can be ruled out on that basis in this case.

In accounting for the wide-ranging nature of the deficit pattern, a traumatic injury is often the most likely choice when the overall picture is of only mild-to-moderate severity. The prominent deficits encompass the entire parietal lobe, with less severe deficits seen in the adjacent areas. This pattern is seen presently in the prominent Tapping, drawing, and TPT results. This explanation accounts for the initial problems in pinpointing the exact location of injury. The case for a traumatic injury is strengthened by the indication that certain functions seem to have recovered. For example, it is unusual to have rather severe deficits such as suppressions and construction dyspraxia while the Trail-making Test part A remains unimpaired. This relationship is common, however, when the patient is tested several months after a trauma in which the initial brain dysfunction caused by the shock and swelling of the actual accident has had the chance to heal and the temporary impairment has recovered. This was in fact the case, as the medical history reveals.

Explanation of the neuropsychological profile on the basis of a traumatic injury also accounts for the troublesome left-hemisphere deficits mentioned—relative TPT deficit on the third trial and bilateral Fingertip Number-writing deficit. As residual contrecoup impairment, these two deficits are what would be expected. They suggest a posterior-parietal-lobe location, which is exactly opposite the site of the right-hemisphere injury. As complex cognitive deficits they are the most likely to be last to recover.

Perhaps the most important point to be gleaned from this case is the necessity for a comprehensive neuropsychological evaluation and a thorough consideration of all possible causes of the resulting deficit pattern. Without a complete test battery, the discrimination of a right-frontal from a right-parietal injury would most likely be impossible. Such a distinction is difficult in any case and was made in the present case based largely upon the relatively intact performance on the Seashore Rhythm Test and the presence of a sensory suppression.

This case also points out the danger of making a diagnosis based on only one or two signs. The presence of a suppression almost always indicates a destructive lesion, which in most cases means either an infiltrating tumor or a severe cerebrovascular process. In this case such a hypothesis was clearly contradictory with the rest of the data and would have led to a wrong diagnosis. It is paramount that all possible etiologies be considered and the one that most succinctly explains all available data then be selected.

Case 71

Background data. This 55-year-old man had last been seen in the hospital for the treatment of lung cancer. The treatment appeared to be effective, but he returned again with complaints of headaches, confusion, dizziness, and clumsiness. A tumor of the left temporal–frontal–parietal areas was found, apparently metastatic and secondary to the lung cancer.

Case Example _71_ Age _55_ Sex _F_ Education _10_ Handedness _R_

General Tests:

    Category (errors) _____ Trail-making: Part A _43"_ Part B _86"_

    TPT: Total time _15 '_ Location _—— _ Memory _—— _

Motor and Sensory Tests:

    Finger-tapping   R _6.8_ L _13.8_ Fingertip

    Finger agnosia   R _7_ L _1_   number-writing R _10_ L _7_

    Supressions: Tactile form

        Visual   R _2_ L _3_   (time)   R _16_ L _16_

        Tactile R _2_ L _0_   (errors)   R _0_ L _0_

        Auditory R _4_ L _0_

    TPT: Time/Block R _1.1_ Q _.4_ Both _———_

Cognitive Tests:

    Speech-Sounds Perception

      (errors)   _49_   Rhythm (errors)   _13_

    WAIS: (scaled score)

Information	10	Picture completion	5
Comprehension	10	Picture arrangement	3
Vocabulary	8	Object assembly	2
Similarities	2	Block design	9
Arithmetic	6	Digit symbol	4
Digit span	8		

        VIQ _88_   PIQ _82_   FSIQ _85_

Aphasia: Drawing (square, cross, key); Spelling Dyspraxia (mild); Right-left confusion

Test results. Dull-normal intelligence is suggested by the full-scale IQ as well as general agreement between the VIQ and the PIQ; however variation in the scale scores with a range from a score of 2 to a score of 10 indicates that a higher premorbid intelligence level probably existed. High scores of 9 and 10 on both verbal and performance subtests suggest a normal premorbid level of ability.

Brain-damaged performance is indicated by the generally sensitive measures, Digit Symbol and Digit Span. General decline is also seen on the performance section, with BD being the only score at an expected level of performance. The most striking impairment is seen on PA and OA which probably indicates left-hemisphere injury in view of the good visuospatial performance on BD. Verbal deficit is definitely indicated by the S and A performances. Borderline impairment is indicated by the V and Digit Span performances.

Three measures of the impairment index are not available (Category Test and TPT Location and Memory measures). The remaining four measures are all impaired, yielding a rating of 1.0. The TPT total-time score reaches only 15 minutes; however, the both-hands trial was not figured into this time. Since the cutoff is only 15.6 minutes and since it can be safely assumed that the person would have taken more than 50 seconds to finish the last trial, the TPT total-time score can be counted as impaired; even at a normal level of performance for the last trial the overall score would have fallen into the brain-damaged range. An index of 1.0 is therefore earned; however, it must be cautiously interpreted, since three measures are not included in the score.

The neuropsychological profile is thoroughly impaired with perhaps the greatest deficits seen on the motor/sensory tests. The Finger-tapping test reflects a large deficit in motor speed for both hands. The right (dominant) hand is more impaired, with scores at almost half the level of performance of the left hand.

There are also clear indications of lateralized impairment to the left hemisphere throughout the sensory measures. The Finger Agnosia and Fingertip Number-writing tests both indicate lateralized left-hemisphere injury with greater impairment to the right hand in both instances. Bilateral impairment on the Fingertip Number-Writing scores is common in left-hemisphere injury, especially where such a lesion is clearly reflected in strongly lateralized Finger Agnosia scores. Suppressions occur in all three modalities, with left-hemisphere disruption exclusively indicated in the auditory and tactile measures. Bilateral visual suppressions occur. The TPT ratio between the right- and left-hand trials bears out the left-hemisphere lateralization.

Cognitive test results largely agree with the motor/sensory tests in the postulation of a left-hemisphere focus of the lesion. A severe deficit on the Speech-Sounds Test strongly indicates left-temporal-lobe dysfunction. A lesser deficit on the Rhythm Test further supports the postulation of a left-hemisphere lesion. The Aphasia Test results also indicate left-hemisphere disruption. Mild spelling dyspraxia and right–left confusion is consistent with a left-parietal-lobe injury. Furthermore, the drawing deficit is consistent with left-parietal-lobe dysfunction, since the square was disrupted, a figure not often in error as a result of right-hemisphere spatial dysfunction.

One result that does not appear to readily fit a left-hemisphere deficit pattern is the Trail-making Test. Trails A is more impaired than Trails B; indeed, part B does not even fall into the brain-damaged range. In view of the other evidence for a left-hemisphere injury, however, this result does not change the conclusion. In fact, it will become obvious that this result helps localize the lesion.

Left-hemisphere injury is fairly obvious from the motor/sensory scores, especially the suppressions of the auditory and tactile modalities. The right hemisphere is implicated by some results, including the bilateral visual suppressions, the Trails A test, and the level-of-performance score on the left-hand trial of the Finger-tapping Test; however, these deficits do not suggest a specific locus of impairment and are inconsistent with the rest of the neuropsychological profile. The BD score fairly strongly indicates the intactness of the right-hemisphere spatial functions. This reason and the fact that almost all test comparisons suggest left-hemisphere dysfunction make a right-hemisphere lesion highly unlikely.

A localized lesion is suggested by the motor and sensory findings, which involve the left motor strip and the middle-to-anterior left temporal lobe. Clear disruption of the motor and sensory areas of the posterior frontal and anterior parietal lobes is seen from the Finger-tapping and Finger Agnosia scores. This lesion is further supported by the tactile suppressions, which by necessity include the primary parietal region. A slight deficit on the right-hand trial of the TPT also reflects the motor/sensory desruption.

The temporal-lobe involvement is largely indicated by the auditory suppressions and the severe Speech-Sounds Test deficit. The Similarities deficit on the WAIS also implicates disruption of the temporal lobe.

The right-hemisphere task deficits also can now be understood in light of the specific lesion location. The posterior frontal lobe includes premotor areas that are responsible for directed eye movements that are instrumental in visual analysis and evaluation of a problem situation. The PC, PA, and Trails A deficits relate to the disruption of the eye-movement region in the left frontal lobe. As a result of the dysfunctional preliminary visual analysis and evaluation of these problem situations, slight-to-moderate deficits arise on tasks normally thought to be associated with right-hemisphere function because of their visuospatial nature. In this case, however, these deficits are secondary to the rest of the neuropsychological profile, which indicates left-hemisphere disruption. One final result is also understood in light of the posterior-frontal-lobe disruption of eye movements, the visual suppressions. In performing this test it is necessary for the person to fixate the gaze. Since motor impersistence is common with these lesion locations, this task can be disrupted not because of primary visual cortical dysfunction but because the gaze cannot be fixated and the visual attention is disrupted. This explanation is likely both in view of the location of the lesion and because of the bilateral nature of the deficit. That is, if the suppressions indicate visual cortex sequelae, then bilateral involvement is necessary, an unlikely occurrence.

The lesion location, then, involves a fairly circumscribed area at the juncture of the left temporal and anterior parietal and posterior frontal lobes. The lesion is quite severe, as indicated by the large number of suppressions in two different modalities. The severity (tissue destructive) and highly localized nature of the lesion points to only one likely etiology, an intrinsic tumor. Such a lesion would account for both the tissue destruction, which is indicated by the suppressions, and the highly localized area of involvement, which is indicated by the overall deficit pattern. A middle-cerebral-artery occlusion might be a likely alternative were it not for the intactness of the posterior parietal lobe as indicated by the lack of severe complex verbal dysphasia and the adequate Trails B performance.

The present case demonstrates the importance of firm motor and sensory signs that suggest a definite locus of injury. The motor/sensory disruption provided a foundation around which the rest of the neuropsychological profile could be interpreted. The suppressions were the operative result that almost by necessity determine the area of injury. Of course, the rest of the profile must agree with this area of injury. In the case of the visual suppressions it can be seen that other explanations were necessary to make sense out of their impairment. Likewise, the few right-hemisphere tasks that did not fit the rest of the profile also needed explanations consistent with the rest of the results. Any neuropsychological test can be disrupted for any number of reasons and should not be rigidly associated with a single brain area. The guiding principle to remember in interpreting neuropsychological results is to make sense out of the entire battery of results and not to overinterpret a single result in isolation from the other tests in the battery.

Case 72

Background data. This 27-year-old female was injured in a barroom brawl during which she was struck frontally with a tire iron. She had a psychiatric history of hospitalization, usually related to alcoholism. The patient refused to take or finish several of the tests in the battery.

Case Example _72_ Age _27_ Sex _F_ Education _12_ Handedness _R_

General Tests:

    Category (errors) _‒‒_ Trail-making: Part A_29"_ Part B_75"_

    TPT: Total time_7' 37"_Location _‒‒‒_ Memory _‒‒‒_

Motor and Sensory Tests:

Finger-tapping	R_51_ L_44_	Fingertip	
Finger agnosia	R_0_ L_0_	number-writing	R_0_ L_0_
Supressions:		Tactile form	
Visual	R_0_ L_0_	(time)	R_14_ L_18_
Tactile	R_0_ L_0_	(errors)	R_0_ L_0_
Auditory	R_0_ L_0_		

    TPT: Time/Block R_.82_ L_.66_Both _.28_

Cognitive Tests:

    Speech-Sounds Perception

    (errors) _2_   Rhythm (errors) _6_

    WAIS: (scaled score)

Information	_12_	Picture completion	_11_
Comprehension	_12_	Picture arrangement	_11_
Vocabulary	_8_	Object assembly	_10_
Similarities	_14_	Block design	_6_
Arithmetic	_10_	Digit symbol	_10_
Digit span	_14_		

        VIQ _109_   PIQ _98_   FSIQ _105_

Aphasia: None

Test results.   Normal intellectual functioning is seen in the WAIS full-scale IQ. Both the VIQ and the PIQ agree with this estimate of intellectual ability, although a nine-point difference exists between the two scores. Despite the PIQ being the lowest score, there are two deficits on the verbal section but only one deficit on the performance section. The V and A subtests are below the average of the other verbal subtests and seem to represent brain-related deficits. The performance section, on the other hand, is essentially without scatter except for BD, which is more than four scale score points below the overall average of the other performance subtests and which therefore appears to represent a brain-related deficit.

An impairment index of 0.75 is earned, although only four of the tests on the index are available for inclusion in the calculation. Of these four tests, three are impaired (TPT total-time score, a slight deficit on the Finger-tapping Test left-hand trial, and a slight deficit on the Rhythm Test). Despite the relatively large rating, the index must be interpreted with caution, since three of the measures are not included in the ratio.

Motor and sensory measures do not suggest any strongly lateralized lesions or lesions that focally involve the motor/sensory strip. Sensory tests are too well performed to make such hypothesis. There are some slight indications of left-sided motor difficulties, however. The Finger-tapping Test yields a slight advantage in favor of the right hand. The left hand is 14 percent worse than the right hand, where only a 10 percent difference is normally expected. This difference would be overlooked were it not for confirmatory evidence provided by the left-hand trials the TPT. Again, a slight deficit is seen on the TPT, involving only a 20 percent difference where a 33 percent difference is expected. These TPT and Tapping results argue for slight dysfunction of the right-hemisphere motor/sensory strip.

Generally adequate scores are obtained on the cognitive measures of the neuropsychological test battery. Both Trails A and Trails B are performed within normal limits. Except for the Vocabulary subtest of the WAIS, no verbal deficits are apparent, with excellent performance on the Speech-Sounds test and the Aphasia Test.

Limited deficits do occur on the test battery, however. The TPT shows an interesting pattern of deficit which includes generally slow performance on all three trials (right, left, and both hands) besides the slight deficiency on the left-hand trial in comparison to the other trials. The BD deficit accompanies the TPT difficulty, and these two deficits occur in the absence of construction dyspraxia. Apart from the VIQ–PIQ difference and the Rhythm and Arithmetic results already mentioned, no other deficits occur on the test battery.

Brain damage is clearly suggested by the 0.75 impairment index, although this figure may be misleading. The deficient tests do not reveal any severely impaired abilities, and three crucial tests are not available for inclusion in the ratio. The question of whether or not brain damage is, in fact, evident is perhaps better answered by examining the overall pattern of results to determine if a specific lesion is suggested.

Indeed, the deficit pattern does suggest a specific lesion and one that encompasses a rather circumscribed area of the brain. The lateralized motor dysfunction seen in the Tapping and TPT results indicates dysfunction in the right frontal lobe. The Rhythm Test deficit confirms this lesion locus since it is one of the most severe deficits. A deficit on the Rhythm Test that because of its severity seems to be a primary deficit (not due to general effects of brain damage or secondary effects from a deficit on the Speech-Sounds Test) is indicative of right-anterior-hemisphere dysfunction.

The other neuropsychological deficits are consistent with this lesion location. The BD deficit involves spatial difficulties, which can be associated with either anterior- or posterior-right-hemisphere dysfunction. The Vocabulary deficit is also consistent with receptive speech deficits, which have been found in recent literature to be associated with right-frontal-lobe disorders. Likewise, the Arithmetic difficulty is consistent with spatial-thinking deficits, which occur in right-frontal-lobe disturbance.

There are some results that argue against a significant or acute lesion in the right anterior hemisphere. The lack of deficits on the Digit Symbol and Trails A tests is unusual in acute lesions involving this area of the brain. Other results are absent, such as body positioning or right–left-confusion errors on the Aphasia Test, that might be expected in significant or acute right-hemisphere disorders. The lack of these kinds of problems suggests that the lesion is both mild and chronic or static.

The most likely etiological alternative for a fairly localized and static lesion in the right frontal lobe is a trauma. The trauma must not have occurred recently, since there is no evidence of contrecoup involvement and since several deficits are absent that would otherwise be expected. An impairment index of 0.75 might also initially appear inconsistent with a right-frontal-lobe traumatic injury; however, it must be recognized that the entire index cannot be calculated and that the actual rating (were all tests included) might be much lower. The included tests also are only mildly impaired, therefore making the 0.75 rating somewhat inflated.

Case 73

Background data. This 27-year-old male had a history of repeated hospitalizations for paranoid schizophrenia. Owing to the
chronicity of the case and the failure of the patient to respond to any
of a large number of medications, the psychiatrist referred the patient
to see if any organic dysfunction was present. The patient was also
referred for EEG and CT scan, both of which were negative.

Case Example __73__ Age __27__ Sex __M__   Education __12__ Handedness __R__

General Tests:

    Category (errors) __57__ Trail-making: Part A __29__ Part B __103__

    TPT: Total time __10'29"__ Location __3__ Memory __9__

Motor and Sensory Tests:

Finger-tapping	R __54__ L __52__	Fingertip	
Finger agnosia	R __0__ L __0__	number-writing	R __4__ L __2__
Supressions:		Tactile form	
Visual	R __0__ L __0__	(time)	R __24__ L __20__
Tactile	R __0__ L __0__	(errors)	R __0__ L __0__
Auditory	R __0__ L __0__		

    TPT: Time/Block R __.37__ L __.34__ Both __.33__

Cognitive Tests:

    Speech-Sounds Perception

(errors)	__1__	Rhythm (errors)	__2__

    WAIS: (scaled score)

Information	__7__	Picture completion	__8__
Comprehension	__9__	Picture arrangement	__13__
Vocabulary	__8__	Object assembly	__9__
Similarities	__10__	Block design	__9__
Arithmetic	__12__	Digit symbol	__12__
Digit span	__8__		

        VIQ __93__   PIQ __102__   FSIQ __97__

Aphasia: Reading (#30), ideational dyspraxia
    (#32)

Test results. The full-scale IQ gives the impression of normal intellectual functioning; however, the VIQ–PIQ difference indicates the possibility of brain-related verbal deficits from the nine-point difference in scores. Essentially normal to bright-normal performance is seen on the highest individual subtest scores. If a scaled score of 12 is assumed to represent the premorbid level of attainment, then some mild deficiency is currently manifested on the WAIS IQs.

Of the three most sensitive WAIS subtests to brain damage— Digit Symbol, Digit Span, Arithmetic—only one appears to manifest a deficiency (Digit Span). The overall pattern of deficits does not reflect a typical brain-damaged profile, as well. The I, V, and C subtests represent the pattern of deficits on the verbal section. These subtests are the three least sensitive subtests on the WAIS to brain impairment and do not suggest any specific locus of brain injury; however, the performance-subtest pattern consisting of BD and OA do indicate right-hemisphere dysfunction of a kind typical of posterior-parietal-lobe injury. This lesion locus is less likely to occur, however, when Digit Symbol is not impaired.

The WAIS results, then, are by no means clear. On the one hand, a familiar brain-related deficit pattern occurs. This pattern, however, occurs in the face of adequate performance on the generally sensitive subtests to brain damage and the lack of a reasonable deficit pattern on the verbal subtests. It is necessary to rely on the other neuropsychological measures to determine how to make sense of the WAIS results.

Impairment on two of the seven tests making up the impairment index yields a rating of only 0.3. Dysfunction occurs on two cognitively complex tasks, the Category and TPT Location measures. Dysfunction on these two tasks may represent a poor ability to learn from experience. The tasks involve the ability to test hypotheses in the face of reinforcement (Category Test) and incidental memory (TPT Location). Such a deficit may or may not be related to brain dysfunction.

Very little motor/sensory dysfunction is seen. There are some deficits on the Fingertip Number-writing Test and the TPT. No consistent lateralization is suggested by the overall pattern of deficits, however. The Fingertip Number-writing deficit weakly indicates a left hemisphere dysfunction. The TPT deficit pattern essentially agrees with the hypothesis suggested from the impairment index measures, that the person does not learn well from experience. No improvement is seen across the three trials of the TPT. The overall motor/sensory disruption, then, does not suggest strong involvement of the motor/sensory strip of either hemisphere.

Of the cognitive neurospsychological measures, deficits occur with complex abilities, while the basic perceptual tasks remain intact. For example, Trails A, Speech-Sounds, and Rhythm are excellently performed, with no indications of brain-related dysfunction. The more difficult or cognitively complex tasks, such as Trails B, Category, and some of the Aphasia items, do show deficit and seem to suggest an inability for the subject to consistently focus intellectual abilities when faced with a complex cognitive task.

Some complex tasks are adequately performed, such as Picture Arrangement and Arithmetic. These tasks necessitate formulating a single plan and then executing it. The other complex tasks (Category, Trails B) are somewhat more difficult in that they require that some cognitive flexibility be maintained, since the person must work within the framework of two competing plans of execution.

The striking inconsistency between the number of neuropsychological deficits and the relatively low impairment index seems to be the focal point of the interpretation. Since the Category Test is the single most sensitive indicator of brain injury on the entire test battery, deficit there raises cause for concern. Likewise, the Trails B, TPT, and WAIS deficits may or may not represent a brain-related disorder.

The impairment index and the lack of a deficit complex pointing to a specified brain lesion indicate that a brain lesion does not explain the neuropsychological deficits manifested on the profile. If no familiar brain-related deficit patterns are present, then the prominent deficits must be analyzed to determine what might be causing their poor performance.

Poor performance is most marked on Category, TPT, and Trails B. No lateralized deficit on the TPT trials is manifested, thereby indicating that there is no specific localized lesion. These three deficits sometimes occur concurrently in frontal-lobe dysfunction. If the frontal lobes are involved, then the Category Test would be expected to demonstrate more severe deficit. It would appear, then, that these deficits also suggest no specific brain lesion, localized or diffuse. In light of MMPI results, a chronic schizophrenic disorder must be considered as an explanation for the deficits.

It is always necessary to rule out all diffuse and subcortical disorders as well as the localized ones. In this case the lack of motor/sensory dysfunction rules out the possibility of a subcortical disorder. The inconsistent neuropsychological results also rule out a diffuse disorder. If some diffuse process is present, then several other tests should be disrupted, such as Speech-Sounds and Rhythm. As it happens, only those tests that necessitate complex cognitive functioning are disrupted, a result associated with functional disorders.

Schizophrenia is further indicated by the inconsistent test performance. The Digit Symbol test is well performed in the face of several other results that would tend to suggest that it should be poorly performed. For example, the Digit Span Test is poorly performed, yet this test, requiring several of the same skills as Digit Symbol, should be dysfunctional as one of the generally sensitive tests to brain injury.

In light of the results, a psychiatric disorder such as chronic paranoid schizophrenia seems to account for the test results in this profile. The deficits are seen only on those tests that measure higher cognitive functioning. Deficits are not seen on motor/sensory measures, and inconsistent test performance is present. This pattern of results is common to a psychiatric neuropsychological profile, and no indications of a diffuse or a subcortical brain lesion are found. Thus the diagnosis of paranoid schizophrenia of a chronic nature, based upon MMPI findings, appears in order.

Case 74

Background data.   This 55-year-old man was found to have an aneurysm in the right temporal area accompanied by some bleeding that had spontaneously stopped without treatment. Testing was ordered to establish baseline levels for the patient.

Case Example _74_   Age _55_   Sex _M_   Education _____   Handedness _R_

General Tests:

    Category (errors) _56_   Trail-making: Part A _30"_ Part B _48"_

    TPT: Total time _10'11"_ Location _4_   Memory _7_

Motor and Sensory Tests:

    Finger-tapping   R _53.6_ L _47.9_ Fingertip

    Finger agnosia   R _0_   L _0_   number-writing R _4_   L _3_

    Supressions: Tactile form

        Visual   R _0_   L _0_   (time)   R _18_ L _26_

        Tactile   R _0_   L _0_   (errors)   R _0_ L _0_

        Auditory   R _0_   L _1_

    TPT: Time/Block   R _.35_ L _.43_ Both _.23_

Cognitive Tests:

    Speech-Sounds Perception

      (errors)   _3_   Rhythm (errors)   _3_

    WAIS: (scaled score)

Information	12	Picture completion	11
Comprehension	11	Picture arrangement	9
Vocabulary	18	Object assembly	8
Similarities	13	Block design	12
Arithmetic	11	Digit symbol	8
Digit span	10		

        VIQ _119_   PIQ _114_   FSIQ _118_

Aphasia: None

Test results.   Bright-normal intellectual functioning is suggested by all three IQ measures, and premorbid function appears to be in this range as well. The only indication that premorbid level should be estimated differently is from the Vocabulary score, which is in the superior range. Since this score is widely affected by learning, it would appear to represent an isolated intellectual acquisition rather than a general measure of intellectual level of function. This interpretation is supported by the fact that no other subtest score matches this level of ability.

There are indications, however, of brain-related deficits on the WAIS. The performance section shows two deficits (Digit Symbol, Object Assembly). The PA score may also represent a brain-related deficit, although the performance-section premorbid level of functioning appears to be between scaled scores of 11 and 12, less than 3 points above the PA score. If the verbal premorbid level of function were generously estimated at 13 (in view of the Vocabulary score), then the Digit Span performance could be construed as a deficit, albeit a weak one.

Two of the seven measures of the impairment index are disrupted, yielding a rating of 0.28. These two tests are only mildly disrupted. The Category Test and the TPT Location score both fall barely within the brain-damaged range of performance. All other measures fall well within the normal limits of performance. The impairment rating may therefore represent either no brain dysfunction or only a mild disorder that is highly circumscribed.

No sensory impairment is found on the Finger Agnosia Test; however, one left-ear auditory suppression is present. Complex sensory deficits are seen on the Fingertip Number-writing Test, although no specific lateralization arises. The overall result is a right-hemisphere indicator in the auditory suppression.

In addition to the WAIS performance-section deficits and the Category and TPT Location deficits, there are few cognitive indications of brain dysfunction. The Aphasia Test shows no dysfunction, nor do the general tests—Trails A or B, Speech-Sounds, Rhythm—show deficit. Likewise, the TPT total-time and Memory measures show no brain-related dysfunction.

While the absolute performance levels show no dysfunction, there are two test comparisons that yield significant information. First, Trails A, while within absolute levels of normal performance, is discrepant when compared to Trails B. This result is perhaps indicative of some visuospatial slowing and is generally confirmed by results that also indicate right-hemisphere involvement such as PIQ, auditory suppression, and the TPT. The TPT is dysfunctional not only in the Location measure but also in the ratio between the right- and left-hand trials; the left-hand trial is much slower than the right-hand trial.

The obvious question is whether or not a brain injury exists. On the one hand, the low impairment index and lack of any dysphasia argue against a brain lesion. On the other hand, however, an auditory suppression is present and other mild but consistent signs are evident, suggesting a specific lesion. The deficit complex must be further analyzed to determine if a common and specific dysfunction is present that could arise from a known lesion.

The most outstanding sign is the auditory suppression. A specific right-temporal-lobe lesion is suggested, which causes severe yet localized disruption of brain function. Very specific concomitant deficits must be present if the deficit pattern is consistent with such a lesion. The right temporal lobe is involved in complex visual analysis. The OA and Trails A deficits are consistent with a loss in this ability.

A spatial component is also associated with the visual-analysis function of the right temporal lobe. In this vein, several deficits corroborate the hypothesis of a right-temporal-lobe disorder. TPT deficits on the left-hand trial and the Location measure both represent spatial difficulties. The general deficit on the Fingertip Number-writing Test may also represent a spatial difficulty in which the person cannot mentally visualize the spatial aspect of the tactile stimulus. This interpretation gains support when it is recognized that no simple sensory signs involving tactile/kinesthetic abilities that would otherwise explain the Fingertip deficits are present.

While the deficit pattern is weak and is made up of several mild deficits and "near deficits," the overall consistency of the pattern strengthens the interpretation. Such a mild picture can represent only one lesion type when such a localized lesion is suggested. An aneurysm involving a temporal-lobe branch of the right middle cerebral artery is the etiological possibility that fully explains the test pattern. The very specific locus suggested by the auditory suppression indicates a severe lesion but one that does not encompass a large cortical area. The other deficits, then, involve cognitive tasks that are only mildly disrupted because of the small area of involvement.

This difference in severity of deficit between the sensory sign and the cognitive deficits may also indicate a traumatic injury in which some recovery of function now makes the discrepancy apparent. This explanation is unlikely, however, because a traumatic injury severe enough to cause a suppression is not likely to leave so few residual deficits. Construction dyspraxia and more motor dysfunction would be expected, and the Rhythm Test should be more poorly performed.

This case represents the necessity of taking seriously such pathognomonic signs as suppression and the brain-damaged performance on the Category Test. These deficits must be logically explained before brain damage can be ruled out even in such a well-performed neuropsychological protocol as the present one.

Case 75

Background data.   This 47-year-old man was a security guard who was hit in the right parietal area in the course of an armed robbery. The patient was unconcious for 6 hours. Testing was performed 4 weeks later to measure any deficits present.

Case Example __75__ Age __47__ Sex __M__ Education __16__ Handedness __R__

General Tests:

Category (errors) __70__ Trail-making: Part A __38"__ Part B __60"__

TPT: Total time __20'24"__ Location __3__ Memory __10__

Motor and Sensory Tests:

Finger-tapping   R __58.6__ L __52.0__ Fingertip

Finger agnosia   R __0/20__ L __4/20__   number-writing R __2/20__ L __4/20__

Supressions: Tactile form

    Visual   R __0__   L __0__   (time)   R __18__   L __32__

    Tactile   R __0__   L __0__   (errors)   R __0__   L __1__

    Auditory   R __0__   L __0__

TPT: Time/Block   R __.5__ L __1.0__ Both __.51__

Cognitive Tests:

Speech-Sounds Perception

    (errors)   __6__   Rhythm (errors)   __3__

WAIS: (scaled score)

Information	9	Picture completion	9
Comprehension	11	Picture arrangement	13
Vocabulary	9	Object assembly	7
Similarities	9	Block design	7
Arithmetic	9	Digit symbol	7
Digit span	10		

VIQ __100__   PIQ __92__   FSIQ __96__

Aphasia: Drawing (all figures), right-left confusion

Test results. The full-scale IQ of the WAIS indicates normal intelligence, and the VIQ agrees with this assessment. The VIQ–PIQ difference suggests the possibility of a brain-related dysfunction on the WAIS. Further evaluation of the individual subtests is needed to determine if in fact the VIQ–PIQ difference is related to brain damage.

Three deficits that deviate markedly from the mean level of performance and therefore indicate brain-related deficits are apparent. The Digit Symbol, OA, and BD scores of 7 indicate definite deviations. Other scores may indicate brain dysfunction if corroborated by the overall neuropsychological pattern of results. The PC score of 9 may represent a brain deficit when compared to the PA score of 13. These results fit into an overall picture suggesting right-hemisphere dysfunction.

Three of seven tests in the impairment index show impairment. An index of only 0.43 tends to argue against a brain-damage interpretation of the test results. The rest of tbe neuropsychological profile must be evaluated, however, before one reaches a final conclusion.

Motor and sensory performance suggest a lateralized focus. A slight left hand deficit is evident on the Finger-Tapping Test. Corroboratory evidence for the motor deficits is provided by TPT, Finger Agnosia, and Fingertip Number-writing.

Several general cognitive measures remain intact. The Trail-making, Speech-Sounds, and Rhythm tests are all adequately performed. There are some higher cortical functions that appear to be disrupted and seem to support, to some extent, the deficits seen on the WAIS. The Aphasia Test shows drawing difficulties on all four figures as well as evidence of right–left confusion. The left-hand deficit on the TPT test can also be considered a cognitive deficit, especially in view of the concomitant deficit on the Location measure. These deficits all seem to involve visuospatial aspects of cortical function and fall in line with the deficits on BD and perhaps even PC and OA.

The TPT left-hand and Location deficits immediately suggest a right-hemisphere, posterior-parietal-lobe lesion. The spatial deficits suggested by BD and Aphasia Test deficits (drawing and right–left confusion) support the posterior-parietal-lobe focus. This deficit complex can also be associated with right-frontal-lobe dysfunction. However, the motor deficit seen on Finger-Tapping are milder than the sensory deficit on the TPT. In addition, there are clear, lateralized sensory signs. This combination of deficits clearly points to a right parietal focus for this patient, consistent with the history. As all signs are mild, the injury is likely to be chronic, accounting for the low Impairment Index and normal performance on such tests as Trails A.

Case 76

Background data. This 35-year-old male psychiatrist was injured when he drove his car into a freeway embankment late at night. The patient struck his head and was unconcious for 12 hours. He was tested for residual deficits.

Case Example __76__ Age __35__ Sex __M__ Education __16+__ Handedness __R__

General Tests:

Category (errors) __– – –__ Trail-making: Part A __27"__ Part B __167"__

TPT: Total time __10'15"__ Location __8__ Memory __8__

Motor and Sensory Tests:

Finger-tapping	R __39__ L __44__	Fingertip	
Finger agnosia	R __0__ L __0__	number-writing	R __0__ L __0__

Supressions: Tactile form

Visual	R __0__ L __0__	(time)	R __12__ L __10__
Tactile	R __0__ L __0__	(errors)	R __0__ L __0__
Auditory	R __0__ L __0__		

TPT: Time/Block R __.53__ L __.37__ Both __.13__

Cognitive Tests:

Speech-Sounds Perception

(errors) __3__   Rhythm (errors) __1__

WAIS: (scaled score)

Information	__11__	Picture completion	__11__
Comprehension	__18__	Picture arrangement	__13__
Vocabulary	__15__	Object assembly	__12__
Similarities	__14__	Block design	__14__
Arithmetic	__19__	Digit symbol	__13__
Digit span	__13__		

VIQ __129__   PIQ __122__   FSIQ __128__

Aphasia: Drawing (cross, triangle)

Test results. A superior intelligence is evident from the WAIS full-scale IQ. Little difference is noted between the VIQ and the PIQ or among the individual subtest scores. The Information subtest, however, is significantly different from the other verbal subtests. This discrepancy does not seem to represent strongly any particular brain deficit in view of the other excellent verbal abilities. Both of the generally sensitive tests (Digit Span, Digit Symbol) are excellently performed, also indicating a brain-related deficit on the WAIS to be unlikely.

The low impairment index of 0.16 corroborates the notion that a brain lesion is unlikely. While all other tests of the index are adequately performed, a relative as well as an absolute deficit is seen on the dominant-hand trial of the Finger-tapping Test. This result is highly unlikely in a non-brain-damaged subject and strongly argues for a brain-related explanation.

Only two other deficits occur on the entire neuropsychological test battery. Trails B is severely dysfunctional especially in view of the superior intelligence scores and the relative performance on Trails A. Two drawing items on the Aphasia Test are dysfunctional as well; both the cross and the triangle are poorly drawn. The deficit probably does not involve spatial difficulties, since a triangle requires little spatial ability to draw. These two deficits are extremely unusual in view of the intelligence of this subject and almost certainly indicate serious problems. Otherwise, the neuropsychological record is excellent. No nondominant-hand motor problems are evident, and likewise no sensory deficits are apparent on either body side. The TPT is well performed, with no indication of lateralized deficit. Auditory perceptual measures (Speech-Sounds, Rhythm) are almost flawlessly performed. Trails A is very well done, and no speech or language problems are noted. The Category Test was not given.

Essentially three deficits (Tapping–right hand, Trails B, and construction dyspraxia) make up the pattern of results. Each considered individually could hardly make a case for suspecting brain injury in light of the otherwise excellent neuropsychological record. When they are considered together, however, the possibility of a brain lesion becomes more likely. The large disparity between the two parts of the Trail-making Test is difficult to ignore when it occurs in a subject of such high intelligence. Add to this the fact that a motor deficit occurs that implicates the left frontal lobe, an area in which the Trails B deficit is often seen, and the deficit complex begins to assume the character of a localized lesion. Finally, a drawing dysfunction occurs in someone who achieves a superior performance IQ, and the results cannot be considered the result of normal brain function.

It is apparent that simple and complex motor behavior is behind this pattern of deficits. The Finger-tapping Test is an obvious indication of this motor problem. The deficits on the Aphasia Test are also those of motor dysfunction. Since spatial difficulties are not apparent and since motor problems exist on the Finger-tapping test (dominant hand), it would seem that the errors on the drawing items probably represent simple or complex motor difficulties that interfere with the execution of a motoric behavior plan. This function is intimately associated with the left frontal lobe, especially, as in the present case, where the right hand is dominant.

The final deficit, Trails B, does not appear to be a strict motor problem, since Trails A is well performed. The difficulty must involve either the added verbal complexity or the cognitive flexibility necessary to switch between two plans of action (number–letter alternation). Since no other verbal deficits are seen, the cognitive flexibility aspect of the test must be responsible for the deficit. Such an explanation of the deficit again points to left-frontal-lobe dysfunction; here, however, the prefrontal area of the left frontal lobe is implicated.

The area of involvement covers the left prefrontal area, as indicated by the Trails B deficit, and the posterior, primary area of the left frontal lobe (motor strip), as demonstrated by the Tapping deficit. It is difficult to localize the drawing deficit, since it may represent either location mentioned above as well as the premotor areas of the left frontal lobe. The entire left frontal lobe seems to be generally involved but, in view of the low impairment index, in only a mild manner. A lesion that would fit the data, then, would have to be capable of involving a large area without causing a great deal of disruption.

Such a deficit pattern rules out many lesions, including tumors, severe vascular problems, and aneurysms. All of these cause either too much disruption to yield an impairment index of only 0.16 or involve too small an area to produce general involvement of the entire left frontal lobe. Perhaps the most likely possibility to explain the deficit complex is a trauma to the left frontal area that is past the acute stage. This alternative allows a generalized disruption of brain area without leading to severe disruption of individual tests. The severe disruption is not seen because the lesion is chronic and the initial edema has subsided.

Case 77

Background data. This 38-year-old female was tested to evaluate deficits related to multiple sclerosis. The patient refused several tests that she thought "looked too hard."

Case Example _77_ Age _38_ Sex _F_ Education _12_ Handedness _____

General Tests:

Category (errors) _--_ Trail-making: Part A _30"_ Part B _84"_

TPT: Total time _--_ Location _--_ Memory _--_

Motor and Sensory Tests:

Finger-tapping   R_41.4_ L_37.0_ Fingertip

Finger agnosia   R _-___ L _-___   number-writing R _4_ L _0_

Supressions: Tactile form

    Visual   R_0___ L_10___   (time)   R _13_ L_19_

    Tactile   R_0___ L_11___   (errors)   R _0_ L_0_

    Auditory   R_0___ L_3___

TPT: Time/Block R _-___ L _-___ Both _-___

Cognitive Tests:

Speech-Sounds Perception

  (errors)   _1_   Rhythm (errors)   _0_

WAIS: (scaled score)

Information	11	Picture completion	8
Comprehension	10	Picture arrangement	9
Vocabulary	8	Object assembly	8
Similarities	11	Block design	10
Arithmetic	9	Digit symbol	8
Digit span	10		

VIQ _99_   PIQ _96_   FSIQ _97_

Aphasia: Drawing (cross, key); spelling
(triangle); pronunciation

Test results. Intelligence testing reveals an overall IQ within normal limits with no significant difference between verbal and performance functions. With the individual subtests uniform performance is seen, with no indications of absolute or relative deficiencies. The current level of functioning appears to represent accurately this woman's premorbid psychometric abilities. Unfortunately, a WRAT is not available to confirm estimates of the premorbid level of ability.

Consistent with the lack of deficit apparent on the WAIS, an impairment index of only 0.3 is earned. This finding must be carefully weighed in view of the fact that four of the seven tests were not administered, including the Category Test and the TPT measures. The one test of the index that is impaired is the Finger-tapping Test. Impairment on this measure is seen in the absolute level of performance, but relative skills of the left and right hands do not reveal any lateralized deficit. Furthermore, the two remaining tests, Speech-Sounds and Rhythm, were excellently performed with only one and no errors, respectively.

Several neuropsychological deficits do occur, however. The most striking impairment is seen on the tests of sensory suppressions. Consistent deficit is seen on the left body side in all three modalities. The visual and tactile tests are severely impaired, showing errors on almost every trial. The auditory test is relatively less disrupted, although it still demonstrates clear deficit.

Deficits are seen on two other tests. The Aphasia Tests shows two mild problems that are generally associated with left-hemisphere dysfunction. Difficulties spelling the word triangle and pronouncing multisyllabic words are present. A further left-hemisphere indication is seen from right-hand errors on the Fingertip Number-writing Test. Unfortunately, the Finger Agnosia test results are not available. The Aphasia Test drawing items demonstrate right-hemisphere dysfunction. Errors are made on the Greek cross and the key, the two items most associated with spatial difficulties.

Some gross inconsistencies in the test results seem at first apparent. On the one hand, normal performance is indicated; on the other hand, severe tissue-destructive damage (suppressions) is indicated. The results must be analyzed to determine how unilateral suppressions could occur in all three modalities with only mild, bilateral cognitive deficits present in an otherwise excellent neuropsychological record.

The good impairment index and the uniform pattern of performance on the WAIS indicate that the cortex is relatively intact. Mild cognitive deficits occur on the Aphasis Test, but otherwise the neuropsychological results confirm the impression that no disorder is present in the cortex that would be consistent with the severity suggested by the suppressions. Even without the data from the tests that were not administered, it can be concluded that the suppressions do not represent cortical dysfunction.

It must be concluded, then, that subcortical damage is indicated and that some mild but nonfocal cortical dysfunction is present based upon the dysphasia signs. A subcortical disorder that manifests "spotty" or nonlocalized cortical deficit complexes (the present dysphasia signs) is multiple sclerosis. The present profile is atypical in some respects from characteristic multiple sclerosis patterns. The VIQ is usually significantly larger than the PIQ, auditory deficits are uncommon, and more motor problems would be expected given the level of sensory impairment. The inconsistently lateralized motor/sensory and cognitive deficits and the spotty cortical impairment, however, are unmistakably characteristic of a demyelinating disease. The mixed deficit pattern results from the random-attack course of the disease.

Case 78

Background data. This 57-year-old male was referred for testing because of progressive decline in behavior that had been present for at least 1 year and probably longer. Testing was requested for differentiation between "involutional depression" and organic brain syndrome.

Case Example 78 Age 57 Sex M Education 12 Handedness R

General Tests:

Category (errors) 104 Trail-making: Part A 75" Part B 330"

TPT: Total time 28'30" Location 1 Memory 2

Motor and Sensory Tests:

Finger-tapping	R 42 L 32	Fingertip	
Finger agnosia	R 0 L 5	number-writing R 7 L 9	

Supressions:

Tactile form

Visual	R 0 L 0	(time)	R 16 L 20
Tactile	R 0 L 0	(errors)	R 0 L 0
Auditory	R 0 L 0		

TPT: Time/Block R 10.0 L 9.0 Both 3.3

Cognitive Tests:

Speech-Sounds Perception

(errors)   9   Rhythm (errors)   13

WAIS: (scaled score)

Information	12	Picture completion	6
Comprehension	6	Picture arrangement	8
Vocabulary	6	Object assembly	5
Similarities	7	Block design	4
Arithmetic	7	Digit symbol	4
Digit span	11		

VIQ 93   PIQ 87   FSIQ 90

Aphasia: Drawing (all figures), spelling (cross), reading, pronunciation writing, calculation

Test results. Performance on intelligence testing reveals functioning in the low-normal range with little difference between verbal and performance IQs. High scores on I, PA, and Digit Span indicate premorbid abilities that may have been in the bright-normal range. Otherwise, general decrement on the WAIS is evident. All performance subtests except PA show decline and suggest spatial and motor-manipulative deficits. Verbal deficits are apparent from the C, V, and S. The large differences among scores on these measures and scores on Information and Digit Span strongly suggest brain-related deficits. The relative lack of difference between the overall IQs, however, indicate a chronic or diffuse injury. Since the deficits appear on measures traditionally labelled "hold" tests (V, C, PC) and since no deficit occurs on Digit Span, a test that is usually sensitive to brain injury, the diagnosis of brain damage must be deferred until corroboratory evidence from the other neuropsychological measures substantiates the WAIS indications.

Corroboratory evidence is immediately provided by an impairment index of 1.0. Several of the tests making up the index are not only in the brain-damaged range but are severely disrupted—Category, TPT, Trails B, and Tapping. The Speech-Sounds and Rhythm tests fall into the brain-damaged range, although they are not as severely dysfunctional as the others.

Certain lateralized motor and sensory deficits occur. Motor speed of the left hand is worse than for the right hand, as indicated by the Tapping scores. Unilateral finger dysgnosia on the left hand and bilateral Fingertip Number-writing Test errors, however, indicate the opposite hemisphere. Also, the right-hand motor-speed scores, while better than the left-hand scores, also fall into the brain-damaged range. The apparent lateralized deficits, then, appear to represent differential performance of the two hemispheres rather than a lateralized lesion.

Lateralized cognitive deficits also appear. Trails B is more impaired than Trails A, and Rhythm is more impaired than Speech-Sounds. All tests, however, fall into the brain-damaged range and indicate impairment in both hemispheres. The TPT manifests generalized impairment with no strong indications of greater damage to either hemisphere. Dysphasia errors also indicate damage to the right and left hemispheres. Construction dyspraxia is manifested on all drawing items of the test, indicating either severe left-parietal damage or right-hemisphere dysfunction. The left hemisphere is implicated by spelling dyspraxia, dysarthria, dyslexia, and dysgraphia. Dyscalculia may lateralize to either side given the strong indications for both right- and left-hemisphere dysfunction.

Diffuse disorders in patients of this age range (50s and up) can be difficult to identify unless specific deficit patterns indicate a localized lesion. The present results do not suggest a focal lesion in either the left or right hemisphere. The severe Category deficit suggests left-frontal-lobe involvement while the dysphasia, Speech-Sounds Test results, and sensory impairment indicate the left temporal and parietal lobes. Likewise, in the right hemisphere the motor/sensory strip is implicated by the left-hand Finger-tapping test, the anterior areas are implicated by the Rhythm Test, and the posterior parietal lobe is implicated by the severe construction dyspraxia. Clearly, the entire brain is affected in what appears to be a fairly uniform fashion, with no area strikingly more severely deficient.

Generalized diffuse disorders without specific focal sequelae can assume a variety of forms. The two most common forms in the elderly are Pick's and Alzheimer's disease, which are progressive, degenerative processes. As such, the neuropsychological profiles often appear acute, depending upon the rate of the disease process. With no indications of a focal lesion and the generalized, severe, and acute-looking neuropsychological profile, some sort of a degenerative and diffuse brain disease is the most likely diagnosis. Pick's or Alzheimer's disease in the middle stages and progressing at a moderate rate is indicated by the acuteness and severity of the test results.

Case 79

Background data. This 44-year-old male entered the hospital with numerous complaints, including headache, nausea and vomiting, dysphasia, confusion, and listlessness. He was diagnosed as having a meningioma located over the left temple area. Testing was employed to establish a behavioral baseline prior to surgery.

Case Example __79__ Age __44__ Sex __M__ Education __12__ Handedness __R__

General Tests:

Category (errors)__52__ Trail-making: Part A __41__ Part B discontinued

TPT: Total time 13' 03"ation __8__ Memory __8__

Motor and Sensory Tests:

Finger-tapping   R 26.6 L 23.4 Fingertip

Finger agnosia   R 12 L 8   number-writing R __12__ L __9__

Supressions: Tactile form

Visual   R 0   L 0   (time)   R __20__ L __22__

Tactile   R 0   L 0   (errors)   R __0__ L __0__

Auditory   R 0   L 0

TPT: Time/Block   R .79 L .31 Both .21

Cognitive Tests:

Speech-Sounds Perception

(errors)   __40__   Rhythm (errors)   __14__

WAIS: (scaled score)

Information   __4__   Picture completion   __8__

Comprehension   __4__   Picture arrangement   __7__

Vocabulary   __4__   Object assembly   __9__

Similarities   __2__   Block design   __4__

Arithmetic   __2__   Digit symbol   __6__

Digit span   __0__

VIQ __56__   PIQ __80__   FSIQ __64__

Aphasia: Spelling (all 4 words), naming,
          reading (letters, numbers, words),
          pronunciation, writing calculation

Test results.   The WAIS full-scale IQ indicates mental-defective intellectual functioning; this measure, however, is misleading, as can be seen by looking at the VIQ–PIQ disparity. The PIQ suggests near-normal intellectual functioning on performance tasks. Considerable variation within the performance section suggests that premorbid functioning may have been even higher. The Block Design and Digit Symbol subtests are likely related to brain dysfunction, as is the general decrement on the WAIS subtests, and it follows that the higher scores probably represent the premorbid level of functioning at an average intellectual level.

The extreme loss of verbal skills, in which no verbal subtest is performed well and in which no more than three numbers can be remembered at a time, represents a very serious lesion. The seriousness of the deficit is better understood when it is recognized that average verbal skills existed premorbidly. The great disparity between the verbal and performance IQs also indicates an acute and lateralized lesion. Global verbal dysfunction immediately suggests a left-temporal lesion as well, although this postulate must be confirmed by the other neuropsychological measures.

Despite the serious disruption seen on the WAIS, an impairment index of only 0.57 is earned. All of the TPT measures are adequately performed, and the Category Test is only mildly dysfunctional. The other measures, however, are severely disrupted (Tapping, Speech-Sounds, Rhythm).

Rather generalized dysfunction is apparent, with the left-hemisphere tasks being much more seriously disrupted. The two most striking deficits occur on Trails B and Speech-Sounds. While Trails A is barely into the brain-damaged range, Trails B was not successfully completed. Likewise, serious defects in speech-sounds perception are seen.

Further verbal problems are manifested on the Aphasia Test. The Aphasia Test shows generalized dysphasia with a specific area of weakness in the verbal tasks. Spelling is completely disrupted. Reading of even individual numbers and letters is also deficient. Word-finding difficulties and writing, calculation, and speaking dysfluencies are also evident; however, difficulty is apparent on right–left discrimination, drawing, and body-positioning tasks.

Motor and sensory disruption is seen, which seems also to indicate left-hemisphere dysfunction. Lateralized sensory dysfunction is apparent from the performance of the Finger Agnosia test and the Fingertip Number-writing Test. Motor-speed deficits on Tapping are bilateral; however, they are probably indicative of dominant-left-hemisphere disruption in view of the lateralized verbal and sensory deficits. Also, a lateralized deficit is seen on the TPT right-hand trial, which probably reflects the left-hemisphere motor/sensory disruption and the mild spatial deficits (seen on BD).

Other deficits occur that do not immediately suggest lateralized dysfunction. The BD deficit is usually a fairly strong right-hemisphere indicator; however, in this case there are no accompanying deficits that strongly suggest right-hemisphere spatial problems. In such a case BD deficits may be the result of left-parietal disruption, which itself can cause spatial difficulties. Two more deficits that are typically right-hemisphere indicators include Trails A and Rhythm. In this case both are only mildly impaired when compared to their complements, Trails B and Speech-Sounds. Generally sensitive to most types of brain damage, these tests show deficits representing general dysfunction that occurs simply as a result of the severity of the lesion and that does not represent lateralized damage.

A serious brain injury is apparent from the great VIQ–PIQ disparity and the striking deficits on Speech-Sounds and Trails B. The Speech-Sounds Test deficit immediately suggests a left-temporal-lobe dysfunction. This postulate is confirmed by the generalized loss of verbal skills seen in the WAIS VIQ and the errors on the Aphasia Test. While there are other deficits, these problems are the most severe and indicate a strong localized lesion in the left temporal lobe.

Other deficits occur that seem to suggest involvement beyond the left temporal lobe. For example, the motor/sensory signs and the TPT right-hand deficit indicate the motor/sensory strip and parietal lobe of the left hemisphere. The tertiary parietal lobe is also apparently slightly disrupted, as signified by the TPT and BD deficits, which implicate spatial problems. It would appear, then, that despite the strong left-temporal-lobe focus there is involvement of the left parietal lobe as well.

The lesion still has a very localized pattern of test results. The left prefrontal area does not appear to be significantly involved, since the Category Test is only mildly disrupted. Also, there is an area (left temporal lobe) which is much more severely damaged with a surrounding area (anterior and to a lesser extent the posterior parietal lobe) of a lesser deficit, a pattern that tends to be associated with a neoplastic process causing more severe destruction in the area where it grows, with the surrounding area of lesser deficit representing remote "pressure" affects.

An extrinsic tumor seems the more likely candidate in this case for two reasons. First, extrinsic tumors cause their effects by compressing rather than infiltrating the brain tissue and therefore are more likely to result in remote and less severe effects than intrinsic tumors. While the lesion is definitely severe in its temporal-lobe effects, the overall severity of the lesion is only moderate, as demonstrated by the 0.57 impairment index. This fact points out the second reason why an extrinsic tumor is a more likely explanation of the present case — an intrinsic and fast-growing tumor of the left temporal lobe would more likely result in a greater impairment rating, while an extrinsic tumor generally causes an impairment index of around 0.4 to 0.8.

Case 80

Background data.   This 69-year-old male with 14 years of education suffered from a variety of medical conditions. He was diagnosed as having general arteriosclerosis and had recently had at least one stroke involving the left hemisphere. Further left-hemisphere strokes of a smaller nature or right-hemisphere deficits could not be ruled out of the medical history.

Case Example __80__ Age __69__ Sex __M__ Education __14__ Handedness __R__

General Tests:

Category (errors) __--__ Trail-making: Part A __97"__ Part B __257"__

TPT: Total time _____ Location __1__ Memory __2__

Motor and Sensory Tests: __25' 15"__

Finger-tapping   R __34__ L __36.5__ Fingertip

Finger agnosia   R __2__ L __0__   number-writing R __1__ L __2__

Supressions: Tactile form

Visual   R __0__ L __0__   (time)   R __16__ L __16__

Tactile   R __0__ L __1__   (errors) R __0__ L __0__

Auditory R __2__ L __0__

TPT: Time/Block R __5.0__ L __1.7__ Both __3.3__

Cognitive Tests:

Speech-Sounds Perception

(errors)   __13__   Rhythm (errors)   __7__

WAIS: (scaled score)

Information   __9__   Picture completion   __7__

Comprehension   __13__   Picture arrangement   __3__

Vocabulary   __8__   Object assembly   __7__

Similarities   __10__   Block design   __6__

Arithmetic   __6__   Digit symbol   __5__

Digit span   __13__

VIQ __105__   PIQ __92__   FSIQ __99__

Aphasia: Drawing (cross, key) reading, pronunciation, calculation

Test results. For the WAIS a 13-point difference between the verbal and performance sections immediately indicates the need for more thorough investigation of this person's neuropsychological functioning. The fact that the lower score is on the performance section alerts one to the possibility of a right-hemisphere dysfunction. The scatter on the performance subtests reveals deficits on the Picture Arrangement and Digit Symbol sections relative to the other performance subtests, which themselves are generally depressed. Such general depression of scores is accounted for at least in part by the loss of motor speed represented by the Finger-tapping Test score for the dominant hand. The particular pattern of deficits on the performance section suggest no focal right-hemisphere lesion, however.

The scatter of the subtests on the verbal section gives indications of premorbid level of function as well as some verbal problems that seem to suggest brain-related deficits. An elevated score on the Comprehension subtest indicates premorbid ability that may have been up to 1 standard deviation above the mean. An excellent score on Digit Span demonstrates good immediate auditory memory skills and attentional abilities. Relative deficits on the I, V, and A subtests, however, suggest the possibility of verbal problems that may be related to left-hemisphere dysfunction.

An impairment index of 1.0 confirms the suspicions of brain dysfunction from the WAIS. All tests making up the index are performed in the brain-damaged range and are severely disrupted besides.

Left-hemisphere tasks are most poorly performed, although generalized decrement occurs. Trails B is worse than Trails A, although both are severely disrupted. Likewise, Tapping and TPT show generalized decrement, with the left-hemisphere aspects being more severely dysfunctional than the right-hemisphere aspects. Sensory signs occur with Finger Agnosia, indicating left-parietal-lobe damage, auditory suppressions indicate left-temporal-lobe destruction, and Fingertip Number-writing is mild and not lateralized. A tactile suppression occurs on the left body side, indicating right-parietal-lobe damage. Finally, Speech-Sounds is more poorly performed than Rhythm, although, again, both fall into the brain-damaged range of performance.

Finer analysis of the TPT results reveals that coordination difficulties are evident from the third-trial score, which is worse than the second-trial score in view of the fact that a one-third improvement in performance is expected. This decrement often occurs in left-hemisphere injuries because of the added difficulty of coordinating both hands (a dominant-left-hemisphere ability) to complete the task. The performance deficit on the Memory and Location scores of the TPT indicate incidental, spatial memory problems, which often accompany severe injuries and/or right-hemisphere injuries in which tactual-perceptual deficits arise.

Deficits on the Aphasia Test also follow the pattern of the other results in which bilateral involvement occurs. Right-hemisphere dysfunction is indicated by the moderate-to-severe construction dyspraxia evident on the drawings of the cross and the key. Left-hemisphere damage is suggested by the reading and pronunciation problems. Calculation problems were also demonstrated, which may be related to damage in either hemisphere.

A severe injury is evident, one that involves both hemispheres and that is more severe in the left hemisphere. The pattern of deficits in the left hemisphere does not appear to represent a focal area of involvement. The lesion would appear to be more generalized, encompassing part of the temporal lobe, a large portion of the parietal lobe, and the sensory/motor strip. The parietal lobe is most widely represented in the deficit pattern, including the sensory signs, the TPT, the pronunciation problems, and perhaps the Arithmetic score and the calculation and reading difficulties on the Aphasis Test. The sensory/motor strip is represented by the Tapping deficit.

The left-temporal-lobe dysfunction is somewhat confusing as a result of the serious impairment suggested by the auditory suppressions. The Speech-Sounds and Rhythm tests do not give the appearance of such serious impairment. The type of lesion involved must be one in which the primary projection areas of the left temporal lobe are maximally involved (representing the auditory suppressions) and the secondary areas are less seriously affected (represeting the impaired but less seriously disrupted Speech-Sounds and Rhythm tests). Such a lesion is difficult to imagine at best. The results may make better sense, however, when fitted into the overall picture.

The right-hemisphere deficits are notable in two respects: they are severe enough to be differentiated from the left-hemisphere deficits, and they are not indicative of a localized disorder. Trails A is a rather general right-hemisphere indicator of dysfunction and by itself gives no useful localizing information. Problems in drawing simple geometric figures stem from construction dyspraxia, which is associated with posterior-parietal function. One tactile suppression occurs, indicating more anterior-parietal-lobe involvement. General depression on the WAIS performance subtests suggests a nonspecific right-hemisphere lesion. Overall, the results are consistent with injury to both hemispheres.

References

Balthazar, E. E., & Morrison, D. H. The use of Wechsler Intelligence Scales as diagnostic indicators of predominant left, right, and indeterminate unilateral brain damage. *Journal of Clinical Psychology,* 1961, *17,* 161.

Bannister, R. *Brain's clinical neurology* (4th ed.). London: Oxford University Press, 1973.

Boll, T. J. *The effect of age at onset of brain damage on adaptive abilities in children.* Submitted for publication.

Chusid, J. *Correlative neuroanatomy and functional neurology* (14th ed.). Los Altos: Lange, 1970.

Cleeland, C. S., Matthews, C. G., & Hopper, C. L. MMPI profiles in exacerbation and remission of multiple sclerosis. *Psychological Reports,* 1970, *27,* 373.

Constantindis, J., Richard, J., & Tissot, R. Pick's disease. *European Neurology,* 1974, *11,* 208.

Fisher, M. Left hemiplegia and motor impersistence. *Journal of Nervous and Mental Disease,* 1956, *123,* 201.

Golden, C. J. The validity of the Halstead-Reitan Neuropsychological Battery in a mixed psychiatric and brain damaged population. *Journal of Consulting and Clinical Psychology,* 1977, *45,* 1043–1051.

Golden, C. J. *Diagnosis and rehabilitation in clinical neuropsychology.* Springfield, Ill.: Charles C. Thomas, 1978.

Golden, C. J. *Clinical Interpretation of objective psychological tests.* New York: Grune & Stratton, 1979.

Golden, C. J. & Anderson, S. Short form of the speech sounds perception test. *Perceptual and Motor Skills,* 1977, *45,* 485–486.

Golden, C. J. & Kuperman, S. Graduate training in clinical neuropsychology. *Professional Psychology,* 1980, *11,* 55–63.

Goldstein, G.: The use of clinical neuropsychological methods in the lateralization of brain lesions. In J. Diamond & J. G. Beaumont (Eds.), *Hemisphere function in the brain.* New York: Wiley, 1974.

Goldstein, G., & Neuringer, C. Schizophrenic and organic damage in alcoholics. *Perceptual and Motor Skills,* 1966, *22,* 345–350.

Goldstein, G. Neuringer, C., & Olson, J.: Impairment of abstract reasoning in the brain damaged: Qualitative or quantitative. *Cortex,* 1968, *4,* 372.

Goldstein, G., & Shelley, C. H. Univariate versus multivariate analysis in neuropsychological test assessment of lateralized brain damage. *Cortex,* 1973, *9,* 204.

Goldstein, G., & Shelley, C. H. Neuropsychological diagnosis of multiple sclerosis in a neuropsychiatric setting. *Journal of Nervous and Mental Disease,* 1974, *158,* 280.

Gudeman, H., Craine, J. F., Golden, C. J., & McLaughlin, D. Higher cortical dysfunction associated with long term alcoholism. *International Journal of Neuroscience,* 1977, *8,* 33–40.

Halstead, W. C. *Brain and Intelligence: A quantitative study of the frontal lobes.* Chicago: University of Chicago Press, 1947.

Hebb, D. O. Man's frontal lobes. *Archives of Neurology and Psychiatry,* 1945, *54,* 10.

Hecaen, H. & Angelergues, R. Agnosia for faces (prosopagnosia). *Archives of Neurology,* 1962, *7,* 92.

Kimura, D. Right temporal lobe damage. *Archives of Neurology,* 1963, *8,* 264.

Klonoff, H., & Paris, R. Immediate, short term and residual effects of acute head injuries in children: Neuropsychological and neurological correlates. In R. M. Reitan & L. A. Davison (Eds.), *Clinical neuropsychology: Current status and applications.* Washington, D.C.: Winston, 1974.

Klove, H. Relationship of differential electroencephalographic patterns to distribution of Wechsler-Bellevue scores. *Neurology,* 1959, *9,* 871.

Klove, H., & Matthews, C. G. Psychometric and adaptive abilities in epilepsy. *Epilepsia,* 1966, *7,* 330.

Klove, H., & Matthews, C. G. Neuropsychological evaluation of the epileptic patient. *Wisconsin Medical Journal,* 1969, *68,* 296.

Klove, H., & Matthews, C. G. Neuropsychological studies of patients with epilepsy. In R. M. Reitan & L. A. Davison (Eds.), *Clinical neuropsychology: Current status and applications.* Washington, D.C.: Winston, 1974.

Logue, P. E., & Allen, K. WAIS predicted Category Test score with the Halstead Neuropsychological Battery. *Perceptual and Motor Skills,* 1971, *33,* 1095.

Luria, A. R. *Higher cortical functions in man.* New York: Basic Books, 1966.

Luria, A. R. *The working brain.* New York: Basic Books, 1973.

Matthews, C. G. Applications of neuropsychological test methods in mentally retarded subjects. In R. M. Reitan & L. A. Davison (Eds.), *Clinical neuropsychology: Current status and applications.* Washington, D.C.: Winston, 1974.

Matthews, C. G., Cleeland, C. S., & Hopper, C. L. Neuropsychological patterns in multiple sclerosis. *Diseases of the Nervous System, 1970, 31,* 161.

Matthews, C. G., & Klove, H. Differential psychological performances in major motor, psychomotor, and mixed classifications of known and unknown etiology. *Epilepsia, 1967, 8,* 117.

Mayo Clinic: *Clinical examinations in neurology.* Philadelphia: W. B. Saunders, 1976.

McFie, J. Psychological testing in clinical neurology. *Journal of Nervous and Mental Disease, 1960, 131,* 383.

McFie, J. The diagnostic significance of disorders of higher nervous activity. In P. J. Vinken & G. W. Bruyn (Eds.), *Handbook of clinical neurology* (Vol. 1). New York: Wiley, 1969.

McFie, J. *Assessment of organic intellectual impairment.* New York: Academic Press, 1975.

McFie, J., & Zangwill, O. L. Visual-constructive disabilities associated with lesions of the left cerebral hemisphere. *Brain, 1960, 83,* 243.

Milner, B. Effects of different brain lesions on card sorting. *Archives of Neurology, 1963, 9,* 90.

Milner, B. Sparing of language function after early unilateral brain damage. *Neurosciences Research Program Bulletin, 1974, 12,* 213.

Osmon, D. C., & Golden, C. J. Minnesota Multiphasic Personality Inventory correlates of neuropsychological deficits. *International Journal of Neuroscience, 1978, 8,* 113–122.

Osmon, D. C., Sweet, J. J., & Golden, C. J. Neuropsychological implications of rhythm and aphasia deficits after unilateral left hemisphere injury. *International Journal of Neuroscience, 1978, 8,* 79–82.

Purisch, A. D., Golden, C. J., & Hammeke, T. A. Discrimination of schizophrenic and brain injured patients by a standard version of Luria's neuropsychological tests. *Journal of Consulting and Clinical Psychology, 1978, 46,* 1266–1273.

Rapaport, D., Gill, M. M., & Schafer, R. *Diagnostic Psychological Testing.* New York: International Universities Press, 1968.

Reitan, R. M. Neuropsychological methods of inferring brain damage in adults and children. Unpublished manuscript, undated.

Reitan, R. M. Affective disturbances in brain damaged patients. *Archives of Neurology and Psychiatry, 1955a, 73,* 530.

Reitan, R. M. The distribution according to age of a psychological measure dependent upon organic brain functions. *Journal of Gerontology*, 1955b, *10*, 338.

Reitan, R. M. Investigation of the validity of Halstead's measure of biological intelligence. *Archives of Neurology and Psychiatry*, 1955c, *73*, 28.

Reitan, R. M. The relation of the Trail Making Test to organic brain damage. *Journal of Consulting Psychology*, 1955d, *19*, 393.

Reitan, R. M. Validity of the Trail Making Test as an indicator of organic brain damage. *Perceptual and Motor Skills*, 1958, *8*, 271.

Reitan, R. M. Correlations between the Trail Making Test and the Wechsler-Bellevue scale. *Perceptual and Motor Skills*, 1959a, *9*, 127.

Reitan, R. M. The comparative effects of brain damage on the Halstead Impairment Index and the Wechsler-Bellevue scale. *Journal of Clinical Psychology*, 1959b, *15*, 281.

Reitan, R. M. Manual for administration of neuropsychological test batteries for adults and children. Indianapolis, privately printed, 1959c.

Reitan, R. M. The effect of brain lesions on adaptive abilities in human beings. Unpublished manuscript, 1959d.

Reitan, R. M., & Boll, T. J. Intellectual and cognitive functions in Parkinson's disease. *Journal of Consulting and Clinical Psychology*, 1971, *37*, 364.

Reitan, R. M., & Tarshes, E. L. Differential effects of lateralized brain lesions on the Trail Making Test. *Journal of Nervous and Mental Disease*, 1959, *129*, 257.

Robbins, S. L. *Pathologic basis of disease*. Philadelphia: W. B. Saunders, 1974.

Rudel, R. G., and Denckla, M. B. Relation of forward to backward digit repetition to neurological impairment in children with learning disabilities. *Neuropsychologia*, 1974, *12*, 109.

Russell, E. W. WAIS factor analysis with brain damaged subjects using criterion measures. *Journal of Consulting and Clinical Psychology*, 1972, *39*, 133.

Russell, E. W., Neuringer, C., & Goldstein, G. *Assessment of brain damage— A neuropsychological key approach*. New York: Wiley, 1970.

Sanides, F. Structure and function of the human frontal lobe. *Neuropsychologia*, 1964, *2*, 209.

Schiller, F. Aphasia studied in patients with missile wounds. *Journal of Neurology, Neurosurgery, and Psychiatry*, 1947, *10*, 183.

Smith, A. Neuropsychological testing in neurological disorders. *Advances in Neurology*, 1975, *7*, 49.

Vega, A., & Parsons, O. Cross-validation of the Halstead-Reitan Tests for brain damage. *Journal of Consulting and Clinical Psychology,* 1967, *31,* 619.

Warrington, E. K., & Taylor, A. M. The contribution of the right parietal lobe to object recognition. *Cortex,* 1973, *9,* 152.

Wechsler, D. *The measurement of adult intelligence.* Baltimore: Williams & Wilkins, 1944.

Wechsler, D. *The measurement and appraisal of adult intelligence* (4th ed.). Baltimore: Williams & Wilkins, 1958.

Wheeler, L. Predictions of brain damage from an aphasia screening test, an application of discriminant functions and a comparison with a non-linear method of analysis. *Perceptual and Motor Skills,* 1963, *17,* 63.

Wheeler, L., Burke, C. J., & Reitan, R. M. An application of discriminant functions to the problem of predicting brain damage using behavioral variables. *Perceptual and Motor Skills,* 1963, *16,* 417.

Wheeler, L., & Reitan, R. M. Presence and laterality of brain damage predicted from responses to a short aphasia screening test. *Perceptual and Motor Skills,* 1962, *15,* 783.

Woo-Sam, J. Lateralized brain damage and differential psychological effects: Parsons et al. re-examined. *Perceptual and Motor Skills,* 1971, *33,* 259.

Woo-Sam, J., Zimmerman, I. L., & Rogal, R. Location of injury and Wechsler indices of mental deterioration. *Perceptual and Motor Skills,* 1971, *32,* 407.

Bibliography

The following sources provide further information on the Halstead-Reitan Test Battery and such related topics as brain injury, brain organization, neurological processes, childhood disorders, and neuropsychological theory and practice. These additional sources should aid the reader who wishes to become a neuropsychologist or who wishes to further understand the Halstead-Reitan Battery and other related topics.

Alvarez, R. R. Comparison of depressive and brain injured subjects on the Trail Making Test. *Perceptual and Motor Skills,* 1962, *14,* 91.

Alzheimer, A. On a peculiar disease of the cerebral cortex. *Archives of Neurology,* 1969, *21,* 109.

Annett, M. Laterality of childhood hemiplegia and the growth of speech and intelligence. *Cortex,* 1973, *9,* 4.

Archibald, Y. M., Wepman, J. M., & Jones, L. V. Performance on non-verbal cognitive tests following unilateral cortical injury to the right and left hemisphere. *Journal of Nervous and Mental Disease,* 1967, *145,* 25.

Armitage, S. G. An analysis of certain psychological tests used for the evaluation of brain injury. *Psychology Monographs,* 1946, *60,* 277.

Auld, A. W., Aronson, H. A., & Gargans, F. Aneurysm of the middle meningeal artery. *Archives of Neurology,* 1965, *13,* 369.

Barnes, G. W., & Lucas, G. J. Cerebral dysfunction versus psychogenesis in Halstead-Reitan Tests. *Journal of Nervous Disease,* 1974, *158,* 1405.

Basser, L. S. Hemiplegia of early onset and the faculty of speech with special reference to the effects of hemispherectomy. *Brain,* 1962, *85,* 427.

Beaumont, J. G. The validity of the Category Test administered by online computer. *Journal of Clinical Psychology,* 1975, *31,* 458.

Boll, T. J. Psychological differentiation of patients with schizophrenia versus lateralized cerebrovascular, neoplastic or traumatic brain damage. *Journal of Abnormal Psychology,* 1974a, *83,* 456.

383

Boll, R. J. Behavioral correlates of cerebral damage in children aged 9 through 14. In R. M. Reitan & L. A. Davidson (Eds.), *Clinical neuropsychology: Current status and applications*. Washington, D.C.: Winston, 1974b.

Boll, T. J., & Reitan, R. M. Psychological test results of subjects with known cerebral lesions and Parkinson's disease as compared to controls. *Perceptual and Motor Skills*, 1970, *31*, 824.

Boll, T. J., & Reitan, R. M. Motor and tactile-perceptual deficits in brain damaged children. *Perceptual and Motor Skills*, 1972, *34*, 343.

Boll, T. J., & Reitan, R. M. Effect of age on performance of the Trail Making Test. *Perceptual and Motor Skills*, 1973, *36*, 691.

Chandler, B. C., Vega, A., & Parsons, O. A. Dichotic listening in alcoholics with and without a history of possible brain damage. *Quarterly Journal of Studies on Alcohol*, 1973, *34*, 1099.

Critchley, M. *The parietal lobes*. Baltimore: Williams & Wilkins, 1953.

Dikmen, S., Matthews, C. G., & Hartley, J. P. The effect of early versus late onset of major motor epilepsy upon cognitive-intellectual performance. *Epilepsia*, 1975, *16*, 73.

Doehring, D. G., & Reitan, R. M. MMPI performance of aphasic and non-aphasic brain-damaged patients. *Journal of Clinical Psychology*, 1960, *16*, 307.

Doehring, D. G., Reitan, R. M., & Klove, H. Changes in patterns of intelligence test performance associated with homonymous visual field defects. *Journal of Nervous and Mental Disease*, 1961, *132*, 227.

Donnelly, E. F., Dent, J. K., Murphy, D. L., & Mignone, R. J. Comparison of temporal lobe epileptics and affective disorders on the Halstead-Reitan Test Battery. *Journal of Clinical Psychology*, 1972, *28*, 61.

Drachman, D. A., & Arbit, J. Memory and the hippocampal complex. *Archives of Neurology*, 1964, *10*, 411.

Earle, K. M. Metastatic brain tumors. *Diseases of the Nervous System*, 1955, *16*, 86.

Filskov, S. B., & Goldstein, S. G. Diagnostic validity of the Halstead-Reitan Neuropsychological Battery. *Journal of Consulting and Clinical Psychology*, 1974, *42*, 382.

Fitzhugh, K. B., & Fitzhugh, L. C. WAIS results for S's with longstanding, chronic, lateralized and diffuse cerebral dysfunction. *Perceptual and Motor Skills*, 1964, *19*, 735.

Fitzhugh, K. B., Fitzhugh, L. C., & Reitan, R. M. Wechsler-Bellevue comparisons in groups with "chronic" and "current" lateralized and diffuse brain lesions. *Journal of Consulting Psychology*, 1962, *26*, 306.

Fitzhugh, K. B., Fitzhugh, L. C., & Reitan, R. M. Relation of acuteness of organic brain dysfunction to Trail Making Test performance. *Perceptual and Motor Skills*, 1965, *20*, 1099.

Fitzhugh, L. C., & Fitzhugh, K. B. Relationships between Wechsler Bellevue Form I and WAIS performance of subjects with longstanding cerebral dysfunction. *Perceptual and Motor Skills,* 1964, *19,* 539.

Fitzhugh, L. C., Fitzhugh, K. B., & Reitan, R. M. Sensorimotor deficits of brain damaged S's in relation to intellectual level. *Perceptual and Motor Skills,* 1962, *15,* 603.

Golden, C. J. The identification of brain damage by an abbreviated form of the Halstead-Reitan Neuropsychological Battery. *Journal of Clinical Psychology,* 1976, *32,* 821.

Goldstein, G., & Shelley, C. H. Statistical and normative studies of the Halstead Neuropsychological Test Battery relevant to a neuropsychiatric hospital setting. *Perceptual and Motor Skills,* 1972, *34,* 603.

Gordon, N. G. The Trail Making Test in neuropsychological diagnosis. *Journal of Clinical Psychology,* 1972, *28,* 167.

Halstead, W. C., & Wepman, J. M. The Halstead-Wepman Aphasia Screening Test. *Journal of Speech and Hearing Disorders,* 1949, *14,* 9.

Heimburger, R. F., Demyer, W., & Reitan, R. M. Implications of Gerstmann's syndrome. *Journal of Neurology, Neurosurgery, and Psychiatry,* 1964, *27,* 52.

Heimburger, R. F., & Reitan, R. M. Easily administered written test for lateralizing brain lesions. *Journal of Neurosurgery,* 1961, *18,* 301.

Kaszniak, A. W. *Organic brain syndromes.* In S. Reiss, R. A. Peterson, L. D. Eron, & M. Reiss (Eds.), *Experimental and clinical approaches to abnormality.* New York: Macmillan, 1977.

Kiernan, R. J., & Matthews, C. G. Impairment index versus T-score averaging in neuropsychological assessment. *Journal of Consulting and Clinical Psychology,* 1976, *44,* 951.

Klonoff, H., Fibiger, C. H., & Hutton, G. H. Neuropsychological patterns in chronic schizophrenia. *Journal of Nervous and Mental Disease,* 1970, *150,* 291.

Klonoff, H., & Low, M. Disordered brain function in young children and early adolescents: Neuropsychological and electroencephalographic correlates. In R. M. Reitan & L. A. Davidson (Eds.), *Clinical neuropsychology: Current status and applications.* Washington, D.C.: Winston, 1974.

Klonoff, H., Robinson, G. C., & Thompson, G. Acute and chronic brain syndromes in children. *Developmental Medicine and Child Neurology,* 1969, *11,* 198.

Klove, H. Validation studies in adult clinical neuropsychology. In R. M. Reitan & L. A. Davison (Eds.), *Clinical neuropsychology: Current status and applications.* Washington, D.C.: Winston, 1974.

Klove, H., & Reitan, R. M. Effects of dysphasia and spatial distortion on

Wechsler-Bellevue results. *Archives of Neurology and Psychiatry,* 1939, *42,* 979.

Knights, R. M., & Watson, P. The use of computerized test profiles in neuropsychological assessment. *Journal of Learning Disabilities,* 1968, *1,* 696.

Lezak, M. D. *Neuropsychological assessment.* New York, Oxford University Press, 1976.

Luria, A. R. Brain disorders and language analysis. *Language and Speech,* 1958, *1,* 1.

Luria, A. R. *Restoration of function after brain injury.* New York, Macmillan, 1963.

Luria, A. R. Neuropsychology in the local diagnosis of brain injury. *Cortex,* 1964, *1,* 3.

Luria, A. R. Two kinds of motor persevation in massive injury of the frontal lobes. *Brain,* 1965a, *88,* 1.

Luria, A. R. L.S. Vygotsky and the problem of localization of function. *Neuropsychologia,* 1965b, *3,* 387.

Luria, A. R. *Traumatic aphasia: Its syndromes, psychology and treatment.* The Hague, Mouton, 1970.

Luria, A. R. Memory disturbances in local brain lesions. *Neuropsychologia,* 1971, *9,* 367.

Luria, A. R. Aphasia reconsidered. *Cortex,* 1972, *8,* 34.

Luria, A. R. Towards the mechanisms of naming disturbance. *Neuropsychologia,* 1973b, *11,* 417.

Luria, A. R., Homskaya, E. D., Blinkov, S. M., & Critchley, M. Impaired selectivity of mental processes in association with a lesion of the frontal lobes. *Neuropsychologia,* 1967, *5,* 105.

Luria, A. R., & Karassev, A. Disturbances of auditory speech memory in focal lesions of the deep regions of the left temporal lobe. *Neuropsychologia,* 1968, *6,* 97.

Luria, A. R., Pribram, H., & Homskaya, E. D. An experimental analysis of the behavioral disturbance produced by a left frontal arachnoidal endotheliona (meningioma). *Neuropsychologia,* 1964, *2,* 257.

Luria, A. R., Simernitskaya, E. G., & Tubylevich, B. The structure of psychological processes in relation to cerebral organization. *Neuropsychologia,* 1970, *8,* 13.

Luria, A. R., Sokolov, E. N., & Klimkowski, M. Towards a neurodynamic analysis of memory disturbances with lesions of the left temporal lobe. *Neuropsychologia,* 1967, *5,* 1.

Luria, A. R., & Tsvetkova, L. S. The programming of constructive activity in local brain injuries. *Neuropsychologia,* 1964, *2,* 95.

Matthews, C. G., & Booker, H. E. Pneumoencephalographic measurements and neuropsychological test performance in human adults. *Cortex,* 1972, *8,* 69.

Matthews, C. G., Guertin, W. H., & Reitan, R. M. Wechsler-Bellevue subtest mean rank orders in diverse diagnostic groups. *Psychological Reports,* 1962, *11,* 3.

Matthews, C. G., & Reitan, R. M. Correlations of Wechsler rank orders of subtest means in lateralized and non-lateralized brain damaged groups. *Perceptual and Motor Skills,* 1964, *19,* 391.

Matthews, C. G., Shaw, D. J., & Klove, H. Psychological test performance in neurologic and pseudo-neurologic subjects. *Cortex,* 1966, *2,* 224.

Norton, J. C., & Matthews, C. G. Psychological test performances in patients with subtentorial versus supratentorial CNS disease. *Diseases of the Nervous System,* 1972, *33,* 312.

Parsons, O. A., Vega, A., & Burn, J. Different psychological effects of lateralized brain damage. *Journal of Consulting and Clinical Psychology,* 1969, *33,* 551.

Reed, H. B., & Fitzhugh, D. B. Patterns of deficits in relation to severity of cerebral dysfunction in children and adults. *Journal of Consulting Psychology,* 1966, *30,* 98.

Reed, H. B., Reitan, R. M., & Klove, H. Influence of cerebral lesions on psychological test performance of older children. *Journal of Consulting Psychology,* 1965, *29,* 247.

Reed, J. C., & Reitan, R. M. Verbal and performance differences among brain injured children with lateralized motor deficits. *Perceptual and Motor Skills,* 1979, *29,* 747.

Reitan, R. M. The significance of dysphasia for intelligence and adaptive abilities. *Journal of Psychology,* 1960, *50,* 355.

Reitan, R. M. Relationship of differential abstraction ability levels to psychological test performances in mentally retarded subjects. *American Journal of Mental Deficiency,* 1963, *68,* 235.

Reitan, R. M. Psychological deficits resulting from cerebral lesions in man. In J. M. Warren & D. A. Akert (Eds.), *The frontal granular cortex and behavior.* New York: McGraw-Hill, 1964.

Reitan, R. M. Problems and prospects in studying the psychological correlates of brain lesions. *Cortex,* 1966, *2,* 127.

Reitan, R. M. Examples of children with brain lesions and children with neuropsychological diagnostic problems. Privately printed, 1969.

Reitan, R. M. Trail Making Test results for normal and brain-damaged children. *Perceptual and Motor Skills,* 1971a, *33,* 575.

Reitan, R. M. Verbal problem solving as related to cerebral damage. *Perceptual and Motor Skills,* 1971b, *34,* 515.

Reitan, R. M. Methodological problems in clinical neuropsychology. In R. M.

Reitan & L. A. Davison (Eds.), *Clinical neuropsychology: Current status and applications*. Washington, D.C.: Winston, 1974a.

Reitan, R. M. Psychological effects of cerebral lesions in children of early school age. In R. M. Reitan & L. A. Davison (Eds.), *Clinical neuropsychology: Current status and applications*. Washington, D. C., Winston, 1974b.

Reitan, R. M. Neuropsychology: The vulgarization Luria always wanted. *Contemporary Psychology*, 1976, *21*, 737.

Reitan, R. M., & Boll, R. J. Neuropsychological correlates of minimal brain dysfunction. *Annals of the New York Academy of Sciences*, 1973, *205*, 65.

Reitan, R. M., & Davison, L. A. *Clinical neuropsychology: Current status and applications*. Washington, D.C.: Winston, 1974.

Reitan, R. M., & Fitzhugh, H. Hypotheses supported by clinical evidence that are under current investigation. Unpublished manuscript, undated.

Reitan, R. M., Reed, J. C., & Dyken, M. L. Cognitive, psychomotor and motor correlates of multiple sclerosis. *Journal of Nervous Disease*, 1971, *153*, 218.

Rourke, B. P. Brain-behavior relationships in children with learning disabilities: A research program. *American Psychologist*, 1975, *30*, 911.

Rourke, B. P., Dietrich, D. M., & Young, G. C. Significance of WISC verbal-performance discrepancies for older children with learning disabilities. *Perceptual and Motor Skills*, 1973, *36*, 275.

Rourke, B. P., & Telegdy, G. A. Lateralizing significance of WISC verbal-performance discrepancies for older children with learning disabilities. *Perceptual and Motor Skills*, 1971, *33*, 875.

Rourke, B. P., Yanni, D. W., MacDonald, G. W., & Young, G. C. Neuropsychological significance of lateralized deficits on the grooved pegboard test for older children with learning disabilities. *Journal of Consulting and Clinical Psychology*, 1973, *41*, 128.

Rourke, B. P., Young, G. C., & Flewelling, R. W.: The relationship between WISC verbal performance discrepancies and selected verbal, auditory-perceptual, visual-perceptual, and problem-solving abilities in children with learning disabilities. *Journal of Clinical Psychology*, 1971, *27*, 475.

Russell, E. W. Validation of a brain damage versus schizophrenia MMPI key. *Journal of Clinical Psychology*, 1975, *31*, 659.

Sarno, M. R., & Levita, E. Natural course of recovery in severe aphasia. *Archives of Physical Medicine and Rehabilitation*, 1971, *52*, 175.

Smith, T. E. Relation of the Trail Making Test to mental retardation. *Perceptual and Motor Skills*, 1963, *17*, 719.

Vega, A. Cross-validation of the Halstead-Reitan Tests for brain damage. *Journal of Consulting and Clinical Psychology*, 1967, *31*, 619.

Vygotsky, L. S. Psychology and localization of functions. *Neuropsychologia,* 1965, *3,* 381.

Watson, C. G., Thomas, R. W., Felling, J., & Anderson, D. Differentiation of organics from schizophrenics at two chronicity levels by use of the Reitan-Halstead Organic Test Battery. *Journal of Consulting and Clinical Psychology,* 1968a, *32,* 679.

Watson, C. G., Thomas, R. W., Felling, J., & Anderson, D. Differentiation of organics from schizophrenics with Reitan's sensory perceptual disturbances test. *Perceptual and Motor Skills,* 1968b, *26,* 1191.

Watson, C. G., Thomas, R. W., Felling, J., & Anderson, D. Differentiation of organics from schizophrenics with the Trail Making, dynamometer, critical flicker fusion, and light intensity matching tests. *Journal of Clinical Psychology,* 1969, *25,* 130.

Wheeler, L., & Reitan, R. M. Discriminant functions applied to the problem of predicting cerebral damage from behavioral tests: A cross validation study. *Perceptual and Motor Skills,* 1963, *16,* 681.

Index